TCHAIKOVSKY'S EMPIRE

TCHAIKOVSKY'S EMPIRE

A NEW LIFE OF RUSSIA'S GREATEST COMPOSER

SIMON MORRISON

YALE UNIVERSITY PRESS
NEW HAVEN AND LONDON

Publication is made possible in part by a grant from the Barr Ferree Foundation
Publication Fund, Department of Art and Archeology, Princeton University.

Endpapers: Heritage Images / Hulton Archive via Getty Images

For information about this and other Yale University Press publications, please contact:
U.S. Office: sales.press@yale.edu   yalebooks.com
Europe Office: sales@yaleup.co.uk   yalebooks.co.uk

Set Adobe Caslon Pro by IDSUK (DataConnection) Ltd
Printed in Great Britain by Clays Ltd, Elcograf S.p.A

Library of Congress Control Number: 2024930686

ISBN 978-0-300-19210-0

A catalogue record for this book is available from the British Library.

10 9 8 7 6 5 4 3 2 1

For Kailey

CONTENTS

ILLUSTRATIONS

1. *Tchaikovsky at the Moscow Artistic Circle*, from a painting by Nikolay Kuzmin. Lebrecht Music & Arts / Alamy.
2. Piano vocal score of *Vakula the Smith*, 1876. Author's collection.
3. Tchaikovsky with the Davïdov family at the Kamianka estate, 1875. Heritage Images / Hulton Archive via Getty Images.
4. Tchaikovsky with his brothers Modest and Anatoly, and N. D. Kondratyev, photograph by Ivan Dyagovchenko, 1875. Heritage Images / Hulton Archive via Getty Images.
5. Portrait of the opera singer Mariya Klimentova-Muromtseva, 1879. Heritage Images / Hulton Archive via Getty Images.
6. Bogomir Korsov in the title role of *Mazeppa*, 1884. Lebrecht Music & Arts / Alamy.
7. Tsar Alexander III, Tsarina Maria Fyodorovna, and their children, 1885. World History Archive / Alamy.
8. Grand Prince Konstantin Konstantinovich. Sueddeutsche Zeitung Photo / Alamy.
9. Tchaikovsky in Tiflis, 1889. Heritage Images / Hulton Archive via Getty Images.
10. Tchaikovsky in Kharkiv, 1893. Heritage Images / Hulton Archive via Getty Images.

11. Consecration of the Cathedral of Christ the Savior. Heritage Image Partnership Ltd / Alamy.
12. Tchaikovsky in his garden, 1890. Bojan Brecelj / Corbis Historical via Getty Images.
13. Desk and chair at which the *Pathétique* Symphony was written. Album / Alamy.
14. Tchaikovsky's tomb. BenzA IMG / Alamy.
15. Vera Karalli as Odette in *Swan Lake*, 1906. Russian State Archive of Literature and Art.
16. *The Sleeping Beauty* at the Bolshoi Theater, 1924. Russian State Archive of Literature and Art.

A NOTE ON TRANSLITERATION
AND DATES

The transliteration system used in this book is Gerald Abraham's system from 1980 including Richard Taruskin's adjustments from 1993. The exceptions to the system are generally accepted spellings of Russian and non-Russian names and places (Alexei rather than Aleksey, Dmitri rather than Dmitriy, and Moscow rather than Moskva) and surname suffixes (Poznan*sky* rather than Poznan*skiy*). Anatole is preferred to Anatoly. I chose Tchaikovsky over the other spellings of the composer's name as the most common in the Latin alphabet sphere. It is the French transliteration of Чайковский, which has Polish origins as Czajkowski (an extension of the Polish word *czajka*, a type of bird). In the endnotes, however, the Abraham/Taruskin transliteration system is respected without exception (Dmitriy rather than Dmitri, etc.). Surname suffixes are presented intact and hard and soft signs denoted.

Russia retained use of the Julian calendar from antiquity until January 1, 1918, when the Bolsheviks adopted the Gregorian calendar and gradually, through monopolization of publishing enterprises, implemented language reforms such that -аго masculine genitive endings became -ого. Before the reign of Peter the Great, Russia (Muscovy) marked the start of the year on September 1 rather than

January 1 and numbered years from the beginning of the creation of the earth rather than the birth of Christ. Peter the Great reformed the counting of the years but upheld the use of the Julian calendar in deference to the Russian Orthodox Church. Before the 1917 Revolution, as a result, the Russian calendar was twelve days behind that of the Western European calendar. In this book dates are specified according to the calendar in use in Russia during Tchaikovsky's lifetime: the Julian.

ACKNOWLEDGMENTS

I am grateful to Ilya Magin, Sergey Konaev, Maryana Petyaskina, Galina Zlobina, Alexander Poznansky, Philip Bullock, Alastair Macaulay, Thomas Keenan, Rob Hudson, Ilya Vinitsky, Michael Wachtel, Igor Pilshchikov, Victoria Aschheim, Chester Dunning, and the brilliant participants in my two Princeton University graduate seminars on Tchaikovsky. My thanks to the anonymous readers of the draft and to Martin Brown, Rachael Lonsdale, Julian Loose, Frazer Martin, Meg Pettit, Katie Urquhart, Robert Sargant, and Susan Silver for their design and editorial work. I am most grateful, as ever, to Elizabeth Bergman.

European Russia

  Russia by 1801
  Russia by 1825
  Russia by 1881

500 miles
800 km

Barents Sea

Kola

Samoyediya

Siberia

White Sea

Arkhangelsk

SWEDEN

FINLAND

Petrozavodsk

Olonets
Lake Lagoda

Solikamsk

St. Petersburg

Novgorod

Vologda

Vyatka

Perm

R U S S I A N

Baltic Sea

ESTONIA

LIVONIA

COURLAND

Pskov

Tver

Yaroslav

Kostroma

Nizhny-
Novgorod

Votkinsk

Vitebsk

Klin

Moscow

Vladimir

Kazan

Ural Mountains

PRUSSIA

Smolensk

Kaluga

Tula

Ryazan

Simbirsk

Ufa

Minsk

E   M   P   I   R   E

Samara

POLAND

Orel

Yelets

Tambov

Volga

VOLYN

Chernigov

Voronezh

Saratov

Ural

RUTHENIA

Kyiv

Kursk

U K R A I N E

Kharkiv

AUSTRIAN
EMPIRE

PODILLIA

Dnieper

Pavlovsk

Kamianka

Don Cossacks

BESSARABIA

Ekaterinoslav

Don

MOLDAVIA

Odesa

TAURIDA

Kherson

Rostov

Astrakhan

WALLACHIA

*Sea of
Azov*

Kuban

Stavropol

Caspian Sea

Danube

Bucharest

Simferopol

Kerch

Sevastopol

CHECHNYA

BULGARIA

Black Sea

Tiflis

GEORGIA

O T T O M A N   E M P I R E

Constantinople

Tchaikovsky's Russia.

INTRODUCTION

He was a composer. He worked constantly and drank and smoked too much and aged prematurely. He also traveled constantly—in Russia and Ukraine, throughout Europe, and once to the United States. He became famous but said, in 1878, that he didn't "give a shit" about fame.[1] (He was in a very bad mood that day.) Like his mother, he died of cholera. He was homosexual, but his music is not about his bedroom. Most was produced on commission for the Imperial Russian Musical Society, the Imperial Theaters, and an aggressive publisher who was also his banker. His style bore German Romantic influences at the start, then embraced a Russian nationalist aesthetic before becoming neoclassical. Had he lived longer, Tchaikovsky might have found a place within the Symbolist movement.

The details of his life presented here are fewer than in other books about Tchaikovsky but situated in a broader sociopolitical and historical as well as musical context. The general aim is to distance his music from the letters to his brothers, sister, and trusted friends. Those express emotion in a nineteenth-century language remote from our own. Even the way Tchaikovsky processed grief or dealt with failure is distant. Certain things, however, feel very present: his disdain for pretense; his frustration with himself for profligate spending; the fact that he came from a happy family unlike other happy families; his belief in living life in reverse, getting younger rather than older, becoming less hidebound and more playful.

To produce as much music as he did—an entire empire's worth—Tchaikovsky had to be hyperfocused and hyperdisciplined, not lurching from one personal crisis to another and indulging morbid fantasies. Such is how he continues to be represented even in publications purporting to correct the record. The most recent reconsideration, by Ada Aynbinder, states right up front that Tchaikovsky's life was "one of endless struggle, confrontation, and occasional submission before the 'restless fate' that pursued him and which in one form or another is felt in all his works."[2] The same claim was made back in the Tchaikovsky centennial year of 1940 in the journal *Soviet Music*, though there the "unequal struggle with 'destiny' and fatal inevitability" is squarely blamed on the Romanovs and their "suffocating" rule.[3] Aynbinder allows that Tchaikovsky experienced typical joys and sorrows, recognizing that the composer cultivated "hobbies" like stargazing and, after reading John Lubbock's *Ants, Bees and Wasps: A Record of Observations on the Habits of the Social Hymenoptera* (1881), amateur entomology.[4] He was also a student of his own family genealogy. Distant relatives who lived in Ukraine and Poland, led Cossack uprisings, and served as provincial governors provided fodder for his operas.

Tchaikovsky's instrumental music is the stuff of subjective expression, though the argument advanced in this book is that the subject is not necessarily himself. Russian accounts differ from non-Russian sources in their emphasis on the transcendent nature of his music as opposed to its autobiographical aspects. But one mythology simply substitutes for another, all buttressed by carefully curated archival collections.

The composer studied for three and a half years at the St. Petersburg Conservatory, graduating at age twenty-five in 1865.

He played piano below the level of his peers but bullishly enough to tackle Franz Liszt's transcription of the second-act sextet of Gaetano Donizetti's *dramma tragico Lucia di Lammermoor*. He remarked that he didn't like the fashion for excessive emotion at the keyboard, "playing with feeling," yet that is how his piano music is often played.[5] Tchaikovsky then earned a living as a teacher at the Moscow Conservatory, the institution that now bears his name and has a monument to him at the front. Then a lucky break: a stipend from a reclusive, recently widowed heiress with a deep obsession with music, Nadezhda Filaretovna von Mekk (née Fralovskaya, 1831–94). She grew up on a landed estate near Smolensk and learned music from her cello-playing father. At age seventeen she married Karl Otto Georg von Mekk (1821–76), an engineer who earned millions of rubles as a railroad contractor. He made this fortune after Nadezhda urged him, for the sake of the family they were trying to raise, to abandon his dead-end, low-paying job as a government bureaucrat and turn to projects matching his technical skills.

Von Mekk's support bolstered Tchaikovsky creatively such that he began to compose in the more prestigious genres of the symphony, opera, and ballet. By the mid-1880s, he had outgrown the need for her support, becoming comfortably ensconced in the St. Petersburg court as an imperial artist, his music a simulacrum of Tsar Alexander III's rule in its combination of nationalism and imperialism. Tchaikovsky was reared in the two Russian capitals yet found topics for his works in the empire's provinces, past and present. The Soviets mythologized Tchaikovsky as a symbol of all things Russian; however, he led an international, cosmopolitan existence. All things Russian, for Tchaikovsky, included all things European. Late in life the composer previewed the aesthetic preoccupations of the Silver Age. The younger generation of progressive artists explored the unconscious in search of meaning beyond the sensory realm. Their aesthetics were often convoluted, but Tchaikovsky (with Mozart as his model) kept his music accessible, infectious, and pliant.

His output includes operas about Ivan the Terrible's court, Joan of Arc, the Cossack hero Mazeppa, an innkeeper thought to be a sorceress (*The Enchantress*, which failed to sell tickets and quickly disappeared from the operatic stage), and a blind princess. Tchaikovsky always gave his heroines the best tunes. The lechers mumble and bumble in quasi recitative. He wrote program music based on Byron, Dante, Ostrovsky, and Shakespeare; incidental music for successful and unsuccessful plays; and a trio of ballets on supernatural-fantastical subjects, the first of which, *Swan Lake*, became canonical only after his death. Thanks to international piano competitions and Cold War politics, his First Piano Concerto became one of his most beloved, and contested, scores. (How exactly should those big chords at the start be played?) His liturgical music is much less known but, at the time of its creation, generated fierce debate. He based songs on bittersweet, morbid, and sentimental poems, several that might not otherwise have seen the light of day without his having set them to music, and one became a staple on recital programs: "Net, tol'ko tot, kto znal," or "None But the Lonely Heart."[6] Tchaikovsky's *Pathétique* Symphony is about death; had things turned out differently, it would have paired with another about life.

He wrote pieces for civic occasions. In 1872, for example, Tchaikovsky composed a cantata for the opening of the Moscow Polytechnic Exhibition. Funded by a factory and salt-mine operator, Prince Sergey Golitsïn, the exhibition commemorated the bicentennial of Peter the Great and showcased advances in Russian agriculture, medicine, and manufacturing. A local "Doctor of Medicine" xenophobically argued that the "visitors from the region of India" might spread disease and cause shortages for local citizens; his concern was dismissed as baseless fear-mongering.[7] For 750 rubles Tchaikovsky was hired to compose music to rouse the masses through church singing.[8] This particular directive followed a larger government initiative encouraging choral singing as a means to bolster communal participation in the life of the church. Bureaucrats at the

Ministry of Internal Affairs and Ministry of Education likewise promoted the forming of choral groups in factories, a practice carried through the Soviet era. The Polytechnic Exhibition Cantata was performed outside on a decorated bridge leading into the Kremlin and then at a Bolshoi Theater gala before being forgotten.

His music is distinct: it's hard to mistake the muted strings, bassoon solos, and sinuous nonimitative counterpoint as flowing from someone else's pen, though he did great imitations of Auber, Berlioz, Mozart, Schumann, and composers no one remembers anymore. His music is a manifestation (not a reflection) of his personality, and that personality, like all personalities, greatly changed. His music greatly changed too—less in terms of its emotional and psychological content than the range of influences it absorbed. One hears the world opening up in his art even as he was forced, owing to the demands on his time, to curtail socializing and sequester like a hermit. Collating the scores and letters, trying to find cause-and-effect relationships between his art and life, makes both incomprehensible. Tchaikovsky composed a neoclassical sextet alongside an opera about the supernatural. What he said to von Mekk about these works differs from what he said to Grand Prince Konstantin Romanov, his publisher, and his brother Modest.

Slowly, Tchaikovsky's career expanded from the local and regional to the national, imperial, and beyond. In 1887 the magazine *Nouvelliste* published an article about his rise, how he had "so brilliantly justified the hopes placed in him, held the banner of Russian art so high. Tchaikovsky did not need to become a general or take any official position—in Russia these conditions are almost a cornerstone for success even in the arts—in order to earn popularity."[9] His achievement is documented in his letters, which have been published and republished, interpreted and reinterpreted. Most are available on Tchaikovsky Research Net, and the superb archivist Brett Langston along with his colleagues have been chipping away at their translation. Tchaikovsky shared his self-doubts and vulnerabilities as a composer but—in part because of his highly mannered, sentimental epistolary style—seemed always to offer too much or too little insight into his intentions and his everyday self. His funnier side is revealed in his unexpurgated correspondence with his closest male friends, especially his younger brothers Anatole and Modest. He curses in his letters; he talks about gambling and his digestive system and the rough trade he enjoyed abroad (as opposed to gathering with other gay men— "aunties"—in St. Petersburg's Zoological Garden, the ballet, the circus, and the *cafés chantants*).[10] Referring to performances of his music, he is harder on singers than dancers because he could judge their skills better. Tchaikovsky mostly avoids jawing at his opponents, recognizing, perhaps, their biases and jealous motivations.

He wasn't an elitist but found a home in elite circles at court. He wasn't of aristocratic lineage and knew he didn't look and behave like an aristocrat, so he quickly abandoned any attempt to fit in with Onegins of the world. He shared his thinking about himself and his temperament with his brother Anatole: "It's comical to recall the extent to which I tormented myself for failing to get into high society and become a social success! . . . How much time it took for me to understand that I belong to the category of the reasonably intelligent, but do not belong in the class of those whose minds possess abilities which are out of the ordinary."[11]

He leaned into that unlearned side of himself and stuck up for regular folk, with a tilt toward the kind of people the Enlightenment philosopher and late-blooming composer Jean-Jacques Rousseau privileged for their "proximity, equality, and similarity."[12] Tchaikovsky also read Octave Feuillet, appreciating the writer's representation of the "subtleties of the normal."[13] (His favorite Feuillet novel was *Death* [*La morte*, 1886], which is about marriage—for Tchaikovsky, itself a kind of death.) The composer highlights the plainer side of existence, the unthinking hours, and in his operas focuses on people of all ages who aren't geniuses, liberal, or unique, individuals who lack, or who have been denied, a metaphysical aspect to their existences.

The man of the people was upwardly mobile, lodging in better neighborhoods, dining in good restaurants, and choosing department stores over markets. No one ever caught him at the pie exchange or haggling over the price of a hat. Tchaikovsky liked popular theater, especially vaudeville, and occasionally quoted from it in his compositions. He enjoyed magic shows and acrobatics but avoided baser entertainments—seen on the slummier streets of Moscow, not St. Petersburg—like boxing, wrestling, bearbaiting, and cockfighting (technically illegal but the police could be bribed). He treated his servants very well, and never forgot the people who raised him and helped him out.

Insights into Tchaikovsky's character come from curious places, like this diary entry of June 11, 1886, concerning a Russian anthropologist who left Russia for the island of Papua New Guinea. Tchaikovsky somehow knew about him and responded as follows to the anthropologist's description of the free sale of alcohol in Papua New Guinea:

> It is said that alcohol abuse is harmful. I completely agree with this. But as an unhealthy person prone to neuroses, I can't get by without the poison of the alcohol against which [the anthropologist Nikolay] Miklukho-Maklay rebels. This person, who has such a strange last name, is perfectly content not knowing the delights of vodka and other alcoholic beverages. How unfair it is, however, to judge others and forbid them what you yourself don't like.[14]

Miklukho-Maklay (1846–88) traveled to mysterious shores, endured long years of deprivation and sickness, and took immense personal risks to the benefit of Russian science. He studied ritual penis-piercing in Borneo and butterflies and birds of paradise on the Malay Peninsula, lavishly illustrating his findings in his publications. How does Tchaikovsky react to Miklukho-Maklay's achievement? By joking about being neurotic and needing stiff drinks in the evening. The humor is bland and thin—the humor of a world-famous person trying to keep the world small.

Bourgeois decorum, and the increasing institutional oversight of artists in Russia, counseled him to limit himself, to mingle with trusted friends and exercise forbearance. He could be snippy but he didn't much argue. He wasn't in any palpable sense a rebel or an iconoclast. Tchaikovsky took an interest in civic affairs—the election of an official he admired, Nikolay Alekseyev, as mayor of Moscow in 1885—but seldom discussed the Romanovs or the royal court. He didn't indicate what, if anything, he thought about the Crimean War, the miscalculations of Tsar Nikolay I, the emancipation of the serfs in 1861, or the assassination of Tsar Alexander II in 1881. Despite an interest in Ukrainian history and culture, he didn't weigh in on the oppressive Ems Ukaz (decree) of May 18, 1876, which curtailed the use of the Ukrainian language in the classroom, in print, and in musical settings throughout the empire (despite Russians generally having fewer books and poorer education than Ukrainians). The Ems Ukaz supplemented another notorious document, a "secret administrative instruction to censors" issued by the Minister of Internal Affairs on July 18, 1863, which asserted the nonexistence of the Ukrainian language, based on the contention that Ukrainian was a dialect of Russian that had been contaminated by Polish.[15]

It would be a stretch to claim that Tchaikovsky was an unwavering supporter of Russian imperial ambition and the horrors—invasions, expulsions, pogroms—committed in the service of empire. Certainly, though, Tchaikovsky's compositions supported the state and speak to the imperial effort to Russify conquered territories. He composed for imperial enterprises; his education, friendships, and fraternal connections further implicated him in imperial administrative structures; his music is kaleidoscopic, capacious, and, befitting the imperial subject, decentered. Certain details of his operas suggest recognition of mixed bloodlines, if not the blood spilled in the blood lands. The cultures of Ukraine, Poland, Tiflis, and Caucasus Mountain villages provided creative inspiration without explicit recognition of Russian colonialist oppression and the empire's chief export: violence. Tchaikovsky wouldn't have known the scale of it, and even if he did, he wouldn't have been able to comment on it, censorship and surveillance being intrusive and all-pervasive.[16]

As a subject of the Russian Empire, Tchaikovsky performed the role required of him as a student, bureaucrat, professor, and composer. Fibbing, exaggerating, playing the part others wanted him to play—these things were no sin for him, nor for anyone else. Philip Ross Bullock has made this point with respect to Tchaikovsky's salon music, his songs that "invite us to interpret them—to engage in an exercise of speculative hermeneutics—though they simultaneously deprive us of the material necessary to decode them." There is a queer aspect to the aesthetic, in the broader and narrower sense of the term: "Tchaikovsky was able to translate the personal experience of his sexuality into a method for reading and setting verse in such a way that he could speak directly to his audiences in a language they would recognize, while guarding his privacy in a world where he was, in effect, public property."[17]

There is no avoiding the fact that he talked about "restless fate," meaning inevitability, and wrote a lot of music about it, most explicitly in an 1868 tone poem named *Fatum*, which has a jarring ending of raised fifth and sixth scale degrees. The booklet for the premiere included a short verse called "The Aphorism of Melchizedek" ("Izrecheniye Mel'khisedeka") by a Romantic poet who lost his mind, Konstantin Batyushkov. Melchizedek, a biblical figure seen as an archetype of Christ, comments at the end of his life on humankind's enslavement to fate. Tchaikovsky loved the dysfunctional music that he wrote on the subject; the dedicatee of *Fatum* and conductor of the second performance, Mily Balakirev, condemned it as piecemeal and hastily stitched together. (One suspects that he didn't conduct it very well.) Tchaikovsky destroyed the manuscript after recycling the music in pieces that weren't about fate. It was reconstructed in 1896 based on the surviving orchestral parts.[18]

Like most people, Tchaikovsky didn't want to die, but annual epidemics and incurable sexually transmitted diseases made dying easy in the Russian nineteenth century. Morphine and alcohol addiction took the life of his sister. "Black wings" fluttered over Tchaikovsky's head as they did the head of Brahms, whose music Tchaikovsky profoundly disliked as a "caricature" of another composer obsessed with fate: Beethoven (at least according to his biographer Anton Schindler).[19] Tchaikovsky's own definition of fate excluded anything behavioral. It wasn't a lifestyle choice, or something he or anyone else earned or deserved. Nor was fate the historical imperative or necessity that Homer's *Iliad* references.[20] Fate was a force majeure, a preternatural power. Consider the thematic organization of *Fatum*: ABCAB'C', with a coda based on B (representing life's joys) and C (sorrows). The hammer of fate (A) is heard at the start, in the middle, and at the end: to be born is to be fated to die, and the score folds back on itself to make that point clear. The issue wasn't worth obsessing about, and Tchaikovsky eventually stopped doing so, recognizing, to quote Daniel Dennett, that "fatalism has absolutely nothing to recommend it."[21]

To accept fate is to relax into its existence, its rhythms, its decreasing tempo, its own end. When the future is taken care of, the here and now welcomes imaginative play. And so, in his Second Orchestral Suite of 1883, Tchaikovsky quoted from an opera about fate by another composer (Verdi's *La forza del destino*, premiered in Russia in 1862). That quote encompasses the gorgeous, lyrical texture of a child's dreams—the reverie of a contented person, which Tchaikovsky, for the most part, turned out to be.

PART I

LOCAL AND REGIONAL MATTERS

What might have been an uneventful bureaucratic life

$\mathbf{C}$ hildhoods aren't interesting to read about, and Tchaikovsky's childhood didn't even interest his own parents. As was typical in Russian families of means, he was cared for but not doted upon. Pyotr Ilyich (Peter the son of Ilya) was born in Votkinsk, an industrial town about 630 miles east of Moscow, between Perm and Ufa. He was baptized on May 5, 1840, at the Cathedral of the Annunciation of the Most Holy Mother of God. As of this writing, the city is in disrepair: transport is spotty, café service gruff, the pond dirty and trash-filled, and Votkinsk's symbol, an anchor, has fallen from its pedestal. Still, the park is pleasant and the people generally decent.[1] The church sits on a square named after the ironworks from which the town was built with serf labor. Votkinsk became the administrative center for a sprawling mining operation on the edge of the Ural Mountains. Now, long-range missiles are assembled there. Tchaikovsky's metallurgist father, Ilya Petrovich (1795–1880), ran the ironworks. He's credited on the Museum of the History of Votkinsk website with developing the infrastructure of Votkinsk and, incongruously, with "environmental conservation."[2] Ilya and his second wife, Alexandra Andreyevna Tchaikovskaya (1812–54), lived in a large, classically designed house on Gospodskaya (Master's) Street, the official residence for the mining director. The couple and their younger children stayed there for eleven years. After the Revolution, the house became a workers' club, and in 1940 it was turned into one of several Tchaikovsky Memorial Museums.[3]

His mother's maiden name was Assier. Her distant relatives were French wine merchants, and her grandfather, Michel Victor Acier (1736–99), was a sculptor who created intricate figurines of shepherds and an illustrious piece called "Cupid Disguised as a Dancing Columbine." Decades before the French Revolution, he relocated from Versailles to Meissen, Germany, a center for porcelain and ceramics manufacture.[4] In the 1770s he worked with another court artist, Johann Joachim Kändler, on "a table-service stylistically based on late baroque traditions comprising a total of 40 groups and individual figures for Catherine II, Empress of Russia." This project lent "expression to the ideals of the time, the quest for education, rational behavior and irreproachable family life."[5] Acier's third son— Tchaikovsky's maternal grandfather, Michael Heinrich Maximilian Acier (1778–1835)—moved as an adult from Meissen to St. Petersburg, Russia, where he served as a tutor in French and German to the Artillery and Engineering Corps; later, he held positions in the customs and finance administrations. Michael changed his first name to Andrey and his last to Assier.[6]

The genealogy is revealing: Tchaikovsky's relatives on his mother's side included an artist who served different courts. Besides figurines, his circle produced chandeliers, tassels, silverware, tureens, vases, clocks, snuffboxes, lacquer chests, and other ornamental pieces. Tchaikovsky too would become attached to a court—that of the Romanovs—and create ornate, showy things in the service of empire. He disliked composing for ceremonial occasions, but he did it as needed, and did it well.

Tchaikovsky had an older brother, Nikolay (Kolya, 1838–1911), who followed his father's path into mining before building railroads.

Tchaikovsky's sister, Alexandra (Sasha, 1841–91), married a senior officer in the imperial service, Lev Davïdov, who retired to manage an inherited estate in the mountain riverside settlement of Kamianka (Kam'yanka) in central Ukraine. Tchaikovsky often visited her there, strolled the forests and the orchards, ducked into the grotto in the park, and tried to ignore the smell of disintegrating beets coming from the sugar factory.[7] The Soviets affixed Tchaikovsky's name to a local museum, as they did the conservatory in Kyiv, 50 miles away.[8] His younger brother by three years, Ippolit (1843–1927), trained in the Cadet Corps in St. Petersburg before becoming a midshipman in the Caspian flotilla. After retiring from the Imperial Navy, he joined the Russian Society of Shipping and Trade, which cut through a tangle of tariffs to increase the flow of goods from the Black Sea to the Baltics and St. Petersburg. The cost of nuts, raisins, and tobacco in the imperial capital dropped. Ippolit received one of his promotions because his firm's chairman loved Pyotr's music.[9]

Closest to the composer were his brothers Anatole and Modest, twins born in 1850 who died a year apart in 1915 and 1916, respectively.

Anatole had a distinguished legal career, the kind that Tchaikovsky might have had were it not for his musical genius. Both of them attended the School of Jurisprudence in St. Petersburg, as did Modest, but only Anatole made a name for himself in the legal profession. He became a district prosecutor and then vice-governor in Tiflis, Georgia, a restive, recently annexed part of the Russian Empire whose playhouse had burned down (rebuilding it became a matter of financial interest to him). With Ippolit, Anatole helped to preserve Tchaikovsky's archive after his death and lobbied to keep rights to performances and publications in the family's hands. The Imperial Theaters had other ideas, as did the Bolsheviks. Tchaikovsky's music became the property of the state.[10]

Anatole's twin, Modest, was a semi-successful playwright and translator. He wrote comedies of manners involving milquetoast aristocrats (there's also a play about a young composer's bad romance with a diva) and produced several opera scripts, including the much-maligned libretto of Tchaikovsky's *The Queen of Spades*.

It was an extraordinarily close family; everyone looked out for one another. Mr. Tchaikovsky called Mrs. Tchaikovsky "angel" and moaned about her occasional absences from Votkinsk, filling his late-night letters to her with kisses from head to toe, details about the kids' antics and upset stomachs (the Tchaikovsky family had chronic gastrointestinal issues), the dopes he had to deal with at the factory, and the "Tatars, Ostyaks, Chuvashes, and Cheremishes" who drove his coaches but couldn't speak any Russian, "damn them to hell."[11] Besides his parents and siblings, Pyotr also benefited from the love of an aunt and uncle on his mother's side—they lived in Siberia, and had four daughters—and that of Fanny Dürbach (1822–1902), the family governess from 1844 to 1848. She remembered Pyotr as a delicate boy, a "child of glass," and once found him wailing in bed because he couldn't get the music out of his head.[12] It reverberated throughout his fifty-three years of life, and he often (unjustifiably) felt inadequate in service to his gift.

Under Dürbach's supervision he began to take piano lessons with Mariya Palchikova (Luginova, 1823–88), a local musician once thought to be of balalaika-playing peasant (or serf) descent, a perfect tale to tell in Soviet textbooks about Tchaikovsky's childhood immersion in folklore. In truth Palchikova's father was a tradesman and an amateur composer while her husband was a high-ranking civil servant (a collegiate assessor). Peasants didn't marry people like that. Palchikova also composed and joined her father in sending a musical gift to Tsar Alexander II on the occasion of his coronation.[13] Tchaikovsky did the same.

He never forgot Palchikova and offered her financial assistance in the 1880s. Dürbach, too, stayed in his life. Her letters are thickly sentimental (so too the effort to publish them in a collection of documents marketed as a biographical exposé). His former governess reminisced about the Tchaikovsky family house in Votkinsk and never wanted the great composer to forget that she had once been his teacher:

> I was particularly impressed by those quiet, mild evenings towards the end of summer. The fishermen's boats rocked gently on the mirror-smooth surface of the pond which reflected the sun. From our balcony we could hear sad and tender songs which were the only things to break the silence of those wonderful nights, when none of you wanted to go to bed; surely you remember them. If you still remember any of those tunes, why don't you use them in your music; it would delight those who are unable to hear them in your country.[14]

The description is achingly similar to words sung at the start of the opera *Eugene Onegin*:

Они поют и я, бывало,	They are singing, and I, too,
В давно прошедшие года—	Used to sing that song in years long past.
Ты помнишь ли?—и я певала.	Do you remember? I used to sing it too.

In 1848 his father's work brought the family to Moscow and then to St. Petersburg, where Tchaikovsky briefly attended boarding school. Then, in 1850, his father accepted a position at another Ural Mountain ironworks (in the town of Alapayevsk, where in 1918 Bolshevik guards executed several members of Tsar Nikolay II's family, detonating them in a half-flooded mineshaft).[15] By that time, his parents had decided to educate him at the School of Jurisprudence, having ruled out the Cadet Corps, and Tchaikovsky graduated nine years later, in the spring of 1859, age nineteen. He had lost his mother five years before. During his legal studies, he sang in the school's choir and took piano and music theory lessons with concert pianist Rudolf Kündinger and his brother August. Voice lessons, and a love of Italian opera, came from Luigi Piccioli, who moved from Naples to St. Petersburg in the 1840s. Piccioli owned a private studio and taught at the Women's Patriotic Institute (a charity school that, at the time of its founding, educated the orphaned daughters of officers killed in the War of 1812) and the Imperial Court Singing Chapel. After 1860, he taught under the auspices of the Russian Musical Society (RMS), which, in 1868, became the Imperial Russian Musical Society (IRMS).[16] Tchaikovsky's father arranged and paid for the lessons until 1858, when Ilya lost his fortune in a scam and was forced to find employment in St. Petersburg's Technological Institute.[17]

Upon graduation Tchaikovsky clerked at the Ministry of Justice, located at the time in a neoclassical palace on the Fontanka Embankment. Alexander II had been crowned tsar and had mitigated the penalties for crimes against the state; buried in this matrix, Tchaikovsky appeared destined for an uneventful bureaucratic life as a *stolonachal'nik* (head of a desk). The records of his official service are opaque with some bare-bones information, including the date his first passport was issued, June 24, 1861, for a trip to Europe that included time in Ostend, Belgium, where he was treated "with mineral waters and sea baths" for "thinness" and "abscesses." The passport includes stamps for visits to Hamburg and London, and he made it to Berlin and Paris as well. His salary at the ministry was low: 25 rubles a month, excluding a subsistence allowance, "table money," of just over a third of that amount. He received generous three-month vacations, using the time to travel and visit friends and family.[18]

He also entered the RMS, an institution that, in nineteenth-century Russia, dedicated itself to music education and the elevation of dilettante musicians in Russia's cities and provinces to a professional level, and with it the elaboration and elevation of the folk traditions. Some RMS ensembles served the cause of women's musical education, others functioned as the provincial Russian equivalent of Alcoholics Anonymous, taking the vodka bottles out of people's hands and giving them violins.[19] Tchaikovsky studied thoroughbass for a year in the St. Petersburg branch of the RMS before enrolling in the St. Petersburg Conservatory, which opened, under the auspices of the RMS, on September 8, 1862, in a leased wing of an estate owned by Olga Demidova-Aledinskaya.[20] Tchaikovsky joined the inaugural class of 179 students (a "motley crowd" that included a "coroner's assistant," a "steamboat company clerk," and the "son of a junior French teacher").[21] He retained his position at the Ministry of Justice for the first year, then resigned to devote himself to music for the rest of his life.

Resigning, however, wasn't what it seemed. Tchaikovsky needed to request permission to do so. He received it on April 11, 1863, but remained "attached" to the Ministry of Justice until 1868. In essence Tchaikovsky trained and started his career as a composer while on long-term leave from his position as collegiate assessor. Unless he filed a request with the ministry, he could neither take a break from his music studies nor travel. In 1867, four years after Tchaikovsky had technically but not officially "resigned," the ministry assigned him a research project in a Moscow archive. Tchaikovsky didn't show up for this work. His record of service was otherwise unblemished.[22]

Anton Rubinstein and needing to rejoice

Tchaikovsky studied under Anton Rubinstein (1829–94), whose musical tastes were German and who so admired Beethoven that he started to look like him—his mane a magnificent mess and affect severe. He attacked the piano as did the Beethoven of myth, and became, according to Richard Taruskin, "the greatest instrumental virtuoso Russia has ever produced" and "a bewilderingly prolific composer in all media."[23] The scribomaniacal massiveness of his output meant overexposure during his lifetime and posthumous erasure from the repertoire at home and abroad. No one listens to him anymore; everyone listens to the student he treated like dirt.

Rubinstein had a complicated childhood and became a cantankerous adult: headstrong, self-doubting, frequently jealous, often frustrated, and prone to ennui. A letter he sent to his sister Sophia also indicates a capacity for self-irony: "Today I conduct an opera here, tomorrow it's a symphony there, and then I give a charity concert in some other place. So it goes on repeating itself without end—but always with enormous success!!! That is my life in total. I am bored to death."[24] Rubinstein recognized Tchaikovsky's talent but treated him gruffly from his student days to the premiere of the *Pathétique*.

Born to Jewish parents in a village in Ukraine on the border with Moldova, Rubinstein moved to Moscow with his family at age four. Later, on the advice of his grandfather, he converted to Orthodoxy. His father operated a pin- and pencil-making operation while his mother ran the household and taught music. Recognizing Anton's potential, she passed him on to a French émigré virtuoso, Alexander Villoing, for lessons. Villoing took Anton to Paris in hopes of enrolling him at the Conservatoire, but the effort failed so they returned to Russia. He and his younger brother Nikolay, also a phenomenal pianist, toured around together, played for the tsar, Nikolay I, and banked enough for professional training in composition with (on Giacomo Meyerbeer's recommendation) Siegfried Dehn in Berlin in 1845. Nikolay quit after a year, ostensibly to be with his gravely ill father. Anton continued his studies with music theorist A. B. Marx, absorbing the latter's organicist, pseudo-Hegelian conception of form (as the combination of a musical thesis, antithesis, and synthesis, becoming a new thesis, and so forth).

Rubinstein supported himself as a performer but could no longer market himself as a child prodigy. Liszt refused to accept him into his piano studio for training as an adult virtuoso. Impoverishment and the Revolution of 1848 convinced him to relocate to St. Petersburg (he thought about emigrating to the United States). There, in the embrace of music-loving nobles, Rubinstein focused on composing and conducting and, through remarkable force of will, establishing what Russia did not have: a music school with a professional faculty and a comprehensive curriculum. Infighting twice forced Rubinstein to resign as director of the school (in 1867 and 1891), and his Eurocentrism brought him into conflict with Russian nationalist composers like Mily Balakirev (1836–1910).

The latter had learned music on a Russian estate supported by a Russian patron and had a formative encounter with Mikhaíl Glinka that contributed to his nationalism (which included elements of the Far East from the Mongols and the southern Muslim regions of imperial conquest). Balakirev's best-known piano piece is *Izlamey* (1869), a knuckle-buster based on themes from the Caucasus and Armenia. Liszt performed it, as did Rubinstein. Russian music, as Balakirev and the *Moguchaya kuchka* (Mighty Heap/Mighty Five/ Mighty Fist/Mighty Handful) defined it, rejected European-style conservatories. As such, they rejected Bachian counterpoint, the teleological forms of the Enlightenment, formal-functional harmonies, and the asymmetrical major and the minor scale along with the leading tone. Russian music found its most resonant sonorities in the mythical steppe. Peasants and serfs, priests and bishops, helmet- and wing-shaped *gusli* (plucked, handheld string instruments) became the inspiration for an aesthetic that wanted to be anything and everything except European, never mind that Glinka's "Russian" operas derive from Italian models. Balakirev antisemitically identified Rubinstein's cosmopolitanism, his conservatory, and his students as a threat to musical nationality and Orthodoxy (though not a threat to the third plank holding up Tsar Nikolay I's regime, autocracy).

When the invective became unbearable, Rubinstein disappeared, concertizing for eight months in the United States and Canada— everywhere from Kalamazoo to Montreal, New Orleans, and Toledo.[25]

Later, Rubinstein played a series of "historical" concerts in Europe. Intended for both the general public and students, the concerts privileged dead composers, especially those buried in Vienna. Rubinstein included his own music on the last of the recital programs as if to prove that he was a European ancestor's imagining—a hard sell for a kid from Moscow.[26] Rubinstein played beautifully until he stopped practicing; he started to leave out the hard parts. In the meantime he wrote piles of quickly forgotten orchestral and piano music that he didn't like editing or revising. (The enormous success he reports to his sister relates to the official recognition of his contribution to Russian music.) Rubinstein's operas are hard work, meaning slogs. Most of them came and went, with only *The Demon* (1875), based on a poem by Mikhaíl Lermontov, catching on. It could be heard as a metaphor for his battle with Balakirev insofar as the mildly folkloric sound of the opening converts to Romantic arioso (following the appearance of a fallen angel seeking to seduce a betrothed maiden).

Russian musical nationalism has been described as a lose-lose proposition.[27] It siloed composers, separating them from the musical mainstream, and relied on a frustratingly limited, partly manufactured vernacular.[28] Balakirev believed that an Orthodox Russian composer could live in different places but belonged to just one. Rubinstein, in contrast, traveled the world promoting "universal" music that, he knew, had nationalistic (antimonarchic) Austro-Germanic origins. He brought this superior (in his opinion) music to Russia and imposed it on his students. In a posthumously published *Gedankenkorb* (*Basket of Thoughts*), Rubinstein wrote about how

everything strives toward the modern, sees the past only from the point of view of historical interest, and desires the transcendental in all branches of art. Will this latest trend in taste last, or will a reaction set in? Or will the question of something else arise? What could this something else be? Folk music? That means starting from the beginning all over again![29]

Neither side compromised until the appointment of Nikolay Rimsky-Korsakov, the most productive member of the *Moguchaya kuchka*, as conservatory professor.[30] Tchaikovsky matured as a composer as the battle waged and, to free himself of one oppressive influence, aligned himself with another.

At the conservatory, Tchaikovsky also studied with Nikolay Zaremba (1821–79), another disciple of A. B. Marx and the first person to teach music theory in Russia. Here is the first riddle of Tchaikovsky's education: his specialization. He majored in music theory at the conservatory, not piano or music theory with piano—he obligatorily took both piano and organ lessons. But what even was "music theory" at the time? It is sometimes named "compositional theory" or "theory of musical composition," plus "orchestration" and "practical composition" are also encountered. What are the differences? The looseness of the language attests to the nascent state of music education at the time but ultimately suggests that music theory meant developing a sufficient command of the craft of composition to fashion a large-scale, vocal-instrumental piece. Another issue concerns the term "Kapellmeister," used to denote "the master of the chapel," but also referring, less nobly, to choral and orchestral conducting. The conservatory didn't educate Kapellmeisters, but Tchaikovsky still learned to conduct. Where? Perhaps being involved in the student orchestra also meant waving a stick in front of it?[31]

Another riddle is Zaremba, lampooned in the sources as a dullard who received a few kopecks an hour for lectures. Tchaikovsky supposedly tired of Zaremba's religious, faith-based approach to teaching, didn't like going to the Lutheran church on Nevsky Prospekt to watch Zaremba conduct chorales, and couldn't countenance Zaremba's love of Mendelssohn over Mozart.[32] A more convincing counternarrative has Zaremba exerting profound influence on Tchaikovsky, educating him in the step-by-step process of transforming sketches into finished forms and instilling in him a pan-European theoretical method that he passed on to his own students.

He encouraged Tchaikovsky to model his student pieces on Mozart, not Mendelssohn, and mandated hours upon hours of score study.

A third riddle concerns Tchaikovsky's employment as a teaching assistant to Zaremba, tutoring twenty-four of his peers (twenty-three after one dropped out). Clearly, he was a prodigious student, prodigious enough, in fact, not to take notes in class. Helping Zaremba kept bread on the table after his resignation from the ministry. But what he taught is unknown. He might have led ear-training sessions or keyboard harmony classes; perhaps he graded harmony assignments, deducting points for parallel fifths and cross-relations. Maybe he did all these things: Zaremba was hideously overworked. One document has Tchaikovsky employed as a teaching assistant from September to December of 1863, and another until 1865, basically his entire time at the conservatory. He earned 40 rubles for each year-long course, while the professors overseeing him brought in 100.[33]

As to "orchestration," Tchaikovsky absorbed the French and Italian opera scores in the library along with Belgian composer François-Auguste Gevaert's *Traité général d'instrumentation* (1863), which in 1865 Rubinstein asked him to translate into Russian.[34] It derives from Berlioz's treatise, tracing the development of the orchestra into the nineteenth century, describing range, register, and the size and function of the string, wind, and percussion sections in different contexts. So far so good, but the organology also has a psychiatric element. Gevaert notes the feistiness of natural contra valved counterparts, the frankness of German oboes and the moodiness of French ones. The flute, which Tchaikovsky studied at the conservatory and played in the student orchestra, comes across as a cheerful churchgoing peasant. The piccolo is happiest when paired with the drum to tighten up "the soldiers' kick." The B♭ clarinet has become more poetic over time but still can't compete with the violin. Gevaert prefers transparent textures to middle-range thickness, adores the harp, and doesn't like trills.[35] Reading the treatise and listening to compositions like Gevaert's 1850 *Fantasía a toda orquesta sobre motivos españoles* greatly illuminate Tchaikovsky's habits as an orchestrator.

Tchaikovsky kept a copy of Otto Jahn's monumental biography of Mozart on his desk and, as music critic Herman Laroche relates, adored Mozart's mature operas (Laroche appends that Tchaikovsky translated Lorenzo Da Ponte's libretto for Mozart's *Le nozze di Figaro* into Russian, "performing the painstaking and quite useless task of fitting a Russian text to the recitativo secco").[36] The student composer excelled in sight-singing and could come up with pieces in the form of a rondo, minuet and trio, and polonaise on the spot (one of Rubinstein's favorite classroom challenges).[37] Although classmates claimed Tchaikovsky wasn't a keen notetaker and avoided all-nighters—and never discussed his teaching-assistant work—he somehow retained enough in later years to develop lesson plans just like those of his teachers.

To graduate from the conservatory, he needed to rejoice. On October 12, 1865, the faculty of the conservatory under Rubinstein perversely assigned Friedrich Schiller's ode "An die Freude" ("To Joy") to Tchaikovsky and another senior, Ivan Rïbasov, as a diploma project.[38] The challenge was to come up with a cantata on the text knowing (but pretending not to know) that Schiller's ode provided the text for the unprecedented choral finale of Beethoven's Ninth Symphony. That work, from 1824, sent Vienna's musically conservative opinionators like Louis Spohr into a tizzy, especially the "monstrous and tasteless" fourth movement and its "trivial" handling of Schiller's ode. "I find in it another proof of what I already remarked in Vienna, that Beethoven was wanting in aesthetical feeling and in a sense of the beautiful," he complained.[39] By the time Tchaikovsky set it, on command, Beethoven had been embraced by millions and the Ninth immortalized for its profundity, not triviality.

The history of *K radosti*, as Tchaikovsky's cantata is known in the Russian translation of Schiller's title, is both brief and incomplete.

During his time at the conservatory, he had played through Beethoven's Ninth at the piano and sung in the chorus. (Tchaikovsky sang in the bass section, giving the lie to all the cinematic depictions of him with a thin, emasculated tenor voice, which might be based on the unnaturally high-pitched recording of him speaking and whistling on Thomas Edison's phonograph.)[40] Much later, in 1889, Tchaikovsky would conduct the Ninth.[41] To pull himself away from Beethoven for his diploma project, he did some background reading about the ode, a freemason's hymn that celebrates fraternity, the canceling of debts, the disappearance of hell, "rescue from the tyrant's fetters," and "pardon at the guillotine!"[42] Beethoven had used the first three of the nine stanzas of Schiller's ode plus part of the fourth. Tchaikovsky also set the first three stanzas, but, as his first distancing move, added part of the seventh with his chorus singing just two refrains. Puzzlingly, Tchaikovsky combined different Russian translations of Schiller's text taken from a complete Russian-language edition of Schiller's writings edited by Nikolay Gerbel. "The task of combining these three different translations was complicated by their disparate poetic meters," the editor of the 2016 critical edition of *K radosti* comments.[43]

Little is known about the genesis of the cantata beyond the typical student problems the composer had to deal with: he was penniless and couldn't pay a tailor; he had a toothache, sore joints, and a cough; the room he rented at his aunt's place was stuffy and the neighbor's doorbell wouldn't stop ringing. He changed addresses, moving to his poet friend Alexei Apukhtin's place after the latter left for Oryol for a couple of months, November and December 1865. There he sketched, drafted, and revised the cantata (Rubinstein demanded a raft of changes) while also preparing for his other graduation tasks.[44] A photograph survives from this period showing Tchaikovsky wearing Apukhtin's boyar-sized raccoon fur coat.

The adjudication of the cantata supposedly involved two performances, the first conducted by Tchaikovsky on December 29 in front of the examination committee and the second presented by Rubinstein to an audience of invited guests and government officials on December 31. This information comes from Tchaikovsky's brother Modest, though he gets the dates wrong and adds the sensational detail that Tchaikovsky was so terrified of a public dressing-down that he skipped the performance on December 31. As punishment, Rubinstein withheld his graduation diploma for several years.[45] There is no evidence to support the claim; in fact, Rubinstein conducted the graduation concert much later, in March 1866. December 29 was the day that half of the graduating students took their exam and December 31 the day that the other half, including Rïbasov, took it.[46] Like his peers, Tchaikovsky received his diploma long after graduating, in his case on May 27, 1870, owing to bureaucratic dillydallying.

The exams and the concert happened at the Mikhaílovsky Palace in the center of St. Petersburg, on what is now called Arts Square. The proprietor, Grand Princess Elena Pavlovna (formerly Princess Charlotte of Württemberg, 1807–73), had married the youngest son of Tsar Pavel I, Mikhaíl, in 1824. She was learned, liberal, and lively; he was affable but apparently something of a saphead. Their incompatible relationship quickly turned cold. Elena Pavlovna founded an order of nurses, imported medicine, and backed several charities. After Mikhaíl's death in 1849, she invested heavily in the arts, becoming the most important patron of music in St. Petersburg's history. Without her, the RMS wouldn't have opened a conservatory, and the conservatory wouldn't have ended up in a building of its own.[47] Her palace hosted the school's fancier and more formal events, including exams. Tchaikovsky's success in those exams brought him into the fold of the musical elite. He received a silver medal (the top medal, gold, wasn't awarded) on May 12, 1866, along with the title of "free artist," exempt from forced recruitment into another profession. It merits adding, as illustrative of the persistence of medieval patriarchal practices in Russia, that the title also exempted Tchaikovsky from corporal punishment, getting flogged in public.

Tchaikovsky clearly excelled in his counterpoint exercises (the strict method he learned came from Heinrich Bellermann's 1862 treatise *Der Kontrapunkt*, an influence on Schoenberg and the Second Viennese School). The cantata relies on four- and (at a stretch) five-part imitation, accelerating the music through proportional rhythmic diminution before triumphant unisons. Tchaikovsky dialogues with the ancients and some more immediate predecessors. For the fourth movement, glorifying the Creator, he uses Haydn's oratorio *The Creation* as a point of departure. Roland John Wiley's assertion that the "opening melody embeds the verbal rhythm of Angel Gabriel's announcement to Mary of the birth of Christ from Luke 1:28" is dubious; measures 4–6 of Schumann's Piano Concerto in A minor (1845) are clearly the source for the unspooling C-minor triadic pattern; even the scoring is similar.[48] There's no doubting, however, the mess of madrigalisms at the end of the third movement, setting stanza 2—though if there is a Renaissance legacy, it is filtered through the *stile antico* choral music of the late eighteenth and early nineteenth centuries. The orchestra falls silent, the texture is emptied out, and the words

Если ж кто благ сих не ведал,—украдкою, С плачем от нас отойди	Whoever did not know—these blessings Stealthily he crept away from us, weeping

are painted with bittersweet semitonal clashes and intonations of lament. In places the singing hovers on the edge of inaudibility, no louder than pianissimo. The strings are kept busy in the other movements, laboriously churning away beneath the singers. Tchaikovsky turns the woodwinds into the solitary souls described by Schiller and uses the brasses to enrich the middle of the texture—though, thanks to the brass, the C-major ending of the cantata is jubilantly noise-filled.

Tchaikovsky follows the lead of the Russian-language translators of "An die Freude" by turning Schiller into an advocate of inner reflection and pure contemplation contra the bombast of the world—at least in the third movement.[49] In the others the subject is overcoming. The cantata sets secular words to sacred music, whose enactment of transcendence has recently been described, by the music critic Vladimir Dudin, as an example of "Russian cosmism, which grew out of the spirit of German philosophy and culture [as reflected in the work of the Orthodox Christian philosopher Nikolay Fyodorov (1829–1903)]."[50] By cosmism, Dudin means the biblical promises of resurrection that are realized repeatedly in Russian history. Catastrophe permits rebirth, which leads to catastrophe and another rebirth, heading towards historical, spiritual, and ethnic apotheosis. The cantata becomes, in Dudin's extreme departure from Fyodorov, a frightening example of Russian nationalism, drawing together Orthodox values, imperialism, and (anachronistically) the Soviet experiment and its repressions into a unified narrative about Russian common purpose over a thousand years. And if the ideology doesn't sit well with you, then you must "stealthily [creep] away from us, weeping." Yet this student composition, which Tchaikovsky never saw published, wasn't heard a single time between 1866 and 1939. It was revived for Tchaikovsky's centenary—on the cusp of the Soviet entry into World War II.

Little Russia

Composer and critic César Cui (1835–1918) reviewed the graduation concert. Like the other members of the Mighty Five, Cui was also an active citizen, a high-ranking officer in the Imperial Army who studied fortifications. His background was French and Lithuanian; he composed operas on foreign subjects; and yet, by the time Tchaikovsky achieved prominence, Cui was championing all things Russian. He wrote for the liberal (meaning: opposition) newspaper *St. Petersburg Register* (*Sankt-Peterburgskiye vedomosti*) and there denounced Tchaikovsky and his music as "feeble." *K radosti* succumbed in pathetic fashion to the German influence rather than keeping it at bay, on the other side of the fortification Cui was building to protect Russian music. "It's true," Cui wrote,

> that Tchaikovsky's composition (a cantata) was written in the most unfavorable circumstances: on command, for a specific date, on a specific subject and in compliance with certain forms. But still, if he had talent, it would have at least broken through the shackles somewhere.

Reading Cui's remarks, Tchaikovsky felt sick: "I don't know what came over me," he recalled to an acquaintance (the mother of a mute boy tutored by his brother Modest) several years later. "My eyes clouded over, my head started spinning, and like a madman I rushed out of the café (where I was reading that newspaper). I was not conscious of what I did or where I ended up. All day long I wandered aimlessly through the city, repeating to myself: I'm useless; I'm a nonentity; nothing good will ever come of me; I have no talent."[51]

Still, he needed income. Two months before Cui's review, Tchaikovsky had taken the twenty-two-hour train ride from St. Petersburg to Moscow, found lodging, and began to teach what he had been taught. He gave lessons at the Moscow branch of the RMS through the spring of 1866 before taking a full-time position at the brand-new Moscow Conservatory.

The student became a professor thanks to Anton Rubinstein's brother Nikolay, who was arguably a better musician but had a narrower existence. At the end of his musically prodigious youth, Nikolay enrolled in law at Moscow University, which got him out of serving in the army. He graduated, then took a job in the office of the governor general (mayor) of Moscow, all the while trying to maintain his musical activities. He couldn't do both, so he resigned to become, like Anton, a composer, conductor, concert pianist, and musical educator at institutions that he founded. Rubinstein hired his brother's prize pupil: Tchaikovsky.

Moscow was the former capital. It was rougher and tougher and poorer than St. Petersburg. Traffic was chaotic (carriages didn't run fixed routes or respect traffic laws); artisans slept where they worked; critters gnawed on the meat sold in the open-air markets; fine dining and balls happened out of sight of hoi polloi in private residences; and sources of financial support for music were scattershot. Nikolay gave his music lessons for free out of his apartment on the Garden Ring Road, then, when the enrollment exceeded the space, out of a larger apartment around the corner on the ancient street of Sretenka (the name references the 1395 meeting, *sreteniye*, of a protective icon of the Mother of God that had been brought to Moscow from Vladimir in defiance of Mongol invaders). By 1864 the two-floor residence itself ran out of room, forcing Rubinstein to relocate to a mansion close to the site of the present-day Russian State (Lenin) Library and finally, as the Moscow Conservatory, into a building on Arbat Square that the Nazis blasted to smithereens during World War II.

Tchaikovsky taught there and at the conservatory's present-day location in an estate on Bolshaya Nikitskaya Street. The building originally belonged to Ekaterina Romanovna Dashkova (1743–1810), an intimate of Catherine the Great and director, from 1783 to 1794, of the Academy of Sciences. Dashkova published dictionaries and collections of plays and greatly elevated the status of Russian as an artistic language. She was also an active composer and folksong collector. The students and faculty of the conservatory would have been grateful to Dashkova for soundproofing her residence. The enrollment expanded from 184 students in 1868 to 430 by 1890, making the building cramped and uncomfortable and forcing the redesign into its present form.

Tchaikovsky composed a *pièce d'occasion* at a pivotal moment in Russian politics; his *Festival Overture on a Danish Hymn* celebrated the marriage of the son of Alexander II to the Danish princess Dagmar. The Romanovs had chosen German spouses for themselves since the era of Peter the Great. These marriages were meant to ensure a strong German presence at the court and in Russian society more broadly. Slavophile ideologues blamed the loss of old Russian customs on the foreign presence and expressed fear of Prussia meddling in Russian affairs through the German communities in the Baltics. The *Moscow Register* (*Moskovskiye vedomosti*) published a series of articles on the "German question" between 1864 and 1867, at which point Tsar Alexander II ordered the newspaper to cease and desist.[52] The question had been addressed by the marriage of his son to an anti-German Dane.

Dagmar was given the Russian name Mariya Fyodorovna. She had been the intended bride of the tsar's older son, Nikolay, but when he unexpectedly died of meningitis the younger son Sasha (later Tsar Alexander III) took her hand. They were married on October 12, 1866. Prussia had gone to war against Denmark and occupied Jutland, and the German states had unified under Prussian leadership. Tchaikovsky represents the consequences of the occupation in his overture with a funeral march.

It wasn't Tchaikovsky's idea. Nikolay Rubinstein arranged an official commission for him to write the music for Dagmar's first visit to Moscow. In November, Tchaikovsky completed it sitting in a tavern, between his classes, only to learn that Dagmar's visit had been postponed until the following spring, April 1867. He also learned that his overture wouldn't be performed, owing to a miscalculation on his part.

His overture has a Balakirev-type nationalist component: the opening flute solo features a chromatic pass between the fifth and sixth scale degree, and there are drones and background variations. The Danish hymn "Kong Christian stod ved højen mast" ("King Christian stood by the lofty mast"), an ode to heroic sailors played at royal and naval occasions, is paraphrased throughout. The overture also includes, in the introduction and the development section, the Russian anthem, Alexei Lvov's "God Save the Tsar" ("Bozhe, Tsarya khrani," 1833), but discordantly harmonized in the minor key. The alteration wasn't a mistake but a marriage: now, after much struggle and anguish, the Russian anthem has united with the Danish hymn. Dagmar and her national tune are the blood of ancient Rus: her lineage reaches back to the age of the Varangians (Vikings) and the original Scandinavian settlers of Tchaikovsky's Russia. Dagmar's betrothal to the future tsar allowed the Romanovs to claim the ancient past in service of the future. This joining of ancient pasts into a new Russian nationalism brings the overture to its triumphant conclusion.

He had carefully thought through his handling of the minor key, but few grasped its meaning or his intentions. The *Festival Overture* was panned for distorting the Russian anthem and excluded from the royal ceremonies. It was instead premiered on January 29, 1867, at a matinee concert of the RMS in Moscow "in aid of the families of the victims of the Christian rebellion [against Ottoman rule] in Crete." Adolphe Adam's "O Holy Night" featured on this "energetically applauded" program, along with Beethoven's "Ah! Perfido," the Chopin Funeral March, and other compositions befitting the somber moment.[53] That's as good as it got. The St. Petersburg newspaper *Voice* (*Golos*) reported that "in the original announcement [of the 1866–67 concert season] a performance of an overture by Tchaikovsky (former student of the conservatory here and a recipient of a silver medal for distinction in composition) had been promised together with a Ukrainian trepak by Alexander Serov. It was decided that Tchaikovsky's overture, conjoining the Russian and Danish national hymns, would not be performed because the talented young composer for some unknown reason decided to set our Russian national hymn in the minor, which altogether changes the character of this well-known tune."[54] Tchaikovsky nonetheless requested, and was granted, the consent of the grand princess and the heir to the throne to dedicate the overture to them, and received in exchange a gift of pearl cufflinks that he didn't want.[55] He sold them to a colleague for a pittance. Such were the vagaries of patronage.

His daytime work on the overture paralleled his nighttime work on the First Symphony, which gave Tchaikovsky such lurid nightmares that he vowed to confine composition to the mornings and afternoons. Nicotine poisoning played a role—he chain-smoked as he immersed himself in the draft between March and November 1866— as did the thought of another denunciation by Cui, who would troll him in print for years, only slowly admitting to Tchaikovsky's talent. Anton Rubinstein ruled out a St. Petersburg premiere, then indulged him by conducting the middle movements on February 11, 1867, at an RMS concert held in the hall of the Russian Merchants Society for Mutual Aid. In Moscow the scherzo was performed before the rest of the symphony, and Tchaikovsky didn't get a sense of the whole until 1868. When he did, he overhauled it. The 1874 revised version didn't itself receive a premiere until 1883.

The first and second movement have titles, "Daydreams of a Winter Journey" and "Land of Gloom, Land of Mist," but not the others. Why not? The fourth movement provides a clue: it uses the tune of a folksong about flowers flowering while maidens are deflowered—not exactly courtly poetry. (Depending on the source consulted, the song goes by the name "Tsveli-tsvetiki" ["Blooming, Blooming Were the Flowers"], or variants like "Ya poseyu l', molodenka, tsvetikov malenko" ["Will I Sow Little Flowers, My Lassie?"] and "Raspashu li ya, mlada-mladen'ka" ["Will I Plow, My Young Little One?"], but the imagery remains the same.) The other untitled movement, the scherzo, reuses music from Tchaikovsky's student piano sonata. Neither movement is about the direct observation of nature, whereas the first two are.

One of the Russian-language sources on the First Symphony likens the first and second movements to the painter Isaak Levitan's "mood landscapes," with an English-language source adding that

Levitan's impulse to "dreaminess—the lightly agitated attraction toward what exists as an image of beauty but cannot be captured—caused [him] to respond by amplifying color and adding dynamism to texture."[56] The parallel with Tchaikovsky's music is obvious, doubly so when considering the emphasis, in the first and second movements, on a single theme. The circular fillip in the flute and bassoon (heard once over two measures, then once over one measure, then twice over one measure) that defines the first movement is commonly described as a representation of solitude, a lone voice in the dull gray void, but the description misses the point.[57] The landscape itself is the protagonist, and Tchaikovsky is less interested in human perceptions of the land than the insignificance of those perceptions in the grand scheme. Russia has a lot of land, too much to fit into a single frame, as evidenced by the form-shattering blast in the French horns before the final iteration of the theme of the second movement. That blast follows a moment of silence and suggests a force beyond the "gloom" and "mist" of nature. The music is a distinct form of abstraction, as was the entire landscape-painting movement in Russia in the nineteenth century, which less glorified the Motherland than radically negated the Imperial Academy of Arts approach to painting and the preferential treatment it gave to the people occupying the Table of Ranks, as opposed to the people roaming the great beyond.

Russian landscape painters escaped one form of burdensome tradition, and the Russian landscape composer another. The "German question" dominated music criticism as it did political discourse in Russia, and Tchaikovsky found a Slavophile solution to it in his First Symphony, which rejects the entire bildungsroman, teleological organicist approach to sonata form. An aristocratic music critic, Prince Vladimir Odoyevsky, summarized it best when he remarked, in a diary entry dated February 3, 1867, "Tchaikovsky's Symphony is a glorious thing, but the Russian aspect isn't brought out clearly enough."[58] He likens folksong to a stream, muddied by Tchaikovsky's orchestration.

Tchaikovsky heard, by contrast, nothing but praise for his Second Symphony, which is perceived as no less nationalistic than the First but invites the opposite claim. The perception is built into its nickname, "Little Russian," which suggests Russian imperial dominance over Ukraine (specifically Kyiv and the Dnipro basin) though it's not about that at all. Back in the fourteenth century, when Moscow barely existed on explorers' maps and St. Petersburg hadn't yet been imagined, the patriarch of the Orthodox Church in Constantinople referred to the Slavic realm nearest to him as Little (Minor) Rus and the distant vistas at the edge of the horizon as Rus Major.[59] Moscow belonged to the boonies, the hinterland; Kyiv was the Slavic heart and, in terms of the establishment of the Russian Orthodox Church, the soul too. Rus Minor was the place that mattered, not the emptier, frostier regions north and east, where spirits and animals vastly outnumbered people. Tchaikovsky knew this history, just as he knew that the Ukraine of his time had once belonged to the Polish-Lithuanian Commonwealth. It took centuries for Russia to conquer the area at the expense of the Poles. Part of that history is obliquely told in Tchaikovsky's 1884 opera *Mazeppa*.

He didn't nickname his Second Symphony "Little Russian." His colleague Nikolay Kashkin did, followed by everyone else, owing to Tchaikovsky's supposed use of Ukrainian folksongs that he is said to have heard (or gathered, or reacquainted himself with) on his sister Sasha's estate in Kamianka in the summer of 1872, when he began the score.[60] The problem with the tale is that Tchaikovsky had arranged the two Ukrainian tunes in question—one an old Volga River tune, the other a children's clap-a-long riffing on the beak and sticklike legs of a crane—before traveling to Sasha's place. Another problem is that the Volga River tune doesn't sound at all like the tune in the first movement. The identification, frankly, is incorrect, a mishearing on Kashkin's part (he taught basic music theory and piano at the conservatory and advocated for Tchaikovsky, but their friendship wasn't as close as advertised). Still another problem is the

"Big [not Little] Russian" tune in the second movement: "Spin, my spinner" ("Pyadi, moya pryakha"). Tchaikovsky's Ukrainian symphony comes down to a single tune—a wisp of a thing—heard in the finale. The composer appears to have plucked this tune from a newly published collection of folksongs edited and annotated by Alexander Rubets, who taught music theory and solfège at the conservatory.[61] Tchaikovsky's variation technique is habitually compared to that in Glinka's *Kamarinskaya,* but that composition is nowhere near as supercharged as this one. The finale builds in excitement up to a short-circuiting blast of the tam-tam.

It's fun, but not simple. Thus argues music theorist Brent Auerbach in an article about the artfulness, as opposed to artlessness, of Tchaikovsky's highly repetitive compositional methods. Auerbach's focus is the final movement of the symphony and the handling of the *do re mi* motive of the opening of the "Crane" folksong. "Melodically," he writes, "we ... observe a process by which myriad small-scale *do re mi* gestures are sequenced to assemble ever-larger but tantalizingly incomplete versions of a giant Crane motive." *Do re mi* is exhaustively explored in the movement: at the start, it is sequenced at intervals of the third and fourth (in interlinked arpeggiations of augmented triads) and then, in the middle section, it is sequenced by second, which recreates the motive at a deeper structural level.[62]

Tchaikovsky quoted a folksong in the finale, and in the second movement, because that's what the Austro-German symphonic tradition taught him to do, even though his handling of the borrowing is fundamentally different from anything Beethoven or Schubert attempted, as Auerbach shows. Tchaikovsky also did so because, in the period of the Great Reforms, kindergarten arrived in Russia, and interest increased in organizing skill-building activities for preschool children.[63] The Second Symphony civic-mindedly reflects this trend. It would be reflected elsewhere in his output, most beautifully in his *Sixteen Songs for Children* (and teenagers), of which fifteen were written in 1883 for the edification and amusement of Sasha's children.[64]

Tchaikovsky orchestrated the Second Symphony in the fall of 1872, and the IRMS scheduled a January 11, 1873, premiere (postponed until January 26 owing to the death of IRMS sponsor Elena Pavlovna). Laroche raved about it in print with a pointed dig at the uneducated Moscow public. The "success or failure" of a composition by a Russian composer was for St. Petersburg to decide, since that's where Russian music is appreciated and taken "seriously" by the "right kind of people," not the dolts living in Russia's second city.[65]

Tchaikovsky refined the orchestration and the Second Symphony was premiered anew on March 27 in Moscow, with a repeat performance on March 29. The removal of the mutes from the strings in the third movement earned a newspaper mention.[66] By this time the score had been heard by St. Petersburg's cognoscenti and properly appreciated. It was the best thing Tchaikovsky had done, according to the consensus, a composition that left all his other compositions behind. Its popularity meant performances abroad and prompted a second round of revisions completed between December 1879 and January 1880. Tchaikovsky touched up the second movement, rescored the third, and abbreviated the first and fourth movements. This version, too, was praised, and for interesting reasons: it didn't take itself too seriously; it wasn't intellectual; it showed that musical variation techniques have a lot in common with nursery rhymes.

Scented suds

Balakirev (and Odoyevsky, and for that matter Tchaikovsky's capacious English chronicler David Brown) would remain disappointed that Tchaikovsky did not become the kind of nationalist that he might or even should have.[67] He didn't realize his Slavic potential, according to the essentializing that eventually rubbed Slavic artists wrong. His music was too urban, too regal, too smitten with the

Romanovs, too idiosyncratic, and frankly too cheerful. Yet the *Romeo and Juliet* fantasy overture, a project foisted on Tchaikovsky by Balakirev, is a paradoxical exception. Russian musical nationalism relies on storytelling, meaning musical narration, program music, in defiance of Germanic transcendent absolutism. Russia, moreover, had become Shakespeare's home away from home. His plays were staged in a manner that explicitly resonated with the Russian experience, and his Renaissance English sounded better in nineteenth-century Russian than it did in other languages. At least that's what the nationalists argued.

Shakespeare became popular in Russia during Catherine the Great's reign (1762–96). The empress was an amateur playwright, and in 1786 she adapted (translated is too strong a word) *The Merry Wives of Windsor* into Russian from a spotty German translation of the original. *Hamlet* had also been adapted from a secondary source, along with some of his other political plays. Napoleon's 1812 invasion tainted everything culturally French and opened the gates for a flood of Shakespeare performances and publications. Alexander Pushkin's 1825 *Boris Godunov* reflects the Bard of Avon's influence. The protorevolutionary Decembrists studied translations of Shakespeare in exile after the brutal liquidation of their cause by Tsar Nikolay I. The quality of these translations began to improve with Nikolay Polenov's 1837 edition of *Hamlet*, which escaped the "trap of excessive literalism" and allowed the Russian language to breathe on its own.[68] Novelist Ivan Turgenev relocated Shakespearean subject matter to the provinces in "Hamlet of Shchigrovsky District" ("Gamlet Shchigrovskogo uyezda," 1848) and "King Lear of the Steppes" ("Stepnoy korol' Lir," 1870), as did Nikolay Leskov in "Lady Macbeth of Mtsensk" ("Ledi Makbet Mtsenskogo uyezda," 1865).

The last, operatically infamous text was a product of comparatively liberal times, as were the St. Petersburg productions of Shakespeare's tragedies and comedies that Tchaikovsky took in. He bought several editions of Shakespeare's plays and, in his later years, started learning English. He wrote music for one of the productions: an 1891 staging of *Hamlet* at the Mikhaílovsky Theater. (It was performed neither in English nor in Russian but in an 1847 French translation by Alexandre Dumas père and Paul Meurice.) Tchaikovsky thought about an *Othello* opera; and in between the first and second versions of the *Romeo and Juliet* fantasy overture, he challenged himself with a tone poem based on *The Tempest*.

The idea for the latter came not from Balakirev but from the prominent historian and critic Vladimir Stasov, during a gathering at Rimsky-Korsakov's apartment in December of 1872. Tchaikovsky asked Stasov if he had any recommendations for a tone poem, and Stasov suggested Walter Scott's *Ivanhoe* (1819) and Nikolay Gogol's Cossack romance *Taras Bulba* (1835). Tchaikovsky showed no interest in these first two subjects, though the mythic Cossacks would recur in his output in the operas *Mazeppa* and, secondarily, *Vakula the Smith*. Stasov's third recommendation, *The Tempest*, caught his fancy, and the two of them exchanged letters about the best approach to representing it in music. The manuscript of the score is lost; a draft of the tone poem preserved in the Russian National Library in St. Petersburg indicates different tempos and instrumentation than the final version.[69]

Allusion is illusion in the score. Minor string arpeggios and Wagnerian horn calls denote the sea and the broader natural world surrounding Prospero's Island. The captured spirit Ariel appears in a hemmed-in version of Mendelssohn's *Midsummer Night's Dream* fairy music; another captive, Caliban, is assigned lumbering, harshly accented string bass music that recalls the Puck-as-Donkey hee-haws from the same Mendelssohn score. Prospero announces himself in a bellicose fanfare before conjuring up the tempest that smashes the opening themes to pieces in an imitation of the shipwreck. It's rough magic, and it's the lovers, rather than Prospero, who abjure it, in a theme potent enough to deflate Prospero's brass pomposity, reducing it to a Rossini galop.

He put much more effort into *Romeo and Juliet* than *The Tempest*, creating both psychological and emotional portraits of the characters and integrating jarringly violent swordfight music into the strains of romance. He also recoded Shakespeare's text, transforming the Verona teenagers into hot-blooded inhabitants of the Turkic Steppe. Juliet's balcony is in Sarai; Romeo is draped in sables and jewels; the tremolos are her thoughts of his touch, his sighs the portamento. Sensuous languor is denoted by a chromatic pass between the fifth and sixth scale degrees and other *Tema vostoka* ("theme of the East") elements, as Taruskin explains by quoting a letter from Balakirev to Tchaikovsky:

> I often play it and have a great wish to kiss you for it. It has everything; *nega* [languor] and love's sweetness, and all the rest ... It appears to me that you are lying all naked in the bath and that Artôt-Padilla herself is rubbing your tummy with hot scented suds. I have just one thing to say against this theme: there is little in it of inner spiritual love, only the physical, passionate torment (colored just a wee bit Italian). Really now, Romeo and Juliet are not Persian lovers but European ...[70]

The quote is weirdly comical. It's also mean-spirited, poking Tchaikovsky about a girl he had a crush on, the Belgian soprano Désirée Artôt, who had spurned him by marrying a Spanish baritone. The letter was also part of a campaign to convince Tchaikovsky to join ranks with the *Moguchaya kuchka*, but Tchaikovsky despised Balakirev for his *khamstvo* (rudeness). His letters to Anatole on the subject pre-date him committing a single note of the baleful-beautiful overture to paper.

August 3:
    The journey from Kyiv to Moscow was awfully tedious for me and, despite the fact that I traveled the whole time in 1st class, I

experienced various inconveniences and slept badly. My arrival in Moscow wasn't without some pleasure; habit has made me love Moscow like something of a native. [Nikolay] Rubinstein isn't here yet, he's in Lipetsk. Then again, Balakirev lives here now, and, I must confess, his presence weighs me down; he demands that I be with him every day, which is somewhat tedious for me. He's a very good person and well disposed towards me personally, but I don't know why, I just cannot get along with him soul-to-soul. I don't entirely like the exclusivity of his musical opinions, and his harsh tone.[71]

August 11:

Balakirev is still here; we see each other often, and I'm more and more convinced that, despite all his virtues, his company would weigh heavily upon me if we lived in the same town. His narrow-mindedness and the stubbornness with which he clings on to his prejudices are especially unpleasant.[72]

Those prejudices included antisemitism, Germanophobia, and insistence that Tchaikovsky compose in the idiom Balakirev preferred—except that Balakirev struggled to write music and so foisted his creative plans onto others.

The tone of Tchaikovsky's correspondence with Balakirev amounts to doing whatever it takes to get him off his back. "In the first place, the overall scheme is yours: an introduction representing the friar; the struggle—allegro, and love—second theme; and secondly, the modulations are yours: the introduction is in E major, the Allegro in B minor, and the second theme in D♭ major," he wrote on October 28, 1869, deferentially adding that "you can then tear it to pieces as much as you like; I shall take note of everything and in my next composition I will try to do things better."[73] Balakirev didn't like the draft music he sight-read, but his explanation makes little sense. The first theme (the friar's) had neither "beauty nor strength," he declared, and he expected the opening chorale to have both a "Catholic" and an "Orthodox" sound.[74] He liked the first iteration of the love theme but called it "overripe," which means what? Too long? Too rich and thick? The best that can be said of his comments is that they are unfair, the worst that they are abusive.

The overture premiered in Moscow on March 4, 1870, the opening of a long concert with several encores. According to Brown, it didn't make a strong impression. The performance suffered, he writes, because Nikolay Rubinstein was "distracted" by the drama surrounding the expulsion of a conservatory student.[75] A female student filed a complaint after Rubinstein scolded her for missing assignments. When she tried to defend herself by opening his grade book, he tore it out of her hands and told her to get the hell out of his office. Rubinstein's side of the story—that the student had been lazy, disruptive, and rude in class and giggled at him in the hall—didn't pass muster with the "assize [court] of the community" hearing her case. Rubinstein was fined 25 rubles and threatened with a week in prison "in case of insolvency." Those who attended the hearing cheered the decision. Humiliated, Rubinstein threatened to quit the conservatory and the IRMS, grousing that it might be time for him to get out of Russia. None of that happened; he stayed put. Though Brown suggests otherwise, Rubinstein's interpretation of *Romeo and Juliet* was praised for its "lyricism."[76]

In keeping with Balakirev's script, the E-major introduction represents the friar and the allegro B-minor music the Montague and Capulet hostilities. Offbeat cymbals, stabbing accents, and the Neapolitan chord illustrate the swordfight. The phrasing expands and contracts, and Tchaikovsky also cleverly threads in the panicky shouts of onlookers. Then the smitten hero and heroine are introduced with heartbeat sounds and the famous butterflies-in-the-stomach theme in Db major. Love blooms and withers amid the feuding. The star-crossed lovers' music recurs in the minor before an ambiguous denouement of plucked harp chords and ascending

B-major sonorities in the strings. Do the teenagers' spirits rise to heaven? Is their double-suicide somehow avoided?

The second version of the overture followed in the summer of 1870 and is the longest of the three versions at 539 measures (about twenty minutes). Much changed, Tchaikovsky told Balakirev: "The introduction is new, the middle section almost entirely new [Tchaikovsky supplants the fugue with a brief canon], and the recapitulation of the second theme has been completely reorchestrated." Balakirev remained unimpressed, despite Tchaikovsky's conscious effort to emulate Balakirev's own music on a Shakespearean theme (the *King Lear* Overture of 1859), and he sent Tchaikovsky back to the drawing board. This time, however, Tchaikovsky stood his ground, declaring the overture finished and himself too tapped out to listen to Balakirev's hectoring about the musical representation of the Montague–Capulet grudge not sounding ancient enough. The second version was premiered on February 5, 1872, in St. Petersburg, with Eduard Nápravník conducting. It proved a success, with a magical introduction featuring rolled chords in the harp that cadence in F minor with the upper voice on the mediant rather than resolving by leading tone to the tonic. Tchaikovsky said that he "wanted in the introduction to represent a lonely soul mentally striving heavenward" and captured in the cor anglais the sentiment of Shakespeare's prologue:

A pair of star-cross'd lovers take their life;
Whose misadventured piteous overthrows
Do with their death bury their parents' strife.
The fearful passage of their death-mark'd love,
And the continuance of their parents' rage,
Which, but their children's end, nought could remove,
Is now the two hours' traffic of our stage;
The which if you with patient ears attend,
What here shall miss, our toil shall strive to mend.[77]

There are other moments of magic in the second version: glimpses of brightness in the major chords threaded into the minor-chord textures (Friar Laurence is this brightness, amid the growing gloom of the introduction), and augmented seconds in the flute, which Tchaikovsky uses to signal erotic danger. The texture thins and deteriorates when F♯ minor sinks to F minor and further down to E. Then, between measures 78 and 90, the dread builds with timpani added (Tchaikovsky exploits all the resources of the St. Petersburg IRMS orchestra), leading to the allegro giusto exposition. The swordfight ends inconclusively with canonic imitation leading to a modulation to G minor then back to B minor. Tchaikovsky heads to the relative major of D in the transition, but takes the music down a semitone, bathing the listener in D♭ major and the timbre of the cor anglais, pitched lower than oboe, with muted violas joined by the throbbing horns, pizzicato cellos and basses. The dynamic softens to pianissimo, dimming the lights. The development involves greater contrast between the music of the introduction and the first subject than between the first and second subject. Unanswerable to their surroundings, Romeo and Juliet keep out of the fray. Tchaikovsky holds their theme in reserve for the recapitulation, which ends with the death knell of the F♯-major dominant of B minor in measures 483–84. The coda is the funeral, though it recalls the rolled harp chords of the introduction. Measures 519–22 bring down the curtain with fortissimo timpani and syncopated tonic chords derived from the first subject.

In the end, Balakirev liked much of what he heard of *Romeo and Juliet*, and Stasov was proud of his role in the composition of *The Tempest*. Both saw a bright nationalist future for Tchaikovsky and wanted him to continue writing program music since he was obviously so good at it. "Now there are six" members of the Mighty Five, Balakirev joked in a letter (unsent) to Tchaikovsky.[78] But five it would stay. Stasov's and Balakirev's personalities were too domineering— Tchaikovsky felt oppressed—and their book of nationalist musical spells less potent than advertised. Tchaikovsky would not join the loose *kuchka* alliance. He would keep his teaching job long past the point of needing the income.

In the classroom

When Tchaikovsky could afford to, he took time off to compose. But these were lean years and he often needed help from friends to make ends meet and took on extra work as an arranger.[79] "I kiss in advance the hand which will be pulling five rubles from his wallet," he wrote in 1870 to his conservatory colleague Karl Albrecht.[80] He sent other notes like this to other people, dozens of them, leaving the impression that he was barely scraping by, sleeping with bedbugs, dining on bread and cabbage soup served out of vats on the streets for kopecks. That Tchaikovsky lived beyond his means is certain: he says as much. But it's also the case that banking in Russia was a supreme hassle. Savings banks followed post-office hours, and transactions were limited. The financial crisis caused by the Crimean War had forced reforms in the banking sector, but the sector remained shaky; people had no choice but to borrow from, and lend to, one another.

To improve his finances, Tchaikovsky organized a benefit for himself—a fundraising concert of his own compositions on March 16, 1871, at the Assembly of the Nobility, a social club near the Bolshoi Theater that included space for concerts and glittering balls (Pushkin describes the space in *Eugene Onegin*, as does Tolstoy in *War and Peace*). Putting the event together proved enough of an ordeal that he never did so again, tasking assistants to deal with the logistics in the future. Albrecht helped him out by organizing the hall rental, putting out chairs, and attending to ticketing. That left Tchaikovsky (according to Alexander Komarov's incredible research on the subject) to "appeal to the directorate of the Imperial Moscow Theaters [which held the monopoly on public performances] for permission to present the concert" and attend to such formalities as donating, as a kind of tax, part of the proceeds to the "Guardianship Council of the Moscow Orphanage."[81]

After receiving permission from the police chief to move forward with his plans, Tchaikovsky placed advertisements in the newspaper *Moscow Register* and its companion, the *Register of the Moscow Police* (*Vedomosti moskovskoy gorodskoy politsii*), which published official information on everything from taxation to road work and dedicated significant space to advertising, at cheap rates.[82] The *Moscow Register* ran a promotional article touting Tchaikovsky's rapid development as a composer. In addition to the premiere of his String Quartet No. 1, the program included several romances, his resetting of the popular French chanson "Comme à vingt ans," piano pieces, a solo violin work, an operatic duet, and a female chorus—quite an extravaganza. Turgenev turned up late but liked what he heard; Tchaikovsky's poet friend Apukhtin was enthralled; most in the audience came to hear the performers Tchaikovsky had contracted, including contralto Elizaveta Lavrovskaya and pianist Nikolay Rubinstein.[83]

Meanwhile, Tchaikovsky taught his classes at the Moscow Conservatory, and did so until 1878, for a total of a dozen years, which is a long time for someone who supposedly disliked the classroom. "Tchaikovsky's hours of teaching theory passed for him in gloomy file. He was clearly bored, barely able to stifle his yawns," a pianist recalled. Worse, "he bemoaned the slowness of most of the female students, the obtuse, superficial attitude toward the essence of art of all these future lady laureates who dreamed only of the stage and were convinced that the audiences applauding would have no interest in their technical knowledge."[84] The attending physical descriptions of him—unkempt, slightly hunched, wearing dusty shoes, and shirts that had never seen irons—are more plausible than the neat and tidy professional photographs dotting the biographies. Other accounts (there aren't a lot) suggest a stronger commitment to his vocation. He cared enough about his students, boys and girls alike, to write a harmony textbook for them. In fact, he wrote it twice.

The archival records are scant and scattered, so it's difficult to determine who studied with Tchaikovsky, when, and for how long. Some of his students started strong but didn't graduate; their disappointments, unsurprisingly, translated into indictments of their teacher. Others graduated but went into other professions, brilliantly and eclectically so. Violinist Mikhaíl Davïdov, for example, became a famous embryologist. He joined Tchaikovsky's orchestration class in 1871 and improved his grade from the equivalent of a low pass to an A, fashioning an E♭-major symphonic first movement that consciously mimicked Tchaikovsky's habit of isolating rather than blending timbres (though the dramatic effect of the low brasses is squandered through overuse).[85] Another student, Raphael von Koeber, ended up teaching German philosophy at Tokyo Imperial University while also giving Russian classes, composing, and facilitating the performance of the first opera in Japan, Christoph Willibald Gluck's *Orpheus*. Von Koeber achieved eminence as a *sensei*, a master teacher of the Meiji Restoration. Under Tchaikovsky's tutelage he composed a Konzertstück for Piano and Orchestra in B minor, cast in a heroic mold with an exceptionally advanced piano part.[86] Two other students, Viktor Paskhalov and Vasily Prokunin, dropped out (as opposed to failing out) after getting what they wanted from Tchaikovsky. Paskhalov remained in music after leaving the conservatory, writing "elegiac romances in the character of, or imitating, Russian folksongs"—*café chantant*-type music.[87] Prokunin entered the conservatory having already established himself as an ethnomusicologist. He completed the second edition of his *Russian Folksongs for Solo Voice with Piano Accompaniment* in 1872 after taking Tchaikovsky's harmony course. In 1873 Tchaikovsky included seven of these folksongs in *The Snow Maiden*.

Tchaikovsky also graduated students who had immense professional careers in Russia. Sergey Taneyev is the outstanding example, likewise pianist Anatole Galli, who would himself teach at the conservatory, and the violinists Iosif Kotek and Andrey Arends, whose graduation exercises involved composing and arranging music for their instrument. Tchaikovsky stayed in touch with his musical progeny and frequently collaborated with them, with Kotek becoming a crucial resource. He studied at the Moscow Conservatory between 1871 and 1876 and took harmony, orchestration, and compositional classes with Tchaikovsky. He motivated all but one of Tchaikovsky's works for violin. (The exception is the *Sérénade mélancolique*, which dates from 1875 and was originally dedicated to the St. Petersburg Conservatory's violin professor Leopold Auer, who asked Tchaikovsky to write it for him.) At Kotek's request Tchaikovsky spent January and February 1877 composing his Valse-Scherzo for violin and orchestra. Kotek partly realized the orchestration, and the manuscript shows Tchaikovsky's penciled-in corrections of his pupil's work. Tchaikovsky's famous (but in its first years of existence, infamous) Violin Concerto of 1878 was likewise composed with Kotek's involvement. The latter edited the solo part and proofread the first version.[88]

Since Auer had lobbied for the chance to premiere it, Tchaikovsky dedicated it to him rather than Kotik, but then Auer rudely called it unidiomatically unplayable (which, for Auer, it was), so Tchaikovsky annulled the dedication along with that of the *Sérénade mélancolique*. The entire situation was a mess, and the composer felt humiliated, fuming in a letter that his

concerto was wanted to be played in Petersburg first by Kotek and then by [the French violinist Émile] Sauret and both could not fulfill their intention, because Auer and [the conductor and composer Karl] Davïdov rebelled against this unfortunate concerto, claiming it was impossible to play, that it was a mockery of the public, etc. I'm perplexed. Auer and Davïdov are my so-called friends, and I even dedicated the concerto in gratitude to Auer, who always presented himself as an ardent lover of my music![89]

While working on the concerto, Tchaikovsky conceived another work for violin and piano with Kotek's involvement: the *Souvenir d'un lieu cher* (*Memory of a beloved place*, 1878). It's seldom played, passed over by celebrity violinists in favor of the daunting concerto. The first movement, "Méditation," was intended as the slow movement of the concerto and is quoted in his opera *The Queen of Spades*.

Several questions remain unanswered, beginning with the supposedly unplayable concerto: did Kotek exceed his own technique, along with Auer's, in advising Tchaikovsky on the solo part? The outer movements are the home of the stunt music, yet the middle movement was the one that Tchaikovsky rewrote: why? Another matter relates to Kotek's studies. To graduate from the Moscow Conservatory, he was tasked with composing the first movement of a violin concerto. Just the orchestral parts survive, not the solo part or the full score, so it remains lamentably unclear if it had an influence on Tchaikovsky's own music for violin.[90]

He left teaching in 1878, giving his last lesson on October 6. The job was no longer manageable; he was overwhelmed with composing. That wasn't quite the end of the matter, however, since he continued to give private lessons and fielded offers to teach in St. Petersburg and Kyiv.[91]

In 1881, Taneyev wrote in hopes of him returning to the conservatory, as he said he might do, to teach a few hours a week—less to "explain the mystery of harmony" to students than simply be an inspiring presence.[92] Nikolay Rubinstein had suddenly died and professors had resigned; the conservatory was bursting at the seams. Tchaikovsky declined the offer, however, in a characteristically self-effacing letter full of wistful remorse:

> Even if I were to take on some post at the Conservatory, I would all the same run away secretly after a month. This is not because I have ceased to love Moscow and the Muscovite musical milieu. Quite the opposite, in fact: I love them too much, and suffer too

much as I realize my utter uselessness for the cause to which I am devoted. I do not want to be there just for the sake of appearances. And as for teaching properly, even if it were just an hour a day, as you suggest, that is something I have never been able to do, and never will. I am incapable of teaching anything, because this is a job that has to be done, if not with love, then at least with patience, and that is something I just don't have. I have become unbelievably irritable. Apart from that, though, whenever I am in Moscow I always experience a whole series of such agonizing feelings, about which I cannot give you even a rough idea. It is a kind of burning anguish at the irrevocability of the past, a kind of excruciating regret over my senselessly spent youth, and many, many other things ... Indeed, I cannot picture to myself my life in Moscow other than in the form of sitting in a tavern and drinking vodka. So, in short, do not exhort me to join the Conservatory. That is impossible now. As for the future, that I cannot vouch for.[93]

PART II

NATIONALISM

Первый блин комом (the first pancake is always lumpy)

He imagined opera in his future. His first remained, in some sense, a rough draft. He struggled to choose the subject, solicited feedback on the draft, and made changes to the score in rehearsal.

As for the subject, Tchaikovsky wasn't an avid reader, but he had friends who were. The Slavophile nationalists among them were fascinated by the distant past as chronicled by Nikolay Karamzin in his twelve-volume *History of the Russian State* (1816–26). An official publication of the Military Printing Office of the General Staff of His Imperial Majesty, the *History* is based on chronicles and hagiographies that Karamzin had exclusive access to as an imperial (not state) historian. Karamzin combined a sentimental central narrative—full of personal details and fictive emotional detail—with a reference apparatus that reproduced the actual historical documents, a goldmine for the academicians who succeeded him. A favorite topic, drawn from the *History*, was the crises of succession and foreign occupation known as the Time of Troubles (1598–1613). The tsar at the center of it all, Boris Godunov (1552–1605), became popular on the stage, as did the outsized ruler before him, Ivan the

Terrible (1530–84). Ivan was given a love life (of sorts), and his acts of depravity downplayed. Historical fiction reached even further back in time to the Kyivian princes, the pre-Christian pagan beliefs of the eastern Slavic peoples, and the magical creatures inhabiting the woods along the Moscow River before Moscow existed, never mind St. Petersburg.

Tchaikovsky would compose music about the *Smuta* (as the Time of Troubles is known in Russian) and Ivan the Terrible, and other Karamzinian topics. He was also, however, taken with the prolific playwright Alexander Ostrovsky (1823–86), including the plays about the people of the Russian heartland and the immense Volga River, spanning over 2,000 miles across boreal forests and desert basins to drain into the Caspian Sea. Ostrovsky focused on average people and average experiences: brides without dowries, drunken louts, the bullies on the block, acts of sin and grace. One of his plays is called *Don't Live as You Like*; another, *Poverty Is No Vice*. There are forty-five more, in both comic and tragic veins.

Tchaikovsky planned to base his first opera on Ostrovsky's most famous play, *The Storm* (*Groza*, 1859), which he had seen as a student and wrote an overture for in 1864. The play is a barbed social critique featuring one of the meanest mothers-in-law on record; she drives the protagonist Katerina to suicide. According to the composer's own description, the overture moves from a representation of Katerina's childhood to her emotional struggles as an adult.[1] She's trapped between her duties to her husband and love for another man. The music, accordingly, oscillates between menacing rhythmic gestures in the brass and timpani and fleeting melodic amorousness in the woodwinds. The score grinds to a halt in indecision, then shifts to an eclectically orchestrated lyrical episode narrating Katerina's adulterous liaison on the Volga. Woodwinds (English horn, flute, and clarinet) are heard in unusual registers, often isolated and exposed, and then doubled with the brass several octaves apart. Tuba is prominent, and harp, and the divided strings shiver in tremolo—"heretical" effects for a pupil of Rubinstein, Herman Laroche declares, though the music critic seems not to have noticed that Tchaikovsky had borrowed the effects from Rubinstein's "Ocean" Symphony of 1857.[2] The storm that holds Katerina in its grip is the provincial social world. Thunder and wind are heard throughout the overture in the recurring timpani rolls, cymbal crashes, soft to loud swells in the strings, and the central fugato.

Tchaikovsky was eager to expand the overture into an opera until Ostrovsky broke the news to him that another composer, Vladimir Kashperov (1826–94), had already written an opera on the same subject. That scuttled Tchaikovsky's plans, although, curiously, the Glinka Museum in Moscow owns a copy of an arrangement of Kashperov's overture in Tchaikovsky's hand. Tchaikovsky had his name removed from it after reading the terrible reviews of Kashperov's opera.[3]

As a replacement, Ostrovsky offered Tchaikovsky a comedy of five acts and sixty characters called *The Voyevoda* (*A Dream on the Volga*, 1865/85). Although it makes for a marvelous theatrical experience, tailoring its sparkling Old Rus language to music proved an almost impossible challenge. Even the title caused problems. *Voyevoda* is an obsolete Russian word meaning warlord or, more politely, troop commander. It morphed over time to describe a provincial governor, since in ancient times the appanages of the Rurik/Kyivian princes were administered by loyal strongmen. (The term fell into disuse during the era of Peter the Great.) Lampooning the loves, lives, and bad behavior of petty tyrants had long been a favorite subject onstage.

The action is set in 1670 in Kostroma among the townsfolk, including merchants, nobles, maidens, brigands, and a nurse named Nedviga, someone who evidently won't be rushed (her name means "can't move").[4] Ostrovsky references Shakespeare's *A Midsummer Night's Dream*, but his *Dream on the Volga* is of *spravedlivost'* (justice), not amorous adventures in the forest. The reckoning with the misdeeds of the title character comes in two different forms in two different editions of the work written two decades apart. In the first, the edition Tchaikovsky turned into an opera, the governor is arrested after an old-timer reports his crimes to the tsar. The people aren't hopeful for the future: "Well, the old [governor] was bad; the new one will be too." "Yes, things will be the same, if not worse."[5] In the second, the governor confesses his sins.

Ostrovsky assisted Tchaikovsky with the libretto, writing the first act and the first scene of the second act. When the composer shared second thoughts about the project, Ostrovsky backed out entirely, leaving Tchaikovsky without an influential support. He had sketched out three of the vocal numbers and worked out a section of the opera that didn't require a libretto: the "Dance of the Hay Maidens," derived from a score that has disappeared, Tchaikovsky's 1865 "Character Dances." He arranged a piano version of the dances for Vera Davïdova, his sister-in-law, with whom he spent part of the summer of 1867, and then sketched another section of the opera that didn't require a libretto: the overture (he would rewrite it a year later).[6] Work stopped until the end of October, when he received a request from a coloratura soprano he greatly admired, Alexandra Menshikova (1840–1902), to create an operatic role for her. Her interest renewed his enthusiasm for the project. Tchaikovsky completed the libretto on his own, writing one number at a time along with the music. The planned four acts were reduced to three, period-specific detail was excised along with Ostrovsky's dream sequences, the scene of the escape of the governor's buffoon, and all the discussions of fairness, freedom, and the search for the truth. (Truth, the characters learn, "has gone to heaven.")[7] Stripped to the bone, the plot involves the governor taking two women of distinct ages and social positions as his mistresses. When he's away, the governor confines the women in his tower chamber. Their lovers hatch a plan to rescue them by getting the governor's guards drunk, but they are captured. Fanfares announce the arrival of a new governor, and the couples are freed.

Musical highlights include the opening women's chorus, the ballet, and the concluding hymn to the tsar, Alexei I (scrapped in the Soviet reconstruction of the opera). Lowlights include the frequent reprises, the contrapuntal filler material, and the rewritten overture, a textbook exercise in background variations, also known as Glinka variations. Tchaikovsky's choice of a full-fledged theme as his ostinato (as opposed to Glinka's preference for melodic fragments) reveals the influence of Mily Balakirev's orchestral pieces, likewise the variations in the first half and their absorption into a sonata structure in the second. Some of the problems in the score date from the 1868-69 rehearsals. According to Tchaikovsky's colleague Nikolay Kashkin, the composer was forced to cut and add entire numbers to accommodate the singers:

> The last number of the first act was a scene in which the governor catches a glimpse of Marya Vlasevna dashing into the bushes. Completely stunned by her beauty he chooses her as his bride over the older sister. This scene ends with a quartet, I think in Eb major, whose music was meant to crown the act, summarizing it and bringing everything together. The composer considered this number if not the best, then at least the most effective in the opera. To his misfortune, he had included within it a rhythmic passage that had a string of triplets in one voice against common time in another—that is, a movement of three against two. It was an insurmountable challenge for the singers. After several failed experiments, the quartet was tossed out and replaced with a perfunctory ending that made a botch of the entire first act.[8]

Tchaikovsky had handpicked the singers for the opera's premiere, privileging quality of tone over quality of technique. The coloratura soprano was undisciplined, in Kashkin's opinion, and the tenor unmusical and better off in a provincial theater. The best moments in the opera, Kashkin believed (and subsequent commentators believed with him), were the simplest: the folksong settings.[9]

The opening women's chorus, "A Duckling Was Swimming on the Sea," is based on a folksong that Ostrovsky transcribed from a villager and included in his play.[10] He passed it along to Tchaikovsky for use in the opera. The chorus is sung by the girlfriends of Praskovya (the older sister of Marya), whose father has betrothed her to the governor. Tchaikovsky mentioned in a letter to Nikolay Rimsky-Korsakov that before arranging Ostrovsky's transcription for the chorus, he removed the leading tone, making it paradoxically more folklike than the folk sang it.[11] The text describes a duckling (the bride) who fears leaving the sea (home) for the world beyond. The waters have turned gray in sadness; the shore looks imposing. Tchaikovsky's setting involves the aforementioned, Balakirev-sanctioned lowered seventh degree, free imitation between the soprano and alto parts, a throbbing tonic pedal point, and some dissonant undervoicing in the middle.

The accompaniment rocks and sways in compound triple meter. The leap of a fourth and the harmonic shift from i to iv6/4 on the first syllable of *u-tush-ka* (duckling) contributes to the effect of bobbing on the waves, as does the ii7 chord on the second syllable of *ku-pa-la-sya* (was swimming). The first two phrases are repeated in variation, after which a developmental middle section begins. Tchaikovsky departs from the source folksong as the chorus becomes a desperate first-person recitation and a cascade of emotion: *I'll leave the blue sea! . . . How can I leave?* The sopranos and altos imitate each other over oscillating sixteenth notes in the orchestral accompaniment before a return of the opening section and a rounding out of the form.

The "Nightingale Song," sung by Marya in the second act, is also based on a folksong, one that Tchaikovsky himself transcribed, as is the choral round dance in the second act (the bookend to the "Dance of the Hay Maidens").[12] That was enough; the composer didn't want to turn his opera into a *style russe* cornucopia, even though the nationalists in his circle, and critics like Laroche, urged him to do just that. (Tchaikovsky had considered Laroche a friend, but the latter's assessment of the opera as derivative of Schumann, likewise his critique of a concert performance of the "Dance of the Hay Maidens" as derivative of Mendelssohn—and "feminine" to boot—so angered Tchaikovsky that he cut Laroche out of his life for years.)[13]

The folksongs provide a certain Old Rus ambience, one that suppresses individual sentiment. Personal feelings are represented in the opera less by individuals themselves than by the collective. Sometimes those feelings are negated, as in the Act II "Dance of the Maidens," which is meant to distract one of the abducted women from her sorrows while also suggesting that the women have no sorrows. Menshikova, as Marya, lends some playfulness to her plight, frequently changing meters and decorating her lines (which fully exploit Menshikova's two-and-a-half-octave range) with melismas and fiorituras that push against the sides of the box she's been placed in. But this is an opera about tradition and subjugation. One must accept one's lot. Those cheerful hay maidens are the governor's serfs: he owns them, but still they dance. Everyone else is owned as well, following the rules of their ancestors and all belonging to the same environment.

The one character who marks a break from tradition is the bass baritone Dubrovin. He's an outsider, a fugitive. Eager to enact revenge on the governor and reclaim his wife Olyona, he engineers the happy ending: he gets the girl, and the governor gets replaced. Dubrovin is the one character with a leitmotif, a scalar passage in mixed rhythmic values that's simple enough to be harmonized in different ways but distinct enough to stick in the ear. Ultimately, not much has changed, however, and the concluding hymn of praise to the tsar celebrates the status quo.

The production at the Bolshoi was rescheduled and rescheduled again for logistical reasons. The chorus was outsourced to a visiting

Italian opera company; the soloists hadn't fully prepared; the dancers didn't show up (and, when they did, treated the young composer with contempt). Worst of all, the administration of the Imperial Theaters long had an aversion to Russian operas on Russian historical themes.[14] By definition, the empire didn't support works about the state. Audiences didn't want to see them, and the tsar didn't want to fund them, except on the cheap, with dusty sets and dirty costumes from the warehouse. The budget for *The Voyevoda* was pathetic, according to Kashkin, compared to what was lavished on Gaetano Donizetti.[15] Ultimately, *The Voyevoda* and its recycled props lasted barely five performances at the Bolshoi Theater, including the January 30, 1869, premiere, which was a benefit for the star soprano.[16] In the opinion of the intendant of the Imperial Theaters, the erstwhile playwright Stepan Gedeonov, the whole thing was a waste of time, and affirmed his position that neither Russian historical dramas nor historical operas should be performed. The premiere of Ostrovsky's *Voyevoda* had been a "fiasco" on the imperial stage, and he predicted the same for Alexander Pushkin's *Boris Godunov*: "Let's scrap it," Gedeonov instructed the head of the repertoire committee.[17]

Reviewers of Tchaikovsky's *Voyevoda* considered it a fiasco too, partly because Gedeonov deliberately underfunded the premiere and partly because of the Ostrovsky/Tchaikovsky libretto, as this caustic takedown in *Voice* attests:

> Let's be honest here: it would be hard to find a sadder, deader plot [than *Dream on the Volga*]. The actors enter, sing, harangue one another without cause or consequence, and exit. Tchaikovsky's music is most peculiar, at once imitating Wagner and Glinka. Although the composer was brought out for countless bows and was given a wreath, the success of the opera is more than doubtful. There's just one aria for the tenor, after which choral singing prevails. As the popular saying goes, and which the audience would have been forgiven for repeating, "thanks but don't do me any

favors." Like Kashperov's [1867 opera] *The Storm*, the accents in the verse don't coincide with the accents in the music; now and then the music anticipates the words and vice versa. I'd quote a passage from the libretto to illustrate why the singers were so unsuccessful, but the whole thing, every verse, is unmusical. Take this example—what Dubrovin sings when he's reunited with his wife:

And I won't ask you,	[А у тебя и спрашивать не стану,
How you've been living. I know	Какъ ты жила. Я знаю, ты охотой
You wouldn't have traded me for anyone else.	Ни на кого меня не промѣняешь.
And don't talk to me about violence:	А про насильство мнѣ не говори:
Be assured I won't spare either of us,	Себя да и тебя не пожалѣю,
Knives and blood-red fog appear	Въ глазахъ туманъ кровавый да ножи
Before my eyes. Best to keep quiet, Olyona.	Мерещатся. Молчи, Олена, лучше.]

The same burdened, unmusical verse typifies the other arias. We might add that Moscow's singers were of no help to Tchaikovsky, though Menshikova successfully carried the role of Marya Vlasevna. The performance was a benefit in her honor and the crowd showered her in diamonds. [The Italian bass Ludovico] Finocchi sang the role of the governor in tune yet tormented the Russian language without mercy. [Alexander] Rapport might have been good in the role of Bastryukov, but he was sick as a dog from an operation the day before. He asked the audience to indulge him. Everyone happily worked together to ensure as bad a performance as possible.[18]

This review echoed other reviews and established the Tchaikovsky's-first-opera-as-failure narrative. The production was impoverished, the libretto weak (though, frankly, the passage singled out in the review isn't that bad: its sentiments are coldly apt for the situation described in the plot), and the music a derivative bricolage. The composer justifiably defended it against the naysayers, taking pride in the instrumental music and the Act III quartet for the reunited lovers. A decade later, however, he had changed his mind and told anyone willing to listen that the opera was a flop that he wished he hadn't composed. He recycled some of it—in the opera *The Oprichnik*, the ballet *Swan Lake*, and the *1812 Overture*—but burned the rest.[19]

Yet there are recordings of the opera. These were made not by retrieving the manuscript from the stove but by finding, and completing, other manuscripts. According to Richard Taruskin, Tchaikovsky's first opera was "twice reconstructed from the composer's sketches and the surviving orchestral and choral parts: first by [musicologist] Sergey Popov in 1927, later by [musicologist] Pavel Lamm with the composers Vissarion Shebalin and Yury Kochurov. Their version was performed (to a Sovietized libretto by S. D. Spassky) in Leningrad (Malïy Theater, 28 September 1949)."[20]

Taruskin is almost correct. The initiative to reconstruct *Voyevoda* came from Modest after his brother's death. From Kashkin and Laroche, Modest had learned that the opera's orchestral parts (excluding the harp) and some of the choral parts had been preserved in the library of the Bolshoi Theater.[21] The restoration proceeded in two phases, the first spearheaded by Popov with assistance from Pavel Lamm and Boris Asafyev, a musicologist and composer who wanted, in the 1940s, to write a ballet based on the sketches of this and other Tchaikovsky compositions.[22] The restoration took a whopping thirteen years, from 1920 to 1933, and relied on materials at the Bolshoi along with an annotated piano score of Act III; the manuscripts and published editions of the "Dance of the Hay Maidens";

and the overture, the published libretto, and the autograph of Ostrovsky's contributions. What Tchaikovsky had recycled in later works was reclaimed for *The Voyevoda*, and Lamm touched up the "Dance of the Hay Maidens," which Pyotr Jurgenson had published in 1873. Lamm could be sloppy, however, and Popov assigned him a problem that required utmost accuracy to solve: updating the libretto to reflect the Russian-language reforms (changes in spellings and phonetics) of 1917–18. In places, that meant changing the music, which set the language of the nineteenth century (and included archaisms from the seventeenth).[23]

Popov's effort ended in 1933. He exchanged some letters with the Stanislavsky Theater in Moscow and the opera house in Smolensk about possibly staging his reconstruction, but it was not to be. Following years of harassment by the secret police (the People's Commissariat for Internal Affairs) for his bourgeois background and presumed anticommunist mindset, Popov was arrested and executed in 1937, a victim of the Stalinist purges. His apartment was ransacked, and his personal belongings, including books and manuscripts, were either sold by the state or disappeared.[24]

The second reconstruction of the opera was initiated by Lamm. It might be that Lamm picked up where Popov left off, and Popov's relatives suspected that Lamm was using Popov's work without due credit, or it might be that Lamm started afresh, passing some of the work on to Shebalin and Kochurov when his health started to fail. Their reconstruction, like Popov's, was based on a flawed "utilitarian" approach to the sources, according to the scholar Alexander Komarov, to whom this overview of the reconstruction of *The Voyevoda* is indebted.[25]

At the time of the 1949 premiere of the reconstruction with the "Sovietized libretto," Kochurov explained how he went about his work. His task, like Lamm's, Popov's, Shebalin's, and Asafyev's,

> was to prepare a stage-worthy score and try to see *The Voyevoda* through the eyes of Tchaikovsky in his later years and thus save

his first opera from complete oblivion. Naturally, we weren't
seeking a total break from the plot of the old libretto, for that
would have meant abandoning some of Tchaikovsky's most valuable and truthful music, thus depriving the performance of *The
Voyevoda* of authenticity. In addition to rethinking the plot of the
framing acts, for which new music was required, a lot of work had
to be done with respect to the formal organization of several
numbers. These had to be changed in a manner that did not
deprive them of expressiveness.[26]

Kochurov adds that the chief problem with the original version of
the opera (which he obviously hadn't seen) was the excessive length
of the arias and choruses. Because the action was so sluggish, he had
to make cuts while also abbreviating and accelerating the plot such
that the Act I quartet became a compact quintet involving the
voyevoda; a merchant; the merchant's daughters Praskovya and
Marya; and Marya's suitor, Stepan Bastryukov. The conclusion of the
first act was abbreviated, the ending of the final act gutted. Kochurov
acknowledges the loss of an Act II duet between the two abducted
women, which he reimagined from the surviving accompaniment.

And so, what we are listening to when we are listening to *Voyevoda*
is what Tchaikovsky might have composed had he lived in the era of
socialist realism. This *Dream on the Volga* is thickly scored and rigid
in its number format; the action is short and sweet and blunt. There's
no mention of the tsar. The reconstruction is as faithful to the original as the surviving sources and the Soviet political context would
allow. It's also, however, bizarrely influenced by the poor reviews of
the original *The Voyevoda*. Because the critics didn't like it, Popov and
Lamm felt that they should fix it. So much for historical accuracy,
and so much for the fact that the negative responses centered less on
the notes than on the rickety staging, the quality of the singing, and
the shift in style between the libretto that Ostrovsky began and
Tchaikovsky finished.

Zhukovsky

Three years before Tchaikovsky was born, in 1837, his parents entertained special visitors: the future Tsar Alexander II and his tutor, the
writer Vasiliy Zhukovsky (1787–1852), who were passing through
Votkinsk on a trip across Russia and spent a night at the Tchaikovskys'
home.[27] Tchaikovsky's parents never tired of talking about this visit, and
their children grew up surrounded by Zhukovsky's (and Pushkin's)
fairytales—those taken from the Russian tradition or adapted to it.
Slavists like Ilya Vinitsky associate Zhukovsky with the beginnings
of Russian Romanticism, and he maintained a place of remarkable
prominence in the aristocracy despite affiliations with the antitsarist,
reform-minded Decembrists.[28] Zhukovsky belongs to the era of
Sentimentalism, but he was also a historian of sorts, a chronicler of
emotion—his own along with the emotional life of his country, past and
present. Tchaikovsky participated in writing that history through opera.

His unperformed, ultimately abandoned second opera, *Undina*,
derives from Zhukovsky's 1835–37 expanded translation of a novella
by Friedrich de la Motte Fouqué, a German author of chivalric
romances. A female water sprite marries a human to gain a soul; her
husband is a Romantic hero for whom a human wife in the real world
is inadequate, and so he craves the other, the supernatural being. It's
unclear if the sprite truly loves the man; perhaps she is interested in
freedom. He betrays her. It's easy to read the tale as a parable about
adultery or taboo love or desire for the unattainable and the unbridge-
able divide between the ideal and the actual, desire and its satiation.
Fouqué's tale in Zhukovsky's telling explores desire and feeling as
having the power to make us strangers to ourselves.[29]

Zhukovsky converted Fouqué's prose into unrhymed dactylic
hexameter with feminine cadence in conscious imitation of Homeric
epics. The meter is distinct in Russian poetic tradition and used to
mimic Undina's frolicking in rising and falling waves. She's more
childlike, guileless, and mischievous than in the source novella, and
floats in a realm of metaphor and allusion. Zhukovsky excised banal

details and passages of explication and rationalization and intensified the tale through the use of direct as opposed to indirect speech.
He's fond of the instrumental case of the Russian language, which
the Symbolists and certainly Futurists also loved because it's so
ambiguous. Focus falls on the heroine's and hero's competing and
conflicting emotional states. Philologist Elizaveta Landa highlights
their first encounter, where Fouqué (in Russian translation) writes

Увидев прекрасного рыцаря, застыла [Ундина] в изумлении.

Seeing the beautiful knight, [Undina] froze in astonishment.

Zhukovsky expands the passage into

Но, увидя рыцаря, вдруг замолчала она, и глаза голубые,
вспыхнув звездами под сумраком черных ресниц, устремились
быстро на гостя.

But, seeing the knight, she suddenly fell silent, and her blue eyes,
flashing like stars under the dusk of her black eyelashes, quickly
fastened themselves on the guest.

Then he enriches the description:

Ундина долго смотрела, пурпурные губки раскрыв, как
младенец; вдруг, встрепенувшись резвою птичкой, она
подбежала к рыцарю, стала пред ним на колена.

Undina gazed at him for a long time, having opened her lilac lips
like a child; then suddenly, quick as a frolicsome little bird, she
rushed to the knight and knelt before him.[30]

Tchaikovsky read these lines as a child and was enthralled by them,
retaining his affection for the pricey (fifteen-ruble) illustrated edition
of *Undina* in his library into adulthood.

Conceiving an opera on the subject, he didn't need to worry about crafting a libretto. Vladimir Sollogub had done this work for another composer, Alexei Lvov, in 1842.[31] Lvov's operatic treatment of *Undina* had greater success with the press than the public on the St. Petersburg stage six years later in 1848, allowing Tchaikovsky to imagine doing better with Sollogub's libretto (which, for theatrical purposes, coarsened Zhukovsky's delicate conception) and getting his version performed with similar (or identical) sets and costumes.[32] Lvov's opera included a ballet in the middle act showcasing dancer and choreographer Marius Petipa and the great ballerina Elena Andreyanova. Tchaikovsky would encounter them again in his life and get to know Petipa exceedingly well.

He composed his own three-act version of *Undina* quickly in the first half of 1869 in between classes at the Moscow Conservatory, then pitched it to Gedeonov, hoping for a production at the Mariinsky Theater. Gedeonov humored him, signaling that if he submitted the orchestral and piano scores of the opera to the Imperial Theaters by September 1, it would be performed in November. Although the composer did as he was asked, he heard nothing back from the Imperial Theaters directorate. Tchaikovsky wrote to Gedeonov on October 12, 1869, distressed by reports in the newspapers that "several new operas are now in preparation" and that his own would be staged "only if some free time remains." Gedeonov didn't respond; Tchaikovsky gave up hope of a Mariinsky premiere. Selections from the first act of *Undina* were performed in Moscow at the Bolshoi on March 16, 1870: the program included the overture, Undina's entrance aria, the chorus of burghers, and the duet between Undina and the knight Huldbrandt. Tchaikovsky thought that the concert might help his case with Gedeonov, but the music didn't have an impact. *Undina* would not be staged, leaving Tchaikovsky to retrieve the score from the Mariinsky Theater library and recycle the music in other compositions, most notably his incidental music for Ostrovsky's "spring legend" *The Snow Maiden*, which he composed over two months, March and April 1873.

The score for this play is a hybrid of accessible dances and songs and a deeply symbolic text that even folklore specialists consider heavy going. The Snow Maiden, the daughter of Ded Moroz (Grandfather Frost) and Vesna Krasa (Spring the Beautiful), wants to leave her forest home for the village. She's attracted to the singing and dancing, and Ostrovsky constructs the first act like a traditional choral round dance. He also infuses it with Shrovetide imagery, wedding rituals, and laments, including one taken from the ancient *Tale of Igor's Campaign* (*Slovo o polku Igoreve*).[33] Tchaikovsky poured the dozen tunes he had mined from folksong collections into the metric and rhythmic patterns Ostrovsky assigned to him—an experience that served him well when it came to ballet composition (as one of the initiators of the *Snow Maiden* project, who was also the author of the scenario of *Swan Lake*, noticed). There's a modal number for blind *gusli* players that falls into a call-and-response structure with strikingly asymmetrical phrasing, the seven-measure orchestral introduction ceding to a 4+4+4 assemblage in the solo voice and a 4+4+5 assemblage in the chorus. The lyrics tell of a "dawn-less darkness" that has closed the singers' eyes forever. Following Ostrovsky's direction, Tchaikovsky also includes a nightmare of a song about a beaver trying to bathe the dirt out of its hide and hunters coming after the beaver—*Ay, leli-leli*—with their dogs wanting to sew a fur coat—*Ay, leli-leli*—to give to thick-browed pubescent girls. It's about matchmaking, sort of, and it's sung by a wandering minstrel with a balalaika (represented by pizzicato strings).

The plot follows the frozen heroine's interactions with Kupava (symbol of summer, earth, and devotion) and two men: Lel (love), to whom Tchaikovsky assigns three songs, and Mizgir (passion). To live among humans is to encounter love, which causes her heart to thaw and the rest of her body to turn to slush. For Ostrovsky, however, love is more than an act of defrosting. It's a sacrifice, one that forces the seasons to change. The sacrifice is atonement for what's been taken from the earth. Unless nature complies, unless it rains, unless it gets warm, unless nature is bountiful and beneficent, people perish. Kupava had been betrothed to Mizgir until he laid his eyes on the Snow Maiden. She ends up with Lel instead, as the beaver song predicted (Kupava semi-rhymes with *kupalsya*, as in *bobyor kupalsya*, the beaver was bathing, and the seemingly nonsensical *leli–leli* refrain points right to Lel). The Snow Maiden, in contrast, ends up with no one. Like Fyodor Dostoyevsky, Ostrovsky was interested in spiritual cleansing through suffering, an idea that has been mapped onto Tchaikovsky's life as much as his art. In Irene Esam's summary, the Snow Maiden has "an inborn, chaste coldness and aloofness" but experiences "a gradual awakening of her aesthetic consciousness." Love, in this interpretation, is the creative wellspring as well as the trench in which the dead, or dissolved, body is destined to lie.[34]

Putting Ostrovsky's five-hour play on the stage of the Malïy Theater was complicated by the absence of stage action. It had about as much going for it in terms of action as a woodcut and invited heckling from the merchants holding the season tickets. It was also complicated by the closing of the Malïy for repairs, as this unimpressed reviewer explains:

Ostrovsky's *The Snow Maiden* (music by Tchaikovsky) has finally seen the light of day. It was performed on Friday, May 11, [1873,] before a full house at the *Bolshoi Theater*, a highly festive occasion … I'll just say the following: first, it's a show that doesn't know the meaning of the word drama; a ballad that's been given the shape of a play; a lyric poem; an acted-out folktale—it's everything you might want with the exception of drama. It doesn't belong on the stage but between the covers of a book. Second, the author borrowed the central poetic conceit from Serbian or Bulgarian legend published in the 1840s [*sic*] in A. F. Veltman's wonderful translation under the title *Troyan and Angelitsa, a Tale Told by the Morning Star to the Clear Moon*. Third, Ostrovsky's latest production, devoid of any element of drama, dragged on and on and was extremely boring on stage, though distinguished in places by the freshness of true poetry and beauty of the verse. Fourth, Tchaikovsky's music was beautiful and the actors, when acting, very good (especially [Nadezhda] Nikulina [as Kupava]). But at the same time the boredom brought about by Ostrovsky's latest production emptied out much of the theater well before the end.[35]

The writer accuses Ostrovsky of pinching material from Veltman's 1856 translation of a legend from Bulgaria. He did, but his main source was the second volume of a folklore collection by Alexander Afanasyev, *Slavic Views of Nature* (*Poeticheskiye vozzreniya slavyan na prirodu*, 1866–69). In Afanasyev's telling, a childless peasant couple fashions a daughter for themselves from a snowdrift. Their love brings the creature to life, but not for long: dared by her friends, she jumps over a fire and turns into steam. In another Afanasyev telling, taken from pagan lore, the heroine comes into being on her own. She is formed in the winter and dissipates in the spring, having fulfilled, or taken away, the desires of humans.

Ostrovsky was tasked with bringing together the artists of the Moscow Imperial Theaters for one big show: actors from the Malïy, singers and dancers from the Bolshoi. He added bawdy filth to the script (the censor-baiting text of the beaver song), and a generous dose of politics. The cast includes a kindhearted and wise Russian ruler, Tsar Berendey, and a tyrant, Frost, from whom the people seek to be liberated—freed of the long feud between Frost and the Sun God that has kept everyone in the cold and the dark. That was the situation in the northern Bulgarian settlement of Troyan, which was on the cusp, in 1873, of liberation from the Turks. Ostrovsky brings a certain form of populism to his play (musicologist Emily Frey identifies "harmonious communal ritual, agrarian prehistory," and "individual feeling" in its pages),[36] but it is also an exercise in pan-Slavism, drawing from the common culture of the Slavic lands and speaking to Slavic solidarity. The characters feature in stories as long ago as twelfth-century Kievan (Kyivian) Rus and recur, in different guises, throughout eastern and southern Europe, including land controlled by the Ottoman Empire.

The Prologue and the first of Lel's songs of the *Snow Maiden*'s incidental music come from *Undina*; other parts of the score ended up in the second movement of his Second Symphony and his ballet *Swan Lake*.[37] Tchaikovsky appreciated the compliments he received, at Ostrovsky's expense, for the repurposing. But the composer felt the loss of *Undina* acutely; he couldn't shrug off its rejection by the Imperial Theaters as he did other rejections. The recovered twenty-five minutes of music attest to Tchaikovsky's intense engagement with, and investment in, the subject matter. The aria begins with water sounds and ends with a simultaneous stretching out and dissolving of sound atop disquieting pulsation in the orchestra. It's a small ternary form that moves from a dialogue with a brook and a waterfall (such as will recur in Tchaikovsky's *Manfred* Symphony) to repeated warnings in the middle section about the dangers of love. The slipperiness of the heroine's situation is captured in the harmonies in the B section, which point to C major, then to F minor, with an augmented sixth chord that revolves not to the tonic but to the dominant (of which it is supposed to be a substitute).[38] The *Undina* storm scene approaches the force of the Dies Irae of Verdi's *Requiem* as the brass tears through the fabric using "experimental horror harmony [occasional tone clusters and triads separated by semitone] of a kind more often found in the work of [Alexander] Dargomïzhsky and the [Mighty] Five."[39] A reviewer of a recent performance of the fragments describes the episode as a battle of light and dark in the soul that neither side wins—and the duet destined for *Swan Lake* is likewise an exploration of opposites—here, pathos and exultation.[40] The exploration of feeling contra thought becomes one of the drivers of Tchaikovsky's career.

He zeroed in on another concept in Zhukovsky's (and Fouqué's) writing: that of a "feminine paradise" that ignores or transcends borders (which would make it a queer paradise).[41] Undina sings too, of an ideal family. "The brook is my uncle, the waterfall my brother." The nymph is liquid, and her realm is flowing, soft, and cool, with trouble in store when she steps onto land. Tchaikovsky never forgot her, even as he turned to other projects. Later he recognized that she belonged in a ballet of her own, not just with Odette in *Swan Lake*. He didn't get to write it; the ballet master of the Imperial Theaters turned it down in favor of another ballet called *The Sleeping Beauty*.

Censorship

In Russia, as in France, stories based on actual historical events usually became operas, while tales of the supernatural typically provided the basis for ballets. *Undina* was the exception that, because it didn't reach the stage, proved this rule. Especially after Napoleon, the French government considered the theatrical arts essential to the promotion of nationhood and generously financed sprawling grand operas with crowd scenes, natural disasters, battles, and broken hearts. In Russia the Imperial Theaters produced Italian operas for the amusement of the sovereign while also permitting the performance of plays, and later operas, about Russia before Russia proper: stories of ancient warriors, marauding Tatar-Mongols, and the formation and fortification of the Tsardom of Muscovy. These productions became popular in the 1860s, after Tsar Alexander II's liberalizing reforms. Imperial censorship still forbade the display of the Romanov rulers on stage, especially in singing roles. Tchaikovsky obviously knew about this prohibition, just as he personally knew some of the censors—who were often sophisticated gentlemen, not dolts with red pens. In place of the Romanovs, the struggles and strife of the preceding Ryurikovichi (Rurik Dynasty princes) became a source of exotic, melodramatic entertainment. Tchaikovsky composed two such Rurik-era operas: the first, *The Oprichnik*, based on a play by Ivan Lazhechnikov; the second, *Mazeppa*, after Pushkin.

Lazhechnikov came from Kolomna, an ancient town on a bend in the Moscow River whose name means just that: Bend in the River.[42] He produced patriotic novels and historical plays, stories, and memoirs along with the script for a burlesque called *Dug In* (*Okopirovalsya*, 1854). Topics range from his experience as a soldier fighting Napoleon's *Grande Armée* to the Winter Palace, a Jewish daughter (*Doch'yevreya*, 1849), and a hunchback (*Gorbun*, 1858). The play *The Oprichnik* (1842) describes rape and murder in sixteenth-century Muscovy. It had to wait a long time for publication and performance owing to its nightmarish representation of Tsar Ivan IV (1530–84).

Ivan is best known as *Ivan Grozniy*, or Ivan the Terrible. European adventurers told lurid tales about him to their patrons after his death, when it was safe to do so. These tales and the politics behind them gave him his nickname.[43] As to what really happened at his court: that is in dispute, since the four surviving eyewitness accounts are at odds with one another.[44] Three of them come from men who had been Ivan's prisoners, though he found uses for them at his court and allowed them some freedom of movement. The fourth comes from an accomplished field commander named Andrey Kurbsky who had defected from Ivan's realm in 1564. He, like the others, had an obvious reason to hate Ivan and fixated, in his recollections, on the gruesome and blackly comedic moments of his rule, like the time he poured boiling soup over the head of a jester too coarse for his taste. (Hearing that the jester had died from the scalding, the tsar snorted, "To hell with him! He made no attempt to recover!")[45] That Ivan did terrible things is certain—the soup anecdote has a sequel involving a giant frying pan—but their scale is unclear.

Increasingly paranoid, Ivan in 1565 established a state within the state: the *oprichnina* (literally, the "widow's land") guarded by henchmen known as *oprichniki*. Most of the guards lived in the Arbat neighborhood around the site of the present-day Lenin (Russian State) Library, abutting the *ostozh'ye*, a meadowland where horses grazed.[46] Their compound encompassed a cluster of fenced-in court-yards, huts, and a renovated palace as its stronghold.[47] Productive enterprises and lavish estates were gradually placed under *oprichnina* administration.[48] Ivan relocated clerks, servants, treasurers, cooks, bakers, and kennel-minders from their homes along the river to the new compound. He left the rest of the administration and the nonsacralized land (*zemshchina*) under the control of hereditary landholders, or boyars.[49]

Lazhechnikov's play is an allegory about Russia's dark, grim past opposing the supposedly enlightened Romanov present. The boyar Andrey Morozov has left his mother and the *zemshchina* to join the *oprichnina*. He and the beautiful maiden Natalya are deeply in love with each other, but Natalya has been promised by her father, a prince, to another man, Molchan Mitkov. The *oprichniki* kill Mitkov, which allows Andrey and Natalya to marry. Before the wedding, however, Ivan demands the "right of the first night" with the bride. Andrey protests and loses his head. Natalya faints in horror before being carted to Ivan's bedchamber.[50]

To get the play into print, Lazhechnikov did something clever that also bailed him out financially. In 1856 he went to work for the people who had banned his play fourteen years prior: the St. Petersburg Censorship Committee. In 1859, just after he resigned from the committee to return to writing, *The Oprichnik* appeared in print in the magazine *Reader's Library* (Biblioteka dlya chteniya). Staging it, however, proved a more challenging matter, requiring a higher level of approval from the Ministry of the Court, which regu-lated the theatrical censors and the Imperial Theaters directorate. Permission was also needed from the division of the tsar's Privy Council responsible for the public image of the monarchy, past and present. That division banned *The Oprichnik* from performance in 1863 owing to its depiction of Ivan the Terrible as a "tyrant."

Karamzin had called Ivan just that in his *History of the Russian State*, but public theaters were held to a different standard because audiences were considered less sophisticated and more susceptible to provocation.[51]

The play came up for review again on April 10, 1867, with different people in charge of the agencies and new policies in place. Censorship relaxed under Tsar Alexander II, and *The Oprichnik* was reinterpreted as a Romeo-and-Juliet-like tale of self-sacrificing love. Lazhechnikov was now seen to have evenhandedly represented Ivan the Terrible as a product of terrible circumstances, a person of "conviction who had consciously subjugated chaotic, egoistic, antiquity."[52] The censor objected neither to the inclusion of the Holy Book in the oath-taking ritual of the *oprichniki*, nor to the tsar and the boyars appearing in monastic garb. Mitkov's murder was all that had to go. The censor was censored, however, by his superior, who insisted that the reading from the epistle ("The Supplication of Daniel the Exile") be excised, Ivan's "beastliness" softened, and crude lines like "any wench anywhere in Rus is yours, just ask" be cut.[53] Those changes allowed the play to be staged in the 1867–68 season of the Malïy Theater and once more in 1869, when Tchaikovsky saw it. The composer immediately recognized its operatic potential, especially since the first act had much in common with the first act of *Voyevoda*, allowing him to recycle some of that abandoned opera's music.

He wrote the libretto of *The Oprichnik* himself (his first mention of the project is February 5, 1870, in a letter to his sister, Sasha) and soon encountered problems of his own with the censor, as evidenced by this report from the fall of 1873:

> The libretto of the opera *The Oprichnik*, taken from the well-known tragedy by Lazhechnikov, represents Ivan the Terrible in the most shameful and immoral manner at the end ... All of Ivan's major shortcomings, his indomitable despotism and brutal

manifestations of his will, have been exhibited in print and on the stage, but the present episode is so morally cynical and outrageous that if the author doesn't agree to a wholesale rewrite, I, as the censor, have no choice but to recommend its prohibition at the discretion of the committee.

November 22, 1873

Resolved: mandate the author to make the changes the censor specifies.[54]

These remarks pertain to the publication of the libretto in antici-pation of the premiere of the opera. The problem was solved not through a rewrite, but by the intervention of Vasily Bessel, one of Tchaikovsky's conservatory classmates. After graduating, Bessel had become a successful music publisher with an attractive storefront on Nevsky Prospekt. He offered to publish *The Oprichnik* before the ink was dry on the page. Tchaikovsky immediately agreed and handed over the rights to *The Oprichnik* to Bessel for 3,000 rubles. (Contra legend, Tchaikovsky wasn't bamboozled; Bessel paid him a hefty fee.) Tchaikovsky confirmed the agreement in a letter to the intendant of the Imperial Theaters: "I have the honor to report that I have sold [to Bessel] the rights to the performances of my opera *The Oprichnik* forever."[55] That last word—forever—caused much unhappiness down the line.[56] In 1873, however, the arrangement with Bessel had the advantage of making the problem with the censor Bessel's problem. The publisher quickly solved it by arguing that the ending of the libretto, like the ending of Lazhechnikov's play, matched the account of Ivan the Terrible's reign being taught in school. The ban was lifted.[57]

The Oprichnik follows the format of French grand opera, including a chorus, ballet, and grand finale for the soloists. Ivan's nickname, Terrible (*Grozniy*), is sometimes rendered as "Thunderous" in Russian. Tchaikovsky brings the thunder in the overture: it opens

with an ominous timpani roll that lands on the leading tone diminished seventh chord of E minor. The theme of the *oprichniki* appears
in A major. The fourth scale degree is sharpened; the *oprichniki*
march to a supercharged major triad on the mediant. The procession
ends; the dynamic softens, and the theme recurs in pizzicato strings
as a seductive accompaniment to a cluster of woodwind melodies
denoting the fraught romantic aspects of the plot—the unraveling
mother–son relationship and the tightening (like a noose) girlfriend–
boyfriend relationship. The overture ends, like the fourth act, with
the *oprichniki* theme rhythmically augmented and a modulation to
D major facilitated by a jarringly inserted German augmented sixth
chord.

Tchaikovsky mined his 1868–69 collection of *Fifty Russian
Folksongs* (commissioned by Jurgenson) for the Act I round dance,
Natalya's opening aria, and the "dance of the *oprichniki* and women"
in Act IV, a kind of Russian capriccio using five tunes of contrasting
character subject to Glinka background variations (which could
alternatively be called fairground variations, given the composer's
cheerful treatment of the orchestra like a hurdy-gurdy in these
passages). The tunes are identified as "Our Wine Cellar," "Floating,
Rising," "Master Andrey Made Merry," "Merry Katya," and "Little
Ivan Wears a Big Hat."[58] The plot is carried by recitatives and ensembles, with Tchaikovsky paying special attention to the finale of the
third act, when Andrey's mother, Morozova, condemns him for
becoming an *oprichnik*. Tchaikovsky dedicates dozens of pages to this
intrigue, beginning with the tremolo-saturated orchestral introduction to Act II, which is all sorts of things: a balalaika singalong, a
lament, a ghost scene, and a funeral procession. The mother, *boyarïna*
Morozova, sings of her humiliation and lost pride. She's submitted to
God's will, and God has repeatedly let her down; now her son is
about to cross over to the dark side. Natalya is of two minds: The
"Nightingale's Song" is the song of a girl who's resigned, like
Morozova, to her lot, while her Act I aria, "I thought I heard voices,"

suggests that she's not resigned after all. Her desire to get out, to be with Andrey, is expressed in orchestral writing so anguished as to overwhelm her vocal line.

The jangling pleasantness of the *zemshchina* is contrasted in the opera with the Bortnyansky-influenced homophonic choral singing and bellicose brass sound of the *oprichnina*, with the force majeure of the evil tsar taking down both sides. Ivan doesn't physically appear, nor sing or speak—not because of some imperial prohibition but because he's part of everyone and everything else. Love is immortal, spiritual, and thus resounds in the unheard music of the spheres, but the lovers are doomed by the white noise of autocracy.

Laroche positively reviewed *The Oprichnik*, and César Cui reflexively condemned it: "I won't say it is immaturity, but we see extreme underdevelopment and childishness throughout the music of *The Oprichnik*," he spewed. Tchaikovsky by now hated him, as did the novelist Ivan Turgenev, who wanted to see Cui's "empty head . . . smashed in with a dirty brick."[59] (That was after Cui threw mud at Mozart.) Laroche, a better-behaved critic, lauded Tchaikovsky's embrace of a lyrical French grand opera idiom that soothed the censors and pleased the public. He complained, however, that *The Oprichnik* lacked Russianness, by which he meant, provocatively, that it needed to sound more oppressive:

> As a musical work *The Oprichnik* is a comforting flowering oasis after the desert of dramatic declamation in which Russian composers have allowed us to languish in recent years. One cannot fail to welcome the freedom with which Tchaikovsky makes use of the words; one cannot fail to welcome his striving for ensembles, that most precious property of dramatic music, and for coherent melodic cantilena in which a character's personality or the mood of the moment is outlined; one cannot fail to admire the rich talent which our composer manifests in both arias and ensembles.
>
> In places, however, this freedom goes too far.[60]

On the one hand Laroche claims that Tchaikovsky has liberated Russian opera from the tuneless realism of compositions like Alexander Dargomïzhsky's *The Stone Guest* (not to mention the first version of Musorgsky's *Boris Godunov*); on the other, he considers Tchaikovsky too digressive, too capricious in his handling of the text, and too invested in representing the freedom that Natalya and Andrey can never find. Much of *The Oprichnik* recalls Bizet's *Carmen*, but the children are nastier and the heroine, Natalya, corseted.[61] She faints before being carted off to Ivan the Terrible. Andrey is led to his execution. Forced to witness the killing, his mother wails in despair as a gong sounds.

The point of this *fabula*? What's notable about *The Oprichnik*, the opera and the play, is the reduction of political terror to a single act of sexual jealousy, which is petty, universal in all cultures, and doesn't address the actual nature of the *oprichnina* and its inhabitants. The *oprichniki* were neither thugs nor henchmen but a combined militia and monastic order that served the tsar and God—but not a Christian God. Russian power (*vlast'*) depended, for its endurance, on an Old Testament God of rage and vengeance. Mindful of the censors, desperate to succeed now in a French operatic format, Tchaikovsky turned this power into a strange form of beauty in his opera. The guardsmen sing a radiant a cappella chorus in praise of Ivan the Terrible as the curtain descends.

The premiere on April 12, 1874, was, like the publication of the libretto, partly Bessel's doing. He submitted the score of *The Oprichnik* to the Mariinsky Theater's maestro, Nápravník, who agreed to conduct it so long as the proceeds from the first performance went directly into his pocket. Nápravník had the muscle needed to get the opera onto the stage. On March 22, 1874, the head of the repertoire committee for the Imperial Theaters informed his supervisor that

the Kapellmeister of the Russian opera [Nápravník didn't conduct foreign operas] has requested permission to premiere [*The*

Oprichnik] as a benefit in his name. In presenting this matter to your discretion, Your Excellency, I have the honor of informing you that the libretto of the opera in question has been approved for performance by the Theater and Literature Committee and by the censor, and the music approved by the Music Committee. According to the regulations pertaining to the remuneration of authors and translators, this opera belongs to the first class— granting the author with one tenth of two thirds of the income from each performance.[62]

A second benefit was arranged for the chorus on April 14, after which the proceeds from the opera went to Bessel. It was a successful production: *The Oprichnik* earned more in its first month than Glinka's ubiquitous operas *A Life for the Tsar* and *Ruslan and Lyudmila*; Weber's *Der Freischütz* (which earned almost nothing in April); and Meyerbeer's *Les Huguenots*, which used the same choral singers as *The Oprichnik* (hence the benefit for them). The premiere run finished on December 8, 1874, eleven performances in all, the ticket sales for the last show a third of those for Richard Wagner's *Tannhäuser* on December 20.[63]

Gogol

Tchaikovsky next tried his hand at comic opera based on Nikolay Gogol's "Christmas Eve" published in 1826 and included in a twinkling collection of Ukrainian tales titled *Evenings on a Farm Near Dikanka* (1832). Several are set during Christian and pagan holidays, Gogol having an interest in seasonal rituals and their mysteries. Tchaikovsky called the opera *Vakula the Smith* (*Kuznets Vakula*) after the metal-working protagonist and completed it in 1874. Eleven years later, in 1885, he pruned and simplified the opera with a different dramatic focus and under a different name, *Cherevichki*, sometimes translated as *Little Slippers* or *Little Golden Slippers*. (The slippers are, in fact, fancy felt boots of silver and gold.) The first version of the opera was a modest success—despite the one-word review in *New Times* (*Novoye vremya*): "colorless"[64]—and the second a bona fide hit from its premiere, with Tchaikovsky conducting, at the Bolshoi Theater on January 19, 1887.[65]

Surrounding it all was Russia's exoticization of Ukraine as a colonial acquisition (the south and west of Ukraine were absorbed into the empire in the late eighteenth century). Gogol, who came from central Ukraine, participated in that process while also caricaturing it, playing the part of the country bumpkin in aristocratic settings. He didn't know how to chitchat in polite Russian society and was altogether too coarse; he needed a haircut and dressed oddly. In his art, as in his life, he is said to have "manipulated stereotypes of the Other [within] the Russian nationalist imagination."[66] His pro-Russian Empire writing does so ambiguously or irrationally.

"Christmas Eve" begins with a devil pocketing the moon and cozying up to a witch, the mother of the protagonist Vakula, a blacksmith and, when work is slow, a painter. The dark and a sudden blizzard (also the devil's doing) conceal the location of the distillery and the church: the plot unfolds in a hedonistic terra incognita. No one knows who's who and what's what. Perhaps your husband is someone else's husband, and the mayor the priest; perhaps the devil living in the chimney is a natty lad about town and those giggling girls a witches' coven. Gogol indulges his grosser side: a Cossack dines on magical stuffed pastries (*vareniki*) that dip themselves in sour cream and stuff themselves into his mouth, smearing the goo all around. Midnights, ends of years, deaths, and births are thresholds: spirits run amok.

Vakula is in love with the local beauty, Oksana, but so is everyone else, which baffles her until she looks in a mirror and concedes that she's indeed a stunner. Oksana humiliates Vakula and he threatens, in despair, to drown himself. She responds with an elaborate demand: she'll marry him if he can bring her the tsarina's fancy footwear. Doing so requires taming the devil (who has long had it in for Vakula for an unflattering painting of the evil spirit) and riding the devil's back across the sky to St. Petersburg. After landing, Vakula spruces himself up for an audience with the empress. Catherine finds Vakula quaintly amusing and gives him the boots, but he doesn't actually need them. Oksana has fallen in love with him in his absence.

The ending is eerier than the rest. Vakula and Oskana are married and have a child. The archbishop turns up and sees Vakula's ugly painting of the devil in hell on the church door. Passersby spit on it, saying "look at that crap head [*yaka kaka*]." Squalling babies are frightened into silence at the sight. "That's Gogol for you," biographer Ekaterina Dmitriyeva summarizes; "something terrible remains in this world."[67]

Tchaikovsky didn't choose this story; the story chose him. Grand Princess Elena Pavlovna, the generous bankroller of the Imperial Russian Musical Society (IRMS) and St. Petersburg Conservatory, had organized an opera competition. Composers were invited to set the libretto that had been taken from Gogol's story by Yakov Polonsky, whom Tchaikovsky knew (he wrote the libretto of the Polytechnic Exhibition Cantata).[68] Submissions were supposed to be anonymous. Instead of his name, Tchaikovsky inscribed the third act of the piano score with the Latin motto *Ars longa, vita brevis*: "art takes time but life is short." The title seems ironic, given that he had drafted the opera in just three months, from June through August 1874.[69] He brazenly violated the rules by pestering the jurors— Nikolay Rimsky-Korsakov (chiefly), Anton Rubinstein, Laroche, and Nápravník—to favor his score.[70] But he didn't need to cheat; the other submissions were amateurish, though one of the other entrants, Nikolay Solovyov, managed to get his setting performed, semiprofessionally, in 1880 and 1882.[71] Tchaikovsky received first prize (there was no second), 1,500 rubles, and the promise of a premiere on the imperial stage.

Polonsky's libretto made it past the print censors but was rejected by the dramatic censors, who found "insurmountable obstacles" for a staging, specifically: "In Act II, scene 3, a clergyman is brought onto the stage, a deacon, comically talking about Father Kondrat, among other things. And the sixth scene in the third act represents the court of Catherine the Great with the Empress Herself brought onto the stage."[72] Although Catherine isn't mentioned by name, the costumes, speeches, events, and all the details of the scene made it obvious that she is the subject. Exception to the rule prohibiting the theatrical portrayal of royal personages could be made for Muscovy's distant rulers, like Boris Godunov, but not for the Hapsburg-Romanovs. The matter wasn't resolved until after the competition was concluded. The Minister of the Court weighed in on special petition of Prince Dmitri Obolensky, who had been acquainted with Gogol and who served as the deputy director of the IRMS. A November 29, 1875, letter to the Imperial Theaters directorate belatedly affirmed the minister's decision "to accept the opera *Vakula the Smith*, by Professor Tchaikovsky of the Moscow Conservatory for staging at the Mariinsky Theater in the 1876–77 season."[73] Tchaikovsky sent a letter of gratitude to the officials involved in the approval process and another to the head of the St. Petersburg division of the IRMS concerning logistics:

Gracious Sir!

Mikhaíl Pavlovich [Azanchevsky]!

In a letter dated December 6 of this year, you were kind enough to inform me that on the fourth of December, in memorandum no. 2214, the Office of the Directorate of the Imperial Theaters requested delivery of the score of *Vakula the Smith*. Accordingly, I have the honor to humbly ask you, Gracious Sir, to deliver to the Office of the Directorate the score of said opera, which is at the St. Petersburg Conservatory. Might I also request of you, Mikhaíl Pavlovich, to take upon yourself the task of providing any and all the explanations and instructions of which the directorate might find need, as my duties in Moscow prevent me from being in

St. Petersburg at the regular disposal of the directorate should the directorate deem it important to contact me as the composer of an opera accepted for production.

With deep respect and unwavering devotion, I have the honor to be, Gracious Sir, your most obedient servant.

P. Tchaikovsky
December 8, 1875[74]

The libretto didn't change much; the deacon became a schoolteacher, and a character called Sir Highness authorized the gift of the shoes as Catherine's stand-in. The standard comic opera episodes of mistaken identities, disguises, and concealment (in coal bags) passed the censor without comment.

Tchaikovsky's music is a potpourri of subtler and gentler humor than the genre demands, with the exception of a near-hysteric choral anthem to the empress. In places, the score seems to laugh at itself, just in case the audiences don't get the jokes, and some of them pass by quickly, like the Cossacks' attempts to speak some French at court (Spanish comes out).[75] The punning of Russian expressions about the devil (*chyort*) is extreme. The opera is set *u chyorta na kulichkakh* (far away); people drink their faces off (*do chyortikov*). The phrase *Chyort vozmi!* is endlessly repeated in its various meanings (The devil take it! Jesus Christ! What the hell!).

Tchaikovsky assigned augmented seconds to the witch; galops to the *chyort*; chromatic and whole-tone segments to the storm together with swirling flute, jingling tambourine, and a chorus of spirits; a glittering polonaise with a cannonade and a rather clogged minuet to the court, and then a Russian and a Cossack dance and the start of a performance of one of the empress's plays as additional aristocratic entertainment. The music trembles and quivers in the devil-induced cold; a solo horn denotes a sterile loneliness; the maidens (*rusalki*) of the Dnieper River complain of frostbite in 5/4 time, and a forest sprite tells them to knock it off.

Tchaikovsky faced criticism for layering too much emotion and somber realism into the vocal parts of the main characters. The reviewer for *New Times* who called the opera "colorless" published a thoughtful piece about exactly what went wrong. Why had Tchaikovsky and Polonsky squandered the opportunity to create the first great Russian comic opera—and the first based on Gogol? The fault wasn't entirely theirs; it was also Russia's: "Our life offers little material for pure comedy," Mikhaíl Ivanov wrote. "Though we are blessed with a robust sense of humor, our nature doesn't indulge cheerful, carefree merriment, we don't have boisterous social lives, and so it's tricky finding comic situations and characters among us." The "Italians, French, and Westerners in general" routinely pause to consider the funnier aspects of life, but for Russians, who conceive of life as a series of tasks to be completed, doing so is "tortuous," a kind of sin. The Ukrainian Gogol had the magic touch owing to his peasant genes, but Polonsky and Tchaikovsky, both highbrow "elegists," did not. Their adaptation was blunt, thick, and heavy; it stripped the devil of wisdom and Vakula of piety. His mother had lost her cackle and was turned into a "*ploshchadnaya shinkarka*" (crude tavern wench). The dances managed to be "sad," pensive," and "cacophonous" all at once, and the Cossack hopak dancers appeared from out of nowhere.[76]

Laroche, in contrast, considered the opera a balanced conception, the "vice" of realism outweighed by the "virtues" of the comic moments, like "the marvelous counterpoint with which the orchestra accompanies the howling and crying of Oksana and [Vakula's mother, the witch] Solokha in Act IV over Vakula's absence: 'Someone said he hanged himself.'" Laroche describes the St. Petersburg music as a juxtaposition of "genuine courage and heroism" and "refined court luxury."[77] He signals—almost—that Tchaikovsky responded to Gogol's grotesquerie with melodramatic excess. Vakula whines, pathetically. His grousing about the lack of ability and loss of strength is parroted in a disintegrating orchestral accompaniment, his inability to think straight captured in botched antiphonal exchanges in the brasses. Oksana doesn't know if she should laugh or cry about her plight; Tchaikovsky threads her opening fairest-in-the-land aria with coquettish lowered fifths and sharp sixths and ends it with ultra-romantic orchestral swells. She's the witch, he implies in his more acerbic musical moments, not Vakula's mother. Oksana's boorish father gets the opera buffa treatment; she can't stand him. Nor does she like the chorus, which is supposed to comment on the action but instead interferes with it. The singers pester Oksana about her love life and bad choices (likewise Vakula's, telling him that suicide is a sin).

There were eighteen performances, "assiduously, competently, and even sumptuously" realized, right down to guardsmen's headwear in the court scene, a fastidious replication of that worn by the Preobrazhensky and Semyonovsky regiments of Catherine's time.[78] Tinkering with the score hadn't helped, and the opera didn't earn enough between 1876 and 1879 to dissuade Tchaikovsky that it was anything but a "failure."[79] Transforming *Vakula the Smith* into *Cherevichki* meant cutting five hundred measures, reorchestrating a thousand others, thinning the texture, adding more singing in place of declamation, and—regrettably—eliminating the Gogolian contrast between Russian literate language and peasant dialect. Tchaikovsky inserted an ode to Russian battlefield prowess against the Turks, which referenced an actual event, Prince Alexander Bezborodko's signing of the Treaty of Jassy with his Ottoman counterpart in 1792 and Russia's annexation of the Crimea. Thus, *Cherevichki* responded to the political moment: the conclusion, in 1878, of another war with the Turks and the ratification of treaties. Tchaikovsky could not have known that this coalition war devolved into an ethnic cleansing operation of barbaric acts of torture and mass rape.

Tchaikovsky's comic opera 2.0 ended with the Gogolian reminder that, after the laughter ends and with it the sorrow, after the guy gets the girl and the devil is stuffed back up the chimney, "something terrible remains."

Jove

As *Vakula the Smith/Cherevichki* illustrates, Tchaikovsky needed to work twice as much to obtain half the result. And he was willing to do so. He multitasked during this period, and he called even successful compositions failures to prevent complacency. To keep his mind buzzing, to bring in income, he stretched himself thin. He worked on genres other than opera, writing his Third Symphony as an exercise in humor as opposed to comedy; even he called it a success.[80] Another pile of paper on his desk was his First Piano Concerto, which had a miserable unveiling but became an all-time classic. Here the issue wasn't the critics or the public but the performers.

Tchaikovsky wrote it for the Moscow branch of the IRMS and its director, Nikolay Rubinstein, the biggest figure in Moscow musical life. Rubinstein decided the repertoire for the concerts and tapped into the aristocratic patronage network to fund commissions, which he awarded to his friends. He was a fabulous pianist and respected conductor, and Tchaikovsky assumed that composing a concerto for him would be of mutual benefit. He completed the draft score in just six weeks, took another week and a half to rough out a four-hand arrangement, then threw himself into the orchestration.[81] The drafts are lost; the completed four-hand version is dated December 21, 1874, and the full score February 9, 1875. Meantime, there was the *incident*: Tchaikovsky's presentation of the draft to Rubinstein and a conservatory theory professor named Nikolay Gubert.

Rubinstein drank. A lot. He was kind when drunk, irritable when sober. Tchaikovsky made the mistake of presenting the concerto to him when he was sober, just before a Christmas holiday party at the conservatory. Playing through the score, he watched Rubinstein's face redden with anger: "Then from [his] lips a torrent of words began to flow, quiet at first, then gradually assuming the tone of Jove the Thunderer. I learned that my concerto was good for nothing, unplayable, that the passages are trivial, awkward and so clumsy as to thwart amendment, that the work was bad and commonplace, that I've stolen this from there and that from here, and that only two or three pages are worth keeping, and the rest must either be tossed out or radically revised."[82] Gubert nodded in agreement, as he always did. Tchaikovsky left the room to calm down, Rubinstein tracked him down, and repeated the criticism, to which Tchaikovsky responded that he wouldn't "change a single note."[83]

It's a great story and might even be true, albeit exaggerated in an effort to secure Nadezhda von Mekk's financial support. Rubinstein's judgment couldn't be trusted; Jove started thundering after hearing just the first movement of the concerto. He didn't hear the rest. He wasn't just stupefied but biased, his perception skewed as a touring virtuoso who considered himself superior to a mere composer. In Russia more so than in Europe at the time, to be revered as a musician required immense command of the keyboard, which Tchaikovsky did not have. Rubinstein did, but he was stunted as a composer, capable of writing polkas and waltzes but little else. He didn't have Tchaikovsky's stubborn patience. He craved attention; he needed to be in the spotlight.

Tchaikovsky changed some of the notes, having received friendlier advice about the concerto from other, fairer judges, including his conservatory colleague Karl Klindworth, a student of Liszt. Klindworth subsequently introduced Tchaikovsky to Hans von Bülow (1830–94), who was both an internationally recognized performer and a conductor, though, at that moment, von Bülow wanted to forget the conducting part of his career. In Munich on June 10, 1865, he had led the premiere of Wagner's music drama *Tristan und Isolde*. He lifted the baton knowing that Wagner was sleeping with his wife Cosima. Eventually, Cosima left von Bülow for Wagner, and von Bülow's life fell apart.

NATIONALISM

He escaped Munich and the unfettered hedonism of German Romanticism's 1865 summer of love. In Moscow he gave a piano recital at the Bolshoi Theater that included Tchaikovsky's op. 19 Theme and Variations. The reviewers described von Bülow as a delicately nuanced, clean-lined performer—no banging—and Tchaikovsky, on Klindworth's encouragement, provided him with a copy of his concerto and an invitation to premiere it. Von Bülow accepted and wrote Tchaikovsky a profusely complimentary letter, for which Tchaikovsky profusely thanked him: "Your praises compensate me one hundredfold for all manner of insults and offensive remarks that I have been and will again be subjected to in my ambition as a composer," he wrote to the pianist on July 1, 1875.[84] There was a scramble to get the parts engraved and into von Bülow's suitcase as he headed west to the United States for a long, lucrative tour of 139 concerts in 39 cities. Audiences were spare and undisciplined, but, at the start of his adventure, the pianist boasted of "living it up," grateful to be free of "the old rotten European world."[85] He premiered Tchaikovsky's concerto on October 25, 1875, at the Music Hall in Boston, about as far away from Wagner, and Rubinstein, as could be imagined.

Von Bülow performed the concerto again in Boston on October 30, before taking it to New York and Philadelphia. The trombones flubbed their entrance on the first night and the conducting was shaky but Bostonians considered it a supreme honor to be the first to hear the concerto.[86] The concert reporter for the *Boston Daily Globe* enjoyed the first movement but couldn't make up his mind about the rest: "[The second] movement is very tender and pleasing throughout, but ends as if the full idea had not taken possession of its [composer], or as if he merely wished to suggest an idea to the hearer to complete. The closing movement contains many points of great breadth and beauty and ends with a most pleasing result for effective scoring; but in spite of this, it has too much in it that is an evident striving after effect, with too little of that nice flow of harmonious fancy which indicates the tuneful soul."[87]

Tchaikovsky regretted not hearing the American premiere, especially since the Russian (St. Petersburg) premiere, by Gustav Kross (1831–85) on November 1, 1875, flopped. Had he heard the American premiere, he would have been no less displeased, but von Bülow painted a bright picture for him and didn't mention the long list of mistakes in the hastily engraved parts. The audience in St. Petersburg had to ensure a pitiful performance of Liszt's *Dante Symphony* before hearing the concerto and so thanked Tchaikovsky for freeing them from hell with his accessible music. Laroche disputed Tchaikovsky's harmonic choices ("in the first Allegro, the incessant sequences of inverted dominant seventh chords and triads are like patches slapped onto tears in a fabric"). He mocked the soloist for liking the concerto too much, since no amount of affection could "save" the piece. Then Laroche unloaded on the conductor: "Either because of an insufficient number of rehearsals or Maestro Nápravník's evident dislike of the concerto (all the tempos were too fast), the orchestra was slipshod and disorganized. I have never heard such badly coordinated playing in the Musical Society. If you closed your eyes and forgot about the piano, you might imagine that you were at the Italian opera."[88]

Tchaikovsky took comfort in the performance by his student Sergey Taneyev with Nikolay Rubinstein conducting. A circle closed when Rubinstein drunkenly decided that the concerto might be good after all and added it to his repertoire. A second, bigger circle closed when Tchaikovsky conducted the concerto during his 1891 visit to the United States, returning to the country where von Bülow premiered it. And a third, even bigger circle closed when Tchaikovsky conducted it in St. Petersburg before the premiere of his *Pathétique Symphony*. It was his last public appearance.

The concerto became popular enough, as the so-called First Russian Piano Concerto, for pianists to leave their mark on the score by adjusting tempos, dynamics, and performance instructions. The Db-major chords of the opening, used for the Russian Olympic

Anthem, were originally rolled, but Alexander Siloti encouraged a more robust sound—solid chords, played with force—and Tchaikovsky heeded the advice.[89] (Siloti was a forceful pianist with a hand span of a tenth.) There are two authorized editions of the score, and a much-disputed third edition. The first was published by Jurgenson in 1875, but erratically. The four-hand arrangement appeared in May, and the orchestral parts in October. In August 1879, Jurgenson published the revised second version of the concerto in full score. Then, in 1889, a third edition was prepared, with a cut of seventeen measures in the final movement that Tchaikovsky might or might not have authorized. This edition was published after Tchaikovsky's death and became the standard performing edition. Note the gap: prepared in 1889, but published in 1894. A German publisher, Daniel Rahter, advertised the third edition based on Jurgenson's printing plates, but because no copies of Rahter's edition survive and because Jurgenson didn't change the numbers on the printing plates, it remains unclear if Rahter issued the third version or merely revised the second version. It's a mess, in short. The concerto had a rough first year of existence. Tchaikovsky accepted the advice, tweaks, and suggestions of the touring pianists who made the concerto famous, incorporating them all into the 1879 edition and perhaps the one after that.[90]

Pianist Kirill Gerstein has recently unaccepted the advice, performing and recording the leaner original version of the concerto. He claims that he researched the history of the concerto—by which he means that he relied on the multivolume 2015 critical edition edited by Polina Vaydman and her daughter Ada Aynbinder. They sort through the alterations and arrangements and devote several pages to the composer's Ukrainian folk music borrowings in the first and third movements and a reference to a French vaudeville in the middle. Gerstein's restoration is the product of their labor.

Scaling back the big nineteenth-century concertos is the trend among pianists, just as bulking them up had been in the twentieth century. Gerstein justifies doing so based on the "tragedy, especially in Russian culture, of geniuses surrounded by less-talented well-wishers":

> Usually the pianist enters with [the opening] chords as powerfully as he can, to show that he's got the goods, and the orchestra immediately responds. It's like a Cold War escalates in the first measures. Now, since the chords are rolled and arpeggiated, one can arpeggiate quicker or slower, and help the flow of the melody in a much more flexible style than what one hears when these chords are symmetrically crashing.[91]

The softer dynamic and lower octave of the rolled chords make the start of the concerto sound like the start, as opposed to dropping the listener into the heat of the moment and throes of passion. As Gerstein notes, the passion became humorlessly hyperaggressive during the international piano competitions of the Cold War. The Texas-born, big-haired wunderkind Van Cliburn won the first of these competitions in Moscow in 1958, stunning the Soviets and inaugurating a musical arms race that bulked up the concerto and excised all subtlety from it. The middle of the middle movement was accelerated, with a harmonically ruminative passage in the finale cut. Trapped in the fame he acquired in 1958, at age twenty-three, Van Cliburn played the concerto throughout his career like a record on repeat, wearing out the grooves.[92]

What Rubinstein hated was the meandering, ruminative looseness of the first movement. Although it is conventionally analyzed, as all first movements seem to be analyzed, as a sonata-allegro form, the music doesn't adhere to formal-functional procedures. The transitions, modulations, and developmental procedures that define the form are absent. The first movement is better described as either a rhapsody, fantasy, or a series of songs strung together and packaged into the loosest three-part structure on the books. The opening trombone blast is in B♭ minor, but the grand theme that launches the proceedings is in D♭ major, the beginning of a protracted tussle between these keys with a diversion into the A♭ major dominant of D♭. The introduction is followed by three themes, of which the first is a borrowing from an epic song of Cossack origins transcribed, Tchaikovsky told von Mekk, from a blind street singer in Ukraine. ("It's remarkable that all the blind singers in the Ukraine play one and the same folk-melody endlessly," he remarked, casually revealing the inspiration for the rotating patterns that serve as nondevelopment bridges to nowhere in his longer works.)[93] The middle theme is sentimental, an ode, if you will, to Nikolay Karamzin's "Poor Liza," and the third is a berceuse. Another, parallel hearing makes the introduction the first theme, the "endless" folk tune the transition, the sentimental tune the second theme, and the berceuse the close. The habit throughout the piece is for the orchestra to pass melodic material to the pianist, who transforms it into a brooding rumination.

The development of the first movement is an exercise in meta-morphosis: the berceuse is passed between orchestra and pianist before morphing into music of comparable force to the opening, its kinetic equivalent. The recap, too, affronts the textbooks: the folk tune is heard in B♭ minor and the sentimental theme and the berceuse in the parallel as opposed to relative major. The seams between the sections are filled, as Laroche complained, either by repeated chords or directionless modal explorations. The point is not to guide the listener from place to place but to distort and destabilize the sound. The pianist gets lost in thought and ends up somewhere unexpected. And in the strangest transition of all, the seventeen measures that the third edition excludes, Tchaikovsky transposes a non-diatonic melodic line by minor second, major second, tritone, and perfect fifth on the flat and sharp of B♭ minor. It might sound like he's evading or delaying a cadence except that no cadence is prepared. The passage is disorienting, with carefully randomized woodwind interjections. It's also amusing, a playful riposte to convention's insistence on logical sequences in tiered dynamics.

The second movement reclaims the sentimental theme in variation for the opening flute solo, and then the pianist takes it up, changing just a single note before the cellos are layered in. The middle section quotes "Faut s'amuser, sauter, et rire" ("You have to have fun, jump, and laugh"), a song-and-dance number from the French vaudeville *La corde sensible* (*Heartstring*, 1851), about two boys trying to find the heartstrings of two girls who don't seem to like having fun, much less jumping and laughing. Efforts to coerce the damsels by force backfire; knight errantry succeeds. The show was cheap to perform and so performed all over, including at the Mikhaílovsky Theater, one of several venues where Tchaikovsky might have seen it.[94] By placing "Faut s'amuser" in dialogue with the heart-on-sleeve theme of his invention, he turns the second movement of his concerto into a musical synopsis of *La corde sensible*.

The final movement opens with the Ukrainian *vesnyanka* (spring song) "Vïydi, vïydi, Ivan'ku" ("Come out, come out, [it's springtime,] Ivanka").[95] It's sung in the round, and it defines Tchaikovsky's rondo, heard six times amid contrasting material, including a hummable tune of the composer's own invention, a heraldic rallying of the full orchestra, and a cadenza that, through all the editions, involves huge leaps, semitonal displacements of ascending scales, and lesser leaps landing on weak pulses that Tchaikovsky wanted played martellato at triple forte.

The borrowings lend the concerto its drama, casual shape, and accessible style. Epic song becomes popular song becomes a spring song in the round, with the piano adding lighter and darker shades of emotion to the complex. The orchestra calls the tunes and consecrates the changes of key, the pianist elaborates those tunes over an accompaniment that replicates lyre and accordion, now regal, now shambolic jamboree. Rolled or unrolled, the chords at the beginning form the introduction (or first theme) that most listeners remember throughout the entire concerto, even though those chords are heard just once. Thickening them, making them more muscular than Tchaikovsky planned, transformed the concerto into *à la russe Sturm und Drang*—an amalgamation of *moshch'* and *dusha*, Soviet might and Slavic soul. Tchaikovsky is credited with an invention not of his making, to the detriment of what he actually invented.

Inflammation

A letter Tchaikovsky sent to his brother Modest from August 8, 1876—during his travels to Paris and Munich and farther on to Bayreuth—mentions two other projects in passing: his *Slavonic March* (*Marche slave*) and his *Francesca da Rimini*. Both are staples of the orchestral repertoire, the first more accessible, hence ubiquitous, than the second. Tchaikovsky's letter is vulgar and banal and not untypical of his letters to the men he trusted (he behaved himself when writing to women, especially the decorous von Mekk). Tchaikovsky repeatedly asks Modest about his recent bout of diarrhea, because

> Such questions are no less interesting to me than the news from the war theater, which, by the way, is grim for the Serbs! As to the circumstances in my own abdomen, I feel great but still occasionally make this face: ☺ My appetite is wondrous, and I'm cheerful and feeling strong, a sign that my health, though iffy, is returning. Now I'm going to have dinner at Peter's [in Paris]. I decided against the theater since it's been hot and there wasn't anything interesting playing. This morning in the carriage I read the 4th [5th] canto of "Inferno" and was inflamed with the desire to write a symphonic poem about Francesca. I embrace you with incredible tenderness. Kiss Kolya for me, on his eyes, neck, and hands. I squeeze his tushy [*fofu obnimayu*].[96]

"The news from the war theater" came from well-paid Russian journalists in the Balkans covering the multisided conflict between the Orthodox populations of the southern Slavic states and the Ottoman Empire. Serbian nationalist groups sought an end to the Turkish influence (and in places, dominance) in the region, and the Ottoman suppression of a revolt in Bulgaria brought those groups into direct conflict with the Turks. In the summer of 1876, while Tchaikovsky was in Paris joking about Modest's gastrointestinal problems, the Ottomans began to repel the Serbs and threaten the Serbian capital of Belgrade. Tsar Alexander II initially sought a peaceful resolution to the conflict, but then, in April of 1877, declared war.

Nikolay Rubinstein commissioned the *Slavonic March* from Tchaikovsky for a charity concert of the IRMS to be held on November 5, 1876. Rubinstein was supposed to direct the funds raised to the Red Cross to help wounded Serbian soldiers. Most of the money, however, went to purchase equipment for "volunteer" Russian soldiers heading to Serbia to fight against the Turks. The charity's dual purpose is reflected in the manuscript title of the *Slavonic March*: "Serbo-Russian March on Slavonic folk themes." Tchaikovsky deployed three Serbian melodies in the march along with, in the middle and at the end, "God Save the Tsar."

The Serbian folk fare comes from the 1862 and 1863 collections of folksongs edited by Kornelije Stanković (1831–65) and published in Vienna, where Tchaikovsky acquired them in 1876. The opening of the march relies on "The Sun Is Bright but Doesn't Always Shine" ("Sunce jarko, ne sijaš jednako"), a punning love song that describes a relationship running hot and cold (my lover kisses me, but not always or not at all). There follows, from measure 86, a tune of sprightlier character, "On the Border of Our Dear Serbia" ("Prag je ovo milog Srba"), and then, from measure 104, the fourth section of "The Serb Gladly Joins the Army" ("Rado ide Srbin u vojnike"). The march is programmatic, representing the rescue of the Serbs from the Turks by the Russian volunteers with a coda celebrating Slavic Christianity after the Muslim tyrants have been driven from the land. The fact that the volunteers were hopelessly incompetent is not reflected in Tchaikovsky's composition (as opposed to Tolstoy's *Anna Karenina*, which caricatures the volunteers as a bunch of drunks, bad soldiers, failed businessmen, and thrill-seeking ne'er-do-wells).[97] The Serbian folk fare is thus but a trivial add-on to the tsar's proud anthem. The Serbs, moreover, are musically paraded around in chains and assigned the strains of lament before a choppily protracted sequence from dominant to tonic and manic sixteenth-note trilling on the tonic, mediant, submediant, and leading tone. Their equipment has broken down; they scream for help; the Russians intervene and the survivors kick up their heels in joy. The *Slavonic March* was such a success at the premiere that Rubinstein conducted it twice.

Jurgenson sought to exploit the patriotic moment and the jejunely realized jingoism of the *Slavonic March* by asking Tchaikovsky to compose another march in honor of General Mikhaíl Skobelev (1843–82). Skobelev was supposedly so brave that he wore white on the battlefield and dared the Turks to shoot him as he crossed the Danube with his squadron. "Soon the music will begin," he told a Russian reporter. "What music?" the reporter asked, just before the shelling started.[98] Tchaikovsky refused to write actual music in Skobelev's honor and considered it an insult to be asked: "that's a bit much," he deadpanned.[99] Jurgenson persisted but changed the assignment. Now it would be a march to raise funds for a Russian "volunteer fleet" established in the spring of 1878. Tchaikovsky obliged with four minutes of C-major pomp that keeps the cymbalist happy. "I have written the march and I'm sending it to you," Tchaikovsky wrote to his publisher on April 24, 1878. "I don't need to be paid, since I too am a patriot, but I ask you not to publish it under my name, but instead under a pseudonym of your choosing."[100] Jurgenson chose "P. Sinopov."

Tchaikovsky was proud to affix his own name to *Francesca da Rimini*. The tone poem (symphonic fantasy) was inspired by a libretto that he might have used for an opera had the librettist Konstantin Zvantsov (1823–90) not behaved so badly. The libretto adapted Canto V of Part I of Dante's *Divina commedia* (1321), a tale of lovers in hell that offered visual effects like iridescent clouds rising from the orchestral pit and references to medieval furnace plays.[101] Zvantsov put it in an envelope addressed to Laroche, who forwarded it to Tchaikovsky. The composer found it "charming" enough to ask Zvantsov to make a second copy for him while the first was under review with the censor.[102] Tchaikovsky's interest ended, however, when Zvantsov overreached, demanding that he compose the opera in imitation of *Tristan und Isolde*. Like Laroche, Zvantsov was a Wagner devotee hoping to bring Tchaikovsky into the fan club.[103] Tchaikovsky declined, probably quite firmly (the rejection letter doesn't survive, but he joked with another friend about falling asleep during *Tristan und Isolde*, so as to avoid getting bored).[104] Rather than an opera, he composed a successful tone poem on the subject that, oddly enough, inspired operas by others. These did not succeed.[105]

Tchaikovsky knew the *Divina commedia*, both in the original Italian (he quotes from Canto V in a July 3, 1876, letter to his brother) and the Russian translation, of which he had access to three: Dmitri Min's diligent but mediocre effort, published in 1855; the 1871 Russian translation by V. A. Petrov, which is dilettantish compared to Min's and completely botches the attempt to replicate Dante's meter; and Dmitri Minayev's translation, published between 1873 and 1879, and partly plagiarized from Min's. This third translation cost much more than the other two because it included Gustave Doré's *Divina commedia* illustrations, which caught Tchaikovsky's eye.[106]

From these sources, Tchaikovsky absorbed the basics, and, if he read the notes to Petrov's translation, broader contextual information. Dante's narrative poem begins with an idealized maternal figure in heaven looking down on a poor soul lost in the woods. She sends a father figure to guide the Pilgrim on a spiritual journey into Inferno, up through Purgatorio and into Paradiso. The father figure is the ancient Roman poet Virgil, whom Dante admired.[107] People and places in Dante's own life populate the flaming circles, through Limbo, Lust, Gluttony, Greed, Anger, Heresy, Violence, Fraud, and Treachery.

In his poetry Dante contrasts emotion with reason and reason with the divine (which was also the project of Thomas Aquinas's *Summa theologica*). Medieval and Renaissance readers privileged Dante's metaphysical musings; Romantic and post-Romantic readers, in contrast, found the spiritual elements less compelling (and certainly less titillating) than the sin. Part I (Inferno) is an encyclopedia of sin and has eclipsed Parts II and III of the *Divina commedia*, Purgatorio and Paradiso, as a source of inspiration to composers, filmmakers, and novelists. Consider the relentlessly unseemly 1995 film *Seven* or Dan Brown's 2013 mystery thriller *Inferno*, which features "screams," "excrement," "disgusting liquid," and "rivers of blood clogged with corpses."[108] Dante's depiction of hell is their source.

Besides the sin, Tchaikovsky adopted some of the formal attributes of the *Divina commedia*. Dante was devoted to the number three, the Trinity, the whole that contains a beginning, middle, and an end. The three sections, or canticas, of the poem comprise thirty-three cantos each. The metric format devised by Dante is also Trinitarian: ABA, BCB, CDC, and so forth, until the end of the canto. The magic of Dante's *terza rima* lies in its impetus. The metric design pulls the reader along, propelling the Pilgrim through the slime of the Inferno and past the grasping hands of condemned souls.

One of them is Francesca da Rimini, whom Dante based on a real person, the beautiful young daughter of an Italian noble. He married her off in 1275, but she fell in love with her husband's brother, the fetching Paolo. The rejected husband, Gianciotto Malatesta, took revenge by stabbing them both in Francesca's bedroom, condemning himself (along with the unfaithful lovers) to the Inferno. Malatesta, whose name means treacherous, presumably lands in the ninth circle with his wife and her lover in the second. The Pilgrim sees Francesca and Paolo trapped in the vortex of an eternal tornado, tortured forever for their illicit desire. Francesca describes the circumstances of her and Paolo's mutual seduction so movingly that the Pilgrim faints.

The ambiguous tale lends itself to competing interpretations. Is Francesca more or less sympathetic than her husband? Is Paolo in any way at fault? Canto V of Inferno suggests that Francesca and Paolo might have exercised forbearance were it not for the influence of literature, namely the Arthurian love story of Lancelot and Guinevere, which Francesca and Paolo recite to each other before embracing. Tchaikovsky represents that recitation and includes within it a pastoral tableau. The harp arpeggiates the tonic chords of C major, G major, and E major while the flutes (three of them, one doubling piccolo) flutter upward through these scales, as if translating these lines from the Lancelot–Guinevere legend:

> The happy winds upon her play'd,
> Blowing the ringlet from the braid.[109]

The happy winds and blowing braid find counterpoint with a motif from Francesca's love theme, and the effect is magical, a moment of bliss in the center of a storm.

The opening of the tone poem sounds like a horror movie soundtrack because horror movies and film noir masterpieces like *Laura* borrow so liberally from it. The cellos and basses slash downward in thirty-second notes on the first beat of *Francesca da Rimini* to outline a tritone, followed by a diminished seventh chord in third inversion, heard in the brass and woodwinds, after which the slashing motion is reversed, at the other end of the cello and bass register, upward from B to F. This is Malatesta's blade, cutting deep into flesh, with the overtones of the tam-tam spraying blood all over the wall.

Inferno is the realm of the diminished seventh chord. Minor thirds, tritones, and juxtapositions of two diminished seventh chords a half step apart govern the first sixty-four measures of the score. Tchaikovsky offers much more than his visual source of inspiration, Doré's illustrations, suggested that he might have. For Canto V, Doré depicted the "blast" in the Inferno that "propel[s] the wicked spirits" through time foregone.[110] Tchaikovsky replicates the blast, but his Inferno is less about pathos than kinky onomatopoeia with no rest for the wicked.[111] The strings slither and squirm; bows scrape and strings tear to expose (for listeners with sufficiently brutal imaginations) severed muscle and bloody ganglia. The inner frame is a chromatic lava flow of eighths, sixteenths, eighths and sixteenths and triplets, eighths and sixteenths and triplets and quintuplets that ignore the bar line and all or part of the downbeat. Tchaikovsky assigns sepulchral fragments of these groups in the brasses and woodwinds. There is no tonal center, no base or ground, and we're in one of those dreams of falling and falling and falling, forever and ever and ever.

Francesca da Rimini is shadowed by Liszt's *Dante Symphony* but, as musicologist Catherine Coppola has shown, Wagner is a presence too.[112] Tchaikovsky composed *Francesca* shortly after attending the premiere of Wagner's *Ring* cycle in August 1876. He went as much for the music as for the stage effects and to see what, in general, the fuss was about. When it was over, he still didn't know. Tchaikovsky authored a five-part overview of the cycle for the *Russian Register* (*Russkiye vedomosti*) that focused more on the plot and the plight of Bayreuth's tourists than Wagner's music. ("The little town billeted and sheltered everyone who came but couldn't feed them, and so on my first day I learned what it means to fight over a crust of bread"; "One woman I met in Bayreuth, the wife of one of the highest-ranking people in Russia, said she hadn't dined the entire time. Coffee was her only subsistence.")[113] He didn't approve of the behavior of his colleagues on the trip, including Laroche, who was drunk the entire time.

Tchaikovsky liked the final act of the final music drama in the *Ring*—the end of the age of the gods, the earth's salvation, and the reappearance of maidens rinsing their hair in the Rhine—chiefly because it was the ending. He wearied of the chromatic harmonies, the grinding in the invisible orchestra, the absence of singing, and Wagner's "aimless Don-Quixotism."[114] He wondered how dilettantes could tolerate what he, as a professional musician, considered unbearable. Still, he acknowledged the hugeness of Wagner's achievement.

The once-in-a-lifetime experience stayed with him, particularly the sounds of *Die Walküre*, the second music drama in the group of four, which lingered in his system like a narcotic. He alluded to the "love" and "ring" leitmotifs in the middle section of *Francesca da Rimini*, forming a link between Wagner's depiction of forced marriage and taboo sex (Sieglinde and Siegmund's incestuous affair) and Francesca and Paolo's relationship.[115]

She and Paolo were willing to die for each other and go to the depths of hell. The musical description of that pledge begins at measure 333 with the introduction of Francesca's tender, erotic theme. Her theme stretches over thirty-nine measures, divided into three sections: a clarinet solo supported by pizzicato strings (the beginning of her explanation); then an appassionato in the strings, reaching higher and higher, riding the tightrope of physical pleasure; and then, in contrast to this upward tonal sequence, a descending chromatic sequence. It will repeat, and repeat again to mimic the turning away, coming back, turning away, and coming back, of Francesca and Paolo's liaison, while also tucking within itself the Lancelot–Guinevere pastorale.

After the third variation of the theme, a cymbal crashes. The reminiscence has come to an end, and Dante's narrator has been brought to tears. A terrible blast of dissonance sends us back into the vortex: a triple forte half-diminished chord on F♯ smeared over four octaves. It's the stabbing again, this time as Francesca feels it. The chord prefaces a diminished-by-half reprise of the opening Inferno music.

The middle section has the stylistic digressiveness and organizational looseness common to symphonic fantasies of the late nineteenth and early twentieth centuries, according to Coppola. She hears a "typical Tchaikovskian balletic-lyrical apotheosis" at the conclusion of the pastorale—though, at the time Tchaikovsky composed *Francesca da Rimini*, his first ballet had not been staged.[116]

It was about to be.

Vladimir Begichev

In the fall of 1875, Tchaikovsky had accepted a commission from the Bolshoi Theater to compose a ballet. His contacts within the theater had gotten his first and second operas on the stage, and now, he was told, it was time to return the favor by lending his craftsmanship and reputation to the Bolshoi's demoralized ballet troupe. Opera composers snobbishly tended to avoid ballet because it lacked prestige. It was the domain of lesser-skilled ballet specialists like Cesare Pugni and Ludwig Minkus. The Bolshoi's troupe had experienced no shortage of controversy in the mid-nineteenth century; it had had its budget slashed owing to low ticket sales; it lacked a permanent ballet master and couldn't hold on to talent. It was deteriorating and needed help. "I accepted this task partly for the money," Tchaikovsky told the ballet-averse Rimsky-Korsakov, "and partly because I have long wanted to try my hand at this sort of music."[117] Tchaikovsky began by recycling the best tunes from *The Voyevoda* and expanding some music that he had improvised at the piano for a children's party. He added music from other sources—not all his own—and imposed a symphonic structure on the whole. The result became the most popular ballet in the global repertoire: *Swan Lake*.

Its origins are unclear, owing to the loss and destruction of records concerning the unprecedented commission, the sources for the scenario, and the 1877 premiere production. Tchaikovsky had mixed feelings about his achievement, though, then again, he had mixed feelings about most of his achievements. In his diary, he said that hearing *Swan Lake* gave him "*a moment—just one—of absolute happiness*"; in a letter to Taneyev, he claimed he was "ashamed" of the ballet because critics had panned it.[118] The choreography, by Wenzel Reisinger (1828–93), was described as bland, boring, and, in Tchaikovsky's opinion, weirdly funny. No voluptuousness, no sensual-erotic harmonization of bodies, no levitation, and ultimately no pleasure: the dancing instead recalled the short comic ballets and divertissements Reisinger had made for pint-sized companies in Prague, Breslau, and Leipzig. "Yesterday, the first rehearsal of some numbers from Act I of this ballet was held in a hall at the Theatrical School," Tchaikovsky informed Modest on March 24, 1876. "If you only knew how comical it was to watch the ballet master creating dances with a most serious and profound air to the sound of one little violin. At the same time, it made one envious to watch the ballerinas and danseurs casting smiles at an imaginary audience and reveling in the easy opportunity for leaping and whirling about, thereby fulfilling their sacred duty." Then a point of pride: "Everyone at the theater raves about my music."[119]

Except Reisinger and his dancers. The choreographer fought with the score, and the premiere of the ballet was postponed from November–December 1876 to February 20, 1877, in part to give him more time to prepare his dancers, but also because Italian operas were taking up most of the rehearsal time. The onstage product failed to impress. *Ports de bras* looked like windmills, the lifts and bends like gymnastic exercises. One reporter insisted that the character dances, the best part of Reisinger's *Swan Lake*, must have come from other ballets and remarked that "only a German could have mistaken the pirouettes excreted by Mlle. Karpakova as a 'Russian' dance."[120] Another critic almost begged the Bolshoi to hire another ballet master. Weaker dances "could not be imagined," so thank goodness the audience "paid no heed at all to them." The reporter found it galling that Reisinger "presumed to have his name printed on the poster" and "took a bow before a public that had no thought or imagining of calling him to the stage. Is not this pointless waving of the legs for four hours a form of torture?"[121]

As staged in Moscow in 1877, *Swan Lake* chronicles the suffering of Odette, a beautiful, guileless princess with an evil stepmother who wants her dead. Odette is protected by the crown that her grandfather gave her, but she and her girlfriends nonetheless live in disguise: at night they are free to be human, inhabiting the ruins of a chapel, while during the day they transform into swans on a lake of tears—the tears shed over the death of Odette's mother. Odette can be saved by a declaration of love from someone who has never been in love before. That someone is Prince Siegfried. He is aimless, restless, and unattached. His mother, a queen, has made it clear that it is time for him to find a bride, so she arranges a matchmaking ball. Meanwhile, he and a companion, the knight Benno, spy a wedge of swans passing overhead and take to the hunt. The birds settle on the lake of tears, led by a majestic swan wearing a crown. Siegfried prepares to sink an arrow into the swan's heart, but just then Odette appears, in human form. She explains her sad plight, and Siegfried falls in love with her. They agree that she will attend the ball, where he will choose her as his bride and thus break the spell. Siegfried awaits Odette, but instead her double appears, Odile, an agent of the demonic Baron von Rothbart. Mistaking her for his true love, Siegfried declares Odile his bride. The stage plunges into darkness; the deception is exposed, leaving both Odette and Siegfried shattered. Odette returns to her companions on the lake of tears. Siegfried begs her forgiveness, to no avail, and Odette dies in his arms. Her stepmother, in the guise of a screeching red-eyed owl, flies overhead, gripping the crown that Siegfried, in despair, has thrown into the water. A storm sweeps the thwarted lovers under the waves.

The ballet establishes a set of oppositions: swans versus humans, lake versus castle, day versus night, good versus evil, truth versus deception, freedom versus enslavement. The usual interpretation has Siegfried seeking escape from the oppressive social order through communion with the ideal. Odette is the ideal, Odile her demonic, carnal opposite. But the plot has its excesses and inconsistencies.

Why, for example, is the knight Benno involved in the first and second acts of the 1877 version, but not the third and fourth? Why do we need both a sorceress and a demon? Do all the swan maidens share the same curse? The biggest problem is the pitiless ending. In productions after 1877, a solution would be found in the music. Tchaikovsky's score concludes with an Orphic apotheosis: a halo of strings suggests spirits still commingling after death, even ascending to heaven.

The inconsistencies suggest decision making by committee, and it was long unknown who put the scenario together. The story of *Swan Lake* was published without attribution in the *Theater Newspaper* on October 19, 1876, close to the time of the intended but postponed premiere. There are distant echoes of Ovid in the plot, likewise the Brothers Grimm and the stories of Johann Musäus. Details also derive from Wagner: the hero is called Siegfried, perhaps after the dragon slayer in Wagner's *Siegfried*; the swannishness calls to mind *Lohengrin*; and when Wagner's Flying Dutchman declares that the feeling in his breast might not be love but the desire for redemption, he seems to be wording what Odette's longing leaves unsaid. Wagner also stages a flood, at the end of *Götterdämmerung*. Some plot devices can be found in other famous ballets, suggesting that Reisinger might have been the author. (The magic crown that Odette wears can be likened, for example, to the wings of the sylph in the iconic Romantic ballet *La sylphide*, which also cannot be removed without causing death.) Tchaikovsky contributed to the scenario, adding some details in his musical manuscript. Later, his brother Modest, a dramatist and librettist, would revise the plot, making the concept of self-sacrificing love explicit. The Soviet ballerina Ekaterina Geltser liked to credit her father, a Bolshoi Theater ballet master, with compiling the scenario, but there is no evidence to support her claim beyond a copy of the scenario with his name on it.

The author turns out to have been Vladimir Begichev (1838–91), a Moscow noble, playwright, and translator who also served as repertoire inspector for the Bolshoi and, for a span in 1881–82, as the director of the Moscow Imperial Theaters. Begichev had knitted all the pieces together for Ostrovsky's *Snow Maiden* production and had nurtured Tchaikovsky's interest in ballet as part of an effort to expand the Bolshoi repertoire. (The two of them had gotten to know each other during the staging of *The Voyevoda*, and had traveled for fun to Paris in 1868 with a mutual friend, the singer and actor Konstanin De Lazari.)[122] Kashkin states that "Begichev himself wrote the scenario for the ballet *Swan Lake*; the composer endorsed the subject—he at first expressed an interest in a fantasy involving knights—and agreed to compose the music for 800 rubles."[123] Case closed, except for the fact that Kashkin's comment came with a disclaimer: "If I am not mistaken." But he wasn't. Begichev excluded his name from the published scenario because he did not want to be seen promoting himself in the imperial service. And ballet work lacked prestige.

The music has a distant antecedent in a children's ballet that Tchaikovsky improvised into existence in 1871 to entertain his nieces (his sister Sasha's three daughters). It was rustic theater of the type that until recently had been performed by serfs, and the composer gamely demonstrated pirouettes amid wooden cutouts of swans. The plot might have been inspired by the Russian folktale *The White Duck*, about a witch who turns a queen into a duck to assume her place on the throne. Four years later, when Tchaikovsky began composing the adult version of *Swan Lake*, he inserted the love duet from the abandoned *Undina*, assigning the mermaid's and knight's vocal courtship to violin and cello. In doing so he consciously or unconsciously placed *Swan Lake* within the cosmos of mermaid stories. The storm and swan song of the final act came from Afanasyev's *Slavic Views of Nature*.[124]

Though he knew some ballet steps, loved *Giselle*, and did his homework, Tchaikovsky's knowledge of the genre was slight. The music gets at the theme of longing and the pursuit of an ideal but ignores the practicalities of moving bodies around a stage. (The lakeside entrance of the swans and the *pas de deux* are exceptions.) Even in those places where he seems to be thinking about the dance, the character of the music is at odds with the dramatic situation. The climactic, devastating exposure of Rothbart's trickery in Act III is assigned mere seconds of music. The passage is jarring, a dense chromatic field, but much too brief to have an impact. The ballet critic Arlene Croce has deduced that, although Tchaikovsky "sought advice from his choreographer, the kind of advice which he was later to obtain from Petipa for *The Sleeping Beauty* and *The Nutcracker*—he appears to have been on his own most of the time. The score, unlike the two later ones, is badly organized in terms of theater logic and stagecraft."[125]

The problem with this assessment is that of the realities of making ballets at the Bolshoi in 1877: Reisinger seems to have had in mind different dramatis personae and different emphases in each of the acts. The Act I *pas de deux*, which later choreographers transposed to the Act III episode where Odile seduces Prince Siegfried, was assigned in 1877 to Siegfried and a character called "villager 1."[126] The lush violin solo is freighted with the kind of mild dissonances—augmented seconds and augmented fourths—heard in gypsy music, suggesting that Siegfried and the girl had some kind of true attraction to each other. Although much is made of the Odette–Odile opposition in the plot, Reisinger, like Tchaikovsky, seems also to have been thinking of an expanded cast wherein this village love interest might parallel a supernatural one. According to the 1877 advertisement, the part was performed by the Bolshoi soloist Mariya Stanislavskaya, a St. Petersburg-trained ballerina who had been a soloist with the Bolshoi since 1871. Stanislavskaya danced in four of the seven numbers of the original Act I, including two dances not labeled as such in Tchaikovsky's score: a polka and a galop. Kashkin claims that Reisinger, baffled by the longer dances in the score, dismissed them as "awkward" and replaced them with easier dances taken from other ballets.[127] Tchaikovsky objected, and Reisinger relented, but only to a point. The crowd-pleasing, ticket-selling polka and galop remained.

The original violin rehearsal score and other materials from the first eight years of the ballet's existence contain some unusual details, like the inclusion of a dance for "12 German women" recycled from an 1874 Parisian ballet titled *Le tour du monde*, after Jules Verne's great adventure novel *Le tour du monde en quatre-vingts jours* (*Around the World in Eighty Days*, 1873). The second section of the dance is labeled a *"pas de séduction à 8."*[128] It became part of *Swan Lake* on the initiative of another, much more experienced choreographer who had come to Russia from Belgium: Joseph Hansen (1842–1907).[129]

Some of the passages that tend to be cut or relocated in current stagings actually took pride of place in the original ballet at the Bolshoi. One such number, critic Alastair Macaulay notes, is the "beautifully poignant *andante con moto* section, which builds up into a tragic climax that makes the ballet's scale seem briefly cosmic." As Macaulay explains, "If you listen to this number with the knowledge that Tchaikovsky intended it as part of the enchantress Odile's dances, you find it completely transforms our idea of her; this music is as poignant, doom-laden, and huge-scaled as anything written for Odette."[130] Yet just who was meant to dance this poignant episode remains unclear. In the rehearsal score, the *andante con moto* is called a *pas de six.* The 1877 playbill, however, lists it as a *pas de cinq*, and a playbill from 1878 as a *pas de dix*, performed by the two principals and eight apprentice dancers. In later years it was cut altogether.[131] There are other examples of this sort. Indeed, apart from the principal characters, their conflicts, and the appeal of Tchaikovsky's music, little was or is stable about *Swan Lake*.

For all his limitations, Reisinger ended up being easier for Tchaikovsky to work with than the two ballerinas who took the part of Odette–Odile. The first of them was Pelageya Karpakova, the second Anna Sobeshchanskaya, who danced Odette–Odile beginning with the fourth performance on April 28. Neither dancer made much sense of the parts, but the 1877 assessments of *Swan Lake* agree that Sobeshchanskaya, who had long carried the Bolshoi repertoire on her generous shoulders, was the superior actor and technician. Of Karpakova, the theater observer Dmitri Mukhin said that "she tried as best she could to represent the fantastic role of the swan, but being a poor mime, she did not leave much of an impression."[132] He added that Tchaikovsky's music vexed most of the cast, being too symphonic, with no clear sense of where numbers began and ended.

Another dancer, Lidiya Geyten, had been offered the lead role. A grey-eyed brunette, Geyten possessed enchanting mannerisms and a filigreed technique. In 1874, she joined the Bolshoi as first dancer after graduating from its school. *Swan Lake* was not the fairytale she wanted to dance, however, for reasons she laid out late in her career, in an interview: "Tchaikovsky wrote his first ballet (*Swan Lake*) for me," she claimed, "but I refused to dance in it, because [he] did not know the technical side of ballet and because it was uninteresting."[133] Geyten softened her opinion of Tchaikovsky's talent after hearing Tchaikovsky's later ballets *The Sleeping Beauty* (1890) and *The Nutcracker* (1892). Yet she still dismissed Tchaikovsky's music as "unrewarding" for dancers, since he was, in her opinion, first and foremost a symphonist. Geyten also proposed, insolently, that everything Tchaikovsky learned about ballet composition came from Yuliy Gerber's ballet *The Fern* (*Paporotnik*, 1867). "Tchaikovsky took the score to his estate and mislaid it. This is why the wonderful ballet *The Fern* isn't staged anymore," she explained. There is no proof to her story, but she enjoyed telling it.[134]

Critics agreed that Sobeshchanskaya danced much better than Karpakova, but, like Geyten, neither ballerina found merit in Tchaikovsky's score. Both gave the composer headaches by demanding that he change his music, though this was perfectly typical of ballerinas to do. Karpakova insisted that he provide her something special for the Act III ball scene. The composer complied, producing an up-tempo Russian dance that stayed in the ballet no longer than

Karpakova did.[135] Sobeshchanskaya wanted a variation of her own for the third act, but ran to the ballet master in St. Petersburg, Marius Petipa, rather than Reisinger or Tchaikovsky, with her demand for the solo. Petipa agreed to choreograph a new dance for her in Act III and asked Ludwig Minkus to compose the music.

When Tchaikovsky discovered what was being done to his score behind his back, he saw red. He calmed himself down by composing a variation of his own for Sobeshchanskaya, with the same tempo, structure, and number of measures as Minkus's insert, so Sobeshchanskaya could dance what she had worked out with Petipa—but to Tchaikovsky's music. She was pleased and even asked Tchaikovsky to compose yet another variation for her. The two variations morphed into a new *pas de deux* for the end of Act III, one that Sobeshchanskaya had willed into being, and one that she danced with her husband as Siegfried. For a while, it replaced the *pas de six* of Act III. Later, the *pas de deux* found its way into *Le corsaire*, and the *pas de six* was restored. There were further changes to *Swan Lake*, more demands. Even Tchaikovsky could not keep track of them.

That the ballet was performed thirty-nine times in the first six seasons at the Bolshoi Theater is less revealing than the fact that box office receipts steadily declined for the twenty-seven performances in the first two seasons, after which Reisinger was dismissed from the Bolshoi. Hansen replaced him in 1879, and the ballet was reconfigured for productions in 1880–81 and 1882–83, after which the sets fell apart and the ballet was retired. Von Mekk saw the Hansen version and was even less impressed with it than Reisinger's original. "Dreadful staging ... so drab and depressing," she wrote to Tchaikovsky on January 14, 1880. She had a stake in saying that she liked the music, so she did: "such a delight."[136] The reviewers demurred. Like the décor and like the dance, the music came across as uninflected, devoid of contrast. It did not help that, for the premiere, there were "just two rehearsals" with the "imprecise" orchestra.[137] The conductor overindulged Tchaikovsky's penchant for bombast, and the principal violinist hacked at his solo while letting the string section disintegrate.

One of the reviewers expressed bewilderment that the Bolshoi had commissioned Tchaikovsky to write music for a ballet based on a "ponderous," "content-free" German fairytale as opposed to something from a Russian source. There was too much water, for one thing, and the prince's love for a swan with a crown on her head was absurd. Most of the plot followed the rules of ballet, though not, to the reviewer's surprise, the end. The thunder and lightning and drowning of the prince and swan princesses was "sad, indeed remarkably so, because ballets tend to end to everyone's satisfaction"—that is, merrily. The invective was tempered only at the end, with the reluctant admission that, despite all its flaws, "the ballet was a success and the public liked it." Tchaikovsky bowed shyly, and Karpakova received "a basket of flowers in the shape of a swan."[138]

The budget was spent on the climactic tempest, as cleverly designed by the Bolshoi's machinist Karl Valts. In his memoirs Valts congratulated himself, deservedly, for making the lake of tears "overflow its banks to flood the entire stage; on Tchaikovsky's insistence I created a true-to-life wind storm; branches and twigs snapped from the trees into the water to be carried along the waves." Odette and Siegfried are seen swimming at the back of the stage. At daybreak the damaged trees were "illuminated by the rays of the rising sun."[139] Observers confirmed his description and, despite scorning the overall production, praised Valts's special effects, including the mechanical construction that allowed wooden swans to swim. He relied on some old tricks, like explosives, as well as batteries for the wind and wave machines. And he used stearin candles and colored gas lighting—or perhaps carbon arc lighting, the production expense records aren't precise enough to know[140]—for Odette's first appearance in Act II and the famous storm scene. The wind and wave sounds drowned out the music, which upset Tchaikovsky more than Reisinger's quirky pantomime and Sobeshchanskaya's demands did. For a composer of operas and symphonies to be involved in the lowly art of ballet was unusual, even radical, and at least one critic was eager to hear the result. But he could not: The music had several wonderful moments but was "perhaps too good for ballet" and, unfortunately, the sound was swallowed up at the end, "owing to the routine, absurd custom of accompanying any fire, flood, etc., on our stage with noise and din such that you would think that you were present at a large artillery drill or gunpowder explosion."[141]

The theatrical fad for astonishing meteorological events eventually subsided. Future versions of the ballet would avoid the storm scene. Odette and Siegfried perish, but their spirits endure as love eternal. The famous swan theme, the B-minor emblem of tragic desire, brings down the curtain as the lovers are seen, in most representations, moving along the surface of the lake.

Odile has come to be known as the black swan, but she did not dress in black in these early versions, nor was she as malevolent a counter to Odette as she has since been made out to be. (The black swan idea dates from World War II.[142]) Odile was, however, meant to be an enigma. The poster for the 1877 premiere assigns Karpakova the role of Odette but does not give the name of the performer of Odile. In its place there is just an ellipsis—three dots. The dancer in the role is not listed, even though the names of dancers in all the other parts, even the trifling ones, appear. The absence has a certain intrigue, but it is obvious from at least one account that Karpakova (and beginning with the fourth performance, Sobeshchanskaya) appeared in both roles—at once the "good" girl and the "bad" one, the femme fatale.

Marriage of inconvenience

In Tchaikovsky lore the role of femme fatale is played by Antonina Ivanovna Milyukova (1848–1917). Her father Ivan's family was of ancient pedigree; she had falconers and regimental governors as distant relatives. Ivan held the title of lieutenant and had inherited three worthless villages outside of Moscow along with forests and meadows of little value.[143] Her mother Olga was the daughter of a general. She and Ivan had ten children together before a fraught separation. Antonina bounced between her parents, her education becoming a mishmash of private boarding school, then tutoring on her father's estate (Karasovo, 27 miles from Klin), followed by enrollment in the Elizabethan Institute (previously called the "House of Diligence"), a school for disadvantaged girls. Milyukova studied languages, geography, history, math, religion, and music.[144] She graduated in 1865, and eight years later, in 1873, she enrolled in the Moscow Conservatory as a member of Eduard Langer's piano studio. She struggled and dropped out after a year.

Milyukova met Tchaikovsky in the spring of 1872 at her brother Alexander's apartment. She was pleasant looking, the composer told friends and family after their relationship had stumbled to its bathetic end, but unpleasant to deal with. She compared herself positively to the other women in Tchaikovsky's life, and in doing so provides some information about the conception of "None But the Lonely Heart," noting that he wrote it for a St. Petersburg Conservatory friend, the contralto Alina Khvostova, and dedicated it to her, but that she didn't like it and excluded it from her concerts—until it became popular with other singers, at which point she included it.[145] Some (perhaps a lot) of the letters between them are lost (destroyed), including a Tatyana-like declaration of love on her part in 1876. Milyukova acknowledged inhabiting Pushkin's heroine, with Tchaikovsky as Eugene, knowing that he had begun writing an opera based on the subject.[146] She gave her father the more plausible role of the provincial landowner Dmitri Larin. Ivan Milyukov died in 1871, leaving her with a pittance of an inheritance tied up with the sale of a forest.[147]

Milyukova's outpourings turned desperate, and she apologized to Tchaikovsky for them. "It's true that in my last letters I wrote a lot of foolish things, but rest assured that actually I'm not so brave and I would never allow myself to do that"—by which she meant hurling herself under a train like Anna Karenina, thus adding another fashionable literary heroine to the role-playing.[148] He kept his distance and contemplated other brides before committing to her. As to why he did so, there are three theories: he felt obligated; he thought she could support him; or, most likely, he resolved to marry for appearances' sake and to save his family possible embarrassment, as homosexual men in polite Russian society often did. The swiftly arranged wedding happened on July 6, 1877, at the Church of St. George, close to the conservatory. Tchaikovsky's brother Anatole and Iosif Kotek served as witnesses on his side. The justice of the peace and a noble stood for the bride.[149] After the ceremony, the newlyweds traveled to St. Petersburg.

Cinematic treatments of these events exaggerate them in contradictory ways. Kenneth Russell's boringly appalling "biopic" *The Music Lovers* (1971) imagines a perspiring Tchaikovsky gulping down vodka—not the wine he preferred—in the nuptial train carriage, resisting his lustful bride in abject terror. The movie's Soviet antipode, the lavish and chaste *Tchaikovsky* (1969), has a train scene of a different sort: a dreamscape in which the composer chats with his patroness as the birch trees whizz by. The two of them conclude that his emotional and carnal life must be sublimated, placed in the greater service of his art.

Clearly, marriage, in this case lavender marriage, was not for him. He never had sex with Milyukova, according to his letters, and showed her little affection and avoided even idle talk with her. Milyukova nonetheless had assembled a comfortable, cheerily decorated apartment and imagined having a family with him, forgetting what he had told her: that the two of them were to live as siblings, not lovers. (In her recollections, published in the *Petersburg Newspaper* in 1894, Milyukova quotes Tchaikovsky saying almost exactly that: "If you will be satisfied with a quiet, calm love, rather like the love of a brother, then I will make you a proposal.")[150] Whatever feelings Tchaikovsky had for Milyukova before the summer of 1877 turned to revulsion and self-loathing. Tchaikovsky briefly idealized suicide; the closest he came was a ridiculous late-night dip in the icy water of the Moscow River in hopes of getting pneumonia.[151] The composer fled to his sister's house in Ukraine on July 27, 1878, and there decided to part company with Milyukova for good. Her mother Olga, who lived until 1881, had some stern words of advice for him about a settlement:

Upon meeting you, I became sincerely fond of you and now I feel hurt to learn of your quick departure and separation from your wife. I swear to God I still don't know how Antonina is guilty toward you that you should punish her so severely and apparently hate her so intensely. I wanted to be helpful but you don't wish to accept my involvement; you want to settle everything in the least expensive way. That is why I take the liberty—though you forbade me to write you—to make a suggestion, for I have spoken to Antonina and came to the conclusion that my plan is simpler, less expensive and faster. Antonina had fallen in love with you deeply and sincerely; she loved you more than anything in the world. Now her life is shattered and joyless; she is not going to marry anyone else; and so, wouldn't it be better to separate peacefully without an expensive and scandalous divorce? You will return her passport, which she can then renew without bothering you. Instead of monthly alimony payments, give her a lump sum, thus sparing yourself and her constant confrontations. She will leave Moscow and move to Petersburg and she will give you her word never to bother you with anything and not even mention you. And you, Pyotr Ilyich, also, I hope, will take steps to ensure that your friends and relatives won't spread any gossip about Antonina, which could hurt the reputation of a young woman. You can take my sincere and honest word that Antonina will faithfully comply with everything and once she has decided to take this step, neither her nor her relatives will bother you; trust me. You are a man of genius. You cherish your good name. Please trust me; we will not stain it, and we'll be faithful to our word as is to be expected from an honest noble family.[152]

He ignored the advice. But he did offer Milyukova a one-time payment (10,000 rubles in borrowed funds) for her participation in divorce proceedings, hoping that if she sued for divorce instead of him the matter could end more quickly than usual in the slow-moving Russian courts. She balked, and after months of effort on his part and Anatole's he abandoned the idea, sending her instead a monthly subsistence payment.

It was a tragicomedy worthy of celebrity tabloids. The episode amounted to six years and six weeks of mutual torture followed by six months of fruitless postmarriage negotiations over a divorce—shaming him and ruining her. Milyukova attempted to maintain good relations with her estranged husband; he did not. Frankly, he hated that poor girl until the end of his life and greatly resented giving her an allowance as compensation for her permanent spinster-hood. One of the anecdotes comes from Anatole Molchanov, editor of the *Yearbook of the Imperial Theaters*, which strangely combines Tchaikovsky's disgust with Milyukova with another frustration: the legal wrangling over his opera *The Oprichnik*:

One evening after the theater a group of us gathered to dine at Dusso's restaurant on Morskaya. There we were, the beautiful people of global fame: Pyotr Ilyich Tchaikovsky; his brother the playwright Modest Ilyich; the great French actors of the Mikhaílovsky Theater, [Lucien] Guitry and [Alix-Marie] Angèle; two or three others; and myself. Pyotr Ilyich took the role of Amphitryon [comic entertainer of Greek myth]. Oysters were served and disappeared with amazing speed from the huge dish, leaving a rather large amount of sea water behind in memoriam. "Do you want to see a magic trick?" asked Pyotr Ilyich. Everyone became concerned. He tipped half a glass of vodka into the oyster dish, causing an immediate disturbance in the sea water. It turned out the ciliates living in the water, which evidently didn't share most of mankind's affection for alcohol, were protesting the extremely unpleasant surprise that he'd dropped onto them.

Dinner continued. Needless to say, our cherished Pyotr Ilyich was the center of attention, even though he didn't want to be. He didn't act the part of an international celebrity and was always courteous with everyone. Suddenly, rather harmonious singing was heard from next door, a chorus from *The Oprichnik*. Pyotr Ilyich made a face like he was struggling to hide an awful feeling. "I can't stand this anymore!" he shouted. Measures were taken to end the singing. It turned out that a group of young people, hearing about Pyotr Ilyich dining nearby, sought to serenade him with his own music. The singing ended but the thought persisted: why such fuss? Why had Pyotr Ilyich, so restrained, gentle, even-keeled, lost his head?

I decided to ask him, and this is what he said: "You know, there's very little I hate in my life but what I hate I hate with all the strength of my soul, namely my *Oprichnik* opera and my wife Antonina Ivanovna. I can't stand [the popular Imperial Theaters soprano] Abarinova, not that she's done anything wrong but simply because her name happens to be the same as my wife's— Antonina Ivanovna." He spoke in a tone the likes of which I'd never heard before, and never would again.[153]

Every letter she wrote to him upset him; he became especially angry hearing of her efforts to find teaching work in noble circles. Milyukova's "social legitimization," Alexander Poznansky speculates, was "a threat to [Tchaikovsky's] prestige."[154] Poznansky doesn't want to state the obvious: Tchaikovsky was a misogynist.

Antonina Ivanovna lived much longer than Tchaikovsky did but in misery. She didn't dine in fancy French restaurants; she had few friends. Milyukova entered an abusive, semilegal relationship with her lawyer Alexander Shlïkov (a poor substitute for *Eugene Onegin*'s Prince Gremin) and had three children with him, each placed in a foundling home on account of her poverty.[155] Paranoid in her final years, certain that Tchaikovsky's siblings were out to destroy her, Milyukova sought help from a priest, John of Kronstadt (Ilya Sergiyev), but he could do nothing for her. She was admitted into the Hospital of Saint Nikolay the Wonderworker before placement in the gentler confines of a "Charitable Institution for the Emotionally Disturbed" outside St. Petersburg. Milyukova succumbed to pneumonia during the February 1917 Revolution.[156]

There's a new movie about her: Kirill Serebrennikov's *Zhena Chaykovskovo* (*Tchaikovsky's Wife*), first shown at the 2022 Cannes Film Festival. She's represented more like Ophelia than Tatyana, pale and mournful and entirely bonkers. She lives in a world as dark as one of the Da Vinci paintings hanging in the Hermitage: a realm of kerosene lamps and cigar smoke, flies and filth, and not a single shot of the sky. Tchaikovsky's unfreedom as a homosexual is tucked inside Milyukova's plight as a nineteenth-century Russian woman. The episode that most harshly and blatantly condemns the pathetically repressed Russian subject shows Milyukova's lawyer coughing up phlegm while masturbating beside a trembling candle.[157]

The salon

On December 18, 1876, Tchaikovsky received his first letter from Nadezhda von Mekk, thanking him, on Kotek's behalf and her own, for making some violin-piano arrangements of his music.[158] It was the start of an almost fourteen-year-long correspondence.

He didn't learn much about her during that long stretch of time. At first, all he knew is that she ran a salon of sorts, inviting musicians to perform in her residences in Moscow and elsewhere for her personal enjoyment. It wasn't a salon like those sponsored by nineteenth-century

Russian, French, or German aristocrats. (For example, the salon hosted in Paris by the Prince and Princesse de Polignac from 1894 served as a haven for the elite connoisseurs of the musical avant-garde, and Joséphin Péladan's *Salons de la Rose-Croix* hosted Symbolist artists.[159]) Von Mekk kept out of sight of the public after the death of her husband Karl, a railroad builder from whom she inherited her fortune (Karl laid down over 9,000 miles of track, monopolizing the transporting of grain from Ukraine to Russia), and her salon consisted—at best—of private performances of newly commissioned pieces by a resident trio. She participated in these nonsoirees as an amateur pianist, playing four hands with, among others, Henryk Pachulski, the son of a forester in her employment. There are no images of the group in action—just photographs of Pachulski, the violinist Kotek, and the cellist Pyotr Danilchenko in other settings.

Yet von Mekk's support proved essential to Tchaikovsky, who established himself as a composer with her help. She did not herself make him a great artist, of course, but her financial support and almost unhealthy commitment to his success helped. His teaching job and instrumental compositions didn't provide enough income to keep him afloat, even with Jurgenson's advocacy and the backing of the IRMS. It took years, a transformation in Russian culture and politics, and the right kind of contacts on high for him to earn recognition as a theatrical composer (Russian opera being less privileged by the Imperial Theaters than the continental European repertoire, and ballet deemed inferior to opera and drama), but when it came, he had von Mekk, as well as Tsar Alexander III and the office of the Imperial Theaters, to thank.

Tchaikovsky's works from the late 1870s, those that von Mekk sponsored, are conceptually richer than his earlier, civic opuses. Tchaikovsky composed romances for the salon, and those songs migrated from the salon to the stage. His theatrical works seem derived from salon convention. Sometimes he sets up a contradiction between an interior world that is real and true and another, exterior world that is less so—a construction, an appearance. That which is real and true is, musically speaking, of the salon. The other world is civic, of the court and the aristocratic Table of Ranks.

But what is the point of this juxtaposition, its meaning? And what of von Mekk's role? She had a large family but lived a lonely life. Her passion for music is described as eccentric, even "pathological."[160] She didn't commission paintings for her homes and homes away from homes; the aromas of flowers did not blend with polite conversation; she did not host a book club. Music was a love that required intimate focus and private concentration—both music with a lowercase m, meaning the actual craft of composing, and Music with a capital M, a religious conduit, music of the spirit. She imagined Tchaikovsky putting the two things together.

Most of the letters from what might loosely be called Tchaikovsky's salon years, or the von Mekk years, survive. Tchaikovsky scholars believe that none of the letters vanished in the Soviet period, when they were published in an attempt to show that Tchaikovsky himself knew that he was living during a time of transition in Russia. Still, the maudlin nature of the letters worried Lenin's Commissar for Enlightenment, Anatole Lunacharsky. "Just how does the sentimental correspondence between Tchaikovsky and von Mekk relate to modern-day concerns?" he asked Vyacheslav Menzhinsky, head of the secret police, the Joint State Political Directorate (OGPU), in 1929.[161] The fact that the letters ended up in OGPU hands is an obvious concern, even if it appears that none of them went missing.

The letters are the bedrock of the literature on the composer. Tchaikovsky articulated his self-doubts in many of them, but, depending on the biases of the interpreter, offered too much or too little insight into his true self, Tchaikovsky the person.

He refrained from delving into highly private matters with his "beloved friend," yet he felt obliged, in a depressed and desperate state, to share the details of his efforts to divorce Milyukova in 1877. Von Mekk reportedly had her own secrets, at least according to the gossipy recollections of her granddaughter Galina, who wrote that Nadezhda bore the burden of having had a daughter out of wedlock and dreaded the truth about the child becoming known out of doors. The revelation of her sin of passion purportedly caused her fifty-five-year-old husband, whom she had married at age seventeen, a fatal stroke, leaving her alone to manage the affairs of the estate.[162] This hidden affair perhaps explains von Mekk's agoraphobia.

The latest (2007–) edition of von Mekk's correspondence with Tchaikovsky reproduces a fifteen-page album of photographs of her estate in Braïliv, Ukraine. Von Mekk sent it to the composer as a gift. It includes images of the wine distillery; the outsized servants' quarters (later turned into a hospital and school); the scrupulously maintained gardens, pavilion, park, and lake; and the gargantuan manor house von Mekk sometimes called home.[163] There are almost no people; the buildings and grounds are the focus of the long-exposure images. It's the kind of place that would look lonely even if crowded with tourists. Tchaikovsky visited the estate four times between 1878 and 1880, but only when von Mekk was away. Its opulent emptiness emerges in a letter to his sister Sasha: "I am living in a palace in the literal sense of the word," he wrote on May 18, 1878. "The furnishings are luxurious, apart from polite and affectionately obliging servants I see no human figures and no one comes to make my acquaintance, the strolls are charming, and at my disposal I have carriages, horses, a library, several pianos, a harmonium, a mass of sheet music—in a word, what could be better?"[164]

Companionship, perhaps, but Tchaikovsky found contentment strolling the grounds, gathering mushrooms in the surrounding woods, reading, and accepting occasional invitations for tea. When the muse arrived (most days right on time in the morning; he seldom had creative blocks), he mentally worked out an opera based on Shakespeare's *Romeo and Juliet* (it went unrealized, save for a duet and the popular, thrice-composed fantasy overture) and drafted six romances, various piano pieces, and his *Liturgy of St. John Chrysostom.*

He gamboled in fair weather and committed to desk and keyboard in foul. Later he moved from Braïliv to another of von Mekk's properties, a six-room cottage a few miles away in the village of Simaki. In his letters to von Mekk, he mixes the fatuous details of his time under her roof with occasional expressions of anxiousness: perhaps she is not being frank with him, stressing only the positive, never the negative, about his music—case in point being his opera *The Oprichnik*, which he called, in a letter from Braïliv dated May 27, 1878, "very weak, over-rushed, and in places an altogether blandly written score . . . Please, my friend, never fear checking my ambition as an artist. I must have only the truth from you, and if now and again it's uncomfortable for me to hear, it will be yet more valuable, as the reaction of my best, most endlessly beloved friend."[165]

Von Mekk declined to criticize, so the letters to and from Braïliv offer little sense of her actual musical tastes, though one imagines the romances and children's piano pieces Tchaikovsky sketched receiving a private hearing at her principal residence on Rozhdestvensky Boulevard in Moscow. He discreetly ("secretly") dedicated three of his works to her, including the famous Fourth Symphony, the first of his orchestral suites, and the Kotek-guided *Souvenir d'un lieu cher*.[166]

Versions of all three of these works were heard in the "salon" in von Mekk's residence on Rozhdestvensky Boulevard. This was less a plush concert or recital space than a kind of shelter, or foster home, for penniless, aspiring performers. Besides Tchaikovsky, the musicians von Mekk brought into her domain included Kotek, who was extremely talented, but, to von Mekk's disappointment, self-destructive. He contracted syphilis from a prostitute—a subject of tragicomedy in one of Tchaikovsky's letters to Anatole—and died at age twenty-nine of consumption.[167] He was not an ideal role model for her children.

Von Mekk also sponsored Henryk Pachulski's brother Władysław, whose ambition as a musician (he played piano and violin and aspired to compose) greatly exceeded his talent, according to his conservatory mentor, namely Tchaikovsky.[168] He nonetheless became a permanent fixture on Rozhdestvensky Boulevard, making himself a part of the furniture in von Mekk's sitting rooms. Her other services to the arts included donating to the Imperial Russian Musical Society; she attended concerts incognito, sitting at the back of the hall to avoid drawing attention to herself. When the Polish violinist Henry Wieniawski took sick on tour in Odesa, she brought him into her home for treatment (too late, as it turned out).[169]

The other musicians von Mekk sponsored included the Symbolist composer Claude Debussy, whom she hosted in Interlaken, Switzerland, following his graduation from the Paris Conservatoire, at age eighteen. He traveled around with her in Italy and France, and Debussy spent August and September of 1882 at von Mekk's estate at Lake Pleshcheyevo, tutoring her children in piano. He dedicated a pleasant if not profound song to one of his pupils, von Mekk's son Alexander, titled "Rondeau." As part of his service to the matriarch, who treated him like an adopted pet, Debussy patiently played piano four hands with her, Tchaikovsky's Fourth Symphony and Suite included. "Yesterday I decided, for the first time, to play *our* symphony with my little Frenchman," she told Tchaikovsky, "and so today I find myself in a terrible nervous state. I can't play it without a fever in every fiber, can't recover from the impression for days . . . I also played your suite with him and he was completely ecstatic about the fugue and expressed himself thus: 'Dans les fugues modernes je n'ai jamais rien vu de si beau. Monsieur Massenet ne pourrait jamais faire rien de pareil' [Among modern fugues I've never seen anything so beautiful. Massenet (whom Tchaikovsky admired) himself could never do anything like it]."[170]

That's basically it; little else is known about von Mekk's private concerts. But the "*our* symphony" remark is telling, insofar as it reflects an "essential feature," in Francis Maes's words, of philanthropy in imperial Russia, namely "the equal footing of patron and artist." "Dedications of works to patrons were expressions of artistic partnership rather than of humble gratitude," Maes comments.[171] In Tchaikovsky and von Mekk's instance, the partnership flourished despite profound differences in their personalities, and it must be stressed, because Maes doesn't, that von Mekk decided the terms of the partnership and the tone of the letters. She was the ardent Romantic, and Tchaikovsky a figure more in keeping with the spirit of the Enlightenment. As the eminent scholar and Tchaikovsky archivist Polina Vaydman has argued, von Mekk idealized, indeed deified Tchaikovsky. He was a demiurge, capable of elevating the listener to the starry heights. In her early letters to him, she calls his music "fantastic," the emotions it evokes "the greatest, the highest of all emotions given to human nature." "So, if you like, Pyotr Ilyich, call me a fantasist, prone to outlandishness, but don't laugh, for it would be amusing if it weren't so sincerely based." "You have written music that transports people into a world of emotions, strivings, and desires inaccessible in life." "I regard the musician-human as the highest creation of nature."[172]

Von Mekk's salon did not need to exist for Tchaikovsky to play the part of a salon composer; nor did the court need to exist for him to adopt its codes. He agreed to serve von Mekk, but she encouraged him instead to serve his talent, free for the most part to follow his muse. Hence the songs, half-rustic, half religious, that he composed following a chance perusal of Massenet's *Marie-Magdeleine* oratorio in her library at Simaki.[173] Von Mekk elevated Tchaikovsky into an ideal, to the detriment of Debussy and the other musicians in her entourage, who suffered by comparison. From that platform, Tchaikovsky ended up using his music to express what is held in common, irrespective of the game of appearances and of the expectations of the world.

During his final visit to Braïliv in 1880, von Mekk sent him a precious gift: a "gold pocket watch with black enamel, studded with stars and golden figures—Joan of Arc, Apollo, and two Muses"—on a gold chain.[174] Von Mekk ordered it for him in Paris in celebration of his completion of the opera *The Maid of Orleans*. Tchaikovsky wore it when he went out for eleven years, until 1891, when it was swiped from the open windowsill of a house that he rented in Maydanovo (the locals of the village were tragically poor, and Tchaikovsky sought to improve the lives of their children by donating funds toward the opening of a school). Suspicion for the theft fell on the valet of a neighboring landowner, whom the police interrogated. To extract a confession, Poznansky relates, "the incensed interrogators deprived their suspect of food, fed him salt herring until he was dying of thirst, got him drunk, arranged with a plainclothes detective a sham escape attempt, and then flogged the youth—all to no avail: his tale got ever more confused."[175] Tchaikovsky never recovered the watch, but he valued it enough to will it to his cherished nephew Vladimir (nicknamed Bob/Bobik from childhood) Davïdov, just in case it turned up.

Rural opera (*Eugene Onegin*)

Milyukova advertised herself as the torrid inspiration for *Eugene Onegin*, but its origins belong more prosaically to the contralto Elizaveta Lavrovskaya, for whom Tchaikovsky conceived the part of Morozova in *The Oprichnik*. In May 1877 she suggested what he called an "impossible" operatic subject to him—Pushkin's novel in verse—and did so with such infectious enthusiasm that he caught the bug. He and Kashkin tried and tried but ultimately failed to cobble together a scenario over a couple of evenings at a restaurant, so he returned to the idea that the project was unrealizable.[176] But he didn't give up. Tchaikovsky had evaluated two other potential opera subjects at the start of 1876, both set in ancient Egypt, but rejected them; pharaohs were not his thing. Pushkin was.

The author of the Egyptology was a friend, Konstantin Shilovsky. He came from a family of Tambov nobles and inherited a manor house in Glebov (40 miles from Moscow) large enough to perform operas. His mother Mariya was a singer whom, like Lavrovskaya,

Tchaikovsky greatly admired. He also admired her second husband and the surrogate father of Konstantin: this was Begichev, the repertoire inspector of the Bolshoi Theater and the author of the *Swan Lake* scenario. The family was keenly passionate about art, all kinds, and Konstantin lost himself in prop making, makeup (about which he wrote a book), acting, composing, and writing. He was remembered as an "extremely susceptible, careless person. Either he immersed himself in alchemy, practiced black magic and studied the life of ancient Egypt, or he was suddenly transported to pre-Petrine Rus, walking around his estate in the summer in boyar garb and adjusting his daily routine to the old Russian ways."[177] Though Tchaikovsky had rejected his pharaoh tales, Konstantin invited the composer to live in Glebov with him, moving the piano from the main house to a cottage so that he could work on *Eugene Onegin* in relative peace.

Konstantin had a younger, no less eclectic brother named Vladimir, whom Tchaikovsky also befriended after giving him compositions lessons at the conservatory. These didn't add up to much, as Vladimir committed himself to a life of leisure with a little music making on the side. Still, he helped with the orchestration of *The Oprichnik* (Tchaikovsky had no problem putting his students to work for him). Vladimir also inherited an estate, in Usovo, and just as Tchaikovsky had stayed with Konstantin while working on *Eugene Onegin*, he had stayed with Vladimir while working on his Third Symphony of 1875, which Tchaikovsky dedicated to him. The picture begins to emerge of a composer destined for global fame and canonic immortality who didn't have a stable home, a fixed address. For most of his life Tchaikovsky lived with family members, rich friends, and in European hotels. He didn't own the house in Klin which became his museum. It was a rental.

Playing house with Milyukova had gone to hell, and moving around increasingly suited him, despite the logistical headaches of obtaining letters of introduction, searching for accommodations, cash exchanges, and predeparture stamps in his passport. He tended to relocate to places that helped with his work, like Braïliv, Kamianka, and Glebov inside Russia and Florence, Paris, and Venice outside. While hosting Tchaikovsky at his estate, Konstantin repeatedly offered to help with *Eugene Onegin*; Tchaikovsky involved him in the editing and expansion of the libretto; Shilovsky wrote the text of a song sung by a Frenchman, Monsieur Triquet, in Act II, scene 1. Part of the draft would have been played through at Glebov, with the participation of Shilovsky family members, in the former serf theater on the property. That the crux of the plot is an anguished letter-writing scene convinced Tchaikovsky (with Shilovsky nodding at his side) to call *Eugene Onegin* not an opera but a group of lyric scenes best suited for chamber singers and conservatory students.

Twenty-two months after Lavrovskaya recommended Pushkin's novel in verse to Tchaikovsky, in March 1879, she sang the role of Olga at a piano-vocal performance at the St. Petersburg residence of another singer, mezzo-soprano Yuliya Abaza, performing as Tatyana. (Olga is sixteen or seventeen at the start of the opera: assigning her a contralto part seems strange, unless one bears in mind that girls are socially conditioned to engage in upspeak as they mature, which might, at a stretch, explain the older Tatyana's higher register.) The opera was calibrated for these private settings and found success in salons and domestic theaters, small dramatic arenas with performers gathered around the piano. Those who heard it liked it. The 1878 engraved piano-vocal score sold in the hundreds, and that popularity took the opera to places it didn't belong: the Moscow and St. Petersburg Imperial Theaters. The premiere was piecemeal; there's no specific date when it privately or publicly happened. "Several productions of *Onegin* make some claim to being the first," Roland John Wiley himself claims, "by students of the Moscow Conservatory on March 17, 1879, by professionals at the Bolshoi Theater in Moscow on January 11, 1881, by amateurs in the first performance in St. Petersburg on April 22, 1883, the first there by professionals on

October 19, 1884, and the first complete performance (with the écossaise) on September 19, 1885."[178]

Some further details: The first performance had been scheduled for December 16, 1878, at the Moscow Conservatory. Just four scenes were seen that day, which was all that the students could pull together. (Another problem, reported in the newspapers, was a student's scandalous resistance to a recent graduate, Taneyev, conducting it, as opposed to a student identified by the initial "K.")[179] For the unveiling at the Maliy Theater, conducted by Nikolay Rubinstein, the orchestra was supplemented with professionals from the Imperial Theaters, since, at the time, the conservatory had only two cellists and one bassist, and just twelve of the seventeen woodwind and brass instruments that the score requires.[180]

The 1881 Bolshoi performance was a benefit for the conductor, the transplanted Neapolitan Enrico Bevignani. Rubinstein convinced the Bolshoi to do it, and the Bolshoi reluctantly agreed, so long as it was preceded, as a kind of "hedge," by a performance of the second act of Daniel Auber's popular comic opera *Fra Diavolo* (1830). The opera's dances were choreographed by Joseph Hansen, who had succeeded Reisinger as the choreographer of *Swan Lake*, and featured Stanislav Gillert, the original Siegfried, in the mazurka. The ballet was soon to disappear from the repertoire while the opera was just getting going. The costumes were stitched in period Pushkin style, a novelty at the time, but the budget didn't allow for many to be made. The dresses worn by the dancers in the country were worn again in the city. This production was revived at the Bolshoi in 1883 and ran until 1889, forty performances in all. Ippolit Altani (1846–1919), a former classmate of Tchaikovsky's who grew up in Ukraine (Ekaterinoslav), conducted most of them. The 1883 Musical-Dramatic Amateur Circle performance in St. Petersburg happened at the Kononov Theater with Karl Zikke of the IRMS conducting. The date Wiley provides is that of the general rehearsal, for which "so many people gathered that it wasn't possible to accommodate all of them in the hall. The rehearsal, or what might be better called a test performance, was a complete success."[181] The 1884 Mariinsky production was choreographed by Lev Ivanov. The écossaise didn't get advertised as part of *Eugene Onegin* until September 19, 1885, but it had been seen on stage before.[182]

The source text is an almost sacred object in Russian culture—one reason Tchaikovsky fretted about turning it into an opera. And when he did, it seems to have been less out of affection for the sacred object than a sense of disquiet. Pushkin's novel in verse is richly parodic and stylized, gamboling through the plushest parts of eighteenth-century culture. Tchaikovsky could play this game, as evidenced by the perfected, glamorized pastness of pieces like his *Variations on a Rococo Theme* (1877), but he didn't play it when he came to Tatyana. He chose in his opera to represent the elasticity of her consciousness, narrating her recognition that love isn't the answer for her unoriginal existence. Love is neither a rescue nor a salvation; it's not transcendent.

Reviews of the first performances took offence at his tampering with Pushkin along with the insufficient realism of the choral singing and the dances. Laroche led the charge by impugning Tchaikovsky's "need to lump together" inferior verses with "the jewels of Pushkin's art."[183] Evgeniya Kavelina, daughter of Pavel Kavelin, administrator of the Moscow Imperial Theaters, remembers a nervous Tchaikovsky coming to her loge in the Bolshoi for the performance on January 11, 1881. She didn't like the opera and complained that the performers in the roles of Tatyana, Onegin, and Lensky were "essentially unsatisfactory, although they were considered decent artists at that time. Everyone criticized the bad libretto, which distorted Pushkin's poem and was not suitable, as they said, for an opera. In a word, the curtain fell after the first act in the deathly silence of the public; Tchaikovsky, who was sitting in the back of the box, got up from his seat and went out the side door to the wings. And we all felt embarrassed, somehow offended for him."[184]

The complaints solidified over the years (Hugh McLean chides Tchaikovsky for turning off Pushkin's "spiritual air-conditioner," and Caryl Emerson described the composer experimentally "break[ing] the vessel he would most honor").[185] Asafyev, a lifelong defender of the opera, reports that in his childhood, in the 1890s, the opera remained a subject of debate, though less about Tchaikovsky's transposition of Pushkin than about the quality of the singers in the lead roles. Asafyev also remembers improvising the central duel scene of the opera between classes at school.[186]

Though written slowly and published in serial form between 1825 and 1831, the novel is "like a perfect curve or parabola," with the plot of the first half mirrored and unraveled in the second.[187] The readership matured alongside the characters, experiencing the creation of a masterpiece that synthesized genres as neither a comedy nor a tragedy but something in between. *Eugene Onegin* adheres to rules of the author's own devising. It comprises eight chapters with 366 fourteen-line stanzas of eight or nine syllables with stress on the even ones. The rhyme scheme is abab ccdd effe gg (or eff egg).[188] Pushkin came up with this structure in 1823, two years before writing the novel. For all its intricacy, it feels effortless, and captures a range of sentiments and sensations.

The first chapter begins and ends with the easily distracted, occasionally sympathetic narrator describing an uncle who has passed away, leaving his fortune to Onegin. The following chapters move Onegin from the city to the rural pile he bought with his inheritance and then back to the city. He's a twenty-six-year-old St. Petersburg dandy and already jaded, burnt out, and unpleasant (*méchant*). Onegin's counter is his personable neighbor, the poet Vladimir Lensky, age eighteen or nineteen. They visit the estate of the Larins, the home of Tatyana, who spends her drowsy days immersed in French novels. Rousseau's 1761 novel, *Julie, ou la nouvelle Héloïse*, is one of her favorites, a teary story of an aristocratic girl who can't marry her tutor because of class difference. Tatyana has a lovingly clueless and rather fickle sister named Olga, to whom Lensky is affianced. Tchaikovsky's Tatyana is a better match for Lensky than Onegin, and he assigns Tatyana and Lensky comparable music, with Lensky mirroring Tatyana's flat-key music on the sharp side, but neither the novel nor the opera is interested in better matches. The focus is Tatyana and Tatyana alone.

While working on the novel, Pushkin stayed in remote manor houses hundreds of miles from St. Petersburg and Moscow, accessible only by horse—much more remote than Glebov. "There's nobody to talk to," novelist James Meek imagines of these places. "All you can do is play billiards, practice with your pistol, go for long walks, listen to the old housekeeper's anecdotes and folk tales, and write."[189] The fictional Larins live in one such house, and it's an exclusively female realm that men don't often visit. Pushkin fashions an exquisite counterpoint of older women talking of former loves and younger ones contemplating relationships that might lie ahead. Crucial in Tchaikovsky's response to Pushkin is the tonic-directed patter motif attached to the words of the nursemaid Filipyevna, in dialogue with Olga and Tatyana's mother about the past, as the two girls perform a duet: "Habit is sent to us from above: it is a substitute for happiness" (Привычка свыше нам дана: замена счастию она). Likewise Filipyevna's "you were young then" refrain.[190] The music attached to these lines will recur at the end of the opera, subtly insinuating itself into Tatyana's rejection of Onegin.

Onegin cares only for himself; he spends hours in front of the mirror, fussing with his mane and shining his nails with his impressive collection of brushes purchased throughout Europe. He doesn't make eye contact with Tatyana, but she falls for him and confesses her love in a letter that he postpones answering. When he does, in person, he's honest about his unsuitableness for marriage. He's also patronizing, which leaves her bereft. Emily Frey, who dubs Onegin a "nowhere" (as opposed to "superfluous") man, describes his "rejection aria" as an "auto-reply": "a highly conventional, well-behaved little romance: two sections in B♭ major, constructed in parallel periods, surround an eight-measure foray into the relative minor, ending neatly with a coda, a perfect cadence, and a long rest. There is no sign of creative struggle here, as there was with Tatyana's letter."[191]

Lensky imagines shaming Onegin by inviting him to Tatyana's Name Day gathering so that he can hear what's being said about him. Onegin bristles at the gossip and, to embarrass Lensky, flirts with Olga. Lensky challenges him to a duel on a snowy day; Lensky is killed, and Onegin escapes to Europe. Here the plot starts to fold back on itself, beginning with Olga's swift recovery from the death of her fiancé and her marriage to a lancer. Tatyana sinks into reveries and reminiscences. She visits Onegin's unlocked house in his absence and looks through his library, where the prototypes of his personality can be found in the books. He's a collection of artifacts, a two-dimensional, choreographed approximation of what he's listlessly browsed. Tchaikovsky doesn't include this episode in his opera, but the irregular, unsettled nature of the music assigned to Onegin in the third act suggests his dandyish mask, or masks, coming off. He never sings a tune; he flails in the minor mode. He repeats the music of others, blandly, because he's never had an original thought.

Years pass. Tatyana moves to Moscow to live with an aunt and find a husband and is noticed by a general from St. Petersburg (the habit of members of the Imperial Court was to shop for brides in Moscow). He's overweight and scarred from a battle somewhere but presentable. She marries him and settles into the comfortable life of a St. Petersburg grande dame, no longer immersed in French romances, fully in control of herself. Onegin, meantime, has returned from his travels. He pesters Tatyana with letters; she need not and does not reply. When Onegin appears in person in a reception room in her house, he's quickly turned out. This climactic event doesn't seem real, according to Emerson; perhaps it's a dream, or the fantasy of the narrator, who wants to give her this dose of revenge by becoming Onegin's "*fatum*," the "weight of his conscience." Onegin, she adds, can't stand being alone but that's where he ends up. Tatyana is also alone, and each event of consequence in the novel increases the loneliness.[192]

Asafyev witnessed the opera's increasing popularity growing up, but for Pushkin purists for 150 years now, the libretto remains a bowdlerization of the novel, a cut-and-paste collage that removes the narrator's doubly and triply parodic sidebars about everything from soles brushing on ballroom floors to ditches (made by witches) to perfume and champagne in favor of what Pushkin and his narrator scorn: sentiment.[193] To the Russian ear, the libretto sounds completely bizarre, with detached third-person speech turned into first-person outpourings. Richard Taruskin counters that the opera is plenty parodic and that the narrator is still present—just listen to the orchestral underpinning of the action, the stormy string crescendo and timpani rolls representing Tatyana and Olga's panic when Lensky and Onegin turn up at their rural house. Olga welcomes the lads into the abode, acting the part of an unfussed lady of rank. Meantime, the bowing and scraping of heels and obsequiousness of Lensky, then Onegin, is represented in woodwind arabesques and buffo rhythmic gestures.[194] Cui, who viciously condemned the opera for its "melancholy uniformity," likening it to St. Petersburg's autumn weather, also picked up on this moment. It was a splash of mirth after a "purely melodramatic crescendo—up to the diminished seventh inclusive."[195]

But Taruskin (like Cui) excludes the true parody: the ghastly recurrence of these foppish sounds in the duel scene, the perverse apotheosis of aristocratic decorum. Two men are threatening to kill each other with pistols cocked, and one of them will in fact die, yet the event is highly regulated, rule-bound, and rationalized. It is as tightly choreographed as the aristocratic ballroom dances that Tchaikovsky added to the score for the St. Petersburg stage, saturated with funeral sounds, including pulsing timpani, that provide justification for a possible rhythmic allusion to the Orthodox funeral service—the kontakian (hymn) "With the saints, give rest"—in Tatyana's music.[196]

In the novel the duel is something that shouldn't have happened: Onegin shows up late and chooses his valet as his second. He wants to get out of the insane, impulsively organized duel and knows that appointing a mere servant to the role of second is against the rules. Onegin hopes he'll be called out on the infraction and the event will be canceled, preserving everyone's honor. Tragically, the referee doesn't notice the infraction and the duel goes ahead. Pushkin includes a description of Onegin's fearful body language and a couple of stanzas about his remorse. The opera is harsher. Onegin shows no remorse whatsoever. "Dead?" he asks Lensky's second. "Dead," the second replies. Tchaikovsky lends the scene pathos by having the two men briefly sing in unison, the only time in the entire opera that they do, to the words "Shouldn't we burst out laughing, rather than staining our hands in blood, shouldn't we part as friends? . . . But no!" (Не засмеяться ль нам, пока. Не обагрилася рука, Не разойтись ли полюбовно? . . . Нет!) In the Pushkin, the narrator poses this question: "Shouldn't they burst out laughing?"

Tchaikovsky's libretto preserves Pushkin's symmetries but in radically abbreviated guise, and sometimes with altogether different text, as in Tatyana's start-of-the-plot address to Onegin and his end-of-the-plot response to her.[197] In the novel, in James Falen's translation, the narrator has Tatyana declaring,

So be it then! Henceforth I place
My faith in you and your affection;
I plead with tears upon my face
And beg you for your kind protection.
You cannot know: I'm so alone,
There's no one here to whom I've spoken,
My mind and will are almost broken,
And I must die without a moan.

I wait for you ... and your decision:
Revive my hopes with but a sign,
Or halt this heavy dream of mine—
Alas, with well-deserved derision![198]

In the libretto this passage is reduced to:

Everywhere, everywhere I look,
I see my fatal tempter
Wherever I look, I see him!

At the end of the novel, Onegin writes the following to Tatyana:

But let it be: it's now too late
For me to struggle at this hour;
The die is cast: I'm in your power,
And I surrender to my fate.[199]

In the opera this passage is reduced to:

I see that beloved, desired image!
Whenever I look, I see her!

The parallelism remains but with different words. The other changes are less extreme. Lensky's speech bidding farewell to life is rewritten and reshaped by Tchaikovsky as follows:

Chapter 6, XXI
~~By chance those verses haven't vanished;~~
~~I have them, and I quote them here:~~
<u>Ah, whither, whither are ye banished,</u>
<u>My springtime's golden days so dear?</u>
What fate will morning bring my lyre?

In vain my searching eyes enquire,
For all lies veiled in misty dust.
No matter; fate's decree is just;
And whether, pierced, I fall
    anointed,
Or arrow passes by—all's right:
The hours of waking and of night
Come each in turn as they're
    appointed;
And blest with all its cares the day,
And blest the dark that comes to
    stay!

XXII
The morning star will gleam
    tomorrow,
And brilliant day begin to bloom;
While I, perhaps, descend in
    sorrow
The secret refuge of the tomb . . .
Slow Lethe, then, with grim
    insistence,
Will drown my memory's brief
    existence;
Of me the world shall soon grow
    dumb;
But thou, fair maiden, wilt thou
    come!
To shed a tear in desolation
And think at my untimely grave:
He loved me and for me he gave
His mournful life in
    consecration! . . .

But thou, thou, Olga . . .
Say, fair maiden, wilt thou come

> Ah, Olga, I loved you!
> I loved you and gave you
> My mournful life in
>   consecration!
> Ah, Olga, I loved you!

Beloved friend, sweet friend.

> Come, come!
> Sweet friend, come, I am thy
>   mate!
> Come, come!
> Sweet friend, I wait,

Oh, come, Oh, come, I am thy
    mate![200]

Tchaikovsky repeats the underlined words at the end of the block. The lines in the right-hand column are his additions to Pushkin's text, serving to enhance Lensky's plea to Olga. He also enhances the ironic pastness of Lensky's pronouncements. He's still alive yet speaking from beyond the grave.

Tchaikovsky began the opera in Glebov with the romances that make up the letter scene. Here Tatyana's consciousness expands along with her passion. The letter is drafted and redrafted, pages are torn up and turned over (the interrupted arpeggios capture this activity), and Tatyana's Russian grammar, a source of derision in the novel, loosens and becomes more casual, the formal *Vï* pronoun shifting to *tï*. The words and the music navigate her inner and outer worlds, and at the end Tatyana is in dialogue with herself in a manner reminiscent of Schubert's "Gretchen am Spinnrade" ("Gretchen at the Spinning Wheel," setting verses from Goethe's *Faust*), while the throbbing horns recall Tchaikovsky's *Romeo and Juliet* fantasy overture. Anton Rubinstein tended in his amorous episodes to mime the intonations of salon songs (*The Demon* provides an example) and perhaps guided Tchaikovsky. The pattern of keys, however, is Tchaikovsky's own:

1) Пускай погибну я (Even it if means I'll die): D♭ major, 4/4, da capo form
2) recitative
3) Я к вам пишу (I am writing to you): D minor, 4/4, strophic form
4) Нет, никому на свете не отдала бы сердце я! (No, there is no one else on earth to whom I'd give my heart): C major, 2/4, da capo form
5) recitative
6) Кто ты, мой ангел-ли хранитель? (Might you be my guardian angel?): D♭ major, 2/4, da capo form[201]

Much is made of the hexachords in the letter scene and the entire three-act opera built around it. Asafyev's "intonational" analysis of the score is the source for Taruskin's description of the music's *sekstovost'*, or "sixthiness." "Tatyana's part, saturated with 6ths encompassing degrees 1-6 or 6-1, or (more characteristically) 5-3 or 3-5, is, with Lensky's, surely the 'sixthiest' in all of opera," he writes, owing to Tchaikovsky's "constant use of the minor submediant (the 'flattened sixth' in the major) as alternate harmonic root or tone center."[202] Scalar descents and ascents by sixth are a cliché of Russian salon songs, and Tchaikovsky's insistence on them would seem to place a clamp on his heroine were it not for the intensity that's achieved. Passionate disorder emerges from decorous syntax, as it does in one of Tchaikovsky's sources of inspiration: Rousseau's *Les consolations des misères de ma vie, ou recueil d'airs, romances et duos* (*The consolations of the sorrows of my life, or a collection of arias, romances, and duets*, 1781).[203]

Tatyana's most prominent leitmotif—the first thing heard in the opera—is a dreamlike construction. Tchaikovsky inserts an augmented second into the descending sixth pattern and detaches it from the governing tonality (as in the first measures of the opera, which are in G minor, but with the sixth pattern concluding in D). The accompaniment to the letter scene furnishes a rising minor sixth pattern representing Tatyana's imagined dialogue with Onegin. The pattern of keys has no forward-moving, formal-functional logic, but if the scene is conceived as a series of layers, the musical equivalent of digressions tucked into digressions, the chromatic displacements of D♭ to D and C to D♭ and the oscillation of major and minor can be understood to capture Tatyana's discursive thinking—and Tchaikovsky's.

Although Pushkin scholars generally hate the music of the opera as much as the libretto, Tchaikovsky finds common ground with Pushkin in throwing Onegin's words, and the music accompanying those words, back at him. He acted toward her like she should be mucking out horse stalls, not dreaming of love, and now it's her turn, the perfect time for the perfect catharsis. The dagger is the music that she uses to reject Onegin for good: a new theme but in an old key, the D♭ major of the letter scene, which will also be, in the expanded version of the opera for the imperial stage, the D♭ major of her appearance at a grand ball with her aristocratic husband.

Tchaikovsky adds an intimate element to Pushkin's metricized plushness, both in the representation of girlhood and in the description of the unrequited romance, where the music becomes emotional and tactile. His sentimentalism might here be better understood as eroticism, the act of writing allowing Tatyana to touch as well as feel, with the orchestra representing her heartbeats and breathing. At the end she begins to talk to herself:

Вообрази: я здесь одна!	Imagine: I am all alone here!
Никто меня не понимает!	No one understands me!

Oscillating sixteenth-note figures in the violins are elaborated from single pitches to thirds to dissonant chords as her agitation increases. She knows that whatever she writes is but a distortion of what she is feeling. The music is that distortion.

Onegin rejects her in Act I, and Tatyana rejects him in Act III, with the duel in between. The cad routine, Onegin learns, doesn't play past middle age (which for Pushkin's generation was thirty, a number that horrified him). Tatyana has a life to live in the aristocratic hall of mirrors, but he's washed up. Their final confrontation is heart-wrenching on this front, recapitulating the governing motif of Gremin's aria, then the governing motif of Lensky's aria, then fragments of the letter scene, then the accompaniment of Filipyevna's "you were young then" and the tune of "habit . . . is a substitute for happiness." Tatyana and Onegin have never been in the right place at the right time. Verbally, and musically, they've never been on the same page, except for a couple of measures here at the end, when their voices align on the words "Tak blizko!" (So close!)[204] But, in truth, they were never close to being in sync. Tchaikovsky is demonstrating that he, too, can be deeply ironic and that the perception of his opera as anti-Pushkinian melodramatic slush is a mishearing. He does something that Pushkin can't do: misalign the enunciated scene and the scene of enunciation. The music brings the characters together to say that they can't be together.[205]

The opera can also be read in an unironic mode as a tale of appearances that can't be trusted, about how people in an aristocratic society conceal their true selves in an effort to be what society expects them to be. Society is the other, the outside force, whose gaze the characters internalize. Tatyana seeks a right to a private life free from society's scrutiny. She exercises that right, only to surrender it, but she's at peace in doing so because of the embarrassment Onegin caused her. The loneliness she experienced by herself was less acute than the loneliness she experienced in the presence of another. It's not that she has surrendered interiority, more that her view of the significance of that interiority has changed.

Two Lions

Work on the lyric scenes happened amid the composition of his Fourth Symphony, dedicated to von Mekk. Tchaikovsky sent her a letter describing what the music seeks to express. He omitted the original name of the composition, "Two Lions," referring to the stone lions seen all over Venice. What they represent changed over the centuries: some are fierce, others docile, and some a blend of aggressiveness and gentleness. The most famous lion, the one with the wings at St. Mark's Square, is "an exotic beast, an apocalyptic sign and a political défi, a *monstre sacré*."[206] The restaurant at the hotel in Venice where Tchaikovsky sketched the first three movements of the symphony is named De Leoni.

The letter to von Mekk excludes the lions. It instead claims that the Fourth Symphony is about fate and fear of a bad end. Tchaikovsky also stresses the pointless point of having "fun," because there are endless reasons to despair and the space his protagonist inhabits is the space of things having no manifest reason, point, or teleology—this is the space of beauty. He told his protégé Taneyev, though not von Mekk, that inspiration for the Fourth Symphony came partly from Alexei Apukhtin's reading of Beethoven's Fifth Symphony and its opening image of fate's cane knocking, or tapping, the floor:[207]

С своей походною клюкой,	With its walking stick,
С своими мрачными очами,	With its dismal eyes,
Судьба, как грозный часовой,	Fate, like a formidable sentinel,
Повсюду следует за нами.	Follows us everywhere.
Бедой лицо её грозит,	Its face threatens misfortune,
Она в угрозах поседела,	Fate's gone gray, making threats,
Она уж многих одолела,	And conquered lots of people
И всё стучит, и всё стучит:	But keeps on knocking and knocking:
Стук, стук, стук . . .	Knock, knock, knock . . .
Полно, друг,	Enough, friend,
Брось за счастием гоняться!	Stop chasing after happiness!
Стук, стук, стук . . .	Knock, knock, knock . . .[208]

The 1863 poem—likewise Turgenev's 1870 story "Knock Knock Knock"—would be great teaching tools for the symphony if they were better known outside of Russian literary circles. Instead, we have Tchaikovsky's summary of the symphony in the form of the letter, which still engages listeners—especially those eager to explore Tchaikovsky's approach to sonata form—Tchaikovsky's use of fanfares to bridge sections and the deployment of "chromatic wedge progressions" as transitions.[209] Musicologists Piero Weiss and Richard Taruskin include the letter in their venerable primary-source reader *Music in the Western World: A History in Documents*.[210]

Taruskin has elsewhere written about Tchaikovsky's approach to form as a clash of genres—dances, marches, and songs—in place of the typical first-subject first-key, transition, second-subject second-key organization. He highlights the lionlike contrast of aggressiveness and gentleness. The opening theme of the Fourth Symphony is a polonaise, more menacing sounding than the theme of the *oprichniki*, and the second is a downward-slithering waltz atop the polonaise pulsations. At the end of the development, the polonaise interrupts the waltz and eventually tears it to pieces, forcing the waltz to match the tempo of the polonaise.[211] All that plus modulations by minor third (F, A♭, B/C♭, and D, before returning to F) which annul the typical tonic and dominant relation. What to make of this? Perhaps the subject stands up to the state, the individual to the mass, or the peasant to the lord? Tchaikovsky, however, was on the side of the state. Alternatively, the first movement could be an ingenious musical exercise in melding one imperial genre into another, given that both the polonaise and waltz have aristocratic associations. The waltz runs a terrible gauntlet, and if this music has a literary counterpart, it's Tolstoy's "After the Ball" ("Posle bala," 1903), a tale of true love eradicated when a fair maiden's suitor finds her father organizing the flaying of a deserter from the Imperial Army. There the mazurka, not the polonaise, is a symbol of the rules of courtship, morphing into the drum cadence of a soldier's horrific punishment.

But the first movement, according to Tchaikovsky's program, has another theme, a barcarolle:

Oh joy! Out of nowhere a sweet and gentle day-dream appears. Some blissful, radiant human image hurries by and beckons us away [Tchaikovsky jots down the opening of the barcarolle, indicating its interruption by the waltz]. How wonderful! How distant the obsessive first theme [the polonaise] of the allegro now sounds! Everything gloomy and joyless is forgotten! Here it is, here it is—happiness! But no! These were daydreams, and Fate awakens us from them [he jots down the opening of the polonaise]. And thus all life is an unbroken alternation of harsh reality with fleeting dreams and visions of happiness . . . No haven exists . . . Drift upon that sea until it engulfs and submerges you in its depths. That, roughly, is the program of the first movement.[212]

So polonaise cedes to waltz, which cedes to barcarolle, which circles back to polonaise. The ensuing movements develop the clashes within the first. The second movement is an "andantino in the style of a canzone" that moves from the tragic mode into the elegiac. As befits the poetic genre of the canzone, the opening musical stanza lasts twenty measures (equivalent to twenty lines). Tchaikovsky likened the music to a book falling from the hand late at night. The third movement is another late-night reverie. The subject is "feeling the first phases of intoxication" and "thinking about nothing in particular, giving free rein to the imagination."[213] The imagination, Tchaikovsky continues, comes up with the image of peasants drunkenly singing a bawdy song and a marching band passing by. The music represents the peasants and marches by translating tipsiness into fantastical pizzicato string playing. The fairies of Mendelssohn's Overture to *A Midsummer Night's Dream* seem to dart and dash through the middle and lower registers. An autobiographical reading indicates that Tchaikovsky was a pretty happy drunk.

The finale is an impossibly fast dance tune framing two versions of the folksong "A Birch Stood in the Field," which the composer had arranged in 1877 on request of the Italian-trained singer, kindergarten teacher, and toy manufacturer Mariya Mamontova. (Tchaikovsky had also arranged a collection of *24 Children's Songs on Russian and Little Russian Tunes with Piano Accompaniment* for her in 1872, but did so reluctantly, demanding a fee of 5 rubles for each setting in expectation that she would refuse, but, to his chagrin, she agreed.)[214] He converted "Birch" from 2/4 into 4/4, inserted rests, and expanded the phrases from 4 x 3 to 2 x 8 measures. Because it outlines a fifth, "Birch" permits effortless harmonization, and the words refer to the fashioning of pipes and a balalaika from the birch. Alas, the polonaise from the first movement brings everything crashing down in the finale's golden section. According to the program tailored for von Mekk, the subject tries to participate in the dancing and singing but "fate" intervenes, sinking him back into morbid thoughts. He's alone; the crowd doesn't care. Still, the movement is a rondo, so he has another chance to join in the revelry. "Have fun with someone else's fun. You can still live," Tchaikovsky concludes.[215]

The poem that became the letter makes the symphony seem like a concentrated outpouring, but it took him close to a year to compose—a long time for Tchaikovsky—amid other projects and an enormous amount of travel. In the autumn of 1877, Tchaikovsky fled Moscow, Milyukova, and his conservatory students for rooms with views in several European cities. Between November 1877 and January 1878, he stayed eleven days at the Villa Richelieu in Clarens, Switzerland; three days in Paris at *Hôtel de Hollande*; three days each in Florence and Rome; a week in Venice at *Hôtel Beau Rivage*; eleven days in Vienna; two weeks back in Venice; two days in Milan; a week in San Remo at *Pension Joly*; three days back in Milan; a day or two in Genoa; thirteen days back in San Remo; and two weeks in Florence. He neither traveled, nor billeted, nor lunched, nor went to the theater alone: either Modest or Anatole or Kotek or the booker of all the trips, his servant Alexei (Lyonya/Alyosha) Sofronov, joined him. His boyfriends always benefited from his largesse, and when the spendthrift ran low on funds von Mekk topped him up without a second thought. Nikolay Rubinstein had arranged for Tchaikovsky to attend the opening of the Exposition Universelle in Paris on May 1, 1878, but Tchaikovsky pointedly refused: "I have never and will never allow the success of my music to depend on my becoming an official representative of Russian music like some prick at a name-day celebration," he vented to his supportive publisher, Jurgenson.[216]

Travel didn't slow his progress as much as work on *Eugene Onegin* did, but in his haste to leave Moscow he had forgotten his manuscript book and needed to ask his slow-witted but sweet assistant to send it to him to Clarens. He broke some news and included some fatherly counsel in the letter:

> I will no longer be living with Ant[onina] Iv[anovna] (but don't tell anyone!) and when I return to Moscow you and I will live together. Now, Lyonya, you will have to be patient for a little and things will be dull for a while; but you can be sure that I will never leave you and until my dying breath I will always love you like my own brother. Write to me and let me know if you need any money. If you do, I'll give you a note for Jurgenson and you'll get some from him. Please Lyonya, don't stint yourself, eat to your heart's content, and if you're bored, go to the theatre or the circus.[217]

Tchaikovsky had instructed Sofronov to clear out his apartment for him, including asking him to deliver a "barrel of white wine" to his employer's (Rubinstein's) apartment.[218]

He wrote to Anatole about a group of Italian pimps (*ruffiani*) offering him "a delightful young creature" (he didn't take the "bait" for fear of being robbed) and joked at his servant's painful expense about syphilis. Tchaikovsky couldn't believe "that such a nice, well-behaved boy, such a naïve, pure and innocent youngster was now going around with his member covered with sores."[219] He by contrast felt good; he was reading Thackeray, eating and sleeping well, and the muse had gotten him out of a funk:

> Of course, it is the symphony that I have to credit for all this, but it's only thanks to the monotony of life here in Venice and the total absence of distractions that I've been able to get down to work so steadily and assiduously. When I was writing [*Eugene Onegin*], I never experienced the same feeling I've been getting from the symphony. With the opera I was just hoping for the best, maybe it will turn out well, and maybe it won't. With the symphony I have every confidence that I am producing something *really special*.[220]

It was special. Both the premiere in Moscow on February 10, 1878, and especially the St. Petersburg performance on November 25 were big successes, the latter receiving broad coverage in the financial press, a popular weekly publication of illustrated news, and a fashion magazine. Von Mekk attended the premiere and gushed to Tchaikovsky about the symphony while also asking him to define it. So he did, tailoring a program that included several musical examples and describing fate and, in the banally cheerful finale, fate's opposite: *avos'*, hope for hope's sake. There's no point in trying to conquer fate, because fate has already overcome a lot of people, Apukhtin's reading of Beethoven's Fifth Symphony cautions.

The letter can't be ignored; it's affixed to Tchaikovsky forever. Hans Keller laments the harm that it has caused in a Time Life-style guide to Tchaikovsky's symphonies published back in 1967:

> To [von Mekk's] inspiring influence we owe much that is profoundest in this music, but we also owe her the profoundest artistic mistake Tchaikovsky ever made: unfortunately, he acceded to her request to explain the "program" of the symphony. The

result has proved noxious ever since. On the one hand, that is to say, almost every writer on the work has welcomed the opportunity of copying this alleged program instead of concerning himself with one of the most towering symphonic structures in our whole literature. On the other hand, Tchaikovsky's strictly private literary attempt has been thrown back at him by sundry anti-romantic, emotion-fearing neurotics.[221]

One problem with this passage is its snobbish definition of creative achievement. To be an artist is to be profound, to be a great artist is to be more profound, the profoundest. Taruskin, in contrast, defends the beautiful in Tchaikovsky as distinct from the profound.[222] Another issue is Keller's affection for "towering symphonic structures." Symphonies inhabit structures of all sorts of sizes, and it's another form of exclusionary bias to ascribe worth to mansions but not the tumbledown and ramshackle edifices that most non-German-Romantic symphonies inhabit (and where most people live). The "emotion-fearing neurotics" are projections.

Throwbacks

Tchaikovsky ruminated about fate in other contexts, suggesting a creative obsession or, worse, a deficit of imagination. Fate becomes a tic that invites sarcasm: Another piece about fate? Imagine that! But his letters to von Mekk skew our perception of his music, and we should not be misled by his flattering of her Romantic sensibility. Most of what he composed in midcareer isn't in fact fate-based but the opposite: luminescent, neoclassical, indebted to eighteenth-century dances and divertissements. It's youthful; it looks back. Certainly, Nikolay Bernard, the publisher of the magazine *Nouvelliste*, wasn't looking for doom and gloom when he commissioned the piano cycle *The Seasons* from Tchaikovsky in the mid-1870s. He was looking for sales, and *The Seasons*, a kind of skip-free album, provided them. *Nouvelliste* lasted a long time, from 1840 to 1916, and made a decent profit catering to the middlebrow. The most popular tunes from operas, operettas, and vaudevilles were published in easy-to-play-and-sing arrangements for the home entertainment of modestly affluent families. Tchaikovsky wrote twelve pieces representing the twelve months of the year; these were published in order in 1876, the composer sending the first five pieces just ahead of the deadlines for them, and the final seven in a single batch in the spring. January represents toes warming round a crackling fire, February the accordions of the Shrovetide festival, and March the song of a lark. April is a waltz that cleverly illustrates drops of water falling from snow-covered branches; May moves from mysterious nighttime sounds to brighter chords for the onset of white nights. June is a barcarolle dedicated to the canals of St. Petersburg, and July a "Song of a Reaper," referencing grass mowing (not, let's be clear, death). August is a harvest-time scherzo. Each month includes an epigraph from a poem that helps the pianist to appreciate the music. These were selected by Bernard, presumably with Tchaikovsky's permission. September opens with a hunting horn sound and includes these lines from Pushkin's "Count Nulin":

Ta-ra! Ta-ra! the bugles blow.
Up since dawn, the hunters sit,
Their horses chafing at the bit.[223]

October is a lament; November is a sleigh ride, and December an invocation of Christmas-time festivities. In sum *The Seasons* offers images of nature amid emotional and psychological reflections, allusions to pagan and Christian traditions, and quirkier comments on aristocratic lollygagging.[224]

Tucked into his retrospective compositions is the experience that he must have had as a child, relocating from the mining town to the imperial center, approaching the Russian capital as it was meant to be approached: from the east. He found himself in a pretend version of an old aristocratic European capital, and, liking games of pretend, started to compose in an old aristocratic manner. Recall the protagonist of Gogol's "Christmas Eve" traveling through the night to Catherine the Great's court. There he encounters French, German, and Italian performers at the empress's grand masquerades. The court was a cosmopolitan place where, Tchaikovsky imagined (with Gogol's help), anyone could be anyone they wanted. The First Orchestral Suite of 1878–79 supposedly followed the example of a German composer named Franz Lachner (1803–90).[225] Tchaikovsky wasn't imitating Lachner himself as much as he was embracing the throwback aesthetics of Lachner's own orchestral suites, likewise his habit of infusing nondance genres with dances.

Tchaikovsky wrote the suite in different places in Europe, Russia, and Ukraine and, as a consequence, on different types of paper.[226] In a well-appointed multiroom apartment in Florence supplied to him by von Mekk, Tchaikovsky first drafted the March, titled the "March of the Lilliputians," which includes in the middle section a teasing snippet of a choral round dance. It's a toy march, with silvery flutes, sparkling percussion, and bejeweled curlicues anticipating, in its scoring, harmonic rhythm, and phrase structure, the overture of *The Nutcracker*.[227] There followed a rondo finale, the "Dance of the Giants," which Tchaikovsky removed from the suite and inserted into a later opera, *The Maid of Orleans*, as the "Dance of the Jesters and Buffoons." He next turned to the Introduction and Fugue (the only self-standing fugue in his output, and the place Lachner had the clearest influence), then the Scherzo, Intermezzo, and Gavotte (replacing the rondo) while staying in St. Petersburg and Kamianka. The Divertissement was the final movement composed and the only one in triple meter. Here Tchaikovsky partly anticipates Act I, scene 6, of *The Nutcracker*, showing the ballet's heroine dancing with her doll. The suite is a score of shared delights and hypnotic forgeries, with an unconvincing return of the fugue theme at the end of the Gavotte (a model for Sergey Prokofiev's Classical Symphony of

1917) that mocks Romanticism's emphasis on integrated wholeness. Reactions were positive: "With this suite," Osip Levenson wrote, "Tchaikovsky will attain for himself that which is called popularity. Without compromising in the slightest, he managed to make this work wholly accessible to the masses in its surface clarity."[228]

The Second Piano Concerto is also a look back in time (as far back as the baroque).[229] Tchaikovsky dedicated it to Nikolay Rubinstein, who was eager to make amends for his castigation of the First Piano Concerto, and he also performed Tchaikovsky's G-Major Piano Sonata in an attempt to make things right. Rubinstein died unexpectedly of liver disease in Paris just after the Second Piano Concerto was completed, however, and there's no knowing if he would have championed it. Jove might have thundered a second time over the organization of the first movement, which withholds the piano for long stretches before the inevitable razzmatazz. Rubinstein might have heard it as a backhanded compliment to Liszt's arrangement of the Polonaise from *Eugene Onegin*.[230] Rubinstein played the arrangement in Moscow in 1880, battling to conceal the decline in his health from the "ladies who so revered" his concerts.[231]

The Second Piano Concerto might seem episodic on initial hearing, but compared to the First Piano Concerto the conception is balanced and highly integrated. The shorter and longer solo interjections in the first movement exposition add up to a massive cadenza in the second half of the development section. For six minutes the musicians in the orchestra take a break to enjoy a recital. Textbooks place the cadenza near the end of the movement, but Tchaikovsky wasn't interested in the textbooks (except his own, which didn't deal with concertos). Those pianists who did read them thought the cadenza better placed at the end of a truncated recapitulation.

The second theme of the first movement is a dialogue between flute and piano with silky cello accompaniment and horn calls. This sets up another, deeply affecting exchange between violin and cello in the second movement. The melodic hook involves a descent from the mediant to the supertonic to the submediant in D major over an ascending chain of seventh chords, with a gentle massaging of the dynamic level. The piano takes over, but the duet between the violin and cello returns. (As in Jules Renard's 1897 play *Le Plaisir de rompre*, the lovers' breakup reminds them of how much they still care about each other.) Tchaikovsky's Second Piano Concerto has aspects of a Triple Concerto, which, again, pianists didn't like. The third movement is a jubilant rondo riding a dotted rhythm from a sun-dappled elsewhere. It follows the nineteenth-century concerto script except that it excludes a cadenza, which makes it more of an eighteenth-century concerto.

Never has such a challenging piece of music for the virtuoso been such a check on the virtuoso's ego. The technical literature finds parallels in Brahms, Chopin (in the second movement), Liszt, Mendelssohn, Saint-Saëns, Schumann (in the third), and even the four piano concertos of Xaver Scharwenka, though only one of these latter predates Tchaikovsky's work. It embraces the comparisons and, like the suites, welcomes all interpretations except those involving suffering: there's nothing but positivity here. Reviewers had nothing to say about the old-new, new-old aspects of the work, nor of Tchaikovsky's shift from symphonic designs toward "suite-ness," and Modest's biography of his brother's career accordingly excludes all mention of the reviews. "Dull" came up in the squibs, "immensely long" but also "skillfully written." Again, reviewers had nothing to say.[232]

Fresh from this achievement, he composed his Serenade for String Orchestra through September and mid-October of 1880. He simultaneously arranged the piece for piano four hands and expressed the hope to von Mekk that she might play it with "Bussy," meaning Debussy.[233] Like the First Orchestral Suite, it was warmly received at its premiere in St. Petersburg, the waltz-based second movement most of all.[234]

The Serenade can be trivially, thus unconvincingly, related to the death of his father at the start of the year or described as an escape from the worries of the present and other losses. One of these losses was short-term. His servant, friend, and pillar of support, Alyosha Sofronov, was lassoed into a five-year stint in the Imperial Army. He served just three owing to pneumonia and Tchaikovsky's advocacy on his behalf; the composer used his influence—the popularity of his music with some of Alyosha's commanders—to improve the lad's living conditions. He feared deeply for Alyosha's safety and sank into a funk equal to, or greater than, the malaise he experienced extricating himself from his marriage.[235] Another loss, pertaining to the Second Piano Concerto, was permanent: Nikolay Rubinstein's death, doubly awful because of Anton Rubinstein's perplexing indifference to it. "Perhaps you are wondering why I didn't go to Moscow to the burial of Nikolay Gr[igoriyevich]?" Tchaikovsky wrote to von Mekk from Paris. "There are two reasons for this: 1) more than ever, I want solitude; and 2) I would have to be a constant witness to the strange, incomprehensible and insulting behavior of Ant[on] Rub[instein] in relation to the loss of his brother. I don't want to throw stones at him—there's no means of entering another's soul, no means of gauging if his outer manifestations correspond to his inner state—so I can only tell you here that he acted as if he was not only *not* crushed by the death of his brother but rejoiced at it. It was strange, incomprehensible, and difficult to witness."[236]

Tchaikovsky's description of his father's passing on January 9, 1880, is uncharacteristically positive. He received the news from Anatole when he was in Rome and told von Mekk that reading Anatole's account of Ilya Tchaikovsky's last days offered catharsis and provided hope. "Shedding these tears over the disappearance from this world of a pure and gifted man with an angelic soul had, I think, some benefit for me. I feel enlightened and reconciled in my soul. As my brother put it, 'his awareness of his death was calm and bright.'"[237] Tchaikovsky might well have been describing his C-Major Serenade, which has the same calm, bright qualities, a departure from the desolate, pitted-out sounds of music written in memoriam from the Renaissance into the modern era. (As Maurice Ravel is said to have said about his own works of remembrance: "The dead are sad enough, in their eternal silence.")[238]

The IRMS premiered the Serenade in Moscow on October 18, 1881 (after a private performance by faculty and students of the conservatory for the composer the previous November), and championed it repeatedly in performance, and the score is perhaps more reflective of the original aspirations of that organization than anything else he wrote for it. Talented amateur musicians can perform it, and it also makes use of folksong borrowings, transformed and beautified through enriched harmonization and string halos.

Tchaikovsky all but specialized in transformations of this sort. He manipulated genres in expectation of generating strange new sounds from them and in the Serenade, took standard slow movement forms and the simplest, plainest of materials (rising scales in the Elegy and the Waltz), then rendered them, for want of a better word, celestial. His Serenade thus becomes much more than aristocratic background music, the conventional function of the eighteenth-century genre. Each of the four ruminative movements is elevated above dilettantish music making. Yet the music never develops, giving the score a sense of stasis in places, so that, for example, the first theme of the first movement is repeated an octave lower, then two octaves higher, at different dynamic levels, and a teased modulation to the relative minor goes unrealized. (Less attuned critics proposed solving the problem of the score's "monotonousness" by adding woodwind and brass instruments.)[239] There are capricious passages, the interpolation of the first-movement processional in the middle of the rapid figurations of the fourth movement, for example, and other signs of human presence, but Tchaikovsky's Serenade, as George Balanchine gleaned in his 1934 choreography of the piece, inhabits a vast singing space, one of periodic emergences and dissolutions in a cosmic abyss.[240]

Wiley notes an emphasis on archlike gestures, palindromes. He points to measures 92–93 of the C major and A minor first movement, where, in his words, "two chords of indeterminate syntax turn upon each other, as if uncertain how to proceed."[241] The eighth notes in the accompaniment move awkwardly down from G♯ to G and then up from F to F♯ to G; meantime, the upper strings, as though ignoring the lower strings of the accompaniment, follow a descending fifth sequence of the eighteenth-century style.

Tchaikovsky acknowledged the Mozart connection, which arose in tandem with his study of *The Magic Flute*, whose overture influenced the Serenade in the opposition of homophonic stateliness and scuttering imitative passages. Mozart also informs Tchaikovsky's Third Orchestral Suite of 1884, and, lest anyone be mistaken, the "Mozartiana" Fourth Orchestral Suite from three years later, recognizing the centennial of Mozart's *Don Giovanni*. The latter isn't just Tchaikovsky's arrangement of Mozart themes; the Fourth Orchestral Suite also includes Tchaikovsky's arrangement of Liszt's arrangement of a Mozart theme and Tchaikovsky's arrangement of Mozart's arrangement of a Gluck theme. Nothing is original; everything is a clone; everyone's borrowing is someone else's borrowing. The eighteenth century is drenched in the perfume of the nineteenth. Taruskin calls this thickly referential music "culinary" and likens Tchaikovsky's suites to Fabergé eggs, the ultimate in kitsch.[242] What Taruskin labels Tchaikovsky's "imperial style" might be more productively compared to Imperial Russian architecture. The Romanovs looked at the palaces of Italy, France, and Austria and wanted theirs to be bigger and bolder, with heavier grease and thicker gold applied to the walls amid a liberal dose of caprice and fantasy. "Mozartiana" is like Catherine's Summer Palace (Yekaterininskiy dvorets), which includes a room coated in fossilized resin (amber) and another covered in mirrors. The palace was repeatedly renovated in its first decades of existence, stripped down to the foundations, then unevenly and asymmetrically expanded to accommodate ever more extra layers of gold leaf. The palace is located about 15 miles south of St. Petersburg in Tsarskoye selo, "Tsar's Village." Such is the combination of poshness and rusticity in Tchaikovsky's neoclassical scores.

Another, less obvious influence on the Serenade is that of the Hungarian composer Robert Volkmann (1815–83), whose compositions he found and played through in von Mekk's library, leading to this exchange in May of 1878 with his patron:

Yesterday I played several Volkmann string serenades with great pleasure. Very nice composer. A lot of simplicity, artless charm. Look, for example, at this charming passage:

Do you know that this Volkmann is a respectable old man who lives in Pest, in woeful poverty? One time in Moscow some musicians organized a subscription for him and sent him 300 rubles, in gratitude for which he dedicated his Second Symphony to the Moscow Musical Society. However, I have never been able to find out why he is so poor.[243]

Tchaikovsky writes too about the alternating aliveness and deadness of his days at the estate. The composer seems at once drowsily comfortable yet can't sleep. "Yes, I know about Volkmann," von Mekk responded:

I know that he's an old man, very poor and lives in Pest. Since I really like his works, I made inquiries about him in Vienna, but could not get his detailed address. I am extremely fond of those unruly harmonies that prevail in his compositions, and the desolate melancholy that is often heard in them.[244]

Volkmann lived in a small apartment overlooking the Danube, teaching at the academy in Pest and living a modest life among a small group of musician friends. He had settled in Pest after trying and failing to establish himself in Vienna. His poverty was the poverty of nonrecognition, the lack of a career—or at least enough of a career to hear his music performed outside the drawing room.[245] There's melancholia in his music, as von Mekk gleaned, and it related to his status as a true Kleinmeister, in the sixteenth-century sense of mastering small forms with impeccable technique and making intimate matters accessible. According to art historian Karl Galle, the Kleinmeister is a perfectionist, not a second-tier talent, and striving for perfection as a means of participating in an immortal process.[246] The warped, sagging sound of the opening of the second movement of Volkmann's Serenade in C offers—in its exposed tritones, the tonicization of A♭ major, the chromatic counterpoint between the outer voices, and the slight stress on the second beat—an example of the unruliness to which von Mekk refers, so too the half-diminished seventh chords presented at the start of phrases in the pathétique final movement.

Tchaikovsky includes unusual sonorities of own, lending, for example, the supertonic more prominence at the start of sections than the tonic. Tonic chords are the late eighteenth-century norm, not Tchaikovsky's and Volkmann's late nineteenth-century preference for chords built on the second scale degree, with added sevenths. The intent, for both of them, was to diffuse or dilute the harmonic sense of key, and to blur the major/minor division for bittersweet effect. The introduction to the Elegy of Tchaikovsky's Serenade consists of four phrases commencing on the supertonic seventh. Each of them avoids cadencing on the D-major tonic; the first phrase ends in a half cadence and the next three phrases tonicize the submediant vi chord, making the chorale sound more minor than major at times. The second phrase ends on a supertonic chord in first inversion. The subdominant and dominant chord tonicize B minor leading up to it; this E minor chord sounds more like a iv chord in B minor rather than a ii chord in D major. It is only in the fifth phrase that D major comes through as the tonic. Tchaikovsky also generates a chorale-like effect in the upper strings against the descending lower strings, creating melodic counterpoint between them that enhances the bitter-suite-ness.

Tchaikovsky works with more instruments in his Serenade in C than does Volkmann. He converted it from a string quintet into a piece for string orchestra and dedicated the whole to the cellist, his colleague Albrecht, whose advice he had sought on the scoring. But the texture remains, like Volkmann's, transparent. Tchaikovsky avoids densities, thicknesses, since these have no interior space, nothing for the listener to mull, to try to understand. The cliché of Romanticism is its subjective immersion, but that comes at the expense of listener engagement. Refutation of contemplation is Romanticism's failing, so too mistaking density for depth. Tchaikovsky spreads the players around to maintain the feeling of openness. The first and second violins trade and divide phrases in the Serenade. The divisions would have made for a "stereophonic" effect in Tchaikovsky's day, since first and second violins sat on opposite sides of the conductor back then. Now performance practice has the second violins sitting behind the first, so the effect is lost.

The beginning of the first movement of the Serenade is heard at the end of the last movement. The magisterial opening theme is reduced to a simple descending pattern which is revealed in turn to be a folksong from Tchaikovsky's 1868–69 collection, "Under the Green Apple Tree" ("Pod yablon'yu zelyonoyu," No. 42). It's one of two folksongs heard in the last movement, the other being "As through the Green Meadow" ("A kak po lugu zelyonomu," No. 28). Both concern love, and both are included in the Serenade not for nationalist reasons or to please Balakirev but because the natural world, the peasant world, rejects time as constructed in the present. It also rejects melancholia, the dominant attribute of the previous movement. Participating in immortal things is the Kleinmeister's means to escape the mortal frame.[247] Such is one explanation of the Serenade: formal perfection, immutable contents.

The Church

There is the past and then there is The Past, the time before symphonies, instruments, diatonicism, concerts, and the concert-going public existed. In 1878, on encouragement from his publisher, Tchaikovsky created his own version of the *Liturgy of St. John Chrysostom*, one of the three most common liturgies in the Orthodox tradition incorporating one of the most frequently arranged hymns: the Cherubic Hymn. It's a song about singing, used as entrance music and as an interlude while priests retrieve sacred utensils and receptables from behind the iconostasis.[248] It bridges the two parts of the service: the first specific to the saint and the second generically reenacting the Last Supper.

An abundance of sermons has survived from John's appointments as deacon in Antioch and bishop in Constantinople in the fourth century. His eloquence gave him the nickname *chrysostomos*, "golden-mouthed."[249] Tchaikovsky hones in on this aspect of John's legacy, imagining how he spoke to create a score of hushed tones, mild dissonances that hook the ear, insistently repeated pitches, and occasional rhetorical flourishes. The *Liturgy* belongs to a brief Slavophile trend seeking to return to the Byzantine roots of the Orthodox faith. Much of the tradition was lost over time (certainly after the seventeenth-century schism in the Orthodox Church), both in the selection of chants heard in the services and in their polyphonic arrangements for chorus. The music had become too florid, too Roman Catholic. Tchaikovsky endeavored to create a more austere sound that would still appeal to singers. His *Liturgy*'s most modern aspect is a decidedly unmodern fugato in No. 14, "Praise the Lord from the Heavens" (the Hallelujah section).

Even No. 6, the Cherubic Hymn, is an exercise in restraint.[250] As an analysis by John Ahern reveals, excluding the opening contrapuntal gesture (measures 1–6, repeated at 44–50), the texture is homophonic and sung slowly in half and whole notes with staggered breathing. At the "Amen," Tchaikovsky interweaves the vocal lines before a concluding pedal point and plagal cadence. The music is in a three-part ABA' form, as opposed to the strophic structure heard in other settings of the Cherubic Hymn, including Glinka's from 1837. While Glinka sends the upper voice heavenward for the description of celestial singing, Tchaikovsky repeats the same midrange pitches. Why do the obvious thing? According to Ahern, another element that distinguishes Tchaikovsky's setting from Glinka's is his effort at suspending time by lingering over chords, such as in measure 7, when a prolonged 6/3 dominant chord interrupts a stepwise descent from C to E. The effect is also manifest in No. 8 of the *Liturgy*, the Creed. Measures 61–67 hold a dominant chord interspersed with a neighbor-tone chord that resolves deceptively to vi in measure 69. Measures 88–90 highlight a half-diminished vii7/V before a pianissimo cadence. These passages, Ahern concludes, recall several other instances of harmonic strangeness in Tchaikovsky's output, like the stuck-in-a-rut churning of the strings in measures 53–58 of his Serbian–Ottoman War piece from 1876: *Marche slave*.[251]

His *All-Night Vigil* of 1881 is no more or less idiosyncratic, though Tchaikovsky thought it prudent to write a preface explaining his method of harmonizing church chants:

> This present work of mine represents an attempt at harmonizing the major portion of the unchanging and some of the changeable liturgical hymns used at Great Vespers and Matins. Some of these authentic church melodies (taken from the chant books published by the Holy Synod) I have left intact; in others I allowed myself to make certain insignificant deviations; in the third category, finally, I departed altogether from following the chant exactly, electing instead to be guided by my own musical instinct. In harmonizing the church melodies I stayed within the narrow boundaries of the so-called "strict style," i.e., avoiding

chromaticism unconditionally and permitting myself to use dissonances in a very limited number of instances.[252]

His intentions were modest, his procedures a model for others to adopt. When Rimsky-Korsakov tried his hand at church music in the mid-1880s, he turned to Tchaikovsky's as well as Glinka's examples. Rimsky-Korsakov's setting of the Cherubic Hymn has exactly the same opening gesture as theirs does: a suspended upper line and a descending lower one.

The 2016 critical edition of the *Liturgy* and *All-Night Vigil* was edited by Hilarion (Grigoriy Alfeyev), the current Metropolitan of Budapest and Hungary. It includes a poorly written preface exaggerating Tchaikovsky's Orthodox upbringing and commitment to the official church. "Thus, before embarking on his work on sacred music," Hilarion writes, "Tchaikovsky had already a serious knowledge in the field, and his aesthetic principles were formed. His own praying and listening experience Tchaikovsky had acquired in Orthodox churches of various Russian and European cities, as well as in monasteries and village parishes." Hilarion also refers to the composer's "profound inner religiousness."[253] Tchaikovsky, however, didn't talk about his personal faith for the simple reason that it was personal, and his relationship to all of those churches and parishes was fraught. Although he composed and arranged sacred music, it wasn't intended for the official church but for concert halls and well-trained singers. He also intended it for publication, which caused a sufficiently nasty scandal that Tchaikovsky forswore additional large-scale religious pieces.

The *Liturgy* was published simultaneously in St. Petersburg and Moscow on January 18, 1879. The publisher, Jurgenson, believed it would have broad appeal to the Orthodox faithful throughout the empire. There was a problem: sacred music had not been printed by a private firm before. The capella of the Russian Imperial Court had long controlled the production and performance of sacred music, preventing its commercialization. Jurgenson knew this and wanted to end the capella's monopoly.

The director of the capella, Nikolay Bakhmetev (1807–91), took him to court. Jurgenson's lawyer Dmitri Stasov, the "conscience" of Russian jurisprudence, defended him and Tchaikovsky on the grounds that the ecclesiastical censor (aka the Moscow Committee for the Censorship of Sacred Books) had approved the *Liturgy* for publication without reservation (and helpfully caught a typo).[254] Stasov also argued that the capella's monopoly on sacred music had expired after the death of Dmitri Bortnyansky in 1825. (Bortnyansky had been awarded the monopoly nine years before, in 1816.)[255] Bakhmetev lost the case, twice in fact, and ended up having to compensate Jurgenson 344 rubles for the copies of the *Liturgy* that the chief of police in Moscow had confiscated (each of them sold for 2 rubles, so presumably 172 of them had been seized). Both the Imperial Court and Governing Senate ruled that, while the capella might have the right to music specifically intended for the church, it had no say over sacred *concert* pieces like Tchaikovsky's *Liturgy* and *All-Night Vigil*. Overshadowing the case, which had considerable implications for the protection of publishers' and composers' rights, was a turf war between the capella, controlled by the Ministry of the Court in St. Petersburg, and the ecclesiastical censor, which operated under the Holy Synod in Moscow. Bakhmetev, who considered the Liturgy an "operatic" profanation of holy cant, sought to prove that he was more Orthodox than the Holy Synod.[256]

There are some ironies here, the first being Bakhmetev's lack of a religious education and musical ignorance. He had served in the cavalry before the capella, and in matters of the church proved himself astonishingly rude, his ire increasing when he received word of priests in the provinces singing salon romances (including Tchaikovsky's) and teaching their choirs melodies by playing them badly on the fiddle.[257]

Another irony, revealed in the court proceedings, was Tchaikovsky's long-time academic study of liturgical music east and west. In 1874, he even wrote a guide to it, adapting the harmony manual that he produced for his Moscow Conservatory students to include sacred compositions by Bortnyansky, Baldassare Galuppi, and Alexei Lvov.[258] Tchaikovsky also edited Bortnyansky's church music and made piano arrangements of it on commission from his publisher.

The third irony is Jurgenson himself, who expected handsome profit from the publication of sacred music and for that reason relished having the fight with the capella. Tchaikovsky was exhibit A in his capitalist religious ambitions. But Jurgenson misjudged the market. Bakhmetev's defeat in the courtroom freed Jurgenson to publish sacred music, but it also freed other publishers as well, which was something Bakhmetev anticipated. "If church musical compositions are not censored," he argued before the court, "then every year there will be countless liturgies."[259]

He didn't personally know Tchaikovsky and didn't make their conflict personal until excerpts of the *Liturgy* were performed at the Moscow Conservatory on November 21 and December 18, 1880, at the Assembly of the Nobility. The *Liturgy* had already been performed in Kyiv, receiving positive notice there in a monarchist newspaper that advocated the Russification of southern Ukraine against the interests of Ukrainian nationalists and Catholic Poland. Tchaikovsky was helping to spread the Orthodox gospel.[260]

The Moscow Conservatory performance was private, the Assembly performance public, and according to Levenson it caused a sensation. "The hall was full. Unexpectedly, given the ban on applause, there was a loud ovation, with an unknown individual presenting a lyre wreath [to the conductor of the Chudov Monastery Choir]."[261] Bakhmetev violently protested the performance. The "nihilism" of "this, *this* concert" is "all the more dangerous for touching the very root of Orthodoxy," he ranted in a letter to the Minister of the Court, claiming that the audience in Moscow was "bewildered" by what they heard—an exercise in "nihilism" and "evil." Everything Bakhmetev had personally tried to do to prevent the secularization of sacred music—going to court; going to the police; confiscating the plates of Tchaikovsky's *Liturgy*; pulling printed copies off the shelves; menacing anyone interested in conducting or singing it—had been for naught and had even backfired on him, adding to the public's curiosity about Tchaikovsky's composition. "We won't even talk about how insulting the combination of the words 'mass' and 'Tchaikovsky' are to the ears of the Orthodox Christian," Bakhmetev added, a personal jab that reflected his anger about losing the power to censor music.[262]

He wasn't alone. The overseer of the Moscow diocese in the late 1870s, Bishop Ambrose (Alexei Klyucharyov, 1820–1901), wanted Tchaikovsky to stick to love songs, *Romeo and Juliet*, and operas. Allowing him to compose church music, Ambrose pseudonymously complained in print, opened the door for anyone to do so, including Jews. "Any Rosenthal and Rosenbloom" could now take a crack at the rites, "and your sacred chants will be jeered and booed. Get ready for that!"[263] Thus, there was an antisemitic element in the fracas. Tchaikovsky later complained to von Mekk that Ambrose had called his *Liturgy* "Catholic," even though he had followed Orthodox practices as reverently as he could.[264]

Such was the conclusion of Stepan Smolensky (1848–1909), a scholar of liturgical music who became the head of the Moscow Synodal College and its choir. (Later, after Tchaikovsky's death, he took over the deposed Bakhmetev's position in St. Petersburg.) Seeking to put his archival findings to use, Smolensky joined Orthodox hardliners in arguing for a return to the corpus of chants that had fallen out of the repertoire. Cleansing the Byzantine-Russian *pesnopeniye* of Western influences and baroque impurities, he believed, would strengthen the power of the church and restore its ancient bond with the people. Quite the opposite happened, however, when, to put it crudely, the people discovered that their favorite hymns had been tossed out.[265] Smolensky softened his position, and his opinion of Tchaikovsky's liturgical music swerved from negative to positive. Purity was impossible, and pragmatism commendable. The *Liturgy* and the *All-Night Vigil*, Smolensky concluded, occupied the perfect middle ground between the ecclesiastical and the artistic.[266]

The case made concerts of spiritual music popular, so much so that by the end of the 1880s the Assembly of the Nobility was hosting concerts of older and newer sacred music sung by opera singers who lent drama and passion to the chants and the scriptures and there was nothing the Russian Orthodox Church could do about it.[267]

No Trifling with Love

Still, Tchaikovsky did as Ambrose advised. He stuck to love songs, *Romeo and Juliet*, and operas. He even tried to combine these things.

He had twice composed a *Romeo and Juliet* overture and was soon to do it a third time, after Jurgenson offered to publish a new work. In May 1878 Tchaikovsky read (or reread) Shakespeare's play in Kyiv while spending time with his sister Sasha and her children. She had gone to the theater with Modest, the kids were in bed, and he had an hour to read.[268] He decided to compose an opera on the subject, declaring that he wasn't intimidated by Bellini's and Gounod's adaptations of the play; in fact, he had serious issues with their interpretations. His *Romeo and Juliet* would be a grand meditation on the power and peril of love, making their operas seem trivial by comparison. But then he balked, stumped by the task he had set himself: composing an opera about transcendent love that would transcend all other operas about transcendent love. Tchaikovsky sketched a duet for the teenage lovers but got no further.[269] Shakespeare's *Romeo and Juliet*, like Pushkin's *Eugene Onegin*, is a chess match of a text, and once Tchaikovsky recognized the strategy behind the sentiment, he pulled back from the project.

Instead, he contemplated setting a comedy or a tragedy by Alfred de Musset, best known for his relationship with the great French novelist and women's rights advocate George Sand. According to essayist Raymond MacKenzie, Musset's "behavior—as described by himself and by others—looked like Romantic Weltschmerz degenerating into hysteria. Werther seemed to be hovering just offstage throughout his life."[270] Undeterred (or inspired) by the gossip, Tchaikovsky wanted to write an opera on Musset's *On ne badine pas avec l'amour* (*No Trifling with Love*, 1835), a deep pool of French pathos guaranteed to elicit howls of protest from Balakirev and an epic rant from Cui. So too *Les caprices de Marianne* (*The Moods of Marianne*, 1833), which opens with an amorous balcony scene—a perfect new home for the composer's *Romeo and Juliet* overture. Tchaikovsky vacillated between Shakespeare and Musset for several more months only to abandon them both in favor of a French historical drama with allegorical relevance to social and political events in Russia. The subject was Joan of Arc, a fifteenth-century girl from Domrémy. Guided by divine forces and/or hearing voices in her head, she contributed to the liberation of France from the English, beginning with the town of Orléans. Charles VII, the new king of France, placed her at the helm of his army. She was captured by Burgundians (allies of the English) and burned at the stake at age nineteen. Tchaikovsky's narration of these events blazes, too, with romance.

The project seems to have come out of the blue, but Tchaikovsky told his brother that he had been thinking about a Joan of Arc opera for years, in part because Giuseppe Verdi had botched the subject so badly in *Giovanna D'Arco* (1845).[271] Tchaikovsky hadn't seen that version but obtained a copy of the score in Florence in 1878. He complained about Verdi crudely merging Schiller's *Die Jungfrau von Orleans* (*The Virgin of Orleans*, 1801) and Voltaire's *La Pucelle d'Orléans* (*The Maid of Orleans*, 1730), a satirical take on the legend that finds "everyone is in love with [Joan], even the king," and features "endless flights of angels and demons soar[ing] down" to the battlefield in the service of a grand choral finale.[272] Tchaikovsky was appalled enough to attempt his own opera, which he composed between December 1878 and August 1879, with two stages of revisions (a habit for him), in 1880 and 1882.

He wrote the libretto while composing the music, using Schiller (as translated into Russian by Zhukovsky) and shunning Voltaire. He wanted his setting of the Joan of Arc legend to be supernatural and sentimental, which also made it ambivalent: Is the heroine a saint or a sinner, sage or dupe? Are her visions Christian or pagan? Schiller embellished the historical sources with family conflict and amorous intrigue; Tchaikovsky retained some of the former and all the latter. Joan disappoints her father by refusing to settle down with the lad he has in mind for her. Later she falls in love with an English soldier, Lionel (whom Tchaikovsky turns into a Burgundian knight), and thus betrays the cause she intended to serve. Schiller assigned the voice of doom to a character called the Black Knight (read, the Black Death), and Joan meets her end on the battlefield instead of burning at the stake. Tchaikovsky removed the Black Knight from the cast list and scrapped Schiller's ending, telling von Mekk that in the final scene he would be consulting another source from the Joan of Arc library he had compiled: Jules Barbier's *Jeanne d'Arc* (1869), the text of Gounod's 1873 opera.

> In Rouen. Joan is led to the fire. Lionel dies at the foot of the scaffold, struck by lightning. Joan is at the pyre. People slowly begin to realize that she is wrongly accused and start to protest. The execution is quickened. She mounts the scaffold. She is crestfallen, but the chorus of angels support her. The first tongues of flame appear at the bottom. Everyone screams in horror, the curtain falls.
>
> This whole scene is set up nicely by *Barbier*, and I am going to borrow it from him.[273]

The libretto calibrates intimate (lyric) and broader cosmic (epic) matters. The operatic Joan, as opposed to the historical Joan, derives her strength from "supernatural sources" as opposed to "will."[274] There's no indication in Tchaikovsky's opera that Joan was motivated, for example, by the dreadfulness she witnessed as a child: the burning down of the church in her hometown and her family's forced flight to Neufchâtel; the stacked corpses of soldiers; and her father's alienating religious fanaticism. Lore represents her as the figure that all of France, not just the places under intermittent siege, needed for its liberation. In the opera, however, Joan is guided by something she doesn't understand. She wonders why her life has become so difficult.

Still, Tchaikovsky attends to factual historical matters. His Joan can't read or write but, as the sources confirm, loves being told stories. The voices in her head come from epics, legends, and scary bedtime tales. The score, accordingly, teems with sounds from the beyond, from within, and from different traditions, pagan and Christian, beginning with the opening of the first act. The right side of the stage features a chapel graced with an image of the Mother of God; the left shows a "druid tree" that maidens (*devushki*) decorate with wreaths. They love the tree; they sing and gather around it when the sun's out. At night, though, they must avoid it because "from the forest, goblins come, mermaids singing in unison, and ghosts [represented by a chromatic scale] roam in the quiet."

Enter Joan's father, a suitor named Raymond, and Joan. The father expresses his concerns about the future of France. Then he shares, more urgently, his worries about his daughter marrying the right man, establishing a link between love for nation and love for the people (symbolized by Raymond). His fears are echoed in a chorus that whispers the following in her ear

Лишь супружеские цепи	Only the bonds of matrimony
Счастье прочное дают	Provide lasting happiness

while also telling her to submit to the husband her father has chosen for her. What this chorus is and where it's coming from isn't specified. By the end of the first act, it will become clear that love for nation and love for people are part of a love for God. Another voice is heard, then a backing chorus of angels, whose singing comes from the druid tree (alternatively, "fairies' tree").[275] Joan hears these words from Zhukovsky's translation of Schiller:

Голос соло

Иди, спеши скорей на поле брани:
Пора, пора, пробил теперь твой час.
Ты меч возьмешь и орифламму в длани
[Возьмешь мою ты орифламму в длани][276]
И мощь врагов сразишь, как жница клас.

Все ангелы

Поставишь их надменной власти грани,
Преобратишь во плач победный глас,
Дашь ратным честь, дашь блеск на силу трону
И Карла в Реймс введешь принять корону.

Solo voice

Go, hasten to the battlefield:
Now's the time, your hour has arrived.
You will take the sword and banner in hand
[Take my banner in hand]
And you will thwart the might of our enemies, like a female
    reaper cuts down a stalk of grain.

All the angels

You will limit their arrogant power,
And turn their shouts of triumph into wails,
And give our soldiers honor and glitter to the power of the
    throne
And bring Charles to Reims to accept the crown.

She's not sure she has the courage to do what's being asked of her, but, frankly, she has no choice. Staying put would keep the voices ringing in her head.

One of those voices is her father's, and she's disappointed him. He introduces her to a "wonderful" potential husband, and she says nothing, albeit in a manner that speaks volumes. She hangs her head, then raises it and shakes it side to side as the clarinet takes a melodic turn in the range of a minor third before floating upward. The figure recurs in the chorus of angels (or druids) as a symbol of Joan's supernatural calling. At the end of Act III, scene 1, as Joan loses consciousness from a wound she's suffered in battle, the same musical figure is elaborated above feverishly undulating strings. Lionel observes that she's bleeding as flute and clarinets develop the motive, which the oboe, bassoon, and French horn pull further and further down, the higher calling now the Black Knight's music, portending her bad end.

Tchaikovsky composed quickly—too quickly for Modernist standards. There are loose ends, rough transitions, and an aria ("Farewell, Ye Native Hills") meant to be packed into a suitcase and performed on recitals without any thought whatsoever of Joan of Arc. Tchaikovsky responded to conditions on the ground as a composer, meaning that he wrote an aria for a specific soprano, Mariya Kamenskaya, to take on the road plus added dances for the ballet dancers of the Mariinsky Theater.

The literature on *The Maid of Orleans* is a protracted argument about its grand operatic Frenchness contra its *Moguchaya kuchka* Russianness.[277] Tchaikovsky assigned a French tune, "Mes belles amourettes," to a group of minstrels in Act II and, as musicologist Marina Frolova-Walker has written, this French tune has been strangely misheard as a Ukrainian (Little Russian) tune in the literature; doubly strangely, the mishearing has been used to criticize the opera. Try as he might, the argument goes, Tchaikovsky couldn't avoid sounding Slavic. Even the mistress of King Charles VII sounds like she's from Muscovy (or lands to the east). Frolova-Walker quotes

Rosa Newmarch paraphrasing Vladimir Cheshikhin as follows: "*The Maid of Orleans* contains incongruous lapses into the Russian style. What have the minstrels at the court of Charles VII in common with a folksong of Malo-Russian origin? Or why is the song of Agnès Sorel so reminiscent of [wait for it!] the land of the steppes and birch forests?"[278] Why indeed.

Tchaikovsky arguably wanted to show that power in fifteenth-century France was diffuse and authority multilayered. The heroine comes from the margins, the borderlands, a place barely France. She defines the centerless center. Complaints in the literature about the opera's lack of Frenchness, or for that matter Russianness, fail to acknowledge that "France," and also "Russia," weren't nation states in the fifteenth century. As medieval historian Janet Nelson writes, "Domrémy straddled the Meuse—or to be precise an arm of that river, whose tendency to meander and divide mirrored political geography—one part lying on the southern bank, in Burgundian territory, the other on the northern bank, in the royal captaincy of Vaucouleurs, acquired less than a century before by the French Crown. The house of Joan's family was situated next door to the church, on the northern bank. It would be hard to imagine a more marginal location."[279] A marginal location is no location at all, of course. It's the *kray*, the edge, and everything about this opera, all the sounds that the heroine hears, occupy an indefinite interspace between here and there.

Joan's trial is another borderline, discussed in the sources as a clash of "two irreducibly opposed cultures . . . learned and popular, written and oral, clerical and lay, Latin and vernacular."[280] Tchaikovsky maintains this clash throughout the opera. Consider how the opening maidens' chorus ends with a wondrous fading pianissimo and how garishly it clashes with the pretentious interlacing of voices for the choral paeans to the French king, who stands surrounded by jesters and dwarfs—a stark contrast with the frescoes and stained glass of the sanctified Joan. The opera moves from a pagan-pastoral mode into a suite of eclectic dances and minstrel singing into royal razzmatazz (nos. 14 and 16 of Act II, combining fanfares, bells, processional music, and a chorus of knights, courtiers, and the people). The middle is filled by the pathos-laden, reverential idiom of Joan's arias, which, as musicologist Sophie Brady has revealed, borrow from a French carol, "La Ballade du Jésus-Christ," published in 1860 and presumably obtained by Tchaikovsky in Paris.[281] The paraphrase links Joan's Act I aria "Farewell, Ye Native Hills" to her Act II aria "Holy Father, My Name Is Joan" to her final farewell, to life itself in Act IV, when a phrase from the carol is assigned to the words "my heart longs and suffers." Joan is an outsider beset by outside forces that take her from her argument with her father (who accuses her of sleeping with the devil) to the court and the battlefield to the land of Romeo and Juliet to the funeral pyre.

Joan's suffering is milder in the opera than in the historical sources Tchaikovsky consulted (and certainly milder than those he didn't). After her trial she rotted in prison for two months, then, just before her execution, she renounced her revelation and promised to wear a dress. Her sentence was changed to permanent imprisonment, but then, perhaps because she was sexually assaulted, her guards discovered her wearing armor and brought her once more before the public to be burned at the stake.[282]

The music of the forest fire at the end of Act I is repurposed for the auto-da-fé. The chorus of angels is joined by the people, soldiers, and nuns who have piled the wood before the crucifix for the baptism by fire. The movement and intensity of the flames are represented metonymically in the upper strings and winds; the texture thickens, with rising hexachords, then rising and falling fifths, building on top of one another, growing louder, moving faster. The rhythms accelerate before Joan's disappearance behind the smoke that fills her lungs and silences her screams. The fire burns itself out as the rhythmic figure of a funeral march resounds.

The ending leaves several questions unanswered. How to explain the behavior of Joan's father and the passive hedonism of the king?

What of the bizarre church odes ending just in time for the ballet divertissement? The conflict of heart versus head seems quaint, even for 1880. What context did Tchaikovsky have in mind when he composed the opera?

According to Ilya Vinitsky, Tchaikovsky was thinking about an event in 1878.[283] The opera allegorically comments on the trial that year of Vera Zasulich (1849–1919), a socialist activist accused of stoking unrest (and colluding with the Russian nihilist Sergey Nechayev). Zasulich was exonerated in a decision deemed a test of Tsar Alexander II's judicial reforms as related to fairness in the courts. That same year, Vinitsky reveals, Ivan Turgenev wrote a prose poem about Zasulich, or someone like her, that could be a *précis* of Tchaikovsky's *Maid of Orleans*. The poem tells of a teenage girl being initiated into the underground People's Will movement or another of the militant groups seeking an end to autocracy. She is told that her future will be defined by extreme hardship: "cold, hunger, hatred, derision, contempt, abuse, prison, sickness, and perhaps even death." She says that she is prepared for "alienation," "loneliness," and "crime":

"Then enter."
The girl stepped over the threshold and a heavy curtain fell behind her.
"Fool," someone said from behind.
"Saint," someone replied.[284]

Turgenev merely hints at the facts, which are as follows. Zasulich was of Polish descent, the daughter of a senior officer in the imperial service. The incident that made her famous, the subject of a series of articles in the "court news" columns of the *Petersburg Leaflet*, involved St. Petersburg's sadistic governor general, Fyodor Trepov. Seeking to avenge a political prisoner, Zasulich turned up at Trepov's office with a pistol, piercing his side with her first shot, missing with the second, then being tackled and arrested. (The prisoner had been subject to "twenty-five rod strokes" for failing to remove his hat in Trepov's presence. The poor sod had actually taken his hat off the first time Trepov passed by him in the prison yard—just not the second time, which was excuse enough for a savage beating.) Given Trepov's record of abuses, the jury acquitted Zasulich.[285]

Once Joan became "an ordinary Russian girl" in Turgenev's political conception, once she became Vera, Tchaikovsky had what he needed to write an opera about her. *Maid of Orleans*, Vinitsky claims, asks a key question about the reforms as related to women's rights: "fool or saint"?[286] Tchaikovsky responds with ambivalence, perhaps even indifference.

To secure a production, he needed Nápravník to write a recommendation to the Imperial Theaters. The Czech conductor obliged in his shaky, repetitive Russian:

> Tchaikovsky's previous operas had a serious drawback: the composer pushed the vocal parts into the background, focusing on the orchestra and the orchestra alone with few exceptions. In this sense he composed not operas but exclusively symphonic music. For all the talent that went into them, the result for these operas was always the same: swift removal from the stage. Things changed for the better with the lyrical scenes of *Eugene Onegin*, a notable success for the composer. The libretto of his opera *Joan of Arc*, skillfully written and presented to you now, overflows with beautiful lyrical scenes most suited to the composer's abilities. It was a lot of effort for the composer not to overshadow the vocal parts with his bright, rich, and colorful orchestration. The singing овладает [this is not a word in Russian; Nápravník doubtless means обладает, "is master of" or "dominates"] almost everything without sacrificing the orchestra as happened in his old operas, whose music was rightly called symphonic and not operatic. Accepting *Joan of Arc* into the repertoire would acknowledge his achievement.[287]

Nápravník conducted the February 13 premiere as a benefit in his own honor. He records the amount he earned along with all the praise he basked in and the astonishing success of the performance. Nápravník picked up the baton to a "brilliant, clamorous, and unanimous reception." The "public" presented him with expensive gifts, including "a massive silver service in the Russian style made by [the silversmith firm] Grachev; a large silver inkwell in the form of a beehive also made by Grachev; and a laurel wreath signed by the around 120 people participating in the presentation of gifts and long unceasing thunders of applause." At the end of the first act, "the entire opera troupe assembled on the stage" after which Nápravník received another wreath with the "pan-Slavic tricolor." The orchestra was cheered at the start of each act, and there were "endless" curtain calls for Nápravník, the soprano in the title role, Mariya Kamenskaya, and Tchaikovsky.[288]

The reviews were a jumble of complaints. Scholarship has amplified them. *The Maid of Orleans* was likened from the start to Meyerbeer's *Le prophète*, which also meant likening it to Musorgsky's *Boris Godunov*, since the title character of *Le prophète* is partly modeled on the False Dmitri.[289] Rutger Helmers lists the librettistic correspondences between Tchaikovsky's and Meyerbeer's operas, specifically the central coronation scenes. Since the libretto of *Le prophète* has *Die Jungfrau von Orleans* as a source, it is reasonable to conclude that the Meyerbeer influence on Tchaikovsky was filtered through Schiller.[290]

Cui predictably savaged Tchaikovsky for simply being Tchaikovsky: composing music that appealed to the public as opposed to recreating, or trying to recreate, the soundscape of fifteenth-century France and the Hundred Years' War.[291] Another problem was the dull, tired-looking décor, which came from a production of Gounod's *Faust*. It had also been used in a performance of Vasily Kyuner's *Taras Bul'ba*, which glorifies a Zaporizhzhian Cossack doing battle against Poles and ends with the hero burned to death while tied to a tree (rather than a stake). The chorus didn't have enough singers and came out sounding pale and thin. Tchaikovsky's French grand opera incongruously lacked grandeur.[292] And Kamenskaya overreached and strained her voice. (Tchaikovsky would revise the score to place it in a more comfortable mezzo-soprano range for her.)

The second performance a week later was a benefit for the stage director, Gennady Kondratyev, after which the theaters closed for Lent. Their reopening was postponed for six months owing to the events of March 1, 1881. Nápravník's diary records an "attempt on the life of Sovereign Emperor Alexander II at 3 p.m. and his death at 3:35 p.m."[293] A member of the People's Will revolutionary organization threw a bomb at the tsar as he was getting out of his armored carriage, tearing off one of his legs and piercing his abdomen. His death brought an end to a period of economic, agricultural, and social reforms, including the emancipation of the serfs and increased freedom of expression in the press and the universities. But even more changes were demanded. Russia's Joan(s) of Arc rebelled, and Alexander II was killed.

1. Nikolay Kuzmin's drawing of Tchaikovsky with artists of the Malïy Theater, Moscow, 1866. Tchaikovsky moved to Moscow from St. Petersburg that year, teaching first at the Moscow branch of the Russian Musical Society and then at the Conservatory.

2. Piano vocal score of Tchaikovsky's sole comic opera, *Vakula the Smith*, based on a tale by Nikolay Gogol. It was composed in 1874 for a competition organized in honor of Grand Princess Elena Pavlovna, St. Petersburg's leading patron of the arts.

3. The composer regularly visited his sister Sasha (Alexandra) at the estate of her husbar Lev Davïdov in Kamianka, Ukraine. Her death from substance abuse in 1891 plunge Tchaikovsky into depression. Memories of their childhood together inform *The Nutcracke* This photograph is from the summer of 1875.

4. Tchaikovsky was clo to his twin brothers Modest, a playwright and librettist, and Anatole, an ambitious lawyer and politician who became vice governor in Tiflis. Thei long-time friend, a lawyer named Nikolay Kondratyev, sits at the desk. The photograph was taken in 1875 in the Moscow studio of Ivan Dyagovchenko.

5. Russian soprano Mariya Klimentova-Muromtseva starred as Tatyana in the 1879 premiere production of *Eugene Onegin* at the Malïy Theater in Moscow. Komentova-Muromtseva also sang the part of the heroine Oksana in Tchaikovsky's *Cherevichki* in 1885.

6. Russian baritone Bogomir Korsov appeared in the title role (which he helped Tchaikovsky create) of *Mazeppa* at the Bolshoi Theater in 1884. Korsov also sang the title roles in Musorgsky's *Boris Godunov*, Rubinstein's *Demon*, and Verdi's *Rigoletto*, and took the part of the devil in Tchaikovsky's *Cherevichki*.

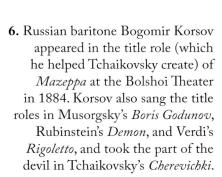

7. Tsar Alexander III, Tsarina Mariya Fyodorovna (Dagmar of Denmark), and their children posed for this photograph in 1885. The Tsar was a keen admirer of Tchaikovsky's music, attending premieres of his later operas and ballets, authorizing performances of his music at the court, and awarding him a lifetime pension.

8. Grand Prince Konstantin Konstantinovich distinguished himself as a naval officer before settling into a life of art, publishing poems and translations, and performing as a pianist in concerts at his luxurious residence. He became Tchaikovsky's chief benefactor in his later years, after Nadezhda von Mekk withdrew her support.

9. Lunch at the Ortachala Gardens in Tiflis, April 30, 1889. The gathering was organized by the photographer Joseph Andronikashvili, a member of the Tiflis branch of the Imperial Russian Musical society. Varvara Zarudnaya, who sang the part of Tatyana in productions of *Eugene Onegin* in Tbilisi and Kyiv, sits opposite the composer.

10. The composer pictured with the directors of the Kharkiv branch of the Imperial Russian Musical Society. On March 14, 1893, the day this photograph was taken, Tchaikovsky conducted a concert of his *Tempest*, Violin Concerto, Second Symphony, and *1812 Overture* in Kharkiv.

11. In front of the iconostasis and altar solea of the Cathedral of Christ the Savior at the time of the church's consecration in May 1883. For the coronation of Tsar Alexander III that month, Tchaikovsky's *1812 Overture* was performed for the first time—with cannons.

12. From 1888–91, Tchaikovsky rented a house with a garden (no longer extant) outside of Moscow in Frolovskoye, a settlement of fewer than one hundred people. His visitors included Alexander Scriabin and Władysław Pachulski, who took this photograph of Tchaikovsky in 1890.

3. Tchaikovsky's desk in the bedroom on the second floor of his house in Klin. Here, overlooking a garden, Tchaikovsky worked on the *Pathétique* Symphony. After his death, Tchaikovsky's brother Modest converted the house into a museum.

4. Tchaikovsky's gravesite in the Tikhvin Cemetery of the Alexander Nevsky Monastery, St. Petersburg. The sculpture was created by Pavel Kamensky, on the initiative of the intendant of the Imperial Theaters, Ivan Vsevolozhsky. It was unveiled in 1897, four years after Tchaikovsky's death.

15. Vera Karalli in the role of Odette in *Swan Lake*. Karalli performed in Moscow, St. Petersburg, and Paris, acted in silent film, and had a dazzling and dangerous private life as mistress to Grand Prince Dmitri Romanov and agent in the plot to murder Rasputin.

16. Vladimir Ryabtsev in the role of Carabosse in *The Sleeping Beauty*, Bolshoi Theatre 1924 (choreography by Vasiliy Tikhomirov, after Petipa's 1890 original). Ryabtsev died on stage in 1945 while performing a dance in a production of Glinka's opera *Ivan Susanin* (*A Life for the Tsar*).

PART III

IMPERIALISM

Propaganda

Tchaikovsky didn't like Alexander II because, he candidly told his publisher, the tsar didn't like him. Alexander II was averse to his music, "antipathetic."[1] Tchaikovsky didn't record a reaction to the tsar's assassination. Concerning an earlier attempt on his life, in 1879, he told his father that it was "awful for Russia."[2]

He tried to get out of writing official music for the tsar. *The Year 1812*, also known as the *1812 Overture*, is proof that Tchaikovsky didn't succeed. Like Mozart's *Eine kleine Nachtmusik* or Ravel's *Boléro* or Rachmaninoff's C#-minor Prelude, the overture became a concert favorite despite the composer's consistent indifference to it. After Tchaikovsky's own death, the *1812 Overture* became but a bonbon on pop concerts, background music for commercials, sporting events, and of course jingoistic national celebrations. In *The Music Lovers*, the famous cannons fire as chorus girls kick up their legs. The allegorical spermatozoa include champagne corks and curly streamers.

The overture was commissioned for the opening concert of the Arts and Industrial Exhibition in 1881 in Moscow, an "all-Russian" demonstration of imported technologies like water pumps and telegraph stations. The opening was postponed for a year after Alexander II's assassination owing to widespread public fear. The next tsar, Alexander III (1845–94), abandoned his predecessor's reforms by reinstating some of the repressive policies of the past associated with Tsar Nikolay I (1796–1855).

Nikolay Rubinstein, the concert's organizer, told Tchaikovsky that the overture could be about three things: the exhibition itself (meaning the government's achievements under Alexander II, a quarter century on the throne when he died); the building of the Cathedral of Christ the Savior; or the Russian defeat of Napoleon's Grande Armée in 1812 (the Battle of Borodino). The composer said in response that he didn't like fairground and promenade music and didn't care for the design of the cathedral, so he chose the third topic. "There's nothing more loathsome to me than composing for the sake of some *festivities* or other," he vented to von Mekk on September 28, 1880. "What, for instance, might one write for the opening of an exhibition, besides banalities and a lot of noise? However, I don't have it in my heart to refuse such a request, and so I keep accepting these unsympathetic tasks regardless."[3] Although it was not the original plan, the *1812 Overture* ended up musically embracing Nikolay I's trinity of Orthodoxy, Autocracy, and Nationality.

The least appealing of those tasks was a composition called "Montenegro," Tchaikovsky's contribution to the silver jubilee celebrations of Alexander II's rule. He composed it in January 1880. According to Nadezhda Teterina, the project was initiated by historian Sergey Tatishchev, who led a "double life" as a "special assignments" official for the Ministry of the Interior, and by Pyotr Korvin-Krukovsky, a "gatherer of statistics" for the secret police. Together they came up with the idea of a combined concert and portrait exhibition—a concert of "living pictures" to be held in the Bolshoi Theater on February 19, 1880. (Alexander Borodin's *In the Steppes of Central Asia* is the best-known composition to arise from the project.) Tchaikovsky wasn't exactly proud of "Montenegro," which was meant to represent the military alliance between Montenegro and Russia against the Turks; he told Anatole that it was gross-sounding noise. Teterina speculates that he recycled some of that noise in the *1812 Overture*, noting the pressure on him to produce.[4] He did what he had to do: earn a living, mollify the snoops in the Ministry of the Interior, and maintain his most-favored-Russian-composer status with the court. He kept his distance from the results of his obligatory labors, serving yet not serving.

The *1812 Overture* lasts between fifteen and twenty minutes, depending on the conductor and whether or not words are sung and the cannons blasted where indicated (five times in the middle of the piece, eleven more times at the end). The opening hymn, heard in the violas and cellos, is interrupted by the sounds of armies mustering then engaging. Napoleon's bedraggled soldiers are assigned "La Marseillaise." The people of Holy Rus fight back with folksongs, one also used in Act II of *The Voyevoda*, and another, "At My Father's Gate," from Tchaikovsky's 1868–69 folksong collection. The defeat of the French is celebrated at a *ffff* dynamic, with real or imitated church bells and cannons, and Lvov's 1833 "God Save the Tsar." The allegro vivace coda, America's fireworks favorite, derives from the music heard at the start: the Orthodox troparion "Save, O God, Thy People," a prayer for liberation.

Tchaikovsky completed the overture on November 7, 1880, after a week of concentrated work on it. It was premiered on August 8, 1882, inside the arts and crafts hall of the exhibition, part of an all-Tchaikovsky program conducted by Altani of the Bolshoi Theater. The audience cheered; critics seethed. "The string instruments are completely overwhelmed; the roar of the 'winds'; the rattling of the timpani and cymbals, the wall-shaking screech of the tam-tam, and the uninterrupted, breathtaking trilling of the snare drums—all this calls forth but one desire— 'Let it end!' And then more bells."[5] The overture had people covering their ears even without the cannons.[6] Those had to wait until May 26, 1883, to be heard, as part of a performance of the overture for the consecration of the Cathedral of Christ the Savior, a tightly choreographed event requiring a manual signal system to coordinate praying, kneeling, bellringing (in more than one church), and powder-charge igniting. Vasily Kochetkov and other impressively long-lived veterans of 1812–14 gathered in the candlelit northern wing of the cathedral with delegates from the heroic regiments and people's militias that had fought against Napoleon in Moscow, Borodino, and other places. "At 10:15 THEIR MAJESTIES and the members of the IMPERIAL HOUSE entered the altar. The rite of consecration of the Throne began. Meantime, the Clergy returned from the Assumption Cathedral with Holy Relics, banners from the Kremlin Cathedrals and Icons and settled down at the Western Doors. The regimental bands began to play [Dmitri Bortnyansky's hymn] 'How Glorious' and the soldiers removed their caps 'in prayer.' At a quarter past eleven, Metropolitan Joannicius, the Clergy, THEIR MAJESTIES and Their Highnesses, having left the altar, headed for the Western Gate to the thunder of cannons and the ringing of bells."[7]

Construction of the cathedral had taken forty-two years and cost over 15 million rubles.[8] One architect had been replaced by another, the design changed, and so did the address (from Sparrow Hills to a rough neighborhood on the Moscow River close to the Kremlin).[9] Like Tchaikovsky's overture, the cathedral was unapologetically outsized—it rose 340 feet from the base to the top of the highest cross; the interior floor space measured 2,500 square yards; its large cupola had a diameter of 98 feet; and the bells in the four bell towers alone weighed 64 tons.[10] Also like the overture, the cathedral had both religious and historical elements. The western façade depicted Russian soldiers under divine protection; the eastern and northern façades were dedicated to the saints; and the southern façade narrated the events of 1812.

After the *1812 Overture*, Tchaikovsky composed three pieces for imperial Russia's new tsar, Alexander III. He was burly in build, ginger-bearded, and slow-witted. The grammar, punctuation, and spelling of his native language proved difficult for him to master; his diaries and letters are fatuous. In the months following his father's assassination, he felt abandoned, unable to secure counsel from his advisors. Fear and paranoia crept into his thinking. His former teacher, Konstantin Pobedonostsev (1827–1907), provided spiritual and political guidance and helped turn Alexander III into a reactionary conservative. Pobedonostsev was a frightening figure, ultra-nationalist and implicated in political executions, pogroms, and forced resettlement campaigns. Jews were denied university admission and the ability to travel between regions, kicked out of theater companies, and prohibited from giving their children Christian names. Pobedonostsev also involved himself in music (the so-called New Trend in liturgical composition) and boasted of helping Tchaikovsky when his funds ran out, arranging a gift for him of 3,000 rubles from the imperial coffers.[11] That gift partly explains Tchaikovsky's music for Tsar Alexander III's coronation.

His contribution comprised the *1812 Overture* and three other pieces: an arrangement of Glinka's "Slava" chorus for performance when the tsar entered Red Square; a Coronation March; and a cantata about Moscow (for which Anton Rubinstein was originally offered the commission). The last two scores were composed in under three weeks. Tchaikovsky was promised 1,500 rubles as payment, but received instead a diamond ring, which he pawned (again, because finances were tight) for just 375 rubles. He then lost this money, along with the receipt.[12]

The Coronation March was performed on May 23, 1883, in Sokolniki (Falcon Hunt) Park, to commemorate the bicentennial of Russia's two oldest regiments in regular rotation: Preobrazhensky and Semyonovsky. According to the official account, the massive circular pavilion built for the occasion accommodated 12,000 soldiers. There were brass bands on the side and a raised platform for the orchestra in the middle. The colors of the uniforms dazzled, and a thousand waiters in white bustled around the tables. "When Their Majesties entered the royal box, the orchestra played a festive over-ture, Tchaikovsky's March, followed by one of the bands taking up the National Anthem [which the March also quotes, giving the audi-ence a double dose of its pomp]. Rising from the royal box and raising a glass of vodka to the health of the Russian Army, the Emperor and Empress walked around the tables."[13] The representa-tional details of the middle of Tchaikovsky's composition—the singers imitate the sound of humming fields and trace the up and down flight of a lark—were lost in the "thousands-fold hurrahs" of the troops.[14]

Tchaikovsky later himself conducted it in New York City, for the 1891 opening of the Music Hall (later Carnegie Hall), bringing Russian imperial swank to America's Gilded Age.[15]

The Moscow Cantata premiered in the Faceted Palace of the Moscow Kremlin on May 15, 1883. "To the sound of bells, the thunder of cannons and the public's jubilation," *New Times* reported, "the Emperor and Empress walked under canopies to the Archangel and Annunciation Cathedrals around the Ivan the Great Tower. Reaching the top of the Red Porch [the entrance to the Faceted Palace, the lone architectural survivor of the fifteenth-century reign of Ivan the Great], the Sovereign bowed before the people. It was one o'clock. Two hours later, a ceremonial dinner was held in the Palace and Tchaikovsky's 'Moscow' Cantata was heard for the first time."[16] Nápravník conducted the choir and orchestra of the Imperial Theaters, and two of Tchaikovsky's favorite singers, Elizaveta Lavrovskaya and Ivan Mel'nikov, sang the solo parts. The royal couple left at four o'clock sharp to a reprise of "Slava."

The Moscow Cantata placed Tchaikovsky in an archaic mode, comparable to Borodin's and Rimsky-Korsakov's *style russe* tapestries. When it was performed in St. Petersburg at a concert of the Society of Patriotic Ladies—an organization that raised funds for orphans, the wounded, and the poor while also operating several boarding schools—the cantata was described as "elegiac," lacking the "bright cheer" habitual of Romanov agitprop.[17] An official poet, Apollon Maykov (1821–97), wrote the words of the six movements. Tchaikovsky relies at the start on word-painting devices that go back in time to Moscow's first centuries as the putative capital of Rus. The opening movement (in A major, dominant of the D-major tonic key of the cantata) includes sounds of nature—the chittering critters of the bog above which Moscow was built. In polyphonic imitation, the singers list the places where the Tatars laid siege. Tchaikovsky brings the texture into homophonic alignment: Moscow will bring the principalities of Rus together against all enemies. A candle—hope—grows in brightness in the B-minor second movement. The D-major third movement represents a jubilant carillon, after which, in the fourth, the idea of Moscow as the Third Rome is introduced in *bïlina*-type heroic recitation (though the opposite, liturgical *peniye*, might seem more appropriate). Alexander III is addressed like this:

Ты для всех теперь, для восточных стран	Now you are for all Eastern countries
Что звезда взошла Вифлеемская	Like the star of Bethlehem that rose up
Во своей святой Каменной Москве!	Over our Holy Moscow city of stone!
Полюбил тебя и избрал Господь,	God loved you and chose you
Повязать тебе Константинов меч	To strap on the sword of Constantine
И венчаться венцом Мономаховым.	And be crowned with the Cap of Monomakh.

"Constantine" is the Byzantine emperor Constantine XI Palaiologos. In 1834, the Ottoman ambassador to the Russian Imperial Court had given Tsar Nikolay I a jewel-encrusted sword that supposedly once belonged to Palaiologos. It served in Russian imagination as proof of Constantinople's *translatio imperii* to Moscow. The Cap or Crown of Monomakh is another such Byzantine artifact.

The fifth movement, a romance, is the cipher. Maykov describes the sovereign as God's most devoted yet burdened servant. The soprano sings in E♭ minor, close to the D major of the people in one sense but far removed from them in another. Musically, we have reached 1883, Tchaikovsky's and Tsar Alexander III's present. The sixth and final movement is cast in three parts that calibrate E♭ minor and D major, tsar and people, heaven and earth.

Alexander III defined himself as a ruler through the distant past of the Rurik princes. In this regard, the cantata was just what he wanted. After his father's grisly death, he symbolically fled "European" St. Petersburg for "Eurasian" Moscow. Encouraged by his wife, Princess Dagmar of Denmark (crowned Mariya Fyodorovna), he had developed an ardent Teutophobia that blossomed into full-throated Slavophilia. Alexander II had been a liberator, keen to release Russia from feudalism. The son's rule was the *reaktsiya*, the end of the liberal period. Alexander III defended the old traditions, embraced the rhetoric of Moscow as the Third Rome, and claimed Russia for Russians alone, expelling and subduing Germans, Swedes, Poles, and Jews in the process. Tchaikovsky praised him for it.

The Court

Thus, Tchaikovsky entered the stagnant but comfortable world of Alexander III, who reigned through to the end of the composer's life and one year beyond. The entrance was facilitated through his friendship, from his time at the School of Jurisprudence, with Prince Vladimir Meshchersky. The latter was a journalist, novelist, and prominently "out" homosexual with an ingrained prejudice against women (his satiric novel, *The Women of St. Petersburg High Society*, is unsubtly bigoted) and a talent for spreading odious rumors about the men who crossed him. He made enemies up and down the Table of Ranks, but he had the ear of (and, according to his 1914 *New York Times* obit, provided the "brains" for) the last two rulers.[18] Meshchersky likened himself to Oscar Wilde, and he was accordingly lampooned by the religious philosopher Vladimir Solovyov as a "shameless sodomite."[19] Meantime, he told Alexander III what he wanted to hear: that the ruler of Russia was accountable to God alone and was neither to be judged by the people nor to succumb to their baser instincts and trivial desires. The sovereign nonetheless maintained a mystical bond with the *narod*; his judgment, in this convenient formulation, reflected at once the will of God and the will of the people. Meshchersky propagated these ideas in the conservative, antireform newspaper *Grazhdanin*, and added to them a threat: decisions made by the tsar, being a reflection of divine and popular will, were not to be blasphemed, tempered, or otherwise interfered with by government ministers.

Of his other court contacts, Tchaikovsky's relationship with Grand Prince Konstantin Konstantinovich (Konstantin Romanov, K. R. in print) is the best documented, albeit without much mention of the role K. R.'s father had earlier played in Tchaikovsky's career. (The father, Konstantin Nikolayevich Romanov, was the brother of Tsar Alexander III and, among his ceremonial duties, the president of the IRMS. He was one of Tchaikovsky's earliest champions and certainly his most august benefactor and protector. Konstantin Nikolayevich endorsed the premieres of the Second Symphony in both the 1872–73 and 1879–80 versions, along with the operas *Vakula the Smith* and *The Oprichnik*, which Tchaikovsky dedicated to him in most humble gratitude.)[20]

K. R. had studied music with Laroche after piano and cello lessons as a child. The Romanovs awarded their children medals and honors—often for no reason whatsoever, but sometimes in anticipation of future glory. Obliged to serve the empire, K. R. distinguished himself as a naval officer by surviving an attack on his frigate during the Russo-Turkish War of the late 1870s. He returned to

St. Petersburg and reduced his official duties, dedicating himself to his love of writing, publishing poems (much less distinguished than Romanov lore would have us believe), plays, and "a studious but uninspired translation of *Hamlet* [published after Tchaikovsky's death, in 1899] accompanied by two highly praised volumes of annotations, sources, and background materials pertaining to the play."[21] Later in 1889, K. R. became president of the Imperial Academy of Sciences in St. Petersburg and remained in that position until he died in his office in 1915, age fifty-six. Had he lived a couple more years his death would not have been of natural causes. During the period Tchaikovsky knew him, K. R. was a bit of a flibbertigibbet: traveling around; imagining sailing around the world with Tchaikovsky as one of his companions (Tchaikovsky was interested but recognized that the court would not permit the trip); riding in his luxurious carriage from one gala to another; enjoying the collection of art on the second floor of his residence, St. Petersburg's Marble Palace; and attending to the education of his children, of which he had eight who survived infancy. In his final years, he directed a modest portion of his gargantuan inheritance to imperial charities; founded a Pedagogical Institute for women; and, channeling Tolstoy, opened a school and a hospital in a village.[22]

K. R. recounted his first meeting with Tchaikovsky on March 19, 1880, in his diary, which gives a fair sense of his light touch in all matters personal and professional, even on painful subjects like Tchaikovsky's failed marriage:

> Those from my division assigned to [the paddle steamer] *Derzhava* were dispatched to Kronstadt today. Vasily Vereshchagin was exhibited in the concert hall of the Winter Palace, where the Tsar viewed them. I heard that he was dissatisfied by Vereshchagin's approach [as a rather unsparing painter of war scenes] and didn't grant him an audience. There was a concert for disabled veterans at the Bolshoi Theater.

I spent a lovely evening at [Tchaikovsky's sister-in law] Vera Vasilyevna Butakova's residence: she promised to introduce me to Tchaikovsky, our best composer, who had also been invited. His brother Anatole, [Alexei] Apukhtin, and [Prince Nikolay] Shcherbatov were also there.

Pyotr Ilyich Tchaikovsky looks about thirty-five years old [he was forty], although his face and graying hair give him an older appearance. He is short, rather thin, with a short beard and gentle intelligent eyes. His movements, manner of speaking, and whole appearance reveal an extremely well-bred, educated, and amiable person. He was brought up in a law school, was very unhappy in his family life, and is now exclusively engaged in music. Apukhtin is known for his exorbitant corpulence and excellent poetry, which he would never consent to publish: he remembers and recites them by heart. Vera Vasilyevna begged him to read something, anything to us; he recited the little-known "Venice." It's so good that, as he says, you fear it'll end soon. I'd dearly like to hear some more of it.

They asked me to play; I wanted to do a Tchaikovsky romance but I was embarrassed. It turns out that his brother sings; I accompanied him as he sang "A Tear Trembles," then "None But the Lonely Heart" and then a romance in B♭ minor. P. Tchaikovsky was asked to play something from his new, as yet unpublished opera *Joan of Arc*. He sat down at the piano and performed the prayer chorus. We were all in awe of the wonderful music; this is the moment when the people recognize that Joan has a prophetic gift, and she addresses the crowd, calling on them to lift up their prayer to the Lord God. The form of the composition resembles the prayer of the first act of *Lohengrin*: the voices gradually rise, all intensifying, and yet together with the orchestra reach fortissimo at the highest note. This *morceau d'ensemble* must be really good, spectacular to see on stage. After dinner Apukhtin read more verses from his composition. We parted company at two o'clock. Tchaikovsky left a most pleasant impression on me.[23]

Tchaikovsky had to be dragged to the gathering and resented being put on display. Still, after protesting and feigning panic he played along. K. R. subsequently invited him to his home, the Marble Palace, where the pair mooted the trip around the world. Subsequently, he began swapping letters with Tchaikovsky about his music, especially the Fourth Symphony. (The grand prince considered the waltz theme more "disturbing" than the polonaise.)[24] Tchaikovsky thanked him for listening, without responding to his admirer's questions about the score, and the friendship grew. The grand prince enhanced Tchaikovsky's prospects with the Imperial Theaters and helped settle a squabble with the Bolshoi about making the premiere of *Cherevichki* a benefit for the orchestral musicians, as Tchaikovsky, who rehearsed and conducted the performances, and the musicians desired.

K. R. also acted as mediator between the composer and the Russian empress, Mariya Fyodorovna. Tchaikovsky dedicated his opus *60 Romances* to her in the autumn of 1886 and enlisted a calligrapher employed by Jurgenson, Nikolay Langer, to make a beautiful, exhibition-suitable copy in her honor. It took him twelve days to do, after which Tchaikovsky inscribed it and had it bound in "bright blue velvet with blind embossing and endpapers of white waxed paper and moire finish. The frame has a corner ornament. The edge is gilded." (The quoted words come from an affectionately obsessive chronicle of the making of the score by Grigory Moiseyev.) Before surrendering it to K. R. for presenting to the empress, Tchaikovsky proofed the romances and caught several mistakes, changing, for example, the tempo of the standout "Song of the Gypsy."[25] K. R. held onto it long enough to learn the piano part of this song and three others. Another member of the imperial family sang them. Whether or not Mariya Fyodorovna did is unknown. Most likely, she placed the score on a shelf in her *bibliothèque privée* and never looked at it.[26] It's now in St. Petersburg's Hermitage Museum. The pages have turned a buttery color; the ink still looks fresh.

At Tchaikovsky's encouragement, K. R. organized an ambitious concert for himself in the palace, with amateur singers accompanied by St. Petersburg's opera orchestra. He played Mozart's D-Minor Piano Concerto on the first half of the program before a couple of hundred listeners; Mozart's *Requiem* was on the second half, as Tchaikovsky had recommended (he proposed Schumann's oratorio *Paradise and the Peri* as an alternate).[27]

K. R. was a closeted homosexual, all those children aside, and his diaries have been read against his poems and translations as evidence of conflicted feelings about his same-sex encounters in the imperial service and beyond.[28] The letters between him and Tchaikovsky could also be read as allusive, naming things without naming them. After the composer's death, K. R. oversaw Tchaikovsky's immortalization, arranging memorial concerts of the sacred pieces and maintaining, through further acts of promotion and preservation, a "posthumous dialogue" with him.[29] The grand prince could do so because he remained loyal to the last tsar, Nikolay II, even after an unwashed Siberian mystic faith healer named Grigory Rasputin established himself in the court. (His influence on the tsarina in particular was a Romanov family scandal that foretold the end of autocratic rule in Russia. Monarchist assassins ensured that Rasputin himself did not live to see that end.) K. R.'s annotated edition of Modest Tchaikovsky's three-volume biography of his brother is housed in the Library of Congress in Washington, DC, part of a transfer of books from imperial Russia after the Revolution.[30]

Tchaikovsky was now part of the matrix and would soon, in 1884, reach the zenith, fame like no other Russian composer before or after him, Professor Nikolay Rimsky-Korsakov of the St. Petersburg Conservatory included. In March of that year, the tsar conferred the Imperial Order of Saint Prince Vladimir on Tchaikovsky in recognition of his achievement and "the fair attention and favor" paid to him by the public.[31] He received a fourth-class distinction, which assigned Tchaikovsky personal as opposed to hereditary nobility for his civil service, along with a financial award (a 3,000-ruble pension, topped with another 3,000-ruble pension three years later). He traveled from Paris to St. Petersburg for the ceremony on February 23, 1884. Tchaikovsky told von Mekk that, in hindsight, he shouldn't have fretted about the encounter, though his "suffering from shyness" was "deadly terrible."[32]

He would have three operas on the Mariinsky and Bolshoi stages in the year he received the Imperial Order and would earn an amount from the directorate eclipsing his annual allowance of 6,000 rubles from von Mekk. (The 6,000 rubles was twice the amount he would earn as a pension from the *kassa* of the Ministry of the Imperial Court, which was about three times the income of an actor or dancer in the upper middle ranks of the Imperial Theaters. Nápravník earned 7,000 rubles a year as St. Petersburg's maestro.)[33] He had long been a regular on the IRMS concerts—"Tchaikovsky *again!!!*"—his detractors complained of his constant presence on the programs, for which he received trifling amounts.[34] Before his entrée into court society, he had earned 10 percent of two-thirds of box-office receipts for his operas. Afterward, with the enactment of financial reforms within the Imperial Theaters directorate, his payout was 10 percent of all box-office receipts (with small deductions). Ballets, he would learn, if *Swan Lake* hadn't already taught him, were lump-sum payments; he didn't receive royalties on them. Nor, obviously, did he earn them from works that he had sold to publishers.

He had a dependable professional relationship with the intendant of the Imperial Theaters, who neither liked Tchaikovsky as a person nor respected his eclectic musical choices but conducted himself as an official in the imperial service must, at least in public—courteously, decorously. Tchaikovsky was not always the intendant's first choice for commissions, and he didn't script Tchaikovsky's rise to fame.

The intendant was Ivan Alexandrovich Vsevolozhsky (1835–1909), a diplomat turned arts administrator turned dramatist. His uncle had been a friend of Tchaikovsky's father.[35] He spent most of his days mediating between what he considered the unseemly subterranean world of performers and the aristocrats who exploited them. He preferred French and Italian artists to Russians, indulged expensive hobbies (procuring fine European furniture that ended up on the stage), cooked, drew (he was a talented caricaturist), pottered around his dacha, groused about his health, and professed to being too clean and passionless for backstage backstabbing. Vsevolozhsky resented having to cover up scandals and suffered the accusation of playing favorites when he hired one performer over another. He engaged in vulgar frank talk with his assistant Vladimir Pogozhev, joking in his mannered French about a gay flutist who liked flutes of another sort. Vsevolozhsky hired the flutist in question because, he said, the Germanophobic, antisemitic Minister of the Court couldn't countenance the alternatives. "If the flutist is good, then I'm happy to accept him—all the more because the Minister wants there to be as few Germans and Jews as possible."[36] On another occasion, late in his tenure as Imperial Theaters intendant, he mocked a ballerina in mourning. She had draped herself in black crepe for a performance. "If she gets married," he quipped, "then doubtless it'll be to a negro."[37]

Vsevolozhsky's letters suggest that he was indifferent to Russian operas and ballets by Russian composers but heeded, as he had to, Tsar Alexander III's demand for them. Vsevolozhsky's biographer counters that he elevated Russian drama of his own volition, transforming musty potpourris into immortal classics.[38] Glorifying Russia meant, for Tchaikovsky, Vsevolozhsky, and the tsar, glorifying Alexander Pushkin. Tchaikovsky ultimately produced three Pushkin-based operas on Vsevolozhsky's watch: an expanded, imperialized *Eugene Onegin*; the Cossack drama *Mazeppa*; and *The Queen of Spades*. On K. R.'s recommendation, Tchaikovsky also contemplated an opera based on Pushkin's *The Captain's Daughter*, but not for long. Catherine the Great looms large in the story, and no one wanted any problems with the censors. Furthermore, the language of *The Captain's Daughter* needed to be converted from prose to verse, the opposite problem Tchaikovsky confronted with *Eugene Onegin*. Transforming it would take time, and the librettist would receive a third of the income (such was how opera contracts worked out). Tchaikovsky did not like to wait.

He received unsolicited advice in this matter from an admirer named Pavel Pereletsky, who read in a newspaper that Tchaikovsky was considering an opera based on *The Captain's Daughter*. Pereletsky thought the composer would be better off setting something simpler, like Ivan Turgenev's novel *On the Eve*, a romance set during the Crimean War. Tchaikovsky thanked him for writing and politely declined the suggestion. (The letter in question was long thought lost but turned up in a tobacco shop in Kyiv in 1923 and was identified by a smoker named Fyodor Zhukov. He surrendered it to the Tchaikovsky archive in Klin in 1938.)[39]

Tchaikovsky's business dealings with the Imperial Theaters extended far beyond St. Petersburg and Moscow.[40] In 1887 Tchaikovsky went to Tiflis, Georgia, to see his brother Anatole, then serving as the Tiflis district prosecutor (and about to be appointed vice-governor by the Ministry of Internal Affairs in St. Petersburg). Anatole lived in an apartment on Consular Street (now Tchaikovsky Street) with his wealthy spouse, the daughter of a Moscow industrialist and niece of the art collector Pavel Tretyakov.

The composer and his valet made an adventure of the trip, taking the train from Moscow to Nizhny-Novgorod—the setting of Tchaikovsky's opera *The Enchantress*, which he had just completed—then, as Alexander Ostrovsky had inspired him to do back in the 1860s, booking a berth on a steamer for the long trip down the Volga River to Astrakhan on the Caspian Sea. There he and Sofronov ambled the streets of the ancient Silk Road hub before taking another steamer to Baku and finally a train to Tiflis for ten days of café terraces and sulfur baths.[41] It was the composer's second visit, and he would return three more times for performances, since the Tiflis public loved him so much. The imperial Russian newspaper *Caucasus* gushed about a concert held in his imperial Russian honor: "The director's loge was reserved for Pyotr Ilyich and decorated with laurel garlands and adorned with a lyre and the dear guest's monogram. The theater was packed to the rafters and looked most festive and elegant." And so on.[42]

Tchaikovsky subsequently headed west to the Georgian spa of Borjomi (of mineral water fame), where he spent twenty-five days composing and gathering the ingredients for future scores. He also wrote to Tsar Alexander III about the sorrowful history of the Tiflis opera house. It had burned down in 1884 (giving the lie to Polonsky's claim, in a poem written to Pushkin's brother Lev, that "there are never fires in Tiflis/There is simply nothing to burn in Tiflis," and the authorities didn't mind him relighting his extinguished cigar from "flatirons").[43] The theater had been rebuilt (hence the concert in his honor) but without the "affordances" for grand operas and ballets. There weren't enough seats; it lacked a proper roof; and, because of the absence of backstage space, sets had to be stored offsite. A production of *The Maid of Orleans* in December 1886 suffered from "impossibly long intermissions."[44] The dance evenings put on by the charity society were more fun, and the summer theater comfier, but it was itself a fire trap and hardly what the magnificent tsarist hinterlands deserved.

Tchaikovsky recommended an investment of 235,000 silver rubles from the Imperial Treasury for upgrades.[45] The tsar forwarded the letter to his highly decorated commander-in-chief in the Caucasus, Prince Alexander Dondukov-Korsakov, who signed on to it. (He did so in rather hilarious fashion, going into elaborate detail about the conflicts between local and regional authorities that had left the theater unfinished. He praised the previous theater, the one that had burned down, as an "elegant" adornment to Tiflis that included space for markets and for which no expense had been spared, "based on the conviction that the Russian stage and opera, having become indispensable to all the empire's nationalities, would bring into homes and spread around a love of art, and which in turn would, no doubt, help to soften the morals of the locals.")[46] Tchaikovsky seems to have been less concerned about softening morals—taming the Caucasian savages—than opening up a new market that would serve his personal financial interests (the contracts for his operas prohibited their performance in private houses), and would also directly benefit Anatole.

The correspondence is striking for its casualness; Tchaikovsky did not pay obeisance to the Sovereign, did not grovel. And he also received a quick response, though, in truth, the completion of the theater dragged on and on. It wasn't finished until after Tchaikovsky's death.

Four accordions

Serving the court meant writing courtly music, aristocratic assortments for well-heeled listeners. It also meant operatic and balletic imperialism. Tchaikovsky rose to the challenge in eclectic fashion.

He composed his Second Orchestral Suite in 1883. It differs from the First, Third, and Fourth Suites in its digressiveness. It may be court music, but it harkens back to the pretend court of the young Peter the Great and his elaborate fantasies playing outside Moscow in Preobrazhenskoye, far from the Kremlin and the baroque lives of his older relatives. The suite opens with a movement abstractly called "Jeu de sons" with winds and strings in dialogue. The composer manipulates pitches at the edges of tonic space, flirting with illogic, challenging the rules of the harmonic game with frequent diversions. The scumbling of harmonic and tonal relationships and mixing of orchestral colors helps blur the formal outlines. Sonata form is implied but never clearly traced, for example, and the movement seems structured around small-scale repetitions.

The introduction contrasts a pair of melodic ideas somewhere between C major and C minor: the first a pastoral hymn, the second jauntier and dance-like. These general topics draw on and emerge from meanings constructed over centuries by other pieces. A web of associations suggests that perceptions are only ever shaped by experience, never pristine nor even original. An allegro exposition of sorts follows in three sections that suggest a movement to G major, the presumed dominant of the presumed home key of C major, but digresses to B minor. Next comes a fugue, or quasi fugue, involving false entries in diverse keys. The concluding move to C major is interrupted by an E-minor passage further confused by the avoidance of a conventional perfect authentic cadence. The movement might be interpreted as a quest for the familiar, a struggle to reach the safe harbor of chord and key and form, that finds shape only as a fugue—arguably the most formal form of all.

Tellingly, the fourth movement in the suite is titled "Rêves d'enfant," a child's dreams. It too creates a dialogue between that which consoles and might unsettle. (The movement is obvious fodder for Freudian exposé, which needn't be done here.) The opening has the rhythms of a bedtime story; the sound is sad and somber at first, then builds to a regal fanfare over the dominant—suggesting, perhaps, the appearance of a fairytale queen or prince to save the day. The orchestra erases the border between what musicologist Campbell Shiflett calls "the world of the story and that of the narration." The movement, Shiflett adds, switches to an E♭-minor chord far removed from the A minor/major theme of the opening. Woodwinds chase one another in a directionless soundscape. Are these racing thoughts, or the sensation of nodding off? Shiflett believes the latter: "Drowsiness takes over as the music slows and thins out."

The harp music and muted strings of the dream don't last long. Nightmares recur, statically and in variation, but dreams, especially the most pleasant ones, indulge a single sensation and end as soon as they start. Shiflett describes a wash of semitones and syncopation in the bass bringing the child back to consciousness. The dream dissolves into motivic fragments of different sorts—"wedge shapes," "pizzicato figures," semitonal displacements between triads of different modes—before the movement concludes.[47] The title of the movement is plural (*rêves*) but the child seems to have just one dream, unless Tchaikovsky is representing the dream of having a dream.

The second movement is a waltz in A major, the third a "burlesque scherzo" that calls for four accordions to be played ad libitum. Iya Nemirovskaya, an administrator with the Samara Philharmonic, credits Tchaikovsky with bringing the instrument to the world stage, taking it out of the hands of "drunken coachmen and custodians," spurring technical innovations, and encouraging other composers to follow his example (few did).[48] It was not the first time the accordion had been heard in a formal concert setting: that honor goes to Louise Reisner, whose *Thème varié très brillant pour l'accordéon . . . d'après Méthode Reisner* was performed in Paris in 1836.

The fifth movement is a baroque dance "in the style of Dargomïzhsky." The puzzling title (Dargomïzhsky was a nineteenth-century Russian realist) references something that has been lost to time: Dargomïzhsky's sketches for an opera based on Pushkin's 1828 narrative poem "Poltava." While composing his Second Orchestral Suite, Tchaikovsky had finished up and partially revised an opera on the same subject. Completing it, and facing his fears about its reception in St. Petersburg, shattered him; he was so tired that he couldn't attend the premiere of the suite on February 4, 1884, in Moscow. The conductor of that IRMS performance, the newly arrived Max Erdmannsdörfer, was inconsolably disappointed.

"Poltava"

The opera that had exhausted him was the imperialistic *Mazeppa*, loosely based on Viktor Burenin's librettistic adaptation of Pushkin's "Poltava." Burenin had followed his father by going to architecture school before relocating from Moscow to St. Petersburg in hopes of establishing himself as a writer. That he did, outrageously. He wrote novels, stories, and feuilletons insulting women, lawyers, and the "abstract moralizing" that affronted his brand of satire. He was routinely censored and hauled in for interrogation for his radicalism. When Tchaikovsky met him, Burenin was writing antisemitic screeds for *New Times*, a newspaper that had been liberal and leftist in the 1860s (hailing, for example, the Russian translation of Karl Marx's *Das Kapital*) but changed stripes in the later 1870s in support of the government's most conservative policies.[49]

Burenin conceived his "Poltava" libretto for another composer, Karl Davïdov, the director of the St. Petersburg Conservatory, who left it unfinished. (He was a spectacularly proficient cellist, and most of his music is for that instrument.) Tchaikovsky picked up the subject and redid the script, using Burenin in places but also consulting Pushkin's and Byron's Mazeppa poems. Ada Aynbinder, a Tchaikovsky biographer and the director of the Manuscript and Publication Department of the Tchaikovsky Museum and Archive, has the list of these and the other sources he consulted.

She considers the opera to be a direct musical response to the bloodshed of Tchaikovsky's time—meaning Alexander II's assassination and the Russo-Turkish conflicts. And she echoes Soviet scholarship in stressing that the husband of Tchaikovsky's sister was the son of a Ukrainian Decembrist, which might have fueled his interest in the life of a revolutionary.[50] The actual impetus, however, was the composer's namesake Michał Czajkowski (1804–96), a Cossack raised to despise Russia. He participated in the Polish uprising of 1830–31, which Tsar Nikolay I quelled, then fled to Paris, finding safety among the bedraggled survivors of the Napoleonic invasion. From there he traveled to Constantinople and fought in the Crimean War. The Polish independence movement ended any hopes of a Slavic alliance under Turkish leadership, and the sight of the corpses of hanged Jews and Christians twisting in the wind forced a reckoning. He petitioned for Russian clemency, converted to Orthodoxy, and settled in Kyiv. Through it all he wrote fiction, and Pyotr Tchaikovsky would have regularly seen Michał's name in print as the author of *Cossack Tales* (*Powieści kozackie*), *Ukrainian Women* (*Ukrainki*), and *The Strange Lives of Polish Men and Women* (*Dziwne życia Polaków i Polek*). Michał's life—not, let's be clear, Pyotr's—ended in suicide.[51]

Ivan Mazeppa was commander (hetman) of the Cossacks of the southern steppe (Zaporizhzhia). He was a real person who lived from 1639 to 1709. He wrote an overrated folk epic including these lines:

> Even the bee boasts a mother
> Whom it obeys, and no other.
> Have mercy, God, for Ukraine
> Whose sons are scattered o'er the plain.
> Some still are mired in pagan days
> Beseeching others to follow their hasty ways:
> "Our Motherland, to defend, to cherish!
> Let us not permit her to perish!"[52]

His status in legend is that of a nationalist without a nation, an Indigenous presence, a horseback renegade and/or a criminal soldier-of-fortune. His qualities as a leader, however, are ambiguous; the Cossacks lacked an organizing structure and operated more anarchically than an army. Mazeppa was elected by a Cossack *veche* (general assembly) and could be forcibly removed from his post if the collective so chose.

Mazeppa had sided with Peter the Great in several conflicts but broke from him when he learned that the Muscovy ruler sought his removal and the broader liquidation of the Zaporizhzhian host. Mazeppa entered into an alliance of mutual benefit with Peter the Great's northern antagonist, the Swedish king, Karl XII. Russian and Swedish/Cossack forces fought each other in central Ukraine (Poltava) in June 1709. Russia won quite easily, and Peter the Great's fighters pushed toward the Black Sea in an attempt (unsuccessful) to secure a warm-water port for Russia. Karl XII left the battlefield in a litter after a musket ball entered the heel of his foot and lodged behind a toe; Mazeppa and about 3,000 Zaporizhzhians accompanied him as he retreated into Ottoman terrain. Mazeppa was welcomed into the Turkish fortress of Bender (Romanian: Tighina) in modern-day Moldova. Karl XII had a pleasant cottage built for himself and played chess while recovering from the musket-ball wound. (According to Voltaire, he played avidly but lost every game because he insisted on using his king as an offensive piece.)[53] Mazeppa died suddenly in Bender in September 1709. Karl XII continued to support the Zaporizhzhian Cossacks under the leadership of Mazeppa's successor, Pylyp Orlyk.

The Soviets championed Mazeppa as an antitsarist freedom fighter, but in Tchaikovsky's telling, as well as Pushkin's, he is a cruel and lecherous old man, decades past the age of surviving being tied to a horse naked and ridden from Poland to Ukraine, as legend claims happened to him in his youth. (One can only pity the horse, who had been whipped into a state of madness during the ride, an event Tchaikovsky hints at in the fragmented overture to his opera.) The inglorious historical events Pushkin recounts were less important to Tchaikovsky (and Burenin) than the interpersonal horrors. His opera picks up in a sense where *Eugene Onegin* leaves off, with the white-haired Mazeppa wooing a girl more than fifty years younger than him. This is Mariya, the daughter of a pitiful Ukrainian noble named Kochubey, Mazeppa's former confidant. She's also, to add to the queasiness, the hetman's goddaughter. Mazeppa's plans to liberate Ukraine from Russia are, from the nineteenth-century Romanov perspective, equally perverse. When Kochubey resists those plans, Mazeppa has him tortured and beheaded, to music freighted with nonfunctional harmonies, quasi-liturgical chant, and the distant fanfares of the Poltava battle.

There's a glimpse of light. Mariya is courted by Andrey, a character of Tchaikovsky's invention. She considers running off with him but can't: she's stuck with Mazeppa. Mariya loses her mind on the battlefield, amid the snow-covered ruins of her husband's mad dreams of glory.

Work on the opera was slow and frequently interrupted. Tchaikovsky cast it in four acts, but the opera was accepted for production in three, resulting in an argument between the composer and the Imperial Theaters about royalties: he was offered 8 percent, but asked for 10, knowing that the administrators intended to stage *Mazeppa* "luxuriously. Probably all of Petersburg will come to see it."[54] Tchaikovsky first composed the most inflamed romantic music, then received a request to provide some of the battle music long in advance of the staging for a Moscow orchestral concert, which also slowed him down. The ending proved problematic: Tchaikovsky had wanted to represent Mariya going insane followed by a grand operatic horror chorus but elected instead—a brilliant decision—to end with Mariya and the dying Andrey singing an off-kilter duet. It's not a mad scene but the opposite, a sane scene, because the opera occupies a cosmos in which madness reigns.

It's the second such number in the score. The first duet, in Act I, is truly at cross-purposes. Andrey declares his love to Mariya, who describes being drawn like a magnet to the rusted Mazeppa. She pities Andrey, and he sings of Mariya's doom (or, as David Brown always prefers, "Fate").[55] The rhythms in the opening arioso section of the duet contradict one another. The two of them are not operatic lovers but find themselves in that circumstance. They sing past each other, instead of for each other. Their personalities are for others to determine, and, abstractly, they are shown to be pawns to larger forces, their wrecked romance a mirror of Ukraine's foiled struggle.

In their Act III duet, Andrey knows that it's over. He's dying. Mariya thinks that he's a child lying on the ground and sings a berceuse that morphs into a dirge. Mourning is supposed to be private and here it happens in the middle of a killing field, the perfect operatic apotheosis for an opera about the birth and death of nations.

Most lullabies, Tchaikovsky knew, have laments slipped into them: the baby falls from the treetop, cradle and all. For all the efforts in comfortable societies to sanitize it, the berceuse is an unsettling genre, with the wish for infants to sleep bound up with a fear of them not waking up.

The cast includes a small but chilling part for a torturer, Orlyk, which Tchaikovsky hoped the great, growling bass Fyodor Stravinsky (father of Igor Stravinsky) would accept for the St. Petersburg premiere (he did), and a smaller part for a drunken Cossack, though there is no such character in Pushkin.[56] Kochubey's interrogation at the start of the second act—the dungeon scene—is defined by Orlyk's chopped-up recitation and his prisoner's fuller phrases. Tchaikovsky preserves this character's dignity while infusing Orlyk's speech with sounds akin to a cracking lash. He also quotes part of the barcarolle (in distorted 4/4 time) from *The Seasons*. In opera and ballet, the genre has traditionally represented the transition from one world into another, including the realm of the dead on the far side of the River Styx—and that's unfortunately where Kochubey is headed. He declines to confess and refuses to reveal the location of his gold, leaving Mazeppa no choice but to put him away. The execution (at the end of the act) is unseen, represented by rumbling timpani and stinger chords in the brass. Usually in Russian productions, the crowd rushes towards the place of execution but then retreats in horror, arms outstretched.[57]

The drunk is stock-in-trade for nineteenth-century Russian operas. These have one, sometimes two of them stepping out of the Acts II or III crowd scenes, tankard in hand, to sing a cheerful tune with quite the opposite set of verses (the form is invariably strophic). Rimsky-Korsakov's *Legend of the Invisible City of Kitezh* includes a sorrowful, delusional drunk named Grishka, and Borodin's *Prince Igor* and Musorgsky's *Boris Godunov* match him in kind. Like holy fools, drunks tend to be truth-tellers, and Tchaikovsky's sozzled Cossack is no exception. He performs a disgusting version of a chivalrous romance, or wants to: it turns into a description of rape and murder, as boring a routine for the vicious Cossack as the beets and potatoes he boils up for dinner every night. The crowd of Ukrainian villagers doesn't know which side of the multisided conflict to root for. They only know they hate this song. And in truth, it doesn't belong in the scene; it's a bad fit. Tchaikovsky seems to be saying: this is an opera about the construction of history, and I'm going to show you how I constructed it.

Russian and Ukrainian folksongs are included in the score alongside some out-of-time chant borrowings. The execution episode is, pointedly enough, labeled a "folk scene," which is about as bleak a commentary on Russian and Ukrainian history as it gets. Mazeppa's entry is marked by a gopak (hopak) dance, a vigorous 2/4 dance primarily for men whose name derives from the verb "to hop." It originated with the Zaporizhzhian Cossacks and in Tchaikovsky's opera offers pro forma Ukrainian *couleur locale*, with no fixed choreography (the leaps, squats, kicks, and general athleticism of the dance are excluded from productions). That it introduces Mazeppa signals, perhaps, that he'll end up betraying Peter the Great for Ukrainian purposes. The rhythm of this dance follows Mazeppa around the opera, much like Russian imperial polonaise patterns accompany Peter the Great. The gopak is not, however, heard in the opera's introduction; Tchaikovsky didn't assign it broad significance. It appears in Act I, scene 1, as a standalone number (popular enough to be repeated at the premiere), then in the finale of the act when Andrey vows to destroy Mazeppa through the aid of the tsar, and finally in Act II, scene 2, as part of Mazeppa's monologue.

The rush to get the opera onto the stage caused brief confusion about the libretto. It was thought to have been published in Moscow without approval of the Moscow Censorship Committee, resulting in a flurry of panicky letters at the start of 1884 and the red-faced realization that the libretto had been vetted months before. The first edition handles Pushkin with special care, indicating, with asterisks, which lines came directly from his "Poltava" poem as opposed to those that were modified or added.[58] The Moscow premiere on February 3, 1884, preceded the St. Petersburg premiere by just three days. Each was a shocking surprise, especially to those critics who had published preview articles with plot summaries and had prepared themselves to cheer it. But it was a nightmare, and not only because of the plot. The décor was depressing, and the audience left with their ears ringing. The *Petersburg Leaflet* reviewer was nonplussed:

> To everything we've said it can be added that Mr. Tchaikovsky scored *Mazeppa* much too loudly, forgetting that the range and power of the human voice have their limits. Busy with the symphonic development of the orchestral themes, he apparently forgot that in an opera the singers are the focal point and can't compete with a mass of instruments. The libretto is beautiful and appealing, and we're certain that if Mr. Tchaikovsky had applied his great talent to the tasks presented to him more fully and deliberately, as opposed to resorting to the "horror" that defines a good half of the opera, he would have made the proper impression on the audience.[59]

The horror, however, was the point, and it had the intended impact. Though *Mazeppa* earned a quarter as much as *Eugene Onegin*, it remained in the Imperial Theaters repertoire until 1890.

Urban opera (*Eugene Onegin* again)

By this point Tchaikovsky's relationship with Vsevolozhsky had developed into a mutually beneficial creative partnership. After reading the initial reviews of *Mazeppa*, the intendant ordered the sets and costumes gussied up to ensure a successful run. The expansion of *Eugene Onegin* for the St. Petersburg stage is another case in point. The original version of the opera had been comparable in spirit to

Rousseau in *Le devin du village* (*The Village Soothsayer*, 1752). Musically, Tchaikovsky privileged natural impulses over strict codes of conduct, and pluck, to an extent, over rank and Onegin's *amour propre* (egocentrism). Nature had been a construction in Tchaikovsky's opera as it was in Rousseau's—beginning with the pastoral flute and harp music in the opening duet and continuing with laborers singing a contrapuntally sophisticated chorus (with especially beautiful undervoicing in the middle) before being commanded to sing even more happily by Tatyana.

The tsar called *Eugene Onegin* his favorite opera and wanted it on the Mariinsky stage, which resulted in a loss of the delicate Rousseauian elements in the service of dazzling spectacle.[60] The task of elaborating it fell to Vsevolozhsky, who commissioned gleaming new sets, costumes, and music for the revival on September 19, 1885. "Regarding *Onegin*, we have to do what we've been told," he grumbled to his chief assistant about the elaboration, adding that he'd written to the manager of the Imperial Theaters in Moscow, Pavel Pchelnikov, "to meet with Tchaikovsky about adding a number to the ball of the third act."[61]

The expansions might seem merely decorative, but the group scenes, and all the dances, have a dramatic function. Each contributes to the spirit or ambience of the plot while also, in places, advancing it. Tchaikovsky relies, according to Roland John Wiley, on "a network of musical associations" and a "complex substructure of keys which link all the principals with their destinies, often by means of an ironic reversal of circumstance."[62] Still, there is more to the dances than tonal symbolism; rather, their style and structure comment directly on the interactions between the principal characters and the choices that each of them must make contra their desires and what's expected of them. The Act I choral round dance is called "Across the Little Bridge" ("Uzh kak po mostu-mostochku") and is based on a summertime singing game called "Twine Round and Round, Cabbage Leaf" ("Veysya, tï veysya, kapustka").[63] The dance is of ancient pedigree, known for its gentle rustic cheerfulness, but here includes a text "telling of a potentially harmful man and an innocent girl just moments before Onegin arrives for the first time."[64] Indeed, the man is crossing that little bridge with a bludgeon.

Grounded in B♭ major, the choral round dance relies on the relentless repetition of pairs of phrases that curl around each other with slight variations like cabbage leaves; the first and second sections end with a brief move to C♭ (B) major in the orchestra and a return to the first sung phrase as the text becomes increasingly suggestive. The modulation changes the instrumentation and texture of the dance; what had been an assemblage of trills and dense sixteenth-note melismatic passages in the winds, likewise tremolo and sixteenth notes in the strings, becomes a passage of long quarter notes in the bass line (cello, bass, trombone, bassoon) and menacing descending chords in the rest of the orchestra. Thus, the C♭ (B) major detour affirms the grimmer implication of the text, while the governing B♭ major foreshadows Onegin's B♭-major rejection of Tatyana in Act I, scene 3.

Act II includes a waltz to frame Onegin's flirtation with Olga and the jealous conflict between Onegin and Lensky over Olga. This dance doesn't comprise a coherent whole; Tchaikovsky interrupts it with an episode of girls flattering a colonel and then tittering at Onegin, who turns angry with embarrassment and flirts with Olga at Lensky's expense. The waltz is a dance of desire, but here the desire is false and the music accordingly corrupted. It moves from D major to G major before shifting to the E minor of the subsequent debutante dance, the cotillion (petticoat). It has accents on the weak beats in triple meter and foreshadows, in its instability, the conflict between Lensky and Onegin, with Lensky "lament[ing] his fate in E minor before dying from Onegin's pistol shot."[65]

It's a dance of mixed metaphor, a whirling shindig that anticipates events spiraling out of control. Rapidly ascending and descending triplets alternate with extended two-measure hemiola phrases that, by definition, throw off the listener's perception of meter before an abrupt snapping back into the governing 3/4 meter. (These are the moments when, onstage, the dancers change partners.) Wiley calls G major "Onegin's key," associated loosely with Onegin's arrival in Act I, his predatory eyeing of Olga, and his callous treatment of Tatyana.[66] His invitation for her to wise up, so to speak, ends disastrously for him when she actually does wise up and, as an adult, rejects his advances. The Name Day gathering is the beginning of the destruction of Onegin's reputation within Tatyana's circle. The cotillion illustrates this, to a degree, in the abrupt jump—down a minor sixth—from the jovial dancing to the interlude with Onegin and Lensky: the natural, undulating flow of the dance is brought to a screeching halt, and then into jarringly different instrumentation and articulation.

Act III gives us a polonaise in G major. It denotes not just Tatyana's elevation to the noble ranks and her psychological maturation, but her triumph in terms of being true to herself. Lastly, and in direct response to Vsevolozhsky's request for more splendor, Tchaikovsky added an écossaise, a contredanse in an energetic duple meter traditionally performed with a double line of couples, women facing men. It wasn't easy for him to compose, though he recognized the importance of "consolidating *Onegin*'s success," as Vsevolozhsky put it to him, and so turned to Jurgenson in hopes of getting sent some sample écossaises, such as those dashed off by Franz Schubert, on which to model his own.[67] The dance is repeated in the third act, recalled in an odd way at the ball. It is wrong for the romantic situation described, and wrong in general in terms of the sequence of events at a ball. Something is seriously off: what is a French dance whose name means Scottish doing in Russia? Art overtakes realistic description to make a point. The écossaise precedes the final confrontation between Tatyana and Onegin, and it is freighted with ironic references to past events including Lensky's Name Day shaming. Onegin is now represented as the country bumpkin courting the sophisticate, a complete inversion of the opening of the opera, when he was the polished urbanite and she the child of nature.

Parody

Russian Romanticism began with the Russian defeat of Napoleon I. It was patriotic; it came with an ideology that rejected all things French, drawing instead from German and English sources. Lord George Byron had a strong influence on Russian Romanticism and inspired a colossal literature—most of it focused on the mentally damaged antiheroes of "Childe Harold's Pilgrimage" and "Don Juan." Byron himself was a source of fascination wherever his writing appeared. As Harold Bloom flamboyantly relates, Byron "bewildered and fascinated his contemporaries with a vitality overtly erotic, compounded of narcissism, snobbery, sadomasochism, incest, heterosexual sodomy, homosexuality, what you will."[68] Byron put his inner world on display, every lurid fiber of it, and Pushkin couldn't help but refer to "Childe Harold" in *Eugene Onegin*. Tchaikovsky wasn't a fan, but his one-time mentor Mily Balakirev got him thinking about Byron's poem "Manfred" and suggested more than once that he compose a piece of music about it.

The poem's subject is remorse. The antihero, a Faustian count who has exiled himself to a castle in the Bernese Alps, seeks oblivion after the suicide of his sister and presumed lover Astarte. He laments not his deeds (incest isn't a crime in Byron's world) but her absence. Manfred appeals to seven nature spirits to bring her back to life. The Prince of Earth and Air summons her ghost. Astarte looks more beautiful than ever in the afterlife. Before she disappears she casually tells Manfred that he's set to die the next day. An abbot tries to save his soul, but Manfred says he has nothing to repent.

The poem wasn't intended for the stage, but Byron recommended dramatic readings of it. Balakirev advocated turning it into a tone poem or a symphony and pitched a compositional plan to Hector Berlioz. The French composer had traveled to St. Petersburg in November 1867 to conduct a series of concerts. The visit, Berlioz's second, was lavishly financed by Grand Princess Elena Pavlovna. She hosted, and pampered, Berlioz in the Mikhaílovsky Palace. Balakirev acted as Berlioz's translator and assistant during his three months in Russia (Berlioz also visited Moscow). Berlioz was frail and sickly, barely able to conduct, never mind compose, and had to be dragged moaning and groaning out of bed and into formal attire for official events.[69] He wasn't interested in "Manfred." Many years later, in 1882, Balakirev asked Tchaikovsky if he might be interested in the project, describing the poem's representation of "broken" ideals, that left "nothing to placate the spirit beyond bitterness. Hence all the trouble of our time."[70] Tchaikovsky gently hedged. "I don't have a translation of 'Manfred' at hand, and I'd rather not give you a definite answer with respect to your program until I've read through Byron's text," he wrote to Balakirev on November 12, 1882, adding that "Manfred"

> could in all probability serve as a design for a symphonist inclined to imitate Berlioz ... To please you I might perhaps, to use your expression, *make an effort*, and squeeze out of myself a whole series of more or less interesting episodes, in which one would encounter conventionally gloomy music to reproduce Manfred's hopeless disillusionment, and a lot of effective instrumental flashes in the "Alpine fairy" scherzo, sunrise in the violins' high register, and Manfred's death with pianissimo trombones. I would be able to furnish these episodes with harmonic curiosities and piquances, and I would then be able to send all this out into the world under the sonorous title *Manfred. Symphonie d'après*, etc.[71]

Of course, Balakirev himself could have written the music—he was a composer, after all, and had in fact been approached by Vladimir Stasov to base a work on "Manfred"—but he freely admitted that the subject matter didn't sit right with him, meaning that he wasn't up to it. His muse had gone the way of Astarte.

Balakirev expanded his scenario in the fall of 1884, just after the publication of a brand-new Russian-language translation of Byron's writings.[72] He made some changes to the thematic plan and tonal scheme and sent it to Tchaikovsky again. This time, Tchaikovsky said he would seriously consider basing a symphony on it, for personal reasons: "As it happens, I'll shortly be in the Alpine mountains, where the conditions for successfully depicting Manfred in music ought to be very favorable, were it not for the fact that I am going to visit a friend who is dying"—namely Iosif Kotek.[73] The twenty-nine-year-old violinist was in end-stage tuberculosis, coughing up sputum for hours at a time, shaking and feverish. Tchaikovsky had planned to see him in January but moved the trip up to November when he learned that Kotek was close to death. Everything about the visit was horrible, Byron's gothic peaks included.

Tchaikovsky composed the *Manfred* Symphony back in Klin between April and September 1885. He expected the sprawling score to have limited appeal in Russia—a couple of performances over a couple of seasons. It was premiered on March 11, 1886, as part of an Imperial Russian Musical Society concert in memory of Nikolay Rubinstein. Cherubini's *Requiem* rounded out the program. There were just five rehearsals under Erdmannsdörfer's direction, but the symphony generated enough applause for Tchaikovsky to call it a success. The *Moscow Register*, meantime, argued for giving the orchestra another chance at it. The piece was too huge and taxing "to limit to just a single hearing."[74] The first movement was played the best; the last movement made the strongest impression. Tchaikovsky told Balakirev that, according to friends and colleagues who had attended the premiere, the music didn't sound like him; it was as if he had "covered [himself] with a mask."[75] The second performance was at a summer 1886 concert series in the St. Petersburg suburb of Pavlovsk, held in a converted ballroom and restaurant attached to the train station.

Byron was too unbridled in his writing to achieve balanced, integrated poetic designs. "Manfred" is a montage, and so too Tchaikovsky's symphony, with a broodingly protracted and self-absorbed first movement setting up three other movements. These parody Berlioz. The initial reservations he had about imitating the French Romantic composer became the creative spark. He cleaned up Berlioz's voice-leading and harmonic syntax, imitated his orchestration, and made better use of fixed ideas (*idées fixes*) than Berlioz ever could—by tucking one of them inside the other and inside another one yet, so that the double of the original is itself doubled. Throughout, Tchaikovsky also referenced Schumann's *Manfred Overture* as well as Beethoven's *Eroica*, Franz Liszt's *Faust*, Chernomor's beard-tossing March from Glinka's *Ruslan and Lyudmila*, and the love theme from his own *Swan Lake*. Lest anyone think Byron's poem is a tragedy, Tchaikovsky brings out the comedy.

Tchaikovsky relies on a style—"ombra"—borrowed from operas about witches, wizards, and black magic. It involves plagal cadences, Neapolitan sixths, portentous dotted rhythms, syncopations, chromatic displacements, the Phrygian mode, sudden dynamic contrasts, and deceptive cadences. Phrases are asymmetrical, and larger formal designs imbalanced.[76] The *Manfred* Symphony's first movement has been interpreted as a "failed" sonata form, meaning that the recapitulation is truncated, excluding half of the material of the exposition and anything resembling a development.[77] Had it had these components the form might have been judged a success, in which case it would have failed the program. The music represents what Balakirev's narrative tells us it's representing: Manfred's tormented aimlessness, expressed in two fixed ideas followed by a third. The first, in an ambiguous minor mode heading to B, seems to sink before being dragged down (the dialogue between the bass clarinet and bassoons is interrupted by slashing chords in the strings); the second pushes a rock up the hill in unison strings with flutes in their lowest register. Later they'll sound in counterpoint with a third theme, in D major, the double of the double, representing that part of Manfred's consciousness inhabited by Astarte. Neither the exposition nor the recapitulation of the structure comes to a firm halt. The thematic material suffers its own incompleteness.

Movement 2, described in the manuscript as "The Alpine Fairy Appear[ing] to Manfred beneath the Rainbow of a Waterfall," relates to the queen of dreams (*reine Mab*) scherzo in Berlioz's *Romeo and Juliet* choral symphony. Skittering strings and hopping flutes, cascades of sixteenths, incongruous intervallic leaps, and digressions of fleet counterpoint establish an atmosphere so carefree as to exclude melody—until, that is, Manfred appears, blocking out the sun and spoiling the fun. Much of the movement was "insipid," César Cui grumbled in an otherwise generous (for him) review, but the music of the end, narrating the fairy's escape, was of "ravishing refinement."[78] Movement 3, "Pastoral: An image of the simple, free and peaceful life of the mountain folk," begins and ends with a 6/8 siciliana in B major followed by a shift to A minor, parallel fifths, and a hunting-horn call. For Cui, Manfred's entrance in the middle of the movement made "a strong impact"; "is it not depicting his rescue when he intends to throw himself into the abyss? The decline of his strength is graphically portrayed by the gradually clearing harmonic progressions—up to the sustained C, in the woodwinds."[79]

The fourth movement—a bacchanalia becoming a ghost scene and an apotheosis—repurposes passages from Berlioz's *Harold in Italy* and the *Fantastic Symphony* witches' orgy (an episode that has no point of reference in Byron's poem). The music turns Spanish exotic, as though the witches have been replaced by *Carmen*'s gypsies and their proudly punctuating tambourines. Astarte's midpoint apparition is richly scored in the strings and woodwinds in Db, a half step below her sickly seductive music in movement 1. ("Can this be death?" Manfred asks in the poem; "There's bloom upon the cheek.") Tchaikovsky moves into a burlesque fugato portraying the swarm of demons attacking Manfred before the Dies Irae and the concluding B-major chorale with harmonium.

Supposedly, this movement is about death and transfiguration, but its liveliness delighted the audience at the Moscow premiere. The music is morbid with a madcap analgesic. It's also triply self-indulgent, Byron's and Berlioz's personalities sifted through Tchaikovsky's.

Disenchantment

He turned deadly serious after these exercises, composing an opera about an abused, misunderstood woman. Tchaikovsky tried to elevate her into a diva for all time, transcending her condition through the power of her voice, but the clogged libretto wouldn't let him. He could only mourn her plight and condemn her abuser.

The opera is *The Enchantress*. It flopped, or seemed to—there were several performances, just not enough to convince Tchaikovsky that the significant effort he had put into the score had been appreciated or understood. Probably it hadn't. He conducted four performances at the Mariinsky, after which Nápravník (who had been unwell) took over. The latter noted the swift decline in interest in the opera, recording the following in his journal on October 20, 1887: "Premiere of *The Enchantress*. The composer, one of the public's favorites, was warmly received. The artists of the Russian opera presented him with a silver wreath. Success over time is expected." But, Nápravník amended the entry, "This expectation wasn't justified." After the second performance on October 23, and owing to an illness in the cast, *The Enchantress* was replaced by *A Life for the Tsar*.

It returned to the stage on November 2 before a full house. "Might it be a success?" Nápravník asked himself. The tsar and tsarina attended a performance on November 13, after which there were two additional performances at the Mariinsky, both "poorly" attended. *Eugene Onegin*, meantime, continued to garner acclaim, and the premiere of Tchaikovsky's "Mozartiana" Orchestral Suite was lauded. *The Enchantress* was seen four times at the Mariinsky in the fall of 1889, after which the sets and costumes were put on the train to Moscow for a Bolshoi run, which was not a run at all but just one performance, on February 2, 1890.[80] It was at best half-rehearsed, since the singers had been told that it would be performed at the Bolshoi the following season, not slotted into a free week in the schedule of the current one. Getting it on the Moscow stage was a Sisyphean labor, like "pounding water in a mortar," according to Nikolay Kashkin, and no one was satisfied with the result. When the Bolshoi closed for Lent, *The Enchantress* was pulled from the repertoire just as suddenly as it had been added. Kashkin spun the cancellation as a "postponement until the opera can be performed as it should be."[81]

The subject came from a briefly popular play by Ippolit Shpazhinsky (1848–1917) called *The Enchantress* (*Charodeyka*, 1884), which Tchaikovsky didn't see but his brother did. Modest was struck by one of the love scenes and thought Pyotr would be as well. Tales of the people—peasant dramas spoken in arcane jargon—remained in vogue, and Tchaikovsky seriously considered setting a legend from the Novgorod cycle called *Sadko the Rich Trader* (Rimsky-Korsakov did instead, the first of several instances of him following in Tchaikovsky's footsteps and trying to best him). Tchaikovsky was also attracted to a legend, from another ancient port town with a similar name, Nizhny-Novgorod, about a brave girl who defends a fortress tower from invading Tatars—killing ten of them with a yoke (wooden harness) as they scale the walls before losing her life. When his proposed collaborators on these projects fell silent, *The Enchantress* became his choice, with Shpazhinsky eagerly agreeing to produce the libretto for a generous cut of the opera's proceeds.

Tchaikovsky purchased a copy of Shpazhinsky's play in January of 1885, began the first act in September, and finished a draft in December. The second act was drafted two months later. The third act took longer, and the fourth wasn't done until August 1886. He feared the opera had become too long but made it longer. The Mariinsky needed a piano score from him for rehearsals; he finished it in February 1887, then turned to orchestration. In all, it took three years of agonized work, second-guessing, anxieties, and extreme mental pressure. He adjusted the score during the rehearsals and didn't finalize the orchestration until he could hear the vocal-orchestral blend.

It's set in the late fifteenth century in Kanavino, the oldest part of Nizhny-Novgorod and the scene of some of the major events in the history of Rus and the Tsardom of Muscovy into the Time of Troubles. The name of the district presumably derives from the Russian word for ditch, *kanava*, and refers either to a moat or to the spirit-filled rivers (the Volga and the Oka), winding around the Nizhny-Novgorod hillfort and connecting central Russia to the peripheries. The *Kanavskaya legenda* centers on the tragic life and death of Kuma, the "godmother" (keeper) of an inn (her Tchaikovsky antecedent is Vakula the Smith's badly treated mother Solokha). The expression "Kuma, vina!" ("Mother, some wine!") is still sometimes heard there, and an amusing book of Kuma cocktail recipes has been published.[82] Inns have important roles in Russian nationalist operas: There's one in *Boris Godunov*, on the Lithuanian border, and Tchaikovsky might have been thinking of *The Enchantress* as his version of Musorgsky's later opera *Khovanshchina*, about the back-stabbing, corruption, and lethal intrigues that convinced Peter the Great to abandon Moscow for a fortress confiscated from the Swedes that would become the imperial Russian capital of St. Petersburg. The inns of the fifteenth century were odorous bordellos where scandal spread like plague. Those hollering for the wine told tales, and innkeepers became the subject of some of them. The heroine of the *Kanavskaya legenda* can help you make a fortune; she can also cost you your life. She doesn't just encourage drunkenness: she's a marriage-wrecking sorceress who needs to be killed—or at least returned to the fetid, slow-moving river from which she emerged.

Two faiths operated in fifteenth-century Russia, as they did before and after. One was pagan, the other Christian. In rural places, the appearance of priests promising hell and damnation frightened people who had otherwise lived in concord with the spirit world. The devil in *Vakula the Smith* is not a devil in the European Romantic sense but a house spirit, the *domovoy* who lives in the glowing recesses of the chimney. Such figures are benevolent and can be genuinely useful: sewing, sweeping, healing the sick, keeping the scarier forest spirits outside. After priests started chasing house spirits away, the chores piled up. (Some people for this reason rebelled against the arrival of Orthodoxy by fleeing into the forests or attacking hierarchs.) Christians feared these spirits, but pagans did not, except for one of them: the river spirit, a dangerous seductress (= enchantress) who uses her emerald-green tresses to pull unsuspecting men into the deep.

Such is the court's, and church's, perception of the innkeeper in Tchaikovsky's opera—that of a river siren, the wicked witch of the deep. The "enchantress" is none of that. She's a fetching widow both beloved and protected by the men swilling the pints. No one knows what happened to Kuma's husband and no one asks. Like Bizet's Carmen, like the tragic, tuberculosis-suffering heroine of Verdi's *Traviata*, Kuma takes the occasional lover. Those men she spurns spread gossip about her, and the ruling prince of the Nizhny region decides to investigate the purported nest of sedition where Sodom reigns. He falls instantly in love with her as he knew that he would. Kuma pours him wine; he tosses his ring into a goblet as a gift, to the shock and horror of the old men and priests in his retinue. They sing a bizarrely protracted chorus about the ring, which is a pretty object but ultimately a worthless one. The chorus is full of portentous sounds, with a thickly contrapuntal texture, dissonant harmonies, and a lot of repetition. Musically, it's a perversion, and so is the situation: the princes and priests of Nizhny-Novgorod desire Kuma, and they can't deal with the fact of that desire and condemn her for it. It's the Madonna–whore complex, fifteenth-century edition. The prince drinks more wine; minstrels arrive.

Act II opens with a chorus of seamstresses. They sing of the bright day that'll soon be marred by grief and anger. And so it is. The princess learns about her husband's infatuation with Kuma from a meddling deacon. She's disgusted but not surprised. He's a prince after all, nakedly ambitious and ambitiously naked. He has had several other wives and taken other mistresses from inside and outside of Muscovy. Kuma is just his latest acquisition, and the fact that she wants nothing to do with him won't stop him—he'll just kill her if she resists. When the princess confronts her husband about his dalliance with the innkeeper, he threatens to put her in a convent.

The prince is the problem; the princess knows that but tells her son that Kuma is in fact the problem and needs to be done away with. He promises to do so, tidily, but he too falls in love with her, and she with him. They express their feelings near the end of Act III, a rare moment of positivity and the opera's first true duet. But neither the feeling nor the melodicism lasts. Act IV is suffused with overblown, dissonant, metrically displaced, wildly accelerated brass fanfares. Some of the clamor is storm music, the rest a representation of the radical dysfunction of the court. Kuma dies (by poison) in the arms of her lover, the princeling, just as they were about to elope down the Volga. The prince kills his son thinking that he is responsible for the poisoning rather than the princess (and the wizard she has enlisted for the dark deed). The truth causes the prince to lose his mind. The curtain comes down after he falls unconscious to the ground.

Tchaikovsky told Shpazhinsky that the libretto had to be much shorter than the play, so some of the chatter was excised and the opera reduced from five acts to four for the health of the cast (as per the joke: "What killed the soprano?" "The fifth act"). Still, and as all the reviewers agreed, *The Enchantress* would have benefited from deeper cuts and more focus on the main characters—including the deacon.[83] Embellishing the plot are a ludicrous array of churchmen, gardeners, hunters (with hounds), laborers, minstrels, pugilists, serfs, traders, and vagabonds in diverse attire—all of which made staging the opera a nightmare for the Mariinsky and enhanced the criticism.[84] Shpazhinsky was used to it, less so Tchaikovsky, and he bristled at the accusations of melodramatic pretentiousness in his quite earnest effort to represent dysfunctional relationships and feudal rot.

The princeling wants to escape his father and the constraints of his royal title, and Kuma wants to be able to follow her heart without being branded a witch or confined in a convent or a terem. The princess wants them all out of her sight.

Like *Eugene Onegin*, *The Enchantress* had a Soviet-era, socialist realist champion, the musicologist and composer Boris Asafyev, who published an analysis of the opera in 1943.[85] Asafyev sought to make amends for the unjust "failure" of the opera in St. Petersburg and Moscow, which forced it into "semi-exile" in Tiflis, Georgia (there it was successfully performed under the baton of Mikhaíl Ippolitov-Ivanov, a student of Rimsky-Korsakov's running the local music school).[86] Fault for the opera's swift removal from the professional stage lay with the "stupid," "deaf," and "condescending" reviewers of the premiere. Fault also lay with Tchaikovsky's colleagues, who altogether avoided talking about *The Enchantress* in his presence and failed to defend him against the critics. The experience left Tchaikovsky feeling alienated and paradoxically "homesick," despite being totally at home in St. Petersburg. His initial impulse to dedicate the opera to the tsar seemed naïve. He had become like his opera's heroine—stuck in a bad place in a bad time. His music had become ever more enchanting, clearer, brighter, and yet was increasingly misunderstood.

The opera is driven by rhythmic ideas that recur like catchphrases, proverbs, "epithets." Asafyev notes the constant leaps of a fourth followed by a descent of a second—it's the first thing heard in the introduction—with the pattern sometimes reversed. It's present in the cantilena episodes, the romances, the inserted songs, and the opera's other "musical dialects." Corrupting the pattern, turning the fourth into a tritone, signals the "dark kingdom" of the "devil's pranks"—comparable to *Mazeppa*'s diabolical gopak. Asafyev asserts Tchaikovsky's post-Reform interest in representing the liberated "Russian female psyche" in its increasing radiance. Kuma's singing grows in power as the opera unfolds, even though his opera is set in the nightmarish context of folktales like "The Mayoress," which ends with the heroine beaten to a pulp for exceeding her station, getting too big for her britches. The core of Asafyev's analysis concerns Tchaikovsky's allegorizing of the river as the female genus:

> I think Tchaikovsky was captivated by the fact that the plot of *The Enchantress* takes place and culminates on a great Russian river, analogous to his imagination finding stimulus in Russia's wayward course. The movement of the Volga and the different perspectives the grand expanse provides became the central, symphonically developed theme of the opera and stimulus for his imagination. It's no wonder that the introduction to *The Enchantress* unfolds from the melodic kernel of the arioso "Look out from Nizhny," which embodies the magnificent beauty of the primordial expanse, a beauty that cannot be obscured by the predacious intrusion of human passions. "The great river" is a theme, and it is accompanied by another clear, broad expanse— that of Kuma's love, the spiritual world of the Russian goddess.

The arioso in question, which Kuma is asked to sing by a drinker, relies on infinitives, a convention in Russian poetic language for representing a wish:

> Глянуть с Нижнего, со крутой горы
> На кормилицу Волгу-матушку,
> Где в желтых песках, в зеленых лугах
> Обнялась она с Окой сестрой,
> Стариков, попов—позабудешь всё!
> Что за ширь кругом! . . . Конца—краю нет! . . .
> Конца—краю нет!
> И засмотришься, залюбуешься,
> И в самой тебе та же ширь-простор,
> Мне бы птицею вольной туда лететь,
> Во раздолье то душа просится,

Во раздолье то душа просится!
И в самой тебе та же ширь-простор,
Птицею вольною полететь туда,
Душа просится!

Look out from Nizhny, from the steep mountain
Upon our wetnurse, Mother Volga,
Where in the yellow sands, the green meadows
She embraced her sister, the Oka,
Just take a look and you will forget the old men, the priests—
  everything!
What an expanse you'll see all around! . . . There's no end to it,
  no limit! . . .
No end, no limit!
And you will lose yourself in contemplation and admiration,
Of this great space,
How I would want to fly there if I were a free bird,
The soul asks to be in the open expanse,
The soul asks to be in the open expanse!
Lose yourself in this great space,
Fly there like a free bird
The soul is begging you so!

The music is modal, avoiding the leading tone and insisting on plagal
cadences; the harmonic pattern and the melodic pattern are simulacra,
mirroring each other. The slight swells in the dynamic in the first
section increase in the second and third sections. Harp arpeggios
imitate waves, flowing up and down and all around the voice. The
singer is one with nature, her voice blended into the accompaniment; in
the strummed middle section she sings of the souls of others becoming
one with nature. "In contemplation," both the "inside" and the "outside"
of the music open up: Tchaikovsky introduces thicker harmonies,
seventh chords instead of floating first- and second-inversion triads,

and he expands the register. The arioso concludes with a fortissimo E♭ (the lowered seventh degree of F) that moves up to the tonic with a decrease in volume to a piano dynamic. The final pitch, another F, is sung an octave lower and sinks back into the accompaniment.

She's in the stratosphere here, but the other characters are firmly grounded, actually buried in the ground, as expressed in the final scene and the final chorus, following the princeling's murder.

Холопы

Не змея взвилась,
А булатный нож!
Он не наземь пал,
А на белу грудь!

(Зашумел ветер. Молния и в отдалении гул грома. Княжича поднимают и медленно уносят по оврагу к лодкам. Около Княгини, лишившейся чувств, остаются трое из холопов.)

Хор

Рассадить ли беду во тёмном лесу,
Все посохнут древа в нём кудрявые;
Нам спустить ли беду во быстру реку,
Загрузить ли её во озёрышке,
Заболотеет вся быстра реченька,
Заволочет травой всё озёрышко.
Знать нигде той беде нету местечка,
Нету местечка!

Serfs

A snake hasn't bit into him
But a steel knife!
He fell not onto the ground
But onto his white chest!

(The wind rustles. Lightning and in the distance the rumble of thunder. They lift the princeling and slowly carry him along the ravine to the boats. Three of the serfs remain near the princess, who has lost consciousness.)

Chorus
If you bury this grief in a dark forest,
All the leaves of the trees will curl and dry up;
If we take this grief to a fast river,
Or sink it in the little lake,
The entire quick-flowing river will become a swamp,
The entire surface of the lake will be overgrown.
Know that there is no tiny place anywhere to be found for
   this grief,
There's no place!

The chorus is framed by chromatic storm music; trees have been pulled out of the ground by their roots. The singers sound as if from the soil themselves, repeating monotonous eighths. The lowest line is a sub-bass, assigned an A♭ so sunken as to be on the growling edge of audibility, anchoring chords of parallel fifths and octaves. The first phrase moves from iv 6/3, i, iv 6/3, i, i 6/3, ii°7/5, i 6/3; the others are comparable, nothing really changes. The hairpin dynamics, shifts from measures in 6/8 to 9/8, and the isolated string and flute sounds combine to represent dying sighs. The sapping energy of the diminuendo describes leaves drying up, while arpeggios in the accompaniment follow them down to drown the horror in the lake. The final lines, insisting that there is no place to inter grief, are recited a cappella. If you are dead, you can certainly be buried: there are rituals for that, often featuring choral music. But if you've already been buried you cannot be interred. Now Kuma, who had alone existed above the loam, is dead as well.

   Asafyev notes the absence of time- and place-specific sounds in the opera. The music isn't of the fifteenth century, for the simple reason that that music isn't preserved, or doesn't seem to be (ancient music is ancient music, and nothing more specific than that). Nor does he try to manufacture an old-fashioned sound to match the old-fashioned libretto. There are few folksong allusions, Asafyev continues, excluding the use in the fourth act of "Seryozha the Shepherd Lad" ("Seryozha pastushok") as an "intonational slogan" that represents separation, the loss of one's home.[87]

Asafyev wrote from a sociological perspective that differed from the psychological realism practiced by Tchaikovsky in his mature operas. Asafyev couldn't go back in time to 1888 to console the composer about *The Enchantress*. That came instead from Shpazhinsky's wife Yulya, a pianist and amateur writer who communicated with Tchaikovsky much like von Mekk did—praising his music to the skies in a sentimental mode. He was embarrassed by her flattery but enjoyed it.

In time she revealed that her marriage had ended. Her playwright husband abandoned her and their children, and Yulya ended up living far from St. Petersburg in Sevastopol. Tchaikovsky supported her morally though reservedly through the nastiness of the separation, offering counsel in the form of paraphrases from Tolstoy, while also, inter alia, offering his thoughts on why *The Enchantress* didn't engage the public and his fears that his next opera, *The Queen of Spades*, might also have a short life on the stage. As ever, he was of mixed minds about his achievements. He didn't like *The Enchantress* but he liked it; the libretto was bad but good.

"Though it pains me, let me tell you briefly about *The Enchantress*," he wrote to Yulya (before her crisis) on October 28, 1887:

I was always very pleased with the attitude of the performers and the management towards me in rehearsal. So too with the performances, with the exception of [Emiliya] Pavlovskaya, who was entrusted with the lead role in recognition of her service but who has completely lost her voice ... I[ppolit] V[asilyevich] turned up just for the dress rehearsal. The tenor [assigned the part of the princeling], [Mikhaíl] Vasiliyev, was unwell and sang with only a quarter of his voice and didn't act. I[ppolit] V[asilyevich] despaired, but on the other hand he was quite pleased with the other performers, especially [Ivan] Melnikov [as the prince] and [the bass Fyodor] Stravinsky [as the deacon]. He even liked Pavlovskaya's acting.

On the day of the performance, I was very nervous as one would expect. When I appeared at the podium, I was greeted with friendly applause. The first act didn't go well. Pavlovskaya took it into her head to change her headwear and was late with an entrance, which caused confusion, bewilderment, and I had to stop the orchestra. Fortunately, [the bass Mikhaíl] Koryakin [in the role of a street fighter] prompted her with pitches and the words that went with them and everything came together again. After the first act, the performers presented me with a silver wreath. The second act went very well; in the third, Pavlovskaya overacted and sang very distastefully and was poorly received. I liked most of the fourth and the storm with Melnikov's excellent acting made a strong impression. The second performance was smoother and cleaner, but less warmly received, except for the end. The third was supposed to take place yesterday, but because of [Mariya] Sionitskaya's illness (who sings the part of Kuma much better than Pavlovskaya) it had to be postponed.

I'd say that in general, my kind Yulya Petrovna, *The Enchantress* isn't much liked and the fault lies both with me and, chiefly, Ip[polit] Vas[ilyevich]. He knows the stage very well, but he has not yet adapted himself to operatic requirements. He uses too many words; there's too much talking over the music. No matter how much I abbreviated his text, no matter the number of cuts I had to make, all the scenes turned out to be too long. But again, a lot of this is my fault. I'm not down about it and think that this is an opera that just needs getting used to; it'll eventually establish itself in the repertoire once the public actually listens to it. (Don't tell I[ppolit] Vas[ilyevich] my opinion about the lack of success; I haven't told this to anyone except you and don't want to upset him.)[88]

Years later, after the opera's disappearance from the stage—it never did establish itself in the repertoire—he told Yulya that he "was convinced that the libretto of *The Enchantress* was delightful, that my music was worthy of it, but the opera failed in the most despicable fashion."[89]

XXX

Tchaikovsky beat a swift retreat into orchestral composition, highlighted by his Fifth Symphony, composed between May and August of 1888 in a house he rented outside of Moscow in the village of Frolovskoye. It was a pleasant place to be until the owner decided to chop down the surrounding woods, ruining the view and forcing him to move.

It was and is a popular work and, like Tchaikovsky's Sixth Symphony, it came with a question that no one could answer in 1888 and certainly no one can answer now: Is there a program or isn't there? Did he change his mind? Does it matter? Is the mysterious XXX he jotted down a reference to a boy, a girl, or the godmother of an inn in fifteenth-century Nizhny-Novgorod? The dedication doesn't help: Tchaikovsky considered honoring Edvard Grieg with the dedication before giving it to Theodor Avé-Lallemant, who was Hamburg's version of Nikolay Rubinstein, dominant in the local music scene. Tchaikovsky met both of them on an 1888 tour abroad, explaining his preference of Grieg to Brahms in an autobiographical article. He enjoyed Avé-Lallemant's company and appreciated his invitation to live in Hamburg.[90]

The speculation centers on a confessional note that Tchaikovsky jotted down for a possible program that, it seems, he decided not to pursue: "Intr[oduction]. Total submission before fate, or, what amounts to the same thing, the inscrutable designs of Providence. Allegro. 1) Murmurs, doubts, laments, reproaches against . . . XXX; 2) Shall I cast myself into the embrace of *faith*??? A wonderful program, if only it can be fulfilled."[91] Tchaikovsky's reference to faith would seem to exclude an erotic or sexual focus, but that hasn't stopped musicologists from interpreting it as a confession. He might be fleeing his taboo lifestyle for the church. "Whether or not XXX represents an actual person," biographer John Warrack writes, "it seems certain that he is referring to [Tchaikovsky's] central emotional problem, his homosexuality . . . 'Complete resignation' suggests that he had come to terms with his nature, that Fate is no longer something to be struggled against nor even (in spite of what he says) to be regarded in quite the same light as Providence."[92] Another thing that "seems certain," however, is the disconnect between Tchaikovsky's scrap of a nonprogram and the music of the symphony: three of the four movements are dances, and nothing in the symphony sounds like the sketches that he produced for XXX. Alas, even those scholars who rightly reject the homosexual-angst agenda still entertain the idea of so much fate and so little time. Donald Seibert claims that the symphony concerns a triumph over fate, or at least its bypassing, leading us to a "Russian festive" finale.[93] For Timothy Jackson, the most contentiously invested commentator of the bunch, Tchaikovsky's homosexuality made him an "outcast," and anyone with evidence to the contrary is in denial—despite all evidence to the contrary. To prove his salacious claims about Tchaikovsky's Fourth, Fifth, and Sixth Symphonies, Jackson cites other scholars' salacious claims.[94]

Dylan Principi has considered these and other imaginings and admirably analyzed the score, focusing on the sound that sticks in the ear the most, namely the motto theme.[95] It does what motto themes do—it recurs, in different places, usually unannounced, and takes on the role of spoilsport, homewrecker, and party crasher. The motto theme is heard in E minor at the start of the symphony and

E major at the end, with something of both in between: it's somber and ominous in the low clarinets before becoming balefully triumphant in the high brasses. Following its first appearance, Principi observes, Tchaikovsky inflates the register with a half-diminished chord spread over the interval of a nineteenth, the kind of maximalism one encounters in Mahler, and then reduces it to a tenth, draining the tension, soothing raw nerves. Principi interprets the use of plagal cadences (there are a lot of them) as a kind of supplication—perhaps this is Tchaikovsky's embrace of faith, or perhaps the opposite: the renunciation, or abandonment, of faith. All of this happens before the first subject of the first movement is introduced. There's an attitudinal resemblance between the motto and this first subject, suggesting an interest on Tchaikovsky's part in integrating musical ideas more than he likes to do. Listen closely to the strange developmental passages: the Fifth Symphony resents having to behave like other symphonies.

The motto appears twice in the second movement, the first time awkwardly, the second time dreadfully as an act of violence against the movement's romantic theme. Imagine a tranquil ending to a beautiful evening interrupted by a former lover. The mood is ruined, the music damaged: it struggles to remain diatonic. Tchaikovsky detours into an unnatural, artificial octatonic before ending with an earsplitting half-diminished chord that makes the return of the first theme disconcerting.

Of course, we're not done: The motto sounds again in the bassoon at the end of the third movement, just a single time, but in a new key (from A major to the flat submediant of F) and meter. The triple meter of the waltz is distorted by the duple of the motto. And in the fourth movement, the motto is heard several times, suffusing the musical space. Rather than destabilizing the surrounding music, however, it is itself unsettled, pushed into different keys through V-I and IV-I cadences with the brasses thundering in unison in C major. Principi points out the presence in the finale of French overture coup d'archet playing, likewise a high-minded polyphonic style, another waltz, and a processional. It's not quite a highlight reel from the first three movements, because some of these ideas haven't been heard before.[96]

What's it about? Romance? No, not really. There's too much else going on, including funeral and battle sounds and the triumphant-transcendent clichés of German Romanticism. Wiley also invites us to hear a connection between the rhythm of the motto and the pacing of the words in the "Paschal troparion" (Easter hymn) "Christ is risen."[97] Alexander Poznansky thinks the Fifth Symphony might have something to do with the death in 1887 of Nikolay Kondratyev, a gentleman of leisure trained as a lawyer whom Tchaikovsky had long known; the composer had often stayed at Kondratyev's estate in Kharkiv, Ukraine, and the two traveled together. Getting to Kharkiv from Moscow meant long train and carriage rides. Tchaikovsky's most frequently told anecdote concerned the time he missed a connection in central Ukraine and spent a night of terror in an inn with rats in the beds and the walls.[98] They scampered everywhere, threatening him with typhus. He didn't have anyone to help beat them back.

Kondratyev's daughter Nadezhda wrote about her father's friendship with the composer, going into quirky detail about the kind of food Tchaikovsky liked to eat—asparagus! Pineapples from the family greenhouse!—and all the fun they all had when he visited. She recalls her father as a spendthrift and a gadabout who believed that life should be a celebration.[99] He died of nephritis (kidney failure) in Aachen, where he had traveled hoping against hope for the thermal springs to cure him. Tchaikovsky spent several weeks with him there; seeing Kondratyev writhing in agony, swollen and feverish and hopelessly untreatable, gutted him.[100]

The reviews of the Fifth Symphony were mediocre but mattered to him less than ever. Newspapers proliferated in the second half of the nineteenth century and after the success of *Eugene Onegin*,

Tchaikovsky received ever greater attention in St. Petersburg's, Moscow's, Kyiv's, Odesa's, and Tiflis's newspapers. Critics also presented their thoughts on his output in pedagogically focused magazines like *Bayan* (Accordion). The tone can be tough; reviewers considered it their task to advise, not advertise. Unfortunately, they didn't always have the time to reflect on what they had heard in the concert hall or theater. The harshest, most reactionary writers concealed their identities in pseudonyms or the initials of pseudonyms or didn't sign their columns at all. (One of Tchaikovsky's crustier antagonists signed his columns "Old Musician," another chose "Humble Observer," and a third mocked himself as the "Unmusical Reviewer.") Tchaikovsky was an established brand; he generally disliked the press and advised others to dislike the press too. That he had once written tough music reviews himself didn't temper his feelings about the hundreds of articles written about him during his lifetime. Perhaps he took comfort in Cui softening his tone over time, or Laroche devoting four long articles to *Eugene Onegin*. Perhaps he didn't care; he gave few interviews.

The Fifth Symphony motto was misheard by the writer for *Nouvelliste* as self-indulgent self-repetition rather than a unifying device. He liked the first and second movements, loved the third, and hated the fourth. It seemed incoherent, with a "protestant chorale" attached to a "theme in a Russian style" over too much brass.[101] Tchaikovsky was advised to reconsider the orchestration. He didn't. The reviewer for *Petersburg Leaflet* focused on the "lyrical theme," throbbing "syncopations," and "beautiful growth of flowing, majestic sounds" of the second movement. The horn performs a solo over a bed of strings, the clarinet provides solace in counterpoint, and then the English horn takes over with the horn in abeyance. It's wonderful; nothing needed to change. The other movements, in contrast, were too thickly scored and at the same time too "waltzy." Perhaps the success of the dances in *Eugene Onegin* had gone to Tchaikovsky's head? Then a nastier swipe: "Tchaikovsky's previous thematic expressiveness is nowhere to be found in the Fifth Symphony. Instead, there's an effort to forge new, original 'combinations' when repeating old, long familiar themes, likewise a desire to give his music more, as it were, 'masculinity' (the composer has often been reproached for the excessive 'femininity' of his music)."[102] Here there's no advice, just innuendo.

Tchaikovsky's late nineteenth-century Fifth Symphony might well be about the entire tradition of programmatic composition, less as a tribute than a rebuke, a triumph over triumph and the entire nonsensical effort on the part of composers to turn pitches into panegyrics. To make a piece of music about something is to make it about nothing—a point that Tchaikovsky drives home by launching multiple narrative possibilities through the manipulation of a single sound.

Returning to the confession, the nonprogram Tchaikovsky scribbled out besides some musical thoughts: it might have been intended for another symphony, one that Tchaikovsky never finished and crossed out: XXX. Regarding the Fifth Symphony, which he obviously did finish, Tchaikovsky told Konstantin Konstantinovich Romanov that, "at the present time [June 11, 1888] I'm working rather diligently, composing a symphony without a program."[103] That he felt obliged to mention something that the work did not include is telling: he was expected to write program music. That's what Russian composers were supposed to do. Balakirev said so.

Aurora

Of course, he didn't need Balakirev anymore. Or the *kuchka*. Or any of the other guilds that sustained Russian composers outside of the realm of court financing. That sponsorship resulted in the protracted gorgeousness of *The Sleeping Beauty*. No other Russian composer before, during, or after his time could have composed such a work.

Vsevolozhsky's first choice for this project was a foreign composer because he wanted a foreign (French or Italian) sound. The composer in question was Albert Vizentini (1841–1906), who had succeeded Jacques Offenbach as director of the Théâtre de la Gaîté in Paris. He had written music for an earlier ballet choreographed, like *Sleeping Beauty*, by Marius Petipa. "I must confess that I would rather commission the score from Vizentini than Tchaikovsky," Vsevolozhsky informed Pogozhev on July 27, 1888. "Our Frenchman [Vizentini] has exactly the qualities that you want for this ballet, that is, he can write the right kind of music—he has knowledge of the old French tunes. Still, I worry that if I commission the music from him, there'll be rancor and upset in Petersburg. It's not like he'll write the music for free [as he had done before, for Petipa's ballet *The King's Command*]."[104] Tchaikovsky ended up with the commission, having reassured Vsevolozhsky that he could produce intelligent historical pastiche on the cheap. In the end, the intendant got much more than that.

The Sleeping Beauty was Tchaikovsky's first opportunity to collaborate with Petipa, who had specific ideas about music. He liked tutti passages with a clear beat and phrase structure; he didn't like compound meters and overlapping rhythms. Duple and common time and the disequilibrium of combinations of three were sufficient for his purposes. Vsevolozhsky also had specific ideas as the driving force and initiator of the project; most had to do with costumes. And so too the conductor of the premiere, Riccardo Drigo (1846–1930), who helped Tchaikovsky orchestrate the score, an experience that served him well in 1895, when Petipa tasked him with revising the score of *Swan Lake* for a new production. Pogozhev recalled numerous meetings about *The Sleeping Beauty* in the Imperial Theaters directorate, the Mariinsky Theater, and his apartment.[105] Petipa wanted to change the setting from seventeenth-century France to the sixteenth-century Spain of his earlier ballet *Don Quixote*. The idea was rejected.

The collaboration had its highs and lows. The result was a true masterpiece. Everything clicked: scenario, dance, pantomime, music (after Petipa overcame his fear of asymmetrical phrases and two-against-three metric alignments), soloists, coryphées, corps de ballet, orchestra, costumes, props, blocking. *The Sleeping Beauty* dates from roughly the same time as Wagner's final music drama *Parsifal* and, unlike *Swan Lake*, stands as Wagner's complete opposite, privileging melodies over leitmotifs, simple triads and seventh chords over nonharmonic tones, set pieces over unending unfolding. The characters come from picture books rather than German epic poems and Nordic sagas. And had Petipa had more of his way, the ballet would have been filled with flora and fauna and included a dance and a comic skit "for bats, flies and midges [*petite danse scènique de chauves-souris, mouches, et cousins*]."[106] Petipa imagined caprice for no reason, and beautiful things that, by definition, don't have a point, and the biosphere as realm of unconditional female desire. *The Sleeping Beauty* is, with apologies to Friedrich Nietzsche and his *The Birth of Tragedy out of the Spirit of Music*, an "Apollonian" composition for a "Dionysian" age. If Mozart had composed in the late nineteenth century, critic Arlene Croce writes, this is what he might have sounded like.[107]

The skeletal plot comes from Charles Perrault's *La belle au bois dormant* (*The Beauty in the Sleeping Forest*), first published in the 1697 collection *Histoires; ou, Contes du temps passé* (*Tales of Times Past*). Versions appear in Giambattista Basile's *Pentamerone* (1634) and the Grimm Brothers' *Kinder- und Hausmärchen* (*Childrens' and Household Tales*, 1812), under the alternative title *Dornröschen* (*Briar Rose*). When the princess Aurora is born, the king and queen invite twelve of the thirteen wise women (fairies) in the land to celebrate. Carabosse is excluded by the Herald, not because she's evil but because she's unattractive, sadly scarred from smallpox. She crashes the christening party in her rat-drawn carriage and curses the child, promising that, in her teenage years, Aurora will prick her finger and fall asleep forever (the Lilac Fairy weakens the curse so that the sleep lasts under a hundred years). At age sixteen Aurora catches her nail in a spinning wheel. As she sleeps, a briar of roses grows around the castle. In the Grimm Brothers' version, a prince revives her with a heartfelt kiss (not a smooch). Tchaikovsky and Petipa's ballet skips ahead to their wedding, evading the unpleasantness described in the sources. In the fourteenth-century chivalric romance *Perceforest* and in Basile's *Sole, Luna, e Talia* (*Sun, Moon, and Talia*), the sleeping princess isn't roused by the kiss and the prince rapes her. The princess awakens and delivers twins, who are almost cooked alive by the prince's evil wife (Basile) or mother (Perrault). Once again, the prince comes to the rescue in the end.

Tchaikovsky is sympathetic to the villainess insofar as nothing she does is musically marked as especially horrible. Aurora, when pricked, merely mixes up a few of her steps before lying down. The scene is level-headed, the opposite of an operatic mad scene, and the hundred-year sleep is paradoxical: dust settles over the stage set and cobwebs form, but Aurora's parents seem not to have aged at all when she rouses through the good offices of the Lilac Fairy. According to critic Konstantin Skalkovsky, something stranger happened in the premiere production: a gnarl of plants and trees sprouted from the mouths of the courtiers.[108] Désiré is the Lilac Fairy's wholesome, elegantly attired godson, and she has tucked an image of the snoozing heroine into his imagination. The music of this image is a barcarolle, representing the transition from one world into another.

Overall, the score moves from consonant block to consonant block, avoiding suspensions and privileging parallel major–minor modulations. To make sure it was dance-worthy, it was subjected to a series of trial rehearsals in 1889. Those who heard the musicians sight-reading the score gushed about its delights. It seemed perfect for dance.[109]

Tchaikovsky blends familiar musical syntax and structure with passages that emphasize timbre, instrumental color. The score is synesthetic in its sonification of that which applies to the eye (the nonacoustic) rather than the ear (the acoustic). As in Claude Debussy's orchestral works, which bear the influence of Tchaikovsky, the drama in the music lies not in a clash of dissonances, nor in the sequence of modulations by perfect fourth, but in a shifting kaleidoscope of instrumental timbres. The Lilac Fairy is represented in the score by a beautiful melody but also through a discreet blend of orchestral colors. Like the Lilac Fairy herself, these instruments in question guard over Aurora in the first and second acts. Their presence is sufficient to denote that Aurora is under the Lilac Fairy's benevolent protection, even when major turns to minor to fleeting discord.

The Lilac Fairy appears in the last variation of the *pas de six* of the Prologue, to a melody in C major heard in the woodwinds (flute, oboe, cor anglais, bassoon), and first violin and cello. In the finale of the Prologue, the oboe has the melody while the bassoon and clarinet answer with harp glissandi throughout. In the first act she appears after Aurora pricks her finger and orders her to be taken to a castle bedchamber. The harp plays rising broken chords when the Lilac Fairy enters; the cor anglais plays the melody from the finale of the Prologue, with oboes, flute, and bassoon responding. Having accomplished a good deed at the start—ensuring that Aurora's sleep is not eternal, only provisional—the fairy waves her wand and the music begins to evaporate, dissolving into pixie dust. Harmonies cede to isolated pitches, tremolos and their faint echoes. The music becomes inaudible to our ears, but not, it seems, to the lilac-colored keeper of the faith, who continues to shift weight from foot to foot, extending the phrase even after the sound is gone, crossing from the heard to the unheard.

In the second act, she appears before Désiré at the hunt and describes Aurora to him. The passages open with rising and falling arpeggios in the harp. The flute plays the melody from the Prologue finale, with the cor anglais adding a countermelody and piccolo and clarinet providing a response and upper strings playing tremolo chords underneath. In the third act, the Lilac Fairy appears to bless the marriage, but without her melody or the instrumentation that represents her.

In the scenario, the highpoint of Act I is the prick, of Act II the kiss and Aurora's awakening. Act III revolves around the wedding

processional. The guests at the wedding (depending on the complete-
ness of the performance) include Puss in Boots and the White Cat,
Little Red Riding Hood and the Wolf, the Blue Bird and Princess
Florine, Cinderella and Prince Fortuné (these last four join in a *pas
de quatre*), Hop-o'-My-Thumb and his six brothers, and an Ogre
(Maneater) with his Ogress wife (who do a folk dance). The preceding
Gold, Silver, Sapphire, and Diamond Fairies represent the riches of
the Russian Empire. It's a supersumptuous, all-embracing version of
Le bourgeois gentilhomme's *ballet des nations*. The character dances
have vaudevillian touches: the low is embraced along with the high.
The Lilac Fairy seems to have blessed not only Aurora, but the
popular dancers as well. Even Carabosse shows up at the end.

Musically and choreographically, the highlight is Aurora's *pas
d'action* with male suitors from different corners of the Russian
Empire (or, depending on the staging, the entire globe). Before the
dance, the harp outlines the dominant seventh, over and over again,
for so long as to erase the memory of its dominant seventhness. It is
the sour *Tristan* chord sweetened. Time recommences when Aurora
reaches center stage and the chord resolves on the downbeat. The
dance that follows is geometrical, consisting of diagonal lines and
square shapes, beginning, in Wiley's overview, with the four princes
from different parts of the empire with their four attendants framing
the ballerina in an *arabesque* position. Aurora will pose in attitude
with each of them in a line, and favor the last, but nothing will come
of this teenage choice—fortune has another suitor in store for her.
The princes return to the corners of the square. Then there is the
presentation and gathering of the roses. "In the final group each
prince supports Aurora in a turn *en attitude*, then kneels while she
performs a final pair of *tours* and ends the adagio in an *arabesque*."[110]

Tchaikovsky freed his score from the musical conventions of
Pugni and Minkus, which helped Petipa to liberate his heroine. The
original choreography isn't *exactly* preserved: the Stepanov notation,
which covers the bulk of the ballet, dates from 1903–06.[111] But

enough is intact to indicate that the rhythm and phrasing in the music moved in and out of phase with the dance for expressive reasons. Often Aurora ends her phrases on weak rather than strong beats, giving her the carefree fleetness of innocent childhood. She rebels against the constraints of Tchaikovsky's boxier musical shapes as she becomes her own person. Her more difficult, painful-looking movements are matched by strained timbres. She's saying something about what dance does to the body over time.

Croce notes that not all productions of *The Sleeping Beauty* are set in the era of Perrault. Some performances send Aurora to bed in the Enlightenment, or Romantic, or Modernist eras. Manipulating (or, as Croce puts it, "meddling with") the time and place of the action has become a habit among choreographers. In Russia the plot ends in the year of the ballet's premiere, and "a young girl's sexual awakening" was, again referencing Croce, the least of Petipa's concerns.[112]

Ballet critic and historian Alastair Macaulay interviewed choreographer Alexei Ratmansky about his 2015 production of *The Sleeping Beauty* based on the Stepanov notation. In the middle of a very long Q&A he asked about the symbolism of the fairies: "Can you explain why Vsevolozhsky chose these six fairies as godmothers? Candide, *Fleur de farine*, *Miettes qui tombent*, *Canari [qui chante]*, *Violente*, Lilac—they're like a collage from different time zones. What do they have in common?" Macaulay asked. Ratmansky said that he believed the fairies were "a collective portrait of the grown-up Aurora," with each denoting an aspect of an ideal family and a perfect household.[113] Ratmansky demurred as to whether there were deeper folkloric connections, but it's known that *Miettes qui tombent* (*Falling breadcrumbs*) refers to a pagan fertility ritual. The other fairies denote personality traits, including truth (candor), passion, and wisdom.[114]

The lavishness of the whole makes *The Sleeping Beauty*, prologue to apotheosis, a ballet about empire. Russia appropriated and elaborated an art that had its roots in a French monarchic environment of social dances at court, with Italian commedia dell'arte elements inserted. Narrative came later, and ballet embedded itself in opera before its Napoleonic emancipation. *The Sleeping Beauty* is a court ballet for the Romanovs and both Russia's and France's colonialist conquests, though geopolitical realities meant that it wasn't immediately appreciated as such. The blending of dances in the final act looks through the windows of the St. Petersburg Hermitage into the Palace of Versailles. There's a sarabande (Act III, no. 29), originally from Spanish colonies in Latin America, which became popular in Spain in the sixteenth century. In the seventeenth century, the dance was introduced to France and became a favorite of the Sun King. The name sarabande, however, is of central and southern African origin. It comes from the Bantu word *nsala-banda* (let the spirit rip), and zarabanda refers to the god (or spirit) of iron and war.[115] The dance in these baroque contexts is hardly staid. The rhythms (and songs) were part secular, part sacred, and associated with evening performances, ceremonies, and communal gatherings. In Spain the music was fast-paced and percussive and, because of its erotic aspects and association with black bodies, banned by royal decree in the late sixteenth century. All that remains of the zarabanda in the sarabande is the 3/4 time and incidental syncopation with an accent on the second beat. The French appropriation of the Spanish appropriation was slowed down to allow the bulky Louis XIV to perform it at court, and Tchaikovsky's version presumably would have appealed to him.

Act III also includes a polonaise, or polacca (no. 22), which likewise has a complicated history in Poland, France, and Russia. The bellicose version of the polonaise rhythm heard throughout the first movement of Tchaikovsky's Fourth Symphony reflects nothing of this history, but the statelier, held-back version of the 3/4 dance in *The Sleeping Beauty* does. It dates back to a Parisian festival known as the *Ballet des Polonais*. That festival, presented by Catherine de' Medici in celebration of her son, Henri de Valois, ascending to the Polish throne in 1573, involved a "mountain of nymphs," references to Virgil's *Aeneid*, and geometrical formations and dancing of martial character.[116] Court pageants in France in the seventeenth century reliably included the polonaise (along with racist imaginings of what the Polish people looked like). In Russia the polonaise became a pomp-filled ceremonial genre thanks to Józef Kozłowski (Osip Kozlovsky), a Polish transplant to the Russian court who wrote a famous polonaise called "Grom pobedï, razdavaysya!" ("Thunder of Victory, Resound!") that, as Taruskin reveals, became an unofficial Russian imperial anthem.[117] Tchaikovsky would explicitly quote "Grom pobedï" in his musical representation of Catherine the Great's brazen confiscation of Polish culture in the opera *The Queen of Spades*.

The polonaise in *The Sleeping Beauty* opens in G major. (Wiley argues that it connects the resolution of the plot to the Prologue, which features G major. "The Prologue has told us, in effect, where the ballet should end ... G [is] the long-anticipated key of resolution.")[118] The triumphant procession includes Russian nobles, the subjugated peoples of the empire, and folk and fairytale characters. The tonal structure is transparent, modulating from G major to the supertonic A minor, back to G, and then to the subdominant C with the musical flourishes (trills and dotted figures) suggesting, perhaps, the empire's flourishing.

The mazurka of the ballet's apotheosis (Act III, no. 30) adds another dimension of rhetorical significance, owing to the use of the piano in place of the harp. The new orchestration allows "the darker, non-ethereal, material connotations of the sonorities [to] make themselves felt ... The piano returns in the apotheosis to enhance the setting of the French tune, 'Vive Henri IV,' which concludes the ballet with great pomp and ostentation."[119] The change in scoring reflects the shift from the realm of fantasy into reality. The harp had defined the dreaminess, and the piano moves the ballet from that other world into Russia's present. Moreover, the piano has a particular national connotation: In the late nineteenth century, musicologist Lucia Denk reports, a distinct school of Russian pianism emerged (to which the Rubinstein brothers obviously contributed), defined by robust playing techniques and the holistic use of the arms and fingers (as opposed to emphasizing finger technique at the expense of arm power).[120] The Austrian-Polish pianist Theodor Leschetizky (1830–1915) alternately celebrated and exoticized his Russian counterparts: "United to a prodigious technique," the Russians "have passion, dramatic power, elemental force, and extraordinary vitality." Despite their "turbulent natures, difficult to keep within bounds," they make for "wonderful players when they have the patience to endure to the end."[121] For Denk, the music for piano in *The Sleeping Beauty* flexes imperial Russian muscle. Tchaikovsky and other late nineteenth-century Russian composers demonstrated their incomparable gifts for orchestration and likewise their ability, manifest in the apotheosis, to enhance the power of the piano into what she calls a "micro-orchestra all its own, ripe with metaphorical implication."[122]

Ballet has come a long way from the era of the farandole, a community dance associated with Provence, France, thought by some to have ancient Greek origins. That dance, included in the second act with the introduction of Désiré, proved popular with audiences and earned a tepid nod of respect from the judges of the January 3, 1890, premiere, who split down the middle in terms of the merit of the new work. Carlotta Brianza as Aurora and Pavel Gerdt as Désiré were complimented for navigating Tchaikovsky's integrated, "symphonic" music together (though Gerdt accidentally pulled out one of Brianza's lovely locks trying to do so). The press described *The Sleeping Beauty* as a lot, perhaps too much, to take in. Was it actually a ballet?[123]

Certainly it was a spectacle, both on the stage and in the audience. The *Petersburg Journal* described "an ocean of tailcoats, snow white shirtfronts, and dress uniforms. The viewers in the galleries looked like sardines in tins."[124] As to the performance itself:

> *Everything* is done for the eye, but for the choreography, there is almost nothing at all. The *féerie* reminds one of a book in a

luxurious binding with empty pages. The music of Tchaikovsky does not suit the dances at all. It's not even possible to dance to it. In places it is a symphony, and in others unsuccessfully imitates ballet rhythms. There are two or three musical phrases, but the composer repeats them endlessly.[125]

Herman Laroche would temper this specific criticism in his own review of *The Sleeping Beauty*, praising Tchaikovsky's sophisticated musical accessibility, but that review appeared after the composer's death, in the 1893–94 *Yearbook of the Imperial Theaters*. By that time a narrative had been established about the ballet's excesses at the expense of toe-tapping titillation. "Don't even look for any sense!" *Petersburg Newspaper* advised its readers,

> All of Perrault's tales are mixed up, thrown into one pile, and the new ballet doesn't produce any one impression as a result. It is a heap of a whole string of wonderful pictures, with marvelous decors, luxurious costumes—a kaleidoscope that blinds the viewers. It is indeed a fairy tale—a fairy tale for children and old men who have returned to a childish state … but a ballet, as we understand it? No! It is the complete decline of choreographic art![126]

This same reviewer described characters that have long vanished from the cast, including Donkey Skin, from a freakishly horrible Perrault story about a widower king's desire to marry his own daughter; she flees his realm with the Lilac Fairy's (!) help wearing the hide of a magical donkey that produces manure of gold. The reviewer also identified a *ballet des nations* tucked inside a *ballet des nations*, a suite of sarabandes for Indians, Persians, Romans, Turks, and even Americans—though in fact Tchaikovsky composed just the one sarabande, involving four men and four women from each of these nationalities.[127]

Petipa's oldest daughter Marie took the part of the Lilac Fairy and was derided as the beneficiary of nepotism. The rumor spread that she did not dance on pointe, despite images of her in pointe shoes. She was beautiful, according to the consensus, but technically limited. Over the years her image deteriorated: she was overweight, misogynistic Soviet-era balletomanes chortled; she couldn't dance at all.[128] Doug Fullington, an expert on the Stepanov notation of *The Sleeping Beauty*, notes that "only one passage" in her Prologue variation "required consecutive steps on pointe: arriving at upstage center, Marie made six steps on pointe in place as she raised her arms overhead. The choreography also avoids turns—a single turn is indicated in the ground plan at the end of the variation—and its few jumps are modest." Another notation of the variation, presumably for another dancer, "includes more challenging choreography … but what it gains in technical brilliance, it lacks in opportunities for gestural grandeur. The simplicity of Marie's variation and its opportunities for characterization may be the happy if unexpected result of the senior Petipa choreographing to the strengths of the junior."[129]

For Tchaikovsky, neither the criticism nor the praise mattered as much as the opinion of the sovereign, who attended one of the three general rehearsals and offered the composer a condescending "very nice."[130] That hurt, but he knew the reason, as he knew the reason for the harsher reviews: not his music and not, for the most part, Petipa's choreography but the costuming, décor, and the ballet's "Francophilia."[131] Pushkin had written a trove of fairytales, why not stage one of those? Rapprochement between France and Russia came after the premiere, not before. Art leapt ahead of reality, and ideologues lined up to howl about the colossal cost of a show— 42,000 rubles for sets and costumes alone—that should have had more Russian content.[132]

That expensiveness produced an astonishing effect on Alexandre Benois, soon to achieve immortality as a designer for the iconoclastically Modernist, Paris-based Ballets Russes company under the direction of Sergey Diaghilev. Benois considered *The Sleeping Beauty* an affirmation of that which would soon be lost to ballet (the Ballets Russes sumptuously revived it in 1921 in London on Benois's instigation, effectively bankrupting Diaghilev's operation). The "classical" constraints of the second half contrasted the lyricism of the first, Benois recalled, as the story of Aurora's coming of age became an allegorical affirmation of Romanov rule and its continuity. The music was a narcotic: he couldn't keep it out of his head, and he returned again and again to the Mariinsky seeking the high:

> When I try to analyze the feeling that came over me then, it seems to me that I simply could not believe in my own joy; that, subconsciously, I was already in the power of something entirely new, but for which, nevertheless, my soul had been waiting, for a long, long while. As soon as possible I saw *The Sleeping Beauty* a second time, and then a third and a fourth. The more I listened to the music, the more I seemed to discover in it greater and greater beauty—a beauty that was not universally understood but that was absolutely in harmony with me, that aroused the sweetest languor and an almost celestial joy.[133]

Florence

Von Mekk did not share in the joy; she didn't even see *The Sleeping Beauty*. Although Tchaikovsky kept her apprised of his progress on the ballet their relationship was at an end. The von Mekk railroad business was teetering; the government had confiscated the family's shares in the Ryazan branch, lucrative for the shipment of grain, and philanthropic activities had to be curtailed. Pressured by in-laws, fearful, and suffering from a myriad of ailments including tuberculosis, von Mekk cut Tchaikovsky off. By then, the late summer of 1890, he obviously had more than enough to live on and did not need her support. Still, the end of their friendship grieved them both.

Poznansky reports that the actual letter in which von Mekk acknowledged her financial problems to the composer is suspiciously missing, "non-extant," and that the letter Tchaikovsky wrote to her in response from Tiflis on September 22, 1890, might well have been intercepted by the musician Władysław Pachulski, who had married von Mekk's daughter Yuliya and thereafter inserted himself into her business dealings and private affairs. His antipathy toward Tchaikovsky, who had doused Pachulski's compositional aspirations, might have also played a role in the severing of contact between Tchaikovsky and his longtime patron. Such, again, is Poznansky's interpretation of the situation; Aynbinder's is the opposite. Pachulski cared about Tchaikovsky; there was no bad blood between them, and he kept Tchaikovsky apprised of von Mekk's health condition when she stopped doing so.[134]

Sometimes writing to her had been a burden, but she never let him down, and he would miss her. She had made his life easier and his world much bigger, more cosmopolitan, during those years when he had the most energy to enjoy it. Her valets attended to logistics for him when his own valet, the frequently indisposed Alyosha, could not. Von Mekk introduced him to the finer sides of Italian life—the gastronomy and galleries of Milan, Rome, and especially the Tuscan capital of Florence. In 1878 von Mekk paid for his stay on Via Bonciana near the Piazzale Michelangelo, which afforded a panoramic view of the city (requiring, Tchaikovsky learned, a tiring uphill hike).[135] For his visit in 1890, during the final months of her support, he rented rat-free rooms closer to the Arno. There he began his *Souvenir of Florence*, an exercise in *Italyanshchina* that quotes nothing Italian.[136] The score is instead influenced by Florence's visual culture, namely the paintings commissioned by the Medici banking family. Tchaikovsky had contradictory things to say about the city. Sometimes he adored Florence, other times, depending on his mood, he derided it as dull and tumbledown. His feelings about Rome also fluctuated. So too Naples. And everywhere else outside of Moscow and

St. Petersburg and sometimes Paris.[137] Credit von Mekk for at least recommending that he visit the galleries.

The *Souvenir* is a string sextet, a quartet with extra layers, leaving Tchaikovsky with the paradoxical challenge of maintaining distinctness in a homogeneous texture. Solving it eluded him, and he uncharacteristically sought advice from the intended performers (the sextet was written for the St. Petersburg Chamber Music Society, which premiered it on a special program dedicated to "classical and historical music").[138] He received feedback on spacing, dynamic, the tempos required to minimize dissonance as the lines move around each other in the middle registers. After hearing the sextet in a private setting— a hotel sitting room—in St. Petersburg on November 25, 1890, and after taking in the reactions to the premiere three days later, he touched up the coda of the first movement, redid the middle of the third movement (originally a fugato), and revised the second theme and fugato of the finale.[139]

The scoring is that of the two Brahms sextets: two violins, two violas, and two cellos. Tchaikovsky includes much fussed-over imitative passages (including a grand finale fugato), dialogues between violin and cello (the first music sketched), sassy trilling beneath legato lines, *ppp* to *ff* shifts in dynamic at cadences, and go-for-broke solos that leave the theological musings of the Serenade for Strings behind. The opening of Tchaikovsky's score is an expression of nonchalance—*sprezzatura*—that precipitates a hypermetric conflict. The strings casually toss up a first-inversion dominant ninth chord that resolves to a root-position tonic chord in the second measure, followed by the studied carelessness of V 4/3 going to I 6/3 before V 6/5, I, IV, and a V 7/5 chord that doesn't resolve. Instead, the cycle repeats with the same misalignment of harmonic pattern and phrase length, leading, at measure 15, to the sudden introduction of the Neapolitan.[140]

The slow introduction to the D-major second movement moves by block chord through the six measures before allowing the first violin and first cello room to roam. The music elaborates the dominant ninth again, but without the nonchalance. Each of the pitches is lingered over, with a modulation to F contemplated through chromatic alteration of C♯ to C and A to B♭ before being dismissed. The third movement counters the first two movements by stressing the tonic chord of A minor before an impetuous crescendo unexpectedly landing on a fortissimo F♯-major chord: the dominant of the dominant of the dominant. The nonresolutions and harmonic aberrances are the cynosures in his music, the beautiful and strange things that attract attention. The piece ultimately seems akin to the Mannerist paintings in the Uffizi—imagine Rosso Fiorentino's *Cherub Playing a Lute*, or the elegance and coolness of Bronzino's canvases.

Tchaikovsky thought on and off about the *Souvenir* for years but didn't get much done on it until May 1890, after he had drafted his Florentine opera *The Queen of Spades*. The scores came from the same place but inhabit wholly different musical cosmoses. The character at the center of the opera's plot is a countess who has had more than enough of the world. She's close to death and lives a spectral life, a twilight-zone existence as the symbol of a defunct empire. Her Weltschmerz is von Mekk's, and the opening salon scene recycles music from the "Méditation" from his *Souvenir d'un lieu cher*, composed for von Mekk and Braïliv (and originally conceived for Tchaikovsky's Violin Concerto).

Pushkin's story begins in 1833 with a card game at the St. Petersburg home of Narumov, an officer in the Imperial Cavalry. The players include two other imperial military men: Herman, the tale's marginalized protagonist (so marginalized, in fact, that it's unclear if Herman is his first name or surname); and Count Tomsky, the grandson of Countess Anna Fyodorovna. As the game progresses, the count relates that the countess once had a terrible gambling problem and was forced to quit after incurring especially heavy losses at a salon in Paris. She was spared bankruptcy and the poor house, according to the count, by a practitioner of the occult,

Saint-Germain,[141] who gave her the names of three winning cards for use in the game of faro.[142] Having settled her debts with the supernatural combination, she vowed never to gamble again and shared the secret formula only with her husband, who died some time ago.

Herman becomes obsessed with learning the card formula and tries to get to the countess through her ward Liza (a name that evokes the "Poor Liza" of Sentimentalist fiction). Liza misreads his flirtations as a serious effort to win her affections and allows Herman into the countess's bedchamber to await her return from a ball. She turns up tired and angry about everything she's seen that night. Herman emerges from the shadows and demands to know the names of the cards. When she refuses, he threatens her with a gun and causes her a stroke. He didn't load the weapon, but he's still killed her with it.

At the countess's funeral Herman imagines, or sees, the cadaver winking at him as he passes by the casket. He returns to his room drunk; the wind howls; images from the funeral fill his head; and he sees, or imagines, the countess's ghost hovering over him. She's come to him against her will, she whispers, to reveal a secret: Herman can win at faro by playing the *troyka* (three), *semyorka* (seven), and *tuz* (ace) cards. The ghost cautions that he can play the series only once, in order, and must do so over different nights (compressed in the opera to a single night) at the casino. He fails to grasp the instruction as a warning: he shouldn't be dabbling in black magic. Nor does he intuit—though he should, the world has always cheated him—that he's being lied to. In the opera the ghost also counsels him to "marry Liza," which, for a rogue like him, just isn't in the cards. Herman wins on the first night selecting the *troyka* and on the second night with the *semyorka*. He now has a pile of coins on the table, but he can't stop and loses on the third night when the card he plays turns out not to be *tuz* but the *pikovaya dama* (the queen of spades), which the ace defeats ("kills"). In Pushkin's epilogue Herman loses his mind after losing it all and is last seen babbling "three seven ace, three seven ace" in a madhouse, the curse enacted. Liza, whom he mistreated, marries the prosperous son of the countess's steward and adopts a child as she herself was adopted. In Tchaikovsky's transposition the darkness is unrelenting. There's no adoption and no asylum: Liza drowns herself in the Winter Canal and Herman drops dead (or shoots/stabs himself) after seeing the countess's face as the queen of spades. Tchaikovsky drafted a *Don Giovanni*-type chorus of prayer for Herman's soul but abandoned it in rehearsal.

The Queen of Spades was supposed to have been composed by Nikolay Klenovsky (1857–1915), a former student of Tchaikovsky's who served as staff conductor and composer for the Bolshoi. He had composed three ballets, including the exotic-erotic spectacular *The Delights of Hashish* (1885), and wanted to move into the more prestigious realm of opera. With Vsevolozhsky's backing he engaged Modest Tchaikovsky as the librettist for *The Queen of Spades*, which Vsevolozhsky thought had immense potential as a combination of Verdi's *Traviata*, Bizet's *Carmen*, and Massenet's *Manon*. Klenovsky procrastinated, then abandoned the project. It was then offered to Nikolay Solovyov, who declined but later "greatly regretted" doing so.[143] Vsevolozhsky also puzzlingly recommended it to Alexander Villamov, a noble composer of well-behaved salon music without any theatrical experience (his chief occupation was railroad maintenance). The composer next in line for the project was Tchaikovsky, but he remained in such a deep funk over the failure of *The Enchantress* that it seemed pointless to ask him. Still, Modest couldn't help but mention that his libretto lacked a composer. To his surprise, Pyotr agreed

> right away to compose an opera to [it]. In the middle of December
> [1889] there was a meeting in the office of the director of
> the Imperial Theaters attended by designers, office heads,
> [Vsevolozhsky's assistant Vladimir] Pogozhev and [stage designer

Platon] Domershchikov of the administration, where I read through my script. It was decided to shift the action from the time of Alexander I, where I had set it for Klenovsky, to the end of the reign of Catherine II. Accordingly, the script for the third scene—the ball—was entirely changed, and the scene by the Winter Canal, which had no part in my original plan, was added.[144]

Tchaikovsky worked extremely quickly, proof of his powers of invention and his concern with the tight deadline. He rose at eight, working in two shifts with lunch in between, dining at seven (he grew tired of the food in his hotel, so began eating out), and then going to the theater, reading, or writing letters. His brother's valet, Nazar Litrov, stayed with him, helped him dress in the morning, brushed and trimmed his beard, and joined him on his outings until he sprained a foot, at which point Tchaikovsky had to care for him.[145]

Within a week, scenes 1 and 2 of the opera's first act were sketched. Before tackling Act II, scene 1, he skipped forward to Act II, scene 2: Herman's confrontation with the countess in her bedchamber, the plot's pivot point. The rough draft is dated February 11, a day before Lent. That same day, he turned to the middle of Act II, scene 1, the pastoral drama—the opera within the opera—involving Liza, her friend Polina, and Count Tomsky. "Finished the fourth scene and started the interlude," he wrote in his diary. "At first it was difficult; then it went well. Drank *terribly* in the evening." The next day: "Continued the interlude. At times I felt like I was living in the eighteenth century and that there was nothing beyond Mozart. Nazar is worse. Started rubbing and massaging [the foot]." Tchaikovsky "finished and played through" the scene on February 19, then relaxed with a book and took early to bed.[146] The rest of the libretto arrived from Modest, and the composer's pace hastened, the muse at his side, cheering him on. He tweaked some of his brother's lines and disagreed with him about including "some girls among the gamblers" in the climactic scene. "That's out of the question, it would be an outrageous stretch! In any case, apart from tarts, there shouldn't be any women in a gambling den, and certainly not a whole chorus of whores—that would really be too much . . ."[147]

Act III, scene 1, representing the ghost's real-or-hallucinated appearance in Herman's room, took just three days to fashion; scene 2, Herman's last meeting with Liza on the edge of the canal, one more. On February 16 he finished the sixth scene and began the final (seventh) scene and introduction, finishing them on March 2 (with the exception of Herman's concluding monologue) and March 3, respectively. The temperature dropped and it started snowing, but he still went out. Tchaikovsky took sick with a horrible cold which got worse and worse before suddenly ending, but the opera had been worked through. Revisions and writing out the piano-vocal score from the draft absorbed three more weeks. On March 25, just before the rehearsal deadline for the autumn season at the Mariinsky Theater, he sent the final act of the piano-vocal score to Vsevolozhsky for printing. Tchaikovsky vacated his apartment in Florence and took the train to Rome for three weeks. He enjoyed returning to old haunts and seeing old friends as he worked on the orchestration. Traveling back to Russia slowed his work on the orchestration of Acts II and III, but excluding dynamic markings and other perform-ance instructions, work was done on June 8.

Among the finer details are moments of folkloric black humor. Magic cards, a frightful old woman, greed and avarice, a ghost, the rational tripping over in the irrational—such are the elements of *skazki*. In his letters, Tchaikovsky talked about losing himself in the world he had created and of his sympathies for Herman. He wrote to Konstantin Konstantinovich Romanov about his "unbelievable" enthusiasm for the opera and how it had pulled him out of his funk over *The Enchantress*. The composer confessed that he "felt and expe-rienced everything happening within it (at one point I even feared the appearance of the ghost of 'the Queen of Spades') and I hope

that all of my anxiety, nerves, and passion as its author will find reso-
nance in the hearts of those who hear it."[148] He told his diary that he
"wept terribly when Herman expired, the result of exhaustion, or
maybe because the opera is really good."[149] He repeated the description in a letter to his brother, saying he'd cried "uncontrollably" out of
pity for his protagonist. It felt good to do so, because his bond with
Herman was so empathetically strong.[150] Even his brother's hobbled
valet, Litrov, remembered the composer spilling tears on the manuscript: "Pyotr Ilyich said that he had cried all that evening, and his
eyes were still red then, and himself suffering terribly. He was tired,
and, despite this fatigue, he still wanted to cry, it seems."[151]

His feelings were as genuine as the exhaustion. Tchaikovsky knew
that he had created a character for the ages—a man who serves the
empire and seeks synthesis with the state yet who is treated like an
outcast, looked down on, and made to feel like he doesn't belong.
Herman suffers mental illness as a result. He seeks escape, much like
"the man of state" in Andrey Beliy's Symbolist novel *Petersburg*
(1913), who "suddenly expanded out of the black cube in all directions and soared above it." Beliy describes the "boundlessness of
mists" in spectral St. Petersburg as well as the squares and rectangles
formed by its streets. The yellow steam and the roads expand ever
outward, from the real into the fantastic. Such is the language used
by essayist Malcolm Forbes in a piece about the novel titled "The
Moving Tide of Abundance."[152] The language also applies to the
opera and Tchaikovsky's shattered emotional response to his
achievement.

To identify (or pretend to identify) with the fictional Herman,
Tchaikovsky frequented gaming houses and drank to excess (something he didn't need to be encouraged to do). Tchaikovsky read Gogol
and Schopenhauer in idle hours and drew inspiration from them as
he composed the opera. The composer thought from the start about
the staging: whether Herman should live in a barracks or an apartment "behind which door the countess's walking stick should be

heard."[153] He had a singer in mind for the role, the great Mariinsky Theater tenor Nikolay Figner (1857–1918).[154] A specialist in villains with a reputation as a political agitator, Figner struggled through a rocky dress rehearsal and a rough premiere (he had not recovered from breaking his collarbone during a performance of another opera) but ultimately excelled in the part, delighting his claque and stunning even nonpartisan operagoers.[155]

The structure of *The Queen of Spades*—three acts and seven scenes comprising one score—partly mirrors the winning card formula: three, seven, and ace. Likewise, the middle of the middle (the chorus, dance, duet, and finale of the pastoral drama in the third scene) reproduces in miniature the opening chorus, ball, final duet, and the dreadful finale in the casino. There are other symmetries, other reflections that took time to notice and to bring out in the production, owing to the rush to assign parts and rehearse what the conductor called an "interesting novelty."[156] The first, fourth, and seventh scenes start with grand choruses, while the third and the fifth are prefaced by entr'actes. Scene 2 begins with an intimate duet, and scene 6 ends with one. Tomsky performs his two big numbers at opposite ends of the opera, the start of scenes 1 and 7. And the romance, the morbid parlor song sung by Polina in the middle of scene 2, anticipates Liza's presuicide arioso in the middle of scene six.

Moving the time and place of the action from the nineteenth century and Pushkin's era back to the eighteenth century allowed for an expansion in the middle. Vsevolozhsky suggested a Mozartian *intermède* and rummaged through the French song albums in his library for the chanson sung by the countess and the tune of Tomsky's Act I aria.[157] The *intermède* became a beauty-for-beauty's-sake dress-up affair, the singers looking like "Sèvres porcelain figures come to life."[158] One imagines Tchaikovsky endorsing this choice of costuming on behalf of his maternal great-grandfather, the French figurine maker Michel Victor Acier. Petipa choreographed it on dancers brought over from a concurrent production of *The Sleeping Beauty*.[159]

Rehearsal director Osip Palachek remembers the performers descending "from white/light blue pedestals, and in the finale stiffen[ing] into immobility." The costume designs were "copied" from illustrations by the French artists Jean-Antoine Watteau and François Bouchet, who both worked in a rococo style.[160]

Changing the time and action made sections of the libretto irrationally anachronistic. For Liza's and Polina's Act I, scene 2, duet about the magic of twilight and Polina's ballad about the end of childhood, Modest had used texts by Konstantin Batyushkov and Zhukovsky. Liza and Polina remember these songs from their childhood, which, if the plot is set during the reigns of Tsar Alexander I or Nikolay I, would be in the nineteenth century. But now in the eighteenth century, living in the era of Catherine the Great, Liza and Polina cannot possibly know the texts they "recall."

It could be argued that the anachronisms were mistakes left uncorrected in the rush to draft the opera. In his preface to the first edition of the piano-vocal score, Modest noted that he had "looked, where possible, for the opportunity to replace verses of his own invention with verses of actual poets who, despite being later, wrote several things in the spirit of the time."[161] He anticipated criticism of his bricolage and, with his brother, defended the anachronisms as fundamental to the opera's central concept: Liza's world is not Herman's world, and Herman's world is not the countess's world. Time bends and warps and folds over on itself, as past and present, perception and reality, are subject to chance.

Caryl Emerson, a Pushkin scholar who has had a decidedly mixed reaction to Tchaikovsky's Pushkin adaptations (the pathos of *Eugene Onegin* should have been held in check, in her opinion; it's too emotional a departure from the dispassionate novel in verse) hears *The Queen of Spades* unfolding concurrently in three different times.[162] The first of them, according to Emerson, is the "historical backdrop" to the plot: the Enlightenment, specifically the final years of the reign of Catherine the Great, the monarch who Europeanized

Russian culture, improved education, founded the orphanage that funded the Bolshoi Theater, and expanded the empire in all directions. The censors prevented Tchaikovsky from placing Catherine the Great on stage—she is announced to great fanfare (Kozłowski's polonaise) but obscured from view in most productions—but his allusions to Mozart and the pastoral *intermède* bring her to the foreground. The second time is the Romantic era, associated with the accidentally burlesque, "bulky, Napoleonic figure of Herman." He seeks escape from despotic servitude and can't stop thinking about doing so as opposed to actually doing so. He's trapped in his thoughts like Byron's Manfred. The third time, introduced in Act III, scene 1, is the Silver Age, that is, the present—the time of "Tchaikovsky's composing of the opera, forty-four [*sic*] feverish days in Florence in the early spring of 1890, on the brink of Russian Symbolism." Emerson focuses here on the ghost scene. The specter is not a haggard crone but (per Tchaikovsky's lexicon) "a tart," the siren of her days with Condé in Chantilly. The passage, Emerson adds, bears the outlines of "Symbolist aesthetics: the Dionysian that is also demonic; the presentation of primary sexuality as guarantor of knowledge; the genuinely transfiguring experience of dreams; and, mostly, a simultaneous multiplicity of times."[163] The countess is the girl, or the ghost of a girl, Herman desires. Liza is a fresh-faced but pale substitute.

The ghost tells him to marry Liza, but he doesn't and that's his ruin. Liza's too. She drowns in a canal built by slave labor in the fantastical city of St. Petersburg. Herman, too, sinks into the abyss. The other characters remain, for the moment, in the palaces and barracks and casinos of the surface. Life, for them, goes on. The dealer deals; the game continues.

The Queen of Spades would be judged textually deficient (owing to the anachronisms) and musically redundant. Modest tried to get ahead of the press with the curious defense that he didn't have the skill to write a libretto in the style of Catherine the Great's era.[164]

Audiences also missed the merriment: in this bleak opera most of the characters seem to wish that they'd never been born, and Herman is nihilistic. Like the opera itself, the reviews were conflicted. One source noted "the public's indifferent reaction through it all; evidently the Mariinsky Theater's patrons didn't care about Herman's three cards, and even the romances, sung by most of the characters, failed to inspire. The luxuriant staging did its thing and nothing else." Another source claimed wild success, Tchaikovsky summoned to bow after each act and draped in a silver wreath. The accolades "increased with each performance."[165] The harshest invective came from Nikolay Solovyov, in a lengthy article published in a financial newspaper amid advertisements for holiday gifts and a report on the apple-cider industry. Solovyov had received an invitation to compose the opera before Tchaikovsky did and wanted to avenge his career-spoiling loss to Tchaikovsky in the 1874 opera competition for *Vakula the Smith*.[166] He authored a rambling, redundant review much in love with the word *naprasno* (in vain/to no purpose). Solovyov noted the change in epoch and the freighting of the libretto with "superficial" effects, including "gusts of wind, the singing of familiar Orthodox funeral chants in the distance, and the appearance of a shade." The pastoral dances "followed a template and looked cheap," and Tchaikovsky's reliance on couplets failed to replicate the success of *Eugene Onegin*. Solovyov provided several examples of Tchaikovsky spoiling the mood by following a cheerful song with something dreadful.[167]

But the musical juxtapositions, like the anachronisms, were intentional. They define Tchaikovsky as ahead of his time and place him in the company of the decadent artists that Solovyov, like Rimsky-Korsakov, so sincerely despised. The Symbolists welcomed Tchaikovsky as one of their own, irrespective of his anti-Symbolist Romanticism, occasional nationalism, and privileged place at court. Even his final opera, *Iolanta*, and his final ballet, *The Nutcracker*, have been given Symbolist readings, though these are a stretch.

Girlhood

Iolanta is based on Henrik Hertz's Danish (that is, not German) play *Kong Renés Datter* (*King René's Daughter*, 1845). In 1883 the literature and politics journal *Russian Herald* published Fyodor Miller's translation, calling it Hertz's finest work and noting its sensational popularity throughout Europe.[168] Miller, a distinguished translator as well as a prominent poet, had just died, and *King René's Daughter* was his last project. The preface offers a brief history lesson:

> The historical basis of the drama is that of King René, Count of Provence, who after much strife with Antoine, Count of Vaudémont, over the latter's claim of the Duchy of Lorraine, had achieved with him, through the offices of the Duke of Burgundy, a settlement stipulating that the king's daughter Yolande should become the wife of Tristan, Antoine's son. This marriage was eventually consummated, and one of Yolande's sons became the Duke of Lorraine. As much as the tale of King René's oldest daughter and the wife of King Henry VI, Margaret of Anjou, receives a lot of attention in the sources, nothing is said about Yolande. And so the reader can hardly reproach the author for stepping aside from history in what follows.[169]

What follows is a work of deeply Romantic fiction that describes Yolande (Iolanta) living in a beautiful garden paradise. She cannot see its splendors, however, because she is blind. The king fears word of her condition spreading to the outside world, so prohibits everyone in the realm from referring to color, light, or dark.

Tchaikovsky didn't immediately take to the subject. Instead, he mulled an opera adapted from Mikhaíl Lermontov's 1841 novel *A Hero of Our Time*. Titled *Béla*, it would have been set to a libretto by Anton Chekhov. The story concerns a Russian officer who has been sent to the northern Caucasus to suppress a Circassian uprising, only to fall in love with Béla, a beautiful and ultimately doomed Circassian maiden. The score doubtless would have included exoticist *couleur locale* of the *Moguchaya kuchka* type. Tchaikovsky also contemplated writing a comic opera, also in an exotic mode, about an ancient samurai clan fighting demons, dragons, and man-eating hags. That libretto was by the Bolshoi Theater machinist Karl Valts, but Tchaikovsky eventually concluded it was better fit to become a *ballet-féerie*.[170] Lastly, Tchaikovsky entertained adapting Byron's "The Prisoner of Chillon." Ultimately, he told the writer who had sent it to him, Alexander Fyodorov, that the sorrowful tale of the imprisonment of the Genevois monk François Bonivard left him indifferent. "My general avoidance of foreign plots is no small matter," he explained. "I only know, and embrace, a Russian person, a Russian girl, a woman. Medieval dukes and knights and ladies capture my imagination but not my heart, and if the heart isn't touched there can't be any music."[171]

The exception was *King René's Daughter*, whose lyricism had long "charmed" the composer, according to an interview published in *Petersburg Life* in 1892. He delayed turning the tale into an opera owing to "various impediments," namely travel and other projects. The interview also fascinatingly touched on Wagner—"in some majestic solitude stood this man of genius, from whose overwhelming influence not a single European composer of the second half of our century escaped"—the decline and fall of the *kuchka*, and the routine that allowed him to get so much done: "When I need to work, I retire to my Klin abode or to some quiet foreign corner and lead a hermit life. I work from ten in the morning until one in the afternoon and from five to eight in the evening. I never work late in the evening or at night."[172]

He took in a production of Hertz's play at the Maliy Theater in Moscow in 1888, then signed a contract with the Imperial Theaters for a one-act operatic adaptation. That same contract covered *The Nutcracker* and specified an 1891–92 premiere, with the opera to precede the ballet on the same bill. Travel to the United States for the opening of the Music Hall (Carnegie Hall) in New York City slowed his progress on both projects. He told Modest that the pressure was getting to him; he had begun to "hate" the opera and especially the ballet, whose mice (which frightened him no less than rats) and soldiers and gingerbread had infiltrated his dreams.[173] Modest had been busy turning Hertz's play into a singable text and expressed alarm that his brother might give up on the opera. Pyotr didn't; he just needed more time. "Traveling to America I'll hardly be able to concentrate," the composer told Vsevolozhsky—partly because of his "awful state of mind," and partly because he was dreading the travel (was the water safe to drink in New York?) and "the experience of being on the ocean, the hustle and bustle of the ship, its pitching on the waves, and, worse of all, the constant plinking on the piano by the English misses who'll be traveling with me."[174] Nápravník got involved, informing Vsevolozhsky on May 9, 1891, that he'd just

> received a very interesting letter from P. I. Tchaikovsky about his time in New York. First of all, he was struck by the enviable comforts Americans enjoyed and the colossal size of all their undertakings. Despite, however, the brilliant reception he received, he misses his homeland terribly, painfully, and can't wait to get back. He writes that his state of mind and the loss of time make it impossible to get the opera and the ballet done for next season.[175]

The intendant was sympathetic. He bumped *Iolanta* (as *King René's Daughter* was renamed) and *The Nutcracker* from the 1891–92 to the 1892–93 Mariinsky Theater season and sweetened the contract, offering Tchaikovsky 6 percent of box-office receipts on top of the original commission.[176]

Modest's libretto for *Iolanta* derives not from Miller's translation but from the freer, abridged translation by Vladimir Zotov used by the Maliy Theater. As further abridged by Modest, it made for a concise if ambiguous operatic experience. The first thing cut was the backstory. Hertz tells us that Iolanta lost her vision in a fire when she was an infant; in the opera she is born blind. Her caring and wise yet somewhat oppressive father, King René, prays for a cure for her condition before the physician he has recruited for the task turns up. In the opera this character, Ibn-Hakia, offers little more than some amorphous talk about "the two worlds of the flesh and the spirit" over an ostinato, a two-minute-long crescendo, and a pile of Eastern mystical musical clichés.

Hertz based the physician on a famous actual person, Ibn al-Haytham (ca. 965–ca. 1040). He was a celebrated astronomer, mathematician, and physicist who made lasting contributions to optical science.[177] In the play Ibn-Hakia promises Iolanta's father that she will be cured in time for her sixteenth birthday. He uses a magical amulet to put her to sleep in the garden, claiming it will help restore her vision. Meanwhile, the king arranges for Iolanta to be married to the son of a rival. The bridegroom, a Burgundian duke named Robert, turns up at court with a traveling companion, the knight Vaudémont. The latter becomes Iolanta's true love. (Besides switching around roles and changing the names of the characters, the opera sheds a lot of the play's romance.) In the pivotal scene of both the play and the opera, Iolanta is asked by her beloved to pick a red rose for him. She knows nothing of color; she gives him a white rose instead. She's asked again with the same result. Now her secret is out. The king flies into a rage; all his plans are unraveling. Suddenly, Iolanta can see—thanks either to Ibn-Hakia's treatment or the power of love, or both. Danish drama and Russian opera conclude with a communal celebration. Tchaikovsky embraced Christian symbolism and composed a hymnlike ending as riposte to the whole-tone fatefulness of Ibn-Hakia's aria. Sight and light are metaphors for "finding God through suffering and spiritual love," according to a recent dissertation about sacred (evangelical) images in Tchaikovsky's operas. *Iolanta*, the author argues, is Tchaikovsky's "spiritual testament." It tells us that our sorrows are not manifestations of "the hammer of ruthless fate," but of "the caring hand of Providence."[178]

These ideas are undercut by the opera's association of blindness with lack and of lack with longing. Tchaikovsky makes this connection in Iolanta's scene 1 arioso "Why haven't I known this before?" ("Otchego eto prezhde ne znala?"). She's just found out that she's of royal blood and now wonders if other things are being held from her. The arioso has points in common with Tchaikovsky's 1886 romance "Night" ("Noch'"), a setting of a poem by Polonsky about night's consolations. In the opera the night ends when Iolanta meets Vaudémont, who sings more than she does during their love scene. He's ecstatic, while her declamations are filled with dread; the orchestral accompaniment is anxious and agitated. Eventually she decides to trust him—his voice has captivated her—and joins him in a song about all things bright and colorful. She begins to see, and, like the miracle healings described in the Bible, the encroachment of an alien sense on her consciousness is cause for joy, not, as one might reasonably expect, terror. The end of the opera has all the characters, dull- and bright-eyed alike, sharing in Iolanta's jubilation, repeating the same phrase over the same root position chords (I and vi in A♭ major). They fall to their knees in praise of the Almighty. The curtain comes down. It's sunset.

The ironic ending is matched by the ironic beginning. When the curtain goes up, Iolanta is seen singing with a group of musicians. The wife of the castle doorkeeper is there, and two of Iolanta's friends, Brigitta and Laura, are gathering fruit and flowers. The diatonic *parlante* is scored with harp and gentle strings evocative of arcadia. Either blindness is a state of innocence or early music is, or both, and together they rebuke the dark overture, a chromatic, woodwind-dominated paraphrase of Wagner's *Tristan und Isolde* prelude. (Recall that one of the characters in Hertz's play is called Tristan.) The reference is an insubordinate critique. Wagner's music is groping in the dark, as opposed to the sadly pleasurable strains of the curtain-opener. For Tchaikovsky, Wagner is the void.

The opera will tell us that happiness is a hymn, that being a princess and getting married are good things for a southern French girl to do, and that the father will overcome his terrible jealousy of his daughter's suitor. Yet Iolanta was perfectly happy in her garden; for her the night is radiant. When she's ultimately forced to see like others do, we're left to think about what's been lost.

During rehearsals Tchaikovsky stayed in the Grand Hotel in St. Petersburg. The days passed by unnoticed, he wrote to Anatole, neither interestingly nor dully, and he didn't quite know when the *Iolanta* and *The Nutcracker* double bill would be premiered. He assumed December 8, but it happened two days earlier (ticket holders weren't put out by the change of dates; it was a common occurrence).[179] Meanwhile, on November 23, 1892, Tchaikovsky took in the premiere of Modest's latest play, *A Day in St. Petersburg*, at the Alexandrinsky Theater. It was an old-fashioned social satire about a prince, the peasants he's seeking to defend at the Imperial Court, and the clogged-up drawing rooms of the haut monde and nouveau riche. It flopped.[180] Pyotr consoled Modest by reminding him that things looked good for the upcoming production. On December 5, 1892, Tsar Alexander III attended the dress rehearsal of the *Iolanta* and *The Nutcracker* double bill and summoned the composer to his loge to congratulate him.

The opera's conductor, Nápravník, chronicled activities inside the theater. He recalled the tsar describing *Iolanta* as "delightful" at the dress rehearsal and counted three curtain calls for the composer after the premiere.[181] Modest, in contrast, sensed that the audience didn't quite know what to make of the evening. It seemed a "succès d'estime," respected without being enjoyed.[182] The reviews of *Iolanta* trended negative: according to the consensus, Tchaikovsky had clumped a bunch of salon romances together and was starting to repeat himself. Composer and conductor Mikhaíl Ivanov disliked Tchaikovsky's clichéd reliance on the whole-tone scale to represent Iolanta's fantastic discovery of sight and pointed out the resemblance between the final chorus and the end of Gounod's *Faust*. The beginning, the scene 1 ensemble in the garden, was the best part; the opera sagged after that. "It's perhaps obvious," Ivanov wrote, "that Tchaikovsky's music for this scene isn't French, much less Provençal, but it lends the impression of the distant south, of another epoch and different values, and is more evocative than technical contrivances could ever be."[183]

Rimsky-Korsakov panned *Iolanta* in his memoir, albeit disingenuously. He had axes to grind about the "ever-growing adoration of Tchaikovsky" and the fashion for "eclecticism" as well as the French-Italian musical style.[184] He was also miffed that the number of performances of his opera-ballet *Mlada* had been reduced at the Mariinsky to make room for *Iolanta* and Pietro Mascagni's *Cavalleria rusticana* (1890):

> I haven't heard *Cavalleria rusticana*, but I listened to a rehearsal of *Iolanta* and couldn't help but think it one of Tchaikovsky's weakest works. Everything in this opera is unsuccessful, from the shameless borrowings, like the tune "Open my Dungeon Cell" by Rubinstein, to the orchestration, which Tchaikovsky decided to do topsy-turvy this time around; music suitable for the strings is entrusted to winds and vice versa, which is why it sometimes sounds even fantastic in places that are completely inappropriate for this (for example, in the introduction, written for some reason for wind instruments alone).[185]

Clearly, Tchaikovsky knew what he was doing. The "shameless borrowing" Rimsky-Korsakov complains about, an allusion to Rubinstein's 1890 "Longing" ("Zhelaniye") in Vaudémont's declaration of love for Iolanta, "Wondrous Firstborn of Creation" ("Chudnïy pervenets tvoren'ya"), hardly compares to Rimsky-Korsakov's encyclopedia of paraphrases. His gripe about the orchestration centers on Tchaikovsky's subversion of Wagner and the instrumental chiaroscuro, the timbral blending of thick and thin, metal and wood, light and shade. "Within a subdued scheme of timbres," Taruskin writes, "Tchaikovsky discovered myriad exquisite shades, foreshadowing devices commonly associated with 'impressionism'—divided and solo strings, measured tremolos, woodwind arabesques. At the moment of Iolanta's cure in the finale, the first rays of light reaching her newly sensitive eyes are depicted with chords of artificial string harmonics, and her momentary fright is underscored by fugitive whole-tone scales."[186]

The Nutcracker also frustrated him. Nothing in Vsevolozhsky's scenario had initially inspired him, and he rued signing the contract knowing the trip to New York was coming up. Inspiration of the saddest sort came en route. His treasured, much-doted-on sister, Sasha, died on March 28, 1891. Memories of the golden summers he had spent with her in Kamianka came flooding back. He knew that she had been battling alcoholism and morphine addiction, but her death nonetheless came as a shock, doubly so because he learned about it not from a family member but from the newspaper. His brother Modest received a telegram but decided against sharing it with Pyotr, knowing that it would disrupt his travel and concert plans. In Paris, on the first leg of his long trip to the United States and where he conducted his Second Piano Concerto with Vasily Sapelnikov as soloist, Tchaikovsky had stopped in a reading room to catch up on events in Russia. There he saw the announcement in *New Times* about Sasha's memorial and burial in Alexander Nevsky Monastery in St. Petersburg.[187] As Modest predicted, the composer was gutted and thought about canceling his trip. But he couldn't; the trip had been long planned and a portion of the colossal payment for his services from the Music Hall Company of New York and the piano manufacturer Knabe—$5,000, equivalent to $150,000 in today's dollars—had been sent to him in advance.[188] Tchaikovsky composed the sugary second act of *The Nutcracker* for his sister (who lived near a sugar factory) in memoriam.[189]

Lost, too, is the symbolism of the plot, which derives from E. T. A. Hoffmann's 1816 gothic fable "The Nutcracker and the Mouse King" as reimagined by Alexandre Dumas and Vsevolozhsky, who hosted Christmas parties for "students lacking means" much like the gathering depicted in Act I.[190] *The Nutcracker* passed, in short, from a German and French context to a Russian one. In 1890, Vsevolozhsky devised the scenario for which Marius Petipa and his energetic assistant Lev Ivanov created choreography and Tchaikovsky composed music over fourteen months—before, during, and after his effort with *Iolanta*. As with the one-act opera, the composer didn't think he had a hit on his hands with this new, two-act ballet. He left St. Petersburg after the premiere for Switzerland, France, and Ukraine, where he conducted and attended the Odesa premiere of *The Queen of Spades*, receiving a silver wreath from the singers inscribed with the words "from the mortal to the immortal. January 19, 1893."[191] He was asked about *Iolanta* and *The Nutcracker*, but he wasn't in for self-promotion. People enjoyed the opera, he allowed, but not the ballet. "[It] was quite well done. A lavish production, everything turned out perfectly, still, it seemed the public didn't like it and was bored."[192]

The curtain rises on a neatly trimmed eighteenth-century German household belonging to the president of a town council, Silberhaus, in one of Germany's "gingerbread principalities" (as smaller German and French political units were nicknamed). It's Christmas Eve, and the daughter of the family, Marie (alternately Clara), receives a nutcracker from Councilor Drosselmeyer, her godfather, at the end of a magic show. Her bratty brother snatches the gift from her and breaks it. That night Marie dreams of sweet revenge against her sibling specifically and her conventional upbringing more generally. There is a pitched battle between the Nutcracker, flanked by fellow soldiers, and the mice patrolling the kitchen, after which the Christmas tree grows to a humungous size to the world-crossing strains of a barcarolle. Marie and the Nutcracker, morphed into a prince, subsequently travel through a *ballet blanc* dreamscape into a court of illuminated fountains. There they experience a thousand delights in the form of national dances, a glittering *ballet des nations* divertissement.

Tchaikovsky dreamily obscures pulse, meter, and rhythm throughout the score. He uses syncopation, juxtaposition of double and triple rhythms, hemiola (which is nothing new in dance music and central to the waltz since the days of Johann Strauss Jr.), displacement within the measure, and in the most elaborate instances, a recurring developmental pattern where compound rhythms struggle to assert dominance within simple meter. The beat is harder to find after Drosselmeyer's appearance, and meter is distorted in all the dances in the second act, with the exception of the apotheosis and the appearance (in the original version) of a beehive. In measure 73 of Act I (no. 7), the soldier's bugle call of two sixteenths and three eighths begins on the fourth beat, while the music of the mice sounds on the downbeat; thus, the soldiers and the mice attack each other a beat apart. The battle intensifies and grows more uncertain, ceding to sixteenths, dotted militaristic rhythms, and unstable syncopations that give the conflict its feeling of frenzied excitement. The night scene when the tree grows and grows begins with quiet triplets in the French horns. The triplets grow louder, and the horns fill the entire texture, imposing 6/8 on to 4/4. A comparable juxtaposition is heard in the climactic *pas de deux*, even though the two episodes—the anxious *pas d'action* involving the tree, and the Sugar Plum Fairy's duet with the prince—don't have an obvious connection.

The Nutcracker privileges pantomime and social dances in the first act, after which some of the performers, students of the imperial ballet school, sang the textless chorus of the entr'acte leading to the suite of national dances. Keeping social dances and the national dances entirely separate wasn't the original plan. Tchaikovsky drafted the Spanish and Chinese dances, "chocolate" and "tea," for the first act, as well as the French dance, for which he used the folksong

"Giroflé-Giroflá." As the conception matured, these dances were moved to the second act, making room for a boisterous Cossack Trepak, an English gigue, and an "Arabian," "coffee" dance actually based on a Georgian tune called "Iavnana," a lullaby as well as a healing prayer:

Bring relief to our children,	čems bavšvebs ušeɣavatet,
O violet, naninao!	iav-naninao![193]

One of Petipa's cast lists adds "caramel," "pistachios," "macaroons," "nougat," and "peppermint drops" to the confections.[194] These are fancy treats, imported from other places. Blander Russian fare—berries and mead—isn't on the menu.

Ballet can be an imperial—meaning colonialist—artform. Consider, though, that for Tchaikovsky, the "Chinese" dance had less to do with reducing the people of China to the tea shipped along the Silk Road than the sound of the whistling kettle in his sister's kitchen. Same goes for Arabia: Sasha knew the "Iavnana" berceuse. To the imaginative ear, refrains of the *panikhida*, a Russian Orthodox prayer for the dead, can be heard in the concluding *pas de deux*, suggesting a painful nostalgia.[195] The heart of the ballet, the "Waltz of the Snowflakes," imagines bluffs of snow around Sasha's home. That recollection inspired a musical journey into a realm of enlightenment with marvelous new sonorities and a wordless chorus comparable to the guardians of Tamino, Papageno, and Pamina in Mozart's *Magic Flute*.[196] Tchaikovsky, Petipa, and Ivanov further drew on the wizardry of optical illusions, musical tone painting in the impressionist style, and the blizzard images found in poems by the Russian "mystic" Symbolist poets Alexander Blok and Andrey Belïy. And the "Waltz of the Snowflakes" is also a chaconne comprising eight variations over a repeated harmonic sequence. Both these dances have specific connotations: the waltz is associated with desire, the chaconne elegiac.[197]

Within this personal tribute to his sister is also a reminder of Tchaikovsky's civic- and court-mindedness. Chocolate factories had opened all over Russia in the mid- to late 1880s, and the Franco-Russian political alliance had pumped French capital into Russia. The 1891 agreement between the two countries even spurred talk of a mutual defense accord. The original second act of *The Nutcracker* recalled a coronation feast, and the nutcracker soldiers wore outfits from the Napoleonic era, as did some of the guests at the Silberhauses' Christmas party. The ballet ended with an image of a honeycomb and swirling bees, a reference to Catherine the Great's vision of harmonious empire.[198]

Hoffmann's story is eerie, in places downright scary. The mouse king drools blood and squeals and hisses in Marie's ear. Such scenes didn't make it into the ballet yet can still be heard in the discordant chromatic passages assigned to the godfather, Drosselmeyer, whose name roughly translates as "mess-maker." Tchaikovsky excised some of the chromaticism before the premiere along with a passage of pantomime and the less-than-a-minute-long English dance.

The other Hoffmann elements that made it into the ballet are subtle but, once heard, stay in the mind. Consider the second act "Waltz of the Flowers." The orchestration is bafflingly strange, "topsy turvy" in Rimsky-Korsakov's parlance. The tuba grinds those poor flowers into the dirt even before we get to the wilting B minor of the middle section. Another riddle is the harp solo that introduces the tuba. As Sara Cutler writes, the harp cadenzas in *The Nutcracker* and *Sleeping Beauty* are *too* eclectic, "either unplayable or in places so unidiomatically written for the instrument as to prove ineffective."[199] The score requires the left and right hands to rapidly play rising sixteenth notes in tandem, a difficult task made impossible when the hands are cold (the cadenzas are preceded by long rests). Tchaikovsky matches Wagner in treating the harp like a sideways piano (the unidiomatic "Magic Fire" music from *Die Walküre* is a notorious case in point), neglecting, among other things, the taxingly high tension in the upper strings. The cadenza in the Act II lakeside scene in *Swan Lake* allows the harpist to relax their hands and lower their arms; the later cadenzas do not. For this reason the Mariinsky Theater harpist, the German virtuoso Albert Zabel and the founder of the Russian school of harp playing, simplified the "Rose Adagio" and "Waltz of the Flowers" cadenzas, "eliminating the contrary motion and playing the arpeggios as thirty-second-note descending right-left arpeggios."[200] He had Tchaikovsky's blessing to do so, and indeed the manuscript of *The Nutcracker* includes the marking "instead of this cadenza the performer can perform another one of their choosing."[201] Because *The Nutcracker* was premiered under the baton of the Italian-born conductor Riccardo Drigo, Tchaikovsky wrote some of the performance instructions in Italian. The manuscript also, however, includes notes in French and Russian. Tchaikovsky specifies when and where the toy instruments should be deployed; he includes a more complicated string bass part in the battle scene than the ballet currently features (the music has been simplified over time) and remarked that the scoring of Act I, no. 5, "the scene and dance of [Drosselmeyer]," exactly replicates that of the children's march in *The Queen of Spades*.

For the beloved *Nutcracker* variation for the Sugar Plum Fairy, Petipa requested from Tchaikovsky thirty-two measures of music for the seasoned Italian prima ballerina Antonietta Dell'Era, a precise terre à terre dancer who took the part for the first three performances.[202] Tchaikovsky composed the dance for his new toy: the celesta. This instrument was invented in 1886 by Auguste Mustel, a Parisian organ maker whose father had built a comparable instrument called the typophone, used by Vincent d'Indy in his *Le chant de la cloche* (1883) and Ernest Chausson in his incidental music to *The Tempest* (1888).[203] The soft sound of the typophone, produced by tuning forks rather than resonant metal bars, precluded its use in large ensembles, spurring Mustel's invention. "Celesta No. 1" was exhibited at the Paris Exposition Universelle of 1889 and, along with its inventor, received an award. French composers rushed to be the first to use it, as did Tchaikovsky.

In a June 3, 1891, letter to his publisher, he described his encounter with the instrument in Paris on his way to the United States, going into detail about the logistics of purchasing it and transporting it to Russia:

I discovered a new orchestral instrument in Paris, something between a miniature piano and a Glockenspiel, with a divinely wondrous sound. I'm keen to use this instrument in the symphonic poem *The Voyevoda* and in the ballet. It won't be needed in the ballet until the fall of 1892, but I'll need it for *The Voyevoda* next season, since I'm committed to conducting this piece for the Petersburg Musical Society, and I might also get to conduct it in Moscow. The instrument is called the *"Celesta Mustel"* and costs 1,200 francs. It can be obtained only from its Paris inventor, M. Mustel. I'm hoping you'll order this instrument for me. You won't lose anything on it, since you'll be leasing it out for all the concerts where *The Voyevoda* is being given. And after that you can sell it to the Theater directorate when it's needed for the ballet. I'd be happy to order the celesta myself, but 1) I don't know the procedure for doing so, and 2) where would I store it and how would I rent it out and then sell it to the directorate? I don't know how to do any of that. If you can cede to my request, then please contact [your accountant] P. I. Yurasov for him to liaise with M. Mustel about ordering the celesta. After I arrive in Moscow, I'll provide Mustel's address and all the necessary instructions to Yurasov or [Yurasov's assistant] Nina Valeryanovna. Since the instrument will be needed in Petersburg before Moscow, it would be best to send it from Paris to Osip Ivanovich [Jurgenson's older brother]. Please know that I don't want anyone else to see it; I fear that Rimsky-Korsakov and Glazunov will hear about it and deploy its extraordinary effects before I get to do so. I will be in Moscow for a few days and will fill you in on everything at your office; meantime, please place the order so that arrangements can begin with M. Mustel. I predict that this new instrument will have a colossal effect.[204]

Tchaikovsky's orchestral tone poem *The Voyevoda* is a distinct outlier in his output. Its conception dates from his youth and Tsar Alexander II's interest in an organic rapprochement of Slavic nationalities within his empire: Russian, Polish, and Ukrainian. So long as Russia was the dominant player, the occupying power, everything was hunky-dory from the tsar's perspective. Tchaikovsky's composition was specifically inspired by Pushkin's translation of Adam Mickiewicz's *Ambush: A Ukrainian Ballad* (*Czaty [Ballada ukraińska]*, 1828), about a provincial governor's efforts to catch his wife when she's with another man. She's innocent; the man isn't her lover, just an aggrieved resident of the province. Tchaikovsky conducted the November 6, 1891, premiere in Moscow on a robust program including Grieg, Bach, Glazunov, Nápravník, and the "Dance of the Hay Maidens" from his *Voyevoda* opera, then consigned the tone poem to the trash, tearing up the score and canceling additional performances. The general arc of his career as a program-music and opera composer indicates two obsessions: the residents of the Volga heartland and the Muscovy princes and governors oppressing them. Something about good people being conditioned to love bad people fascinated him; so too mutable borders and changing alliances; and so too doomed relationships and the transcendence of that doom, with fairytale overtones. Tchaikovsky tried and tried again to balance the realistic and fantastic elements to an affecting end. He never got it right.

The organizer of the premiere, Tchaikovsky's assistant and advocate Alexander Siloti, irritated the composer by ignoring his request to destroy the orchestral parts, which allowed, down the road, for the score to be restored and recorded. (Touted as the next Liszt in the

Russian press, though he had tidier hair and less flamboyance, Siloti would likewise assemble an edition of the Second Piano Concerto drastically at odds with Tchaikovsky's stated intentions for it.)[205] Taneyev was another annoyance. He bluntly told Tchaikovsky that he should have turned the Pushkin/Mickiewicz text into a vocal scene rather than an orchestral piece.[206] Tchaikovsky agreed with him, sort of, informing Jurgenson that he had no regrets withdrawing *Voyevoda* from publication, since it was a "compromised" score and

> a gray-haired old man needs to keep moving forward (as was even possible for Verdi, still growing as a composer at age eighty [Tchaikovsky is referring to *Falstaff*]) or to remain at the height reached earlier. If it happens again with another score, I'll tear it to shreds and then give up composing for good. The last thing in the world I'd want to be is like A[nton] G[rigoriyevich Rubinstein], who kept scribbling long after he'd fizzled out.[207]

Tchaikovsky at least found use for the tone poem's devastating final chords in his *Pathétique* Symphony of 1893. In the earlier context, the chords represent the murder of the governor by the Cossack enlisted to assassinate the governor's runaway wife.

Had Tchaikovsky not rejected this *Voyevoda* as he had the opera, the tone poem would have been performed in St. Petersburg at a concert of the Imperial Russian Musical Society on February 29, 1892. Instead, Tchaikovsky proposed conducting a suite of dances from the as-yet-unfinished *Nutcracker*. He selected, and then orchestrated, eight numbers grouped into three movements: the *Ouverture miniature*; the Act I, no. 2, March; the Sugar Plum Fairy variation; the Russian, Arabic, and Chinese dances; the Reed-Flutes dance; and the Flowers Waltz. The premiere, on March 7, delighted young and old, and the suite was subsequently performed on July 4 at Moscow's Electrical Exhibition No. 1 before additional performances in St. Petersburg, the audience demanding encores each time.[208]

Electricity arrived in Moscow in time for Alexander III's coronation. "3,500 brilliant Edison lamps" magically "traced the lines of the Kremlin's towers, domes, and crosses" on May 15, 1883. "From the towers beamed intense 'electric suns,'" none, of course, shining brighter than the emperor himself.[209] Electricity began to be marketed to Moscow's residents in 1887, thanks to a generating station capable of sending 120 volts through underground cables to well-to-do subscribers. The 1892 Electrical Exhibition opened in a prime location in Moscow: the corner of the Garden Ring Road and Tverskaya, the central avenue, and included different pavilions demonstrating various "operating control devices," electric fire alarms, handheld telephones, and "photographs on porcelain" made "with the aid of electric light." The exhibition grounds boasted a central garden and strolling area, a tram, and a launchpad from which a hot-air balloon rose, its journey traced by spotlight affixed to the roof of a house.[210] Electricity illuminated the fountains near the outdoor stage where Tchaikovsky's suite was conducted by Vojtěch Hlaváč, a popular local musician leading his first symphonic concert before a friendly summertime audience. Besides the suite, Hlaváč conducted *Manfred*, the *Sérénade mélancolique*, Valse-Scherzo, Italian Capriccio, the Elegy from the Serenade for Strings, the "Dance of the Hay Maidens," and even the polonaise from *Vakula the Smith*. "All three movements of the *Nutcracker* Suite are undeniably original, written in a light, elegant style and in the instrumentation present an inexhaustible richness of colors and sound combinations," the *Moscow Register* reported, adding that, despite a downpour, the audience stayed until the end.[211]

Tchaikovsky's celebrity also meant foreign interest in *Nutcrackers*, as it was first called in America, and *Casse noisette* everywhere else outside of Russia. Audiences in Chicago heard the suite on October 22, and in Detroit a month after that.[212]

The actual ballet didn't fare as well. Reviews of its belated premiere, on Sunday, December 6, 1892, at the Mariinsky Theater, were flat. The *Petersburg Newspaper* offered up the meanest critique, deriding

The Nutcracker as a bore for adults and not much fun for children. The double billing meant that the sold-out crowd had to wait until midnight for Petipa's star dancer, Dell'Era, to finally appear—part of the reason that the ballet almost immediately began to be presented apart from the opera. Dell'Era performed the *pas de deux* with Pavel Gerdt as the prince. "The adagio is replete with combinations and attitudes where the ballerina demonstrates her inimitable grace and plasticity, but it was interminable. The ballerina isn't to blame for this: she wanted to make cuts but that didn't happen," the writer elaborated. Meantime, the stage machines noisily clunked and something smashed offstage. "The lighting was primitive, and the fountains in the final scene most pathetic. The stage crew obviously isn't up to the challenge of *fontaines lumineuses*."[213]

Nonspecialists poked fun at the ballet as well:

The ballet is written for those who like to eat gingerbread and aren't afraid of mice. Balletomanes loudly protest: we don't want gingerbread, and all the mice running around and squeaking interrupts our pleasant tête-à-têtes. The writer of these lines knows nothing of ballet's tricks, and so it seemed to him that Ms. Anderyanon [Anderson] danced in Chinese best of all. What a delightful Chinese girl she was. The snow ensemble was also good. Ballerinas in white tunics decorated with snow puffs with icicles on their heads shook snow-covered branches. And when the corps sat and lay down it was like a pleasurably warm blanketing of snow. Outside, meanwhile, it was also snowing, but it gave no pleasure. That's art for you![214]

The "Waltz of the Snowflakes" had serious admirers, not just among the synesthetes of the World of Art movement. Asafyev ruminated on the ballet throughout his career. He had been a répétiteur pianist in the Mariinsky Theater in 1910 and was involved as a dramatist in productions of the 1930s. He didn't like Vsevolozhsky's scenario and panned Petipa's/Ivanov's choreography and encouraged a later choreographer, Vasily Vainonen, to abandon the fairytale apotheosis in favor of an image of Marie realizing the Land of Sweets was all a dream. Still, the ballet had moments of magic. "The imaginings of the heroine and hero break through into a fresh space—into the forest and nature and the wind, the blizzard, and further to the stars and into the rose sea of hopes." Asafyev wanted to hear the end of childhood in Tchaikovsky's score and imagined the melancholic celesta shedding metal teardrops for the ballerina. As to romance, the throbbing strings are "born of a heartache accumulating in the heart and long repressed." Asafyev also heard (or pretended to hear) the end of the imperial era in the *pas de deux*, a premonition of loss and even doom. No wonder Marie buries her head under the pillow.[215]

In 1892, pairing *The Nutcracker* with *Iolanta* made financial and logistical sense for the Imperial Theaters. For Tchaikovsky, it made sense for another reason. He associated childhood with the divine and sought to preserve, in sound, childhood's blending of reality and fantasy. Growing old encumbers the mind, a development Tchaikovsky resisted in his balletic masterpiece celebrating the joys and sorrows of youth at the end of another year.

And had Tchaikovsky had another year, as opposed to just ten months, there is a chance he would have written something for children's orchestra or choir. Smolensky recalls him taking a keen interest in the toy instruments kept in the Synodal College during a visit in April. Tchaikovsky tried them all.[216]

PART IV

MATTERS OF LIFE AND DEATH

Escape

Alexei Apukhtin died in 1893, a few months before Tchaikovsky's own unexpected end. He and the composer had known each other almost from the start, having studied together at the School of Jurisprudence. Apukhtin wrote for the school's newspaper and was noticed by Ivan Turgenev. Apukhtin worked alongside Tchaikovsky at the Ministry of Justice, then for the governor of the province (Oryol) where he was raised. Tchaikovsky frolicked with him in Oryol during one of his vacations from the ministry. Apukhtin pursued magazine and journal writing and lectured on Alexander Pushkin, his idol and source of inspiration. He angered as he aged, expressing increasingly jaded views about life and art while also upbraiding Tchaikovsky for serving his own talent so zealously, ignoring the upheaval in Russian culture brought about by the Reforms and the rise of the *raznochintsï* (middle-class intelligentsia). He despised Russia's cultural diversification: the rise of avant-garde voices, religious philosophers antagonistic to the church, peasant as well as proletarian figures. "What's the point?" the disenchanted poet asked his composer friend. "Back in the day when some of our nobles pursued literature, I could still imagine myself as a full-time writer. But now no amount of coercion can make me enter a sphere of such corrupted meanness, denunciations, and ... seminarians [*razno-chintsi*]."[1] Apukhtin couldn't countenance Tchaikovsky's efforts to keep classicism alive in an era of transformation—his musical commitment to ideals of "truth, goodness, and beauty."[2] Apukhtin extracted himself from the fray and became a shut-in, spending his days slumped in an armchair reciting Pushkin to himself and beginning to suffer from the edema that took his life. In his final decade the tired bard put out a stuffy collection of poems; he occasionally appeared in public as a fat, red-faced caricature (according to a younger peer) of a man of letters. Joking around and "goofing off" were long behind him.[3] He became serious about historical writing; Alexander III listened to him read, so too Konstantin Romanov (K. R.).

Like Tchaikovsky, Apukhtin was a politically conservative man who had sex with other men, some underage (he was an open pederast). Tchaikovsky turned a half dozen of his poems into songs. Three of them ("To Forget So Soon," "He Loved Me So," and "No Response, No Word, No Greeting") have been interpreted by Philip Ross Bullock as expressions of musical-poetic queerness.[4] Apukhtin had a crucial piece of advice for the composer: ignore the slander about your private life, and Tchaikovsky did. He also told him that artistic creation was antithetical to work, because work was a bitter necessity and artistic creation an act of sensual pleasure. "Could it really be said that my admiration of the beauty of X is work!?" he asked Tchaikovsky, recalling the enigmatic XXX of the unused draft program for the Fifth Symphony.[5]

Apukhtin's funeral notice appeared in an issue of the *Petersburg Journal* that contained no shortage of sensational news from the day before (about the "horrible discovery" of body parts at a construction site; a well-dressed gentleman getting run over by a carriage driven by a ten-year-old; the theft of 400 rubles from a merchant's wife; a plant worker blowing up the apartment of a hated supervisor). Tchaikovsky didn't attend Apukhtin's burial on August 20 in the Nikolskoye Cemetery of the Alexander Nevsky Monastery in St. Petersburg; the ceremony was for family members only. The preceding memorial service was attended by poets and writers and the director of the School of Jurisprudence along with members of the court. Apukhtin was buried next to the crypt of the Kasatkin-Rostov clan.[6]

K. R. suggested that Tchaikovsky set Apukhtin's "Requiem," written around 1869, as a memorial to the poet. Part 4 of the cycle includes these piteous reflections on God:

С воплем бессилия, с криком печали	With a cry of impotence, a cry of sadness
Он повалился недвижен и нем.	He collapsed onto the ground motionless and speechless.
Вот он, смотрите, лежит без дыханья . . .	There he is, look, lying without breathing . . .
Боже! к чему он родился и рос?	God! For what purpose was he born and raised?
Эти сомненья, измены, страданья,—	These doubts, betrayals, sufferings,—
Боже, зачем же он их перенес?	God, why did he have to bear them?
Пусть хоть слеза над усопшим прольется,	Let at least one tear be shed over the deceased,
Пусть хоть теперь замолчит клевета . . .	Let the slander now be silenced . . .
Сердце, горячее сердце не бьется,	A heart, a passionate heart no longer beats,
Вежды сомкнуты, безмолвны уста.	The eyelids are closed, the mouth silent.
Скоро нещадное, грозное тленье	Soon merciless, terrible decay

Ляжет печатью на нем роковой . . .	And the seal of fate will be affixed to him . . .
Дай ему, Боже, грехов отпущенье,	Forgive him, God, for his sins,
Дай ему вечный покой!	Grant him eternal peace!⁷

The composer decided against setting these words, telling Romanov that he didn't agree with Apukhtin's appeal to God for God not to exist and that he had frankly exhausted the subject of death in his *Pathétique* Symphony, which he had composed after abandoning work on a symphony in E♭ major about death's supposed opposite: life. En route to New York City from Rouen, he bought a notepad and began sketching this latter work, with the following programmatic entries: "Motif: For what purpose? Why? Why"; "Origin and basic idea of the whole symphony." Then: "Motif for the finale after the Why. At first, no answer, but then a sudden solemnity." The skimpy plan evolved into a meditation on "love," "disillusionment," "youth," and "difficulties" overcome through positive thinking and soldiering on, moving "forward! Forward!"⁸

He worked on and off on the "Life" Symphony until December 1892, a period of deep unhappiness caused by a miserable trip to Vienna. He had often fantasized about a triumphant engagement in the city but learned that he'd been booked to conduct his First Orchestral Suite in a restaurant. The room was "full of stuffiness and reek[ed] of unpleasant oils" and other consumable items, including "sausages and beer," so, after a day of trying to make the space work, he canceled the humiliating engagement, traveling instead to Mozart's hometown, Salzburg, as a tourist.⁹ He purchased a deluxe edition of Mozart's works and jotted down his own musical ideas on the blank pages. The reaction to the *Iolanta/Nutcracker* premiere further soured his mood, as did the Imperial Theater's decision to pull *The Queen of Spades* from the repertoire. He didn't get the respect he knew he deserved in central Europe and was fed up with jealous mediocrities writing bad reviews of his works in Russia. Tchaikovsky decided that the "Life" Symphony wasn't worth pursuing and so repurposed three of the four movements as a piano concerto. (The other movement became the Scherzo-Fantasie of his Eighteen Pieces for Solo Piano.) The piano concerto would have been his third had he completed it, but he didn't get beyond the bassoon-and-tuba-dominated opening movement (whose supposedly life-affirming cadenza ironically alludes to Liszt's *Danse Macabre*). Taneyev realized the second and third movements after Tchaikovsky's death and published them separately from the first movement.[10]

The *Pathétique* has no obvious pretext, and the dedication to his nephew, Bob Davïdov, is a cipher—academic fantasies of an erastês–erômenos relationship gone wrong notwithstanding.[11] (Tchaikovsky said that the symphony had a secret program but he said that a lot, to generate interest.) People other than Apukhtin had died, and his most morbid songs come from this period: settings of poems by Daniil Rathaus (1868–1937), a twenty-four-year-old student at the University of St. Vladimir in Kyiv and self-declared melancholic. One of the Rathaus-based songs, "Mid Bleak Days" ("Sred' mrachnïkh dney"), has been described by Lucia Denk as a paradoxical preservation and immortalization of "the ephemeral," with reverberations in the piano capturing the mists of recollection and the invigorating ascent into a condition of lightness. Transparent harmonic progressions define the clearest memories, and destabilizing secondary dominants suggest what belongs to the distant, murky past.[12] Another Rathaus setting, which turned out to be Tchaikovsky's last completed song, is called "Again, as Before, Alone" ("Snova, kak prezhde, odin"). It speaks to nature's indifference to the protagonist's solitude, with the voice inhabiting an exceedingly narrow range within A minor (A–C), and the piano iterating its own minor third (E–G). The spare texture is unusual for Tchaikovsky and involves a terse selection of chords: i 6/4, VI 5/3, the tonic seventh chord (converted from minor to major when the focus shifts to nature), and ♯iv°4/3 reflecting pain in the moment. There's one dramatic moment amid the uneventful-ness: a stark articulation of a vii°7 chord atop the tonic for the lines "Everything that's happening to me / I can't convey [Vsyo, chto tvoritsya so mnoy, / Ya peredat' ne berus']." That chord is the nexus of the song, capturing the intense aspects of life, of everything that's happened all at once. The circularity of "alone, as before" is replicated in "Pray for me / I'm already praying for you! [Pomolis' za menya / Ya za tebya uzh molyus'!]." There's no means of conveying what's been happening, since the other is gone for good, leaving the protagonist caught in the loop of memory. Thus, the song ends where it began, where it ended.

After the songs were published by Jurgenson in August 1893, Tchaikovsky wrote to Rathaus expressing the hope that they might one day meet. They never did. He also asked for his photograph and was surprised to see that the author of the bleakest poems he ever set was but a college kid. Tchaikovsky added a personal thought: that he aspired to be "sincere in my music—and as a matter of fact I am predominantly inclined to sad songs, like you, at least in recent years, although I want for nothing and generally consider myself a happy man!"[13] The exclamation point is the giveaway: he's saying that, frankly, there's no other choice but to be happy.

The *Pathétique* (meaning impassioned, pathos-filled) performs the same operation as "Again, as Before, Alone." It's circular, starting where it finished. The secret is a nonsecret: it's about death, which is a typical subject for art, often with the curtain drop of death denied, a transcendent elsewhere invoked, or linked to the immemorial rotation of the seasons. Tchaikovsky's explicit engagement with the subject has turned the symphony into a kind of curse. "The human whose name is written in these notes shall die." Composing the symphony killed him; listening to it might be fatal too.

Musicologist Marina Ritzarev has dedicated an entire book to the *Pathétique*, describing it more hopefully as a musical shrine to Christ's Passion: "The image that might have served as inspiration for

Tchaikovsky's masterpiece was that of Jesus Christ, his life and death, transformed into a general imagery of the Passion." It's a theory, and Ritzarev doesn't oversell it, noting the composer's unknowable intentions. Ritzarev considers Tchaikovsky's knowledge of the Bible, his interest in the religious genres and in Passion and Requiem compositions by Bach and other non-Russian composers, and the prominence of the Christ theme in Russian culture. If the Passion is the symphony's subject, it had to be sublimated, she believes, since the official church prohibited "representation of the gospel theme in the theater or on the concert stage." Defining the "Passion plot," however, is difficult. Ritzarev's technical discussion centers on the echoes of Bach's *St. Matthew Passion*, the incursion of passages from an Offenbach operetta, tonal symbolism, and correspondences between the *Pathétique* and other scores by Tchaikovsky. Much of what she argues is plausible, excluding the strange identification of "the rooster call of anxiety" in the first movement—associated with the crowing apparently heard on Christ's path to Golgotha. Tchaikovsky's rooster, however, is unnaturally chromatic: the call Ritzarev hears in the symphony consists of two eighth notes followed by two quarter notes, moving up by semitone from G to G♯ to A and then back down by semitone to G♯.[14]

One thing is always noticed: the middle of the first movement quotes "With the saints, give rest, Christ, to the souls of Thy servant," a hymn heard in the middle of the Orthodox service for the departed, the memorial gathering before the burial. (It's a feature of the abbreviated service, the supplication or "litiya.")[15] The deceased enters an eternal realm without sickness and sadness. The first movement has something of this double nature: the second theme is a bright contrast to the first, the denial of the acceptance, the mind unable to grasp its nonbeing. Perhaps it's a glimpse of the radiant beyond, but the glimpse is fleeting, obliterated by a quadruple-forte trombone blast.

The second movement is a dance that can't be danced, cast in a spectral 5/4, and generally interpreted as a delirious recollection of a waltz, which makes a certain sense given the evenness of the phrase lengths: eight-measure groups in a transparent three-part structure. The recollection of the dance is there, but something is missing. Memories are subjective, there are gaps, and one parent and one part of the house might be remembered better than others. The instruments that should be providing the sixth beat of the compound duple meter are absent, just empty chairs.

All those symphonies, before and after Tchaikovsky's time, that move from funeral march to triumphant fanfare are delusional. Even worse: they are con acts. Tchaikovsky exposes the con in the third movement of the *Pathétique*, a perpetuo moto that becomes a march in the minor and then the triumphant major that suggests an ending. There is no point in standing up and applauding, however, as the music moves on to a cadential gesture, endlessly iterated. Together with the pendular back-and-forth patterns in the woodwinds and strings, Tchaikovsky relies on descending sequences of perfect fourths and falling scales, cheap filler for a hollow texture.

The first movement occupies ecclesiastical time, quoting, dead center, the prayer; the second movement is a broken metronome; the third a pendulum swaying much too fast. (The paradox of an exceedingly long scherzo movement representing time running out was not lost on the composer.) The theme/nontheme of the concluding adagio lamentoso is another falling pattern: a musical picture of sand draining from the top to the bottom of an hourglass, repeatedly: death isn't an end, Tchaikovsky simply states, because death never ends. The scalar descent is distributed, along with its harmonization, between the blended upper strings and lower woodwinds. The narrow range suggests imprisonment and powerlessness. The glass is dipped back over, the bottom of the theme becoming the top. Pitch is eviscerated: the strings are muted, the reeds of the bassoons loudly buzz, the revival fails only to be reattempted, and reattempted again, before a slow disappearance. B minor becomes D major and briefly C major before the return of the B-minor block, with the symphony ending as it began, in the lowest of the lower depths, an eclipse at sunset.

Composers as sophisticated as Rachmaninoff relied on the Dies Irae chant to spell the end, taking the listener to the isle of the dead and then keeping the music going to affirm that the crossing of the River Styx is an infinite event—everyone will take the trip. Tchaikovsky makes the same point in the *Pathétique*, but without the famous chant. The final measures of the final movement stare unflinchingly at death, as a "darkness in which nothing is hidden," without the allegories.[16] Death is compulsory; there's no avoiding it; no happy endings, neither love nor religion nor art nor psychiatric counseling nor healthy living, can transcend it. Tchaikovsky leaned hard on this point in *Swan Lake* and *The Enchantress*: the lovers think that if they can only just hold on to each other things will be all right, but the river is going to absorb them and frankly they both should have known that they're not going to make it. The absorption is heard in the opening measures of these scores and throughout the *Pathétique*.

No sketches survive, but a short score written in a swift hand does. It's in two, three, and mostly four staves with occasional indications for instrumentation (trombone entrances in the otherwise string- and woodwind-dominanted score). The second movement follows the first, third, and fourth movements, amid sketches for an unrealized composition for cello and piano with funereal intonations of its own. The draft score of the fourth movement is written out of order; measures 38–89 appear before measures 1–37 and 90–171. After each movement Tchaikovsky wrote the Russian equivalent of "Praise the Lord!"[17]

He began rehearsing the *Pathétique* on October 10, 1893, and conducted the premiere six days later on October 16, a concert sponsored as usual by the Imperial Russian Musical Society. It was the first half of a program that had Tchaikovsky also conducting an overture composed in 1868 by Herman Laroche for an unrealized opera based on Musset's comedy *Carmosine* and the dances from Mozart's *tragédie lyrique Idomeneo* (1781). Laroche was but a dabbler in composition, and the overture is a patchwork: turgid string fugue, brass and timpani fanfare, and a mini Konzertstück for Piano and Orchestra. It hadn't been heard since 1869 and was panned back then as an example of composition by number ("glued together according to the rules of music theory").[18] The second half of the program featured Liszt's 1858 *Rhapsodie espagnole* and Tchaikovsky's First Piano Concerto with one of Liszt's protégés, Adele aus der Ohe, as soloist. She had performed the concerto under Tchaikovsky's direction in New York City for the opening of the Music Hall and done so brilliantly.

Several reviews appeared on October 18 and October 19, the critical reaction being cooler than the response in the hall, where Tchaikovsky repeatedly basked in applause. St. Petersburg's commentators looked at one another in bafflement, then, per usual, came up with a joint response to what they'd heard. "The new symphony was doubtless influenced by the composer's travels abroad," *New Times* claimed. "There's much clever insight here, and acumen in the handling of orchestral colors, gracefulness (especially in the middle two movements), and craft, but in terms of inspiration it yields to the composer's other symphonies."[19] The *Petersburg Newspaper* echoed these points: "Gracefulness (especially in the two allegros)" supplanted other composers' "love for din and noise," but "there were inconsistencies in certain movements between their endings and what was heard before. The piece as a whole isn't marred by this, however, and his new symphony, though less inspired than his others, was heard with interest."[20] There's no mention of the music's desolation and morbidity. Tchaikovsky had to die for those things to be heard, for the *Pathétique* to make "a gripping, deeply tragic impression."[21]

He made changes to the symphony ahead of Jurgenson publishing the first edition. During this time the *Pathétique* acquired its name (at the premiere it was simply called Symphony No. 6 in B minor). Tchaikovsky did not get the chance to conduct it in Moscow on

December 4, as he had pledged to do back in July. That concert was in support of a charity that Nikolay Rubinstein had set up a quarter century back to provide pensions to the widows and orphans of musicians. The concert did happen, but without Tchaikovsky. As Aus der Ohe lamented in an interview with the *Chicago Sunday Tribune*,

Tchaikovsky was well and happy, but there seemed to lurk in his mind the presentiment of sudden death. In the intermission he spoke of Gounod's demise and of the great age granted him [the French composer had died in October of 1893 at age seventy-five]. Several times he repeated, "If I could only live twenty years more, how much I could write, what things I might be able to do." The report that the first performance of the Sixth Symphony did not meet with enthusiastic reception was incorrect. The first and last movements were especially well received. Tchaikovsky said with that childlike simplicity that distinguished him, "I am so glad they like those movements best; they are my favorites, too." The symphony was named during its performance the *Pathétique*. His concerto in B♭ minor, which I played on this occasion, was warmly received; and I walked up to the conductor's desk and, taking his hand, made him acknowledge the applause which was due to his work, not mine. The next evening Tchaikovsky invited myself and several friends to dinner. Again the idea of approaching death seemed impressed upon him, although he was apparently in the best of health. He seemed especially anxious to revise his third pianoforte concerto. While the work pleased him he wished to give the solo instruments a greater opportunity. Both that work and his opera *Romeo and Juliet*, however, were doomed never to reach completion. Tuesday he called upon me and heard me play some of his compositions. Wednesday he should have left for Moscow, where, as I was engaged to play there, I hoped to meet him. For some reason he failed to make his departure. Thursday he was taken ill, and the disease was pronounced cholera.

Notwithstanding the dread in which the disease is held, callers besieged his house and the physicians, of whom four were in attendance, were obliged to post bulletins on the door to avoid danger of contagion. He remained unconscious for six hours previous to his death, and then, just before his soul fluttered out, he opened his eyes and smiled a last recognition on his brothers.[22]

It makes sense that he had premonitions of death while working on a symphony about death fresh off a trip to Mozart's birthplace and its reminders of Mozart inadvertently composing his own *Requiem*. Tchaikovsky had always, in fact, feared sudden death and an abrupt bad end. (The final version of his will is dated September 30, 1891, just after Nadezhda von Mekk ended her support.)[23] From childhood he had been plagued with digestive troubles. He does not seem to have aged particularly well, though that perception stems from anecdotes and a falsely attributed photograph of a similar-looking man smoking a cigarette on a balcony with dark circles under the eyes and a bleached-out complexion.[24] Still, in the weeks leading up to the unveiling of the *Pathétique*, he claimed plenty of pep and dismissed all talk of the friends and colleagues he had lost and the "repulsive snub-nosed monster" of death. "I feel I shall live a long time," he boasted in an echo of his letter to Rathaus.[25] He took on new projects fully intending to complete them.

But Asiatic cholera had spread throughout Russia in 1892. The first cases were detected around Astrakhan, on the Caspian Sea. The field hospitals that had been opened along rural transport routes proved ineffective, since rural types, including peasants and Old Believers, viewed urbanites—ministers, cashiers, copiers, doctors, and lawyers—with suspicion. There were antigovernment riots and bizarre stories about people dying after digging for potatoes in infected soil and putting dirty money in their mouths. According to a report prepared by a British epidemiologist, "On July 25, two peasants from Rostov-on-Don, where cholera had prevailed for nearly a month, came to the house of a peasant named S— in the village of Egorovka in order to pay him a debt. The coins were held by S— in his mouth for a considerable time.... On the following day S— died from cholera."[26] The disease moved upstream along the Volga River until it reached the underperforming sewer and water systems of St. Petersburg.

There the homes of the ill were disinfected with lime and chlorine, but the disease could not be eradicated. It lingered for more than a year, taking the lives of ne'er-do-wells, manual laborers, rank-and-file bureaucrats, and eventually nineteenth-century Russia's greatest composer. Cholera bacillus was even found in the pipes leading into the Winter Palace, the residence of the tsar, alarming those in the upper ranks who considered themselves immune to the disease by virtue of their avoidance of untreated water, and regular intakes of ether, camphor, and castor oil.

Tchaikovsky didn't speak of the disease, so it's unclear how much he feared it. Nor did he take the kind of precautions that the intendant of the Imperial Theaters did. In the summer of 1892, Ivan Vsevolozhsky wrote to Vladimir Pogozhev to gripe about a reviewer putting off writing about the Mariinsky and Mikhaílovsky and the miserable state of the Russian postal system—things were going missing, and a letter arrived with the side torn open. He thanked him for sending "instructions for preventing cholera. So far we don't have it and we're regularly eating fruits, mushrooms, etc. etc. Perhaps cholera won't reach St. Petersburg until September, when the cold will destroy it." Vsevolozhsky had a scare in August: "My stomach hurts and I have diarrhea. I hope it's not cholera." The illness lasted a week. It wasn't cholera.[27]

Tchaikovsky presumably contracted it by drinking unpurified water at (as Aus der Ohe and others claimed) one of the restaurants he frequented with family and friends. He was staying at Modest's apartment on Malaya Morskaya Street, where his room looked out at the "House of the Queen of Spades," the one-time residence of Princess

Natalya Golitsïna, the prototype of the countess in Pushkin's tale. On October 20 Tchaikovsky was at Leiner's Restaurant on the corner of Nevsky Prospekt and Moika Embankment, dining past midnight. He complained of a stomachache on the morning of October 21. Loss of appetite led to headache, nausea, severe cramps, and diarrhea. Word of the illness "thundered" throughout St. Petersburg; there was hope for a recovery amid the grim tallies of all the others who had been diagnosed with cholera in St. Petersburg that same week.[28] Tchaikovsky's heart stopped in the middle of the night on October 25. His doctors, including the esteemed court physician Lev Bertenson, would be vilified for their flatfootedness in treating the composer with hot baths and doses of perfume (musk). The funeral was held on October 28 at a packed Kazan Cathedral; the tsar covered all the expenses. Tchaikovsky was buried as a national icon not far from Apukhin in the Tikhvin Cemetery of the Alexander Nevsky Monastery. The cemetery is also the final resting place of the *Moguchaya kuchka*. The funeral procession was the longest ever seen for a Russian artist, tsarist authorities having suppressed the public response to Pushkin's premature passing to avoid unrest. Only those members of the public who had obtained tickets the day before at the office of the Imperial Theaters could attend Tchaikovsky's internment.[29]

Memorial concerts in February 1894 included the Moscow premiere of the *Pathétique* and a little-noticed performance of the second act of *Swan Lake*. Modest was subsequently enlisted by the Imperial Theaters to revise the entire scenario of the ballet. Petipa was in his mid-eighties when he received the go-ahead to stage his own version of *Swan Lake* in St. Petersburg. He had himself been brought low in previous years by a serious illness, suffering from the skin disease pemphigus. The itching depressed him, and it persisted for years, right up to the proto-revolutionary year of 1905, when rioting broke out in the streets of St. Petersburg, and he could not make it to the pharmacy for ointments. It thus can hardly be argued that he brought the same level of energy and imagination to *Swan*

Lake that he had brought to *The Sleeping Beauty*. And he had left most of the 1892 St. Petersburg staging of Tchaikovsky's last ballet, *The Nutcracker*, to his amiable second-in-command, Ivanov.

His (and Ivanov's) *Swan Lake* was performed sixteen times during the 1894–95 season, including three performances at the Bolshoi Theater. The premiere concluded the official period of mourning for Tsar Alexander III, and the three performances at the Bolshoi celebrated the coronation of Tsar Nikolay II. The original version had disappeared; the revival entered the canon. Had Tchaikovsky lived longer, it might not have. The *Pathétique*, too, would not have earned the reputation as the ultimate expression of the ultimate experience.

Imperial Russia did not have much longer to live. Miscalculation, overreach, disease, war, and profound indifference to the restiveness in the regions would soon bring the Romanov dynasty to an end. St. Petersburg would witness the February and October Revolutions, and the Bolsheviks would install themselves in Tchaikovsky's beloved Moscow, though little of what he loved survived Vladimir Lenin's coup d'état. Distinguished nineteenth-century families, including the Volkonskys and Trubetskoys, lived in the Old Arbat area near the conservatory, as did the poets Pushkin and Marina Tsvetaeva. Their stucco homes, with intricate balconies and fanciful facades, would be torn up in the early twentieth century as pedestrian lanes were expanded and pavement slapped over tram rails. Former artistic salons became museums: one on Kudrinskaya Square dedicated to Tchaikovsky (he lived in the building in question in 1872–73), another to the Napoleonic invasion, and still another to optical illusions. There's also—because such things are popular everywhere—a Museum of Death.

The Arbat and its side streets housed the artists of Moscow's Silver Age, which extended from the 1890s through the Russian Revolution and beyond. In St. Petersburg, these artists gathered in the Dernov Apartment House—and it's odd to think that the cultural output of the largest country on earth came from just a dozen or so buildings like this one. Symbolism tried, in poetic and musical form, to bridge the knowable and unknowable and catch echoes of the past. Its spiritualism was rooted in the ancient Russian church, the Orthodox faith as practiced in Muscovy before Peter the Great's ascension. The aesthetic had an eschatological dimension but was also a mode of being, a worldview.

Tchaikovsky entered this arena in his final works, though the idea that he anticipated the experimentalism of the Silver Age runs somewhat counter to his conservatism as an imperial subject and an imperial artist, his reverence for the music of eighteenth-century composers, reliance on a compact number format in his operas, general adherence to the diatonic system, and predilection for German augmented sixth chords. But he embraced these things either to affront or to highlight and enhance them with his own unmistakable signature, just as he embraced the highs and lows of regular human experience and his immediate cultural context to take us to a place where nothing is real. In his final works, meters are scrambled and gestures displaced over the registers before fading into nothingness. The *Pathétique* exemplifies the trend. There is no escaping death, Tchaikovsky despaired, but there is a means of escaping life, at least the rudderless day-to-day of a humdrum, banally punitive, unoriginal mode of existence.

Through music.

NOTES

Introduction

1. Marina Kostalevsky, ed., *The Tchaikovsky Papers: Unlocking the Family Archive*, trans. Stephen Pearl (New Haven and London: Yale University Press, 2018), 125 (letter to Pyotr Jurgenson, January 17, 1878). This book is a translation of *Neizvestnïy Chaykovskiy* (The unknown Tchaikovsky), ed. Polina Vaydman (Moscow: Yurgenson, 2009). It provides marvelous new information about the composer, albeit incompletely so. The documents included were carefully selected in the venerable Soviet tradition of suppressing information that challenges the officially/unofficially agreed-on image of an artist. Vaydman reports that the Klin archive has ninety letters among Tchaikovsky's papers, but just twenty-six of them are included in her publication, with the criteria for their selection never explained or justified. Of the 248 letters excluded from the Soviet Tchaikovsky *Polnoye sobraniye sochineniy* (Complete collected works) edition, published in 107 volumes over 50 years (1940–90), just 46 are included in *The Tchaikovsky Papers* and *Neizvestnïy Chaykovskiy*.
2. Ada Aynbinder, *Pyotr Chaykovskiy* (Moscow: Molodaya gvardiya, 2022), cover text.
3. "Pyotr Il'yich Chaykovskiy," *Sovetskaya muzïka*, no. 1 (1940): 7.
4. Aynbinder, *Pyotr Chaykovskiy*, 8.
5. Alexander Poznansky, ed., *Tchaikovsky through Others' Eyes*, trans. Ralph C. Burr Jr. and Robert Bird (Bloomington: Indiana University Press, 1999), 35.
6. "[I]n some cases," Philip Ross Bullock comments, "Tchaikovsky's songs are the only known source for poetry that was not otherwise published" ("Tchaikovsky's Songs: Music as Poetry," in *The Edinburgh Companion to Literature and Music*, ed. Delia da Sousa Correa [Edinburgh: Edinburgh University Press, 2020], 478).
7. Rossiyskiy gosudarstvennïy istoricheskiy arkhiv (henceforth RGIA) f. 733, op. 142, d. 466, ll. 1, 3, 308.
8. Ibid., l. 461. The cantata's libretto, by Yakov Polonsky, is a historical survey spanning—ambitiously—from the days of monks in dugouts to the era of

Peter the Great up to Tsar Alexander II. Among Polonsky's borrowings is an explicit quotation from Pushkin's mock epic *Ruslan and Lyudmila*. Institut russkoy literaturï (Pushkinskiy dom) f. 241, d. 37.

9. "Muzïkal'noye obozreniye," *Nuvellist*, no. 4 (April 1887): 1.

10. V. V. Bersen'yev and A. R. Markov, "Politsiya i gei: Epizod iz epokhi Aleksandra III," in *RISK: Al'manakh*, ed. Dmitriy Kuz'min (Moscow: ARGO-RISK, 1998), http://www.vavilon.ru/metatext/risk3/repressions.html.

11. Kostalevsky, *Tchaikovsky Papers*, 132 (February 13, 1878).

12. Jean-Jacques Rousseau, *The Basic Political Writings*, trans. Donald A. Cross; introd. David Wootton (Indianapolis: Hackett, 2011), xxii. Tchaikovsky valued Rousseau's ideas about natural goodness and the origins of language, but he was appalled by Rousseau as a person and couldn't get over the fact that the philosopher had abandoned five of his own children to an orphanage. Kostalevsky, *Tchaikovsky Papers*, 270n230.

13. Henry Harland, "Octave Feuillet's Novels," in Octave Feuillet, *The Romance of a Poor Young Man* (London: Heinemann, 1902), xiv.

14. Aleksandr Poznanskiy, *Pyotr Chaykovskiy. Biografiya*, 2 vols. (St. Petersburg: Vita nova, 2009), 1: 73.

15. Johannes Remy, "The Valuev Circular and Censorship of Ukrainian Publications in the Russian Empire," *Canadian Slavonic Papers* 49, nos. 1–2 (March–June 2007): 87, 92.

16. Nor would he have seen pictures from Russia's wars, save for heroic prints sold on the streets together with Church-sanctioned paintings of the Last Judgment and the miracles of Saint Nikolay (and popular prints meant for children, like "How the Mice Buried the Cat"). Ivan Belousov, *Ushedshaya Moskva. Zapiski po lichnïm vospominaniyam. S nachala 1870 godov* (Moscow: Moskovskoye tovarishchestvo pisateley, 1927), 52.

17. Philip Ross Bullock, "Ambiguous Speech and Eloquent Silence: The Queerness of Tchaikovsky's Songs," *19th-Century Music* 32, no. 1 (2008): 127–28.

18. E. A. Mikhaylova, "'Etu veshch' ya khotel bï posvyatit' Vam . . .': Tvorcheskiye svyazi P. I. Chaykovskogo i M. A. Balakireva," RNB Virtual'nïye vïstavki, accessed June 22, 2023, https://expositions.nlr.ru/ve/RA3941/simfonicheskaya-poema.

19. Reinhold Brinkmann, *Late Idyll: The Second Symphony of Johannes Brahms* (Cambridge, MA: Harvard University Press, 1995), 134; Richard Taruskin, *Defining Russia Musically: Historical and Hermeneutical Essays* (Princeton: Princeton University Press, 1997), 254.

20. Robert C. Solomon, "On Fate and Fatalism," *Philosophy East and West* 53, no. 4 (October 2003): 444.

21. Quoted in ibid., 435.

Part I Local and Regional Matters

1. "Otzïvï o Votkinske," Komandirovka.ru, accessed February 19, 2023, https://www.komandirovka.ru/cities/votkinsk/reviews/.

2. "Istoriya goroda," Muzey istorii i kul'turï g. Votkinska, accessed February 6, 2023, http://www.votmuseum.ru/node/21.

3. "Istoriya muzeya," Muzey—usad'ba P. I. Chaykovskogo, accessed February 6, 2023, https://tchaikovskyhome.ru/stories.

NOTES

4. Lucinde Braun, "Michel Victor Acier," *Sächsische Biografie*, May 19, 2005, https://saebi.isgv.de/biografie/Michel_Victor_Acier_(1736-1799).

5. Gordon Campbell, ed., *The Grove Encyclopedia of Decorative Arts*, 2 vols. (Oxford: Oxford University Press, 2006), 2:93–98.

6. "Andrey Assier," Tchaikovsky Research Net, August 26, 2023, https://en.tchaikovsky-research.net/pages/Andrey_Assier.

7. E. Chernaya, "Kamenka," *Sovetskaya muzika*, no. 6 (1949): 27.

8. Debate about renaming the conservatory, Tchaikovsky's relationship to Ukraine as a person, and his borrowings from (and contributions to) Ukrainian culture as a composer, has intensified since Vladimir Putin's 2022 invasion of Ukraine.

9. See M. N. Barïshnikov, "I. I. Chaykovskiy v upravlenii chernomorsko-baltiyskoy sudokhodnoy liniyey v 1894–1896 godakh," *Nauchnïy dialog* 12, no. 3 (2023): 361–81.

10. Rossiyskiy gosudarstvennïy arkhiv literaturï i iskusstv (henceforth RGALI) f. 648, op. 2, yed. khr. 234. This file contains records from 1898 to 1925 concerning the payment of royalties for Tchaikovsky's ballets *Swan Lake* and *The Sleeping Beauty*.

11. Kostalevsky, *Tchaikovsky Papers*, 18 ("Votkinsk Factory, March 27, 1837, Saturday, 11 p.m.").

12. Poznanskiy, *Pyotr Chaykovskiy. Biografiya*, 1:29, 33.

13. "Pervaya uchitel'nitsa muzïki," RNB Virtual'nïye vïstavki, accessed February 6, 2023, https://expositions.nlr.ru/ex_manus/Chaikovsky/teacher_music.php.

14. Kostalevsky, *Tchaikovsky Papers*, 74 (letter of July 24, 1893).

15. Simon Sebag Montefiore, *The Romanovs: 1613–1918* (New York: Alfred A. Knopf, 2016), 648–50.

16. I. A. Mishkina, "Picchioli, Luigi (Luigi Piccioli) (1812–1868)," 2013, https://www.conservatory.ru/esweb/pichchioli-luidzhi-luigi-piccioli-1812-1868.

17. In 1857, Ilya Tchaikovsky had entrusted his fortune to the widow of an engineer he had known. In a disastrous business dealing, the widow lost both Ilya's money and her own. Kündinger recollects in his memoirs that "in 1858 owing to changed circumstances, Tchaikovsky's father was no longer able to pay for lessons and I completely lost sight of my pupil." R. V. Kyundinger, "Zanyatiya s molodïm Chaykovskim," in *Vospominaniya o P. I. Chaykovskim*, ed. V. V. Protopopov (Moscow: Muzïka, 1973), 36. My thanks to Alexander Poznansky for this information and reference.

18. RGIA f. 1404, op. 63, d. 3356 (Delo o sluzhbe P. I. Chaykovskogo), ll. 1–20. He traveled to Europe in the capacity of translator and assistant to one of his father's engineering friends, who paid for the train tickets and hotels.

19. The history of the RMS is told by Lynn M. Sargeant, *Harmony and Discord: Music and the Transformation of Russian Cultural Life* (New York: Oxford University Press, 2011).

20. "Kak Konservatoriya iskala svoy dom?," Arkhivï Sankt-Peterburga, September 13, 2019, https://vk.com/@spbarchives-kak-konservatoriya-iskala-svoi-dom.

21. Herman Laroche, quoted in Philip S. Taylor, *Anton Rubinstein: A Life in Music* (Bloomington: Indiana University Press, 2007), 101.

22. RGIA f. 1404, op. 63, d. 3356, ll. 25–51.

23. Richard Taruskin, "Rubinstein, Anton Grigor'yevich," in *The New Grove Dictionary of Opera*, ed. Stanley Sadie, 4 vols. (London: Macmillan, 1994), 4:80.

24. P. Taylor, *Anton Rubinstein*, 235.

25. See R. Allen Lott, *From Paris to Peoria: How European Piano Virtuosos Brought Classical Music to the American Heartland* (New York: Oxford University Press, 2003), 171–85, 197–214.

26. The programs are listed in ibid., 269–71.

27. Richard Taruskin, "Others: A Mythology and a Demurrer (by Way of Preface)," in Taruskin, *Defining Russia Musically*, xi–xviii.

28. Cliché defines Russian music as: essentially but variously modal; plagal; leading-tone-resistant and dominant-seventh-allergic; fond of the augmented triad and the whole-tone scale; and hypersensitive, in text settings, to the accents and stresses of the Russian language. Melancholic *protyazhnaya* ("drawn-out") singing is also an element—the opening of Tchaikovsky's opera *Eugene Onegin* provides a richly stylized example—likewise heterophonic undervoicing, tone-semitone-tone tetrachords, and abundant bellringing. According to Marina Frolova-Walker, the Russian recipe enjoyed by Nikolay Rimsky-Korsakov included "tritones"; "the juxtaposition of keys in augmented-fourth (or diminished-fifth) relationship"; "parallel fifths"; "Borodinian epic parallel seconds"; and the "Balakirevian keys of B minor and D flat major." *Russian Music and Nationalism: From Glinka to Stalin* (New Haven and London: Yale University Press, 2007), 162.

29. P. Taylor, *Anton Rubinstein*, 275.

30. Sargeant, *Harmony and Discord*, 89.

31. Yelena Yevgen'yevna Polotskaya, "P. I. Chaykovskiy i stanovleniye kompozitor-skogo obrazovaniya v Rossii" (PhD diss., Gnesin Russian Academy of Music, 2009), 85–96.

32. Poznansky, *Tchaikovsky through Others' Eyes*, 27, 44–45.

33. Tamara Skvirskaya, "P. I. Chaykovskiy—prepodavatel' Sankt-Peterburgskoy konservatorii," *Opera Musicologica*, no. 2 (2012): 54–61.

34. Poznansky, *Tchaikovsky through Others' Eyes*, 28.

35. Information in this paragraph from Katja Messwarb, "Die Instrumentations-lehre von François-Auguste Gevaert im Spiegel seiner Kompositionen," *Revue Belge de Musicologie* 64 (2010): 89–97, esp. 92.

36. Poznansky, *Tchaikovsky through Others' Eyes*, 37. Another source reports that Tchaikovsky translated the libretto "from German" as opposed to the original language of Italian in 1876 for a student performance of the opera at the Moscow Conservatory. This translation was published by Jurgenson in 1884. Polotskaya, "P. I. Chaykovskiy i stanovleniye kompozitorskogo obrazovaniya," 147.

37. Poznansky, *Tchaikovsky through Others' Eyes*, 46–47.

38. Kostalevsky, *Tchaikovsky Papers*, 203.

39. Louis Spohr, *Autobiography* (London: Longman, Green, Longman, Roberts, and Green, 1865), 189.

40. Tim Edwards, "What Did Tchaikovsky's Voice Sound Like? Here's a Rare Recording," Classic FM, August 2, 2017, https://www.classicfm.com/composers /tchaikovsky/news/voice-speaks-phonograph/. Everyone captured on the recording sounds strange.

41. Pyotr Il'yich Chaykovskiy, *Akademicheskoye polnoye sobraniye sochineniy. Seriya IV. T. 1. Muzïka k gimnu 'K radosti' F. Shillera dlya solistov, smeshannogo khora i orkestra. 1865*, ed. T. Z. Skvirskaya (Chelyabinsk: Music Production International, 2016), lxviii.

42. Friedrich Schiller, "Ode to Joy," trans. William F. Wertz, Schiller Institute, accessed February 6, 2023, https://archive.schillerinstitute.com/transl/trans_schil_2poems.html.

43. Chaykovskiy, *Akademicheskoye polnoye sobraniye sochineniy. Seriya IV. T. 1*, lxxi.

44. Ibid., lxxiii.

45. M. Chaykovskiy, *Zhizn' Petra Il'yicha Chaykovskogo. Po dokumentam, khranyash-chimsya v arkhive imeni pokoynogo kompozitora v Klinu*, 3 vols. (Moscow and Leipzig: Jurgenson, 1901–03), 1:203; P. Taylor, *Anton Rubinstein*, 116.

46. Polotskaya, "P. I. Chaykovskiy i stanovleniye kompozitorskogo obrazovaniya," 108. The other student assigned the Schiller cantata project, Rïbasov, didn't complete it. He instead graduated in piano performance.

47. Seeing that the school was struggling to pay the rent at Demidova-Aledinskaya's estate, the grand princess allocated a building of twelve rooms (eight in converted hallway spaces) to the school; from there, the school relocated to the Medical Department of the Ministry of Internal Affairs. The current, menthol-colored building of the St. Petersburg Conservatory didn't open until three years after Tchaikovsky's death. "Kak Konservatoriya iskala svoy dom?"

48. Roland John Wiley, *Tchaikovsky* (New York: Oxford University Press, 2009), 40.

49. I am grateful to Rachel Glodo for this observation.

50. Vladimir Dudin, "V Russkom muzeye ispolnili kantatu Chaykovskogo 'K radosti,'" *Rossiyskaya gazeta*, April 27, 2017, https://rg.ru/2017/04/27/reg-szfo/v-russkom-muzee-ispolnili-kantatu-chajkovskogo-k-radosti.html. Dudin's Eurasianist reading of the cantata considerably exaggerates Fyodorov's credentials. He was much less a philosopher than an eccentric librarian and pseudopagan mystic.

51. Iosif Rayskin, "Petya i Folk. Retseptsiya Chaykovskogo v slushatel'skoy audi-torii i v professional'noy kritike," *Musicus*, no. 2 (April–June 2012): 5 (quoting Cui in the March 24, 1866, issue of *Sankt-Peterburgskiye vedomosti* and the memoirs of Alina Bryullova).

52. Terry Martin, "The German Question in Russia, 1848–1896," *Russian History* 18, no. 4 (1991): 373–434.

53. N. Panovskiy, "Kontsert v pol'zu khristian postradavshikh v Kandii," *Moskovskiye vedomosti*, February 2, 1867, p. 3.

54. Rostislav, "Kratkiy obzor minuvshego kontsertnogo sezona," *Golos*, April 12, 1867, p. 1.

55. Kostalevsky, *Tchaikovsky Papers*, 207–08.

56. Andrei D. Serebianov, "Isaak Ilyich Levitan," *Britannica.com*, accessed March 17, 2023, https://www.britannica.com/biography/Isaak-Ilyich-Levitan.

57. L. Mikheyeva, "Chaykovskiy. Simfoniya No. 1 ('Zimniye gryozï')," belcanto.ru, accessed March 17, 2023, https://www.belcanto.ru/s_tchaikovsky_1.html.

58. Knyaz' Vladimir Odoyevskiy, *Dnevnik. Perepiska. Materialï*, ed. M. P. Rakhmanova (Moscow: Deka-VS, 2005), 204.

59. Rory Finnin, "How the West Gets Ukraine Wrong—and Helps Putin as a Result," *Politico*, February 12, 2022, https://www.politico.com/news/magazine/2022/02/12/west-gets-ukraine-wrong-helps-putin-little-russia-00007977.

60. N. Kashkin, *Vospominaniya o P. I. Chaykovskom* (Moscow: Yurgenson, 1896), 94.

61. Richard Taruskin, "Chaikovsky as Symphonist," in *On Russian Music* (Oakland: University of California Press, 2008), 129–30. "The Crane" ("Povadilsya zhuravel'") is No. 53 in A. I. Rubets, *Dvesti shestnadtsat' narodnïkh napevov: Dlya peniya bez soprovozhdeniya* (Moscow: Yurgenson, 1872). Rubets collected the folksongs close to Kharkiv in the present-day Ukrainian–Russian border-lands of Chernihiv and Bryansk.

62. Brent Auerbach, "Tchaikovsky's Triumphant Repetitions: Block Composition as a Key to Dynamic Form in the Symphonies Nos. 2 and 3," *Theory and Practice* 37/38 (2012–13): 89–103, esp. 92.

63. O. N. Kislova, "Russkiy detskiy muzïkal'nïy fol'klor vtoroy polovinï XIX veka v istoricheskom, teoreticheskom i pedagogicheskom aspektakh," *Muzïkal'noye iskusstvo i obrazovaniye* 9, no. 3 (2021): 154.

64. Most of the settings are poems by Alexei Pleshcheyev (1825–93), who turned to childhood in his later years, at the end of a hard life that included arrest and exile on charges of sedition. The point about childhood extending through teenagerhood in the Russian context comes from Rachel M. Glodo, who likens Tchaikovsky's *Sixteen Songs for Children* to "a garden . . . of carefully cultivated selections that balance theme, mode, tempo, texture, and tone. The arrange-ment of the songs is much like childhood itself—defined not by narrative or temporal distinctions, but by the ever-flowing cycle of seasons, play, the school year, and holidays." "Tchaikovsky's Sixteen Songs for Children (Op. 54): Domestic and Public Childhood in Nineteenth-Century Russia" (research paper for Princeton University Music Department seminar MUS 514: Tchaikovsky, submitted May 9, 2023). Tchaikovsky's childhood ended earlier than most: he was packed off to boarding school; he lost his mother; his father went broke.

65. G. A. Larosh, "Muzïkal'nïye ocherki," *Golos*, February 7, 1873, p. 1.

66. Postoronniy, "Arabeski," *Moskovskiye vedomosti*, March 29, 1873, p. 4.

67. David Brown generalizes about what "many" and "most" Russian composers excel at ("decorative counterpoint") and what defies them ("organic counter-point"), and praises Tchaikovsky's folksong adaptations—all of them, no exceptions—as a reflection of his salt-of-the-earth Russianness. "It is one of the greatest causes for regret in all Tchaikovsky's work that he never again attempted something of the same sort," he writes of the folksong-based ending of the Second Symphony. *Tchaikovsky: The Early Years* (London: Victor Gollancz, 1978), 108, 269.

68. Yury D. Levin, "Shakespeare and Russian Literature: Nineteenth Century Attitudes," in *Russian Essays on Shakespeare and his Contemporaries*, ed. Alexandr Parfenov and Joseph G. Price (Cranbury, NJ: Associated University Presses, 1998), 85–86; John Givens, "Shakespeare and Russian Literature," *Russian Studies in Literature* 50, no. 3 (Summer 2014): 3.

69. "Burya v 'Burye,'" RNB Virtual'nïye vïstavki, accessed March 16, 2023, https://expositions.nlr.ru/ex_manus/Chaikovsky/burya.php.

70. Richard Taruskin, "Russian Musical Orientalism: A Postscript," *Cambridge Opera Journal* 6, no. 1 (March 1994): 81–82. Since Romeo and Juliet are tech-nically Italian, the Italian flavoring of the theme is appropriate.

71. "Letter 143," trans. Brett Langston, Tchaikovsky Research Net, August 3, 1869, https://en.tchaikovsky-research.net/pages/Letter_143.

72. "Letter 145," trans. Brett Langston, Tchaikovsky Research Net, August 11, 1869, https://en.tchaikovsky-research.net/pages/Letter_145.
73. "Letter 156," trans. Luis Sundkvist, Tchaikovsky Research Net, October 28, 1869, https://en.tchaikovsky-research.net/pages/Letter_156.
74. "*Romeo and Juliet*," Tchaikovsky Research Net, December 1, 1869, https://en.tchaikovsky-research.net/pages/Romeo_and_Juliet.
75. Brown, *Tchaikovsky: The Early Years*, 185 n.48.
76. "Moskovskiy fel'yeton," *Novoye vremya*, January 17, 1870, pp. 1, 3; "Moskovskiy fel'yeton," *Novoye vremya*, March 7, 1870, pp. 1–2; "Moskovskiy fel'yeton," *Novoye vremya*, March 24, 1870, pp. 1–2.
77. "Letter 212," trans. Luis Sundkvist, Tchaikovsky Research Net, ca. October 20, 1870, https://en.tchaikovsky-research.net/pages/Letter_212; the quotation from the Act I Prologue of the 1597 play is from William Shakespeare, *Romeo and Juliet*, accessed March 14, 2023, shakespeare.mit.edu/romeo_juliet/romeo_juliet.1.0.html. My thanks to Lucia Denk and Brooke Burkhart for this reference.
78. "*Romeo and Juliet*," Tchaikovsky Research Net, March 16, 1870, https://en.tchaikovsky-research.net/pages/Romeo_and_Juliet.
79. Philip Ross Bullock reports that Tchaikovsky's annual salary at the conservatory was 600 rubles in 1866, 1,500 in 1871, and 2,300 a year after that. "Chaikovsky and the Economics of Art Music in Late Nineteenth-Century Russia," *Journal of Musicology* 36, no. 2 (2019): 202.
80. "Letter 220," trans. Brett Langston, Tchaikovsky Research Net, 1870, https://en.tchaikovsky-research.net/pages/Letter_220.
81. Aleksandr Komarov, "Pervïy avtorskiy kontsert P. I. Chaykovskogo v 1871 godu. Opït rekonstruktsii muzïkal'no-istoricheskogo sobïtiya," *Nauchnïy vestnik Moskovskoy konservatorii* 12, no. 4 (2021): 116. Additional information in this paragraph is from pages 69–70 and 79–92.
82. Aleksandr Danilkin, "'Vedomosti moskovskoy gorodskoy politsii' upolnomochenï zayavit'," *Petrovka* 38, July 20, 2021, https://petrovka-38.com/arkhiv/item/vedomosti-moskovskoj-gorodskoj-politsii-upolnomocheny-zayavit.
83. The quartet was the biggest success, the second movement in particular, a setting of a folksong that Tchaikovsky heard a carpenter sing on his sister's estate in Ukraine (the melody is also included in his 1868–69 collection of *Fifty Russian Folksongs*). In 1876, the movement was performed at a conservatory reception for Leo Tolstoy, who had traveled to Moscow from his home in Yasnaya Polyana to attend to the publication of *Anna Karenina*. Tchaikovsky revered him as a fiction writer—the trilogy *Childhood, Boyhood, Youth* and the *Confession* especially—but disagreed with pretty much everything Tolstoy had to say about music (they had two evenings together to chat) and altogether disliked the proselytizing of his later years. "When I met Leo Tolstoy," Tchaikovsky wrote in his diary, "I was seized with fear and a feeling of embarrassment in front of him. It seemed to me that this greatest expert on the heart could penetrate the deepest recesses of my soul with just a single glance. Being before him, I surmised, it wouldn't be possible to successfully hide all the rubbish that was at the bottom of the soul and expose only the casual side." But the conversation was benign, and Tolstoy, to Tchaikovsky's amazement, was moved to tears by the String Quartet. P. I. Chaykovskiy, *Dnevniki*

1873–1891, ed. S. Chemodanov (1923; repr., St. Petersburg: Severnïy olen', 1993), 210–11.
84. Poznansky, *Tchaikovsky through Others' Eyes*, 57.
85. Polotskaya, "P. I. Chaykovskiy i stanovleniye kompozitorskogo obrazovaniya," 172–74.
86. Ibid., 168–69.
87. Ibid., 167.
88. Ibid., 170–71.
89. "Letter 1916," Tchaikovsky Research Net, December 23, 1881, https://en.tchaikovsky-research.net/pages/Letter_1916.
90. Polotskaya, "P. I. Chaykovskiy i stanovleniye kompozitorskogo obrazovaniya," 170–71.
91. Ibid., 158, 161.
92. Ibid., 159.
93. "Letter 1839," trans. Luis Sundkvist, Tchaikovsky Research Net, August 25, 1881, https://en.tchaikovsky-research.net/pages/Letter_1839.

Part II Nationalism

1. "*The Storm*," Tchaikovsky Research Net, last modified August 2, 2023, https://en.tchaikovsky-research.net/pages/The_Storm.
2. P. Taylor, *Anton Rubinstein*, 111, 296 n.92.
3. "Samaya plokhaya opera," Rossiyskiy natsional'nïy muzey muzïki, October 30, 2022, https://music-museum.ru/about/news/samaya-ploxaya-opera.html.
4. Wiley, *Tchaikovsky*, 69.
5. A. N. Ostrovskiy, "Voyevoda (Son na Volge) (1865)," Lib.ru, January 27, 2009, http://az.lib.ru/o/ostrowskij_a_n/text_0092.shtml.
6. Aleksandr Komarov, "Vosstanovleniye proizvedeniy P. I. Chaykovskogo v istorii russkoy muzïkal'noy tekstologii" (PhD diss., Moscow Conservatory, 2006), 99–104.
7. Anastasiya Chernova, "Chto prisnilos' voyevode," *Sotï*, April 4, 2019, https://litsota.ru/chto-prisnilos-voevode/.
8. Kashkin, *Vospominaniya*, 56–57.
9. Brown is nothing if not insistent in declaring the Russianness of this or that episode in *The Voyevoda*, and yearning for more of it, despite never actually explaining what exactly makes Russian music Russian. "The traveler through the scrublands and featureless dramatic plains of *The Voyevoda*'s landscape will remember with most pleasure coming upon those fresh springs of Russian inspiration which constantly break the surface," he concludes his Kashkin- and Laroche-derived takedown of the opera. Brown, *Tchaikovsky: The Early Years*, 139–55.
10. Tat'yana Yevgen'yevna Zimnukhova, "Zhenskiy khor 'Na more utushka . . .' iz operï P. I. Chaykovskogo 'Oprichnik': K probleme prochteniya fol'klornogo teksta," in *Muzika v sovremennom mire: Nauka, pedagogika, ispolnitel'stvo*, ed. O. V. Nemkova (Tambov: Izdaniye Tambovskogo gosudarstvennogo muzïkal'no-pedagogicheskogo instituta im. S. V. Rakhmaninova, 2018), 449–54.
11. "Letter 493," trans. Anna-Maria Leonard, Tchaikovsky Research Net, September 7, 1876, https://en.tchaikovsky-research.net/pages/Letter_493.

12. *The Voyevoda* (Opera)," Tchaikovsky Research Net, last modified September 2, 2023, https://en.tchaikovsky-research.net/pages/The_Voyevoda_(opera).

13. Poznanskiy, *Pyotr Chaykovskiy. Biografiya*, 1:257–58; Poznansky, *Tchaikovsky through Others' Eyes*, 64–65.

14. RGIA f. 776, op. 2, d. 5, l. 312 ob.

15. Kashkin, *Vospominaniya*, 57.

16. There was a standalone performance of the dance-centered second act on February 25, 1869.

17. RGIA f. 497, op. 2, d. 25506, ll. 17–18. Pushkin's drama was partially premiered in 1870, with sixteen of the twenty-four scenes staged at the Mariinsky Theater.

18. S. P., "Moskovskaya zhizn'," *Golos*, March 4, 1869, p. 1. Rapport's problem wasn't an operation but a sprained thumb that kept him up for several nights.

19. Wiley, *Tchaikovsky*, 68.

20. Richard Taruskin, "Voyevoda," in Sadie, *New Grove Dictionary of Opera*, 4:1046.

21. Komarov, "Vosstanovleniye proizvedeniy P. I. Chaykovskogo," 174.

22. See Polina Vaydman, "'Zapis' stanovitsya *kosim dozhdem, livnem.*' 'Klinskaya tetrad' B. V. Asaf'yeva," *Sovetskaya muzika*, no. 6 (1990): 114–17. The title of this article quotes Asafyev's description of Tchaikovsky's sketches: the shorter ones seem to have been "quickly dashed off to capture the fleeting thought," the longer like "*slanting rain, a downpour.*" Tchaikovsky isn't "trying things out or improvising at the piano," he's turning "his inner spiritual life into sound."

23. Komarov, "Vosstanovleniye proizvedeniy P. I. Chaykovskogo," 79–80.

24. Ibid., 90–91, 130–35.

25. Ibid., 78.

26. Ibid., 235–37.

27. Pyotr Il'yich Chaykovskiy, *Akademicheskoye polnoye sobraniye sochineniy. Seriya I. T. 3. Undina*, ed. A. E. Maksimova (Chelyabinsk: Music Production International, 2016), lxxvi–lxxvii.

28. Ilya Vinitsky, *Vasily Zhukovsky's Romanticism and the Emotional History of Russia* (Evanston: Northwestern University Press, 2015), 3–4.

29. Alastair Macaulay, "What Do Aquawomen Want?," *New York Times*, March 1, 2009, https://www.nytimes.com/2009/03/01/arts/music/01alas.html.

30. E. V. Landa, "'Undina' v perevode V. A. Zhukovskogo i russkaya kul'tura," Lib. ru/Klassika, November 30, 2017, http://az.lib.ru/z/zhukowskij_w_a/text_0150.shtml.

31. The two of them swam in the same circles as high-ranking nobles. According to the consensus, Lvov's skills as a composer—and virtuoso violinist—exceeded Sollogub's as a writer.

32. Lvov's opera had a brief run in a hall-full theater in 1848 before being performed in Vienna; it returned to the St. Petersburg stage as a benefit for the tenor Fyodor Nikolsky in 1863. The longer reviews are flattering. A. E., "Teatral'naya khronika," *Sankt-Peterburgskiye vedomosti*, September 19, 1948, p. 2; "Russkaya opera v Peterburge," *Golos*, December 6, 1863, p. 2.

33. Irene Esam, "Folkloric Elements as Communication Devices—Ostrovsky's Plays," *New Zealand Slavonic Journal* (Summer 1968), 77–79.

34. Ibid., 76.

35. "Moskovskiye zametki," *Golos*, May 15, 1873, p. 3. This same reviewer wrote a second, longer piece about the production that went into detail about the plot, performers, and music (more of it was needed; the chorus in the Prologue saying goodbye to winter, Frost's verses, and the chorus of the blind men contained some real gems or, as the writer preferred, "pearls"). "Moskovskiye zametki," *Golos*, May 26, 1873, p. 2.

36. Emily Frey, "Rimsky-Korsakov, Snegoruchka, and Populism," in *Rimsky-Korsakov and His World*, ed. Marina Frolova-Walker (Princeton: Princeton University Press, 2018), 85.

37. Chaykovskiy, *Akademicheskoye polnoye sobraniye sochineniy. Seriya I. T. 3*, lxxvii–lxxix.

38. My thanks to Aster Zhang for this information.

39. Richard Taruskin, "Undina," in Sadie, *New Grove Dictionary of Opera*, 4:865.

40. Margarita Bednyakova, "Undina: Zachem mï vozrozhdayem zabïtoye?," *Muzïkal'nïy klondayk,* accessed April 7, 2023, https://www.muzklondike.ru/events/zachem_my_vozrozhdaem.

41. Vinitsky, *Vasily Zhukovsky's Romanticism*, 284.

42. Lazhechnikov is a local hero. Kolomna's Literary Café sells some of the food described in his books: goose with lingonberry sauce, noodles on egg yolks, and berry tea brewed with water from a coal-heated samovar. "Literaturnoye kafe 'Lazhechnikov,'" kolomnapastila.ru, accessed February 13, 2023, https://kolomnapastila.ru/orchard/lazhechikov/.

43. Edward L. Keenan, "How Ivan Became 'Terrible,'" *Harvard Ukrainian Studies* 28, nos. 1–4 (2006): 521–42. The nickname dates from the mid-eighteenth century, and was first used in Europe before being accepted, hesitantly, in Russia.

44. James Meek, "In Fonder Times, the Tsar Scalded and Stabbed to Death a Prince," *London Review of Books* 27, no. 3 (December 1, 2005), https://www.lrb.co.uk/the-paper/v27/n23/james-meek/in-fonder-times-the-tsar-scalded-and-stabbed-to-death-a-prince.

45. Hugh F. Graham, "A Brief Account of the Brutal Rule of Vasil'evich, Tyrant of Muscovy (Albert Schlichting on Ivan Groznyi)," *Canadian-American Slavic Studies* 9, no. 2 (January 1975): 254.

46. Ivan Zabelin, *Domashniy bït russkago naroda v XVI i XVII st.*, vol. 1 (Moscow: Tovarishchestvo tipografii A. I. Mamontova, 1895), 16.

47. M. N. Tikhomirov, "Maloizvestnïye letopisnïye pamyatniki XVI v.," *Istoricheskiye zapiski* 10 (1941), https://www.vostlit.info/Texts/Dokumenty/Russ/XVI/1520-1540/Kratk_otr_opric/text.htm.

48. Isabel de Madariaga, *Ivan the Terrible: First Tsar of Russia* (New Haven and London: Yale University Press, 2005), 182, Kindle.

49. *Polnoye sobraniye russkikh letopisey. Tom 13. Chast' 2. Dopolneniya k Nikonovskoy letopisi*, ed. S. F. Platonov (St. Petersburg: Tipografiya I. N. Skorokhodova, 1906), 394–95.

50. Lazhechnikov's representation of Ivan as a shameless womanizer intent on defiling the bride-to-be of his most trusted guard draws on tales of Vasilisa Melentyeva, one of Ivan's wives who may or may not be a historical fabrication. If real, she might have been a mistress or one of Ivan's random conquests, abandoned as opposed to being initiated into marriage through rape. Because she was not of a noble line, she was disposable.

51. K. Yu. Zubkov, "Ivan Grozniy na russkoy stsene 1860-x gg.: Reprezentatsiya monarkhicheskoy vlasti i dramaticheskaya tsenzura," in *Tsenzura v Rossii: Istoriya i sovremennost'*, ed. M. B. Konashev (St. Petersburg: Rossiyskaya natsional'naya biblioteka, 2017), 93.
52. Ibid., 97.
53. Ibid., 98.
54. RGIA f. 777, op. 2, d. 12, l. 43.
55. RGIA f. 497, op. 18, d. 1151, l. 1.
56. *The Oprichnik* received performances in St. Petersburg, Moscow, Kyiv, and Odesa in 1874–75. Plans for a revival in 1879–80 came to naught; *The Oprichnik* only returned to the stage in 1906. The Imperial Theaters rejected Bessel's claim to the rights, conflictingly arguing that (a) the rights had been transferred to Tchaikovsky's heir, Anatole, and (b) the rights expired with Tchaikovsky's death. RGIA f. 468, op. 13, d. 2397.
57. Still, the problems with the libretto persisted. For a production of *The Oprichnik* in 1906 at the People's House (a cultural center for the general public) in St. Petersburg, the ending was rewritten to "eliminate" Ivan the Terrible from the plot. "Andrey Morozov's execution is the fault of [Prince] Vyazemsky's intrigues," the censor summarized. "It's no longer the Tsar's revenge for Andrey's refusal to surrender his beautiful bride to him." RGIA f. 776, op. 26, d. 25, l. 120.
58. Actually, little Ivan is in a long Kazakh robe, *Na Ivanushke chapan*, but no matter. The melodies are identified in *"The Oprichnik,"* Tchaikovsky Research Net, last modified January 14, 2023, https://en.tchaikovsky-research.net/pages/The_Oprichnik.
59. Ts. A. Kyui, "Muzïkal'nïye zametki. 'Oprichnik,' opera g. Chaykovskago," *Sankt-Peterburgskiye vedomosti*, April 23, 1874, 2; "César Cui," Tchaikovsky Research Net, last modified August 26, 2023, https://en.tchaikovsky-research.net/pages/C%C3%A9sar_Cui. My thanks to Céleste Pagniello for these references and the translation of the quoted sentence.
60. G. A. Laroche, *"The Oprichnik,"* April 17, 1874, in *Russians on Russian Music, 1830–1880: An Anthology*, ed. and trans. Stuart Campbell (Cambridge: Cambridge University Press, 1994), 242.
61. Bizet himself composed an Ivan the Terrible opera in 1862 or 1863, as did Gounod four or five years before, using the same libretto. Neither was staged in Paris and Tchaikovsky knew nothing about them. (Bizet's opera received a much belated premiere in Bordeaux in 1951; Gounod tore up his score for use in later works.) The shared libretto transforms Ivan's personal life into an exotic-erotic adventure. He's in love with the daughter of a Muslim prince. She and her underling are pursued by assassins. Ivan recovers from an epileptic seizure to triumph over his foes.
62. RGIA f. 497, op. 18, d. 1151, l. 1 ob.
63. RGIA f. 497, op. 4, d. 3406, ll. 15–16.
64. [M. Ivanov], "Teatr i muzïka," *Novoye vremya*, November 26, 1876, p. 2.
65. "Vnutrennaya pochta," *Peterburgskiy listok*, January 21, 1887, p. 3: "The opera was a success. A brilliant production. After the final act the singers and composer were summoned to take bows without end. The theater was completely full."
66. Yuliya Ilchuk, "Nikolai Gogol's Self-Fashioning in the 1830s: The Postcolonial Perspective," *Canadian Slavonic Papers* 51, nos. 2–3 (June–September 2009):

206; see also Edyta M. Bojanowska, "Confronting Russia," in *Nikolai Gogol: Between Ukrainian and Russian Nationalism* (Cambridge, MA: Harvard University Press, 2007), 170–254.

67. Anastasiya Rogacheva, "The Night before Christmas—Gogol's Nativity Scene," *Nauchnaya Rossiya*, January 3, 2022, https://en.scientificrussia.ru/articles/noc-pered-rozdestvom-vertepnyj-teatr-nv-gogola-2.

68. The libretto had been written for Alexander Serov, but Serov died in 1871. Pavlovna organized the competition in memoriam. Richard Taruskin, "Cherevichki," in Sadie, *New Grove Dictionary of Opera*, 1:831.

69. *Kuznets Vakula*, kul'tura.rf, accessed May 7, 2023, https://www.culture.ru/catalog/tchaikovsky/ru/item/archiv/opera-kuznec-vakula.

70. "Letter 401," trans. Anna-Maria Leonard, Tchaikovsky Research Net, May 18, 1875, https://en.tchaikovsky-research.net/pages/Letter_401.

71. "Teatral'nïy kur'yer," *Peterburgskiy listok*, January 17, 1882, p. 3, compares it positively to Tchaikovsky's opera.

72. RGIA f. 776, op. 25, d. 199, l. 2.

73. RGIA f. 497, op. 2, d. 23766, l. 1.

74. Ibid., l. 6.

75. Yuliya Ilchuk argues that, in Gogol's story, the Cossacks "intersperse their speech with Ukrainian words and phrases, thereby making a political statement about their free spirit and demonstrating their defiance to imperial authority." *Nikolai Gogol: Performing Hybrid Identity* (Toronto: University of Toronto Press, 2021), 60.

76. M. Ivanov, "Muzïkal'naya khronika," *Novoye vremya*, November 29, 1876, p. 3.

77. G. A. Larosh, "P. I. Chaykovskiy kak dramaticheskiy kompozitor," in *Sobraniye muzïkal'no-kriticheskikh statey. Tom. II. O P. I. Chaykovskom*, ed. Vas. Yakovlev (Moscow and Petrograd: Gosudarstvennoye izdatel'stvo muzïkal'nïy sektor, 1924), 103–04.

78. RGIA f. 497, op. 2, d. 23766, l. 9.

79. Kostalevsky, *Tchaikovsky Papers*, 254–55n54 (letter to Taneyev, December 2, 1876).

80. Composed in the summer of 1875, the Third Symphony reaches back to the time before the consolidation of the symphony as a genre. The middle movement of the five is an elegy, and it's framed by a scherzo in duple meter instead of triple (movement 4) and a waltz labeled "alla tedesca" (movement 2). Tedesco comes from the late antique Latin *theodiscus*, originally meaning "the language of the people" (the vernacular as opposed to the learned language of Latin) and eventually extended to represent the German people as well. The scherzo anticipates the ghost scene in *The Queen of Spades* with its augmented sonorities. The movement also includes, near the middle, a quotation of the rapid arpeggios from the *passa calle* of Luigi Boccherini's popular *Night Music of the Streets of Madrid* (1780). The tune of the waltz is fetchingly off-kilter, lolloping on the off-beat, taking itself out for a walk and meeting another tune.

The frame of the frame, the first and fifth movements, comprises a sonata-allegro prefaced by a funeral march and a rondo based on the rhythm of a polonaise. The Third Symphony picked up the inappropriate nickname "Polish" because of the polonaise—and, frankly, because the Second Symphony had a nickname too.

81. Pyotr Il'yich Chaykovskiy, *Akademicheskoye polnoye sobraniye sochineniy. Seriya III. T. 3. Kontsert No 1 dlya fortepiano s orkestrom si-bemol' minor. Soch. 23*, ed. P. E. Vaydman and A. G. Aynbinder (Chelyabinsk: Music Production International, 2015), cxxii–cxxiii.

82. Ibid., cxxvi.

83. Ibid.

84. "Letter 406a," trans. Alex Guster, Tchaikovsky Research Net, July 1, 1875, https://en.tchaikovsky-research.net/pages/Letter_406a.

85. R. Allen Lott, "'A Continuous Trance': Hans von Bülow's Tour of America," *Journal of Musicology* 12, no. 4 (Autumn 1994): 531, 536.

86. "Von Bülow," *Boston Daily Globe*, October 25, 1875, p. 5.

87. "Music and the Stage: The Von Bülow Concert," *Boston Daily Globe*, October 26, 1875, p. 4.

88. Chaykovskiy, *Akademicheskoye polnoye sobraniye sochineniy. Seriya III. T. 3*, cxxxii.

89. Ibid., cxxxvi.

90. Ibid., cxxxv–cxxxvi.

91. David Allen, "A Concerto Minus its Sequins," *New York Times*, February 1, 2017, sec. C, p. 4.

92. Richard Taruskin, "Flesh and Blood Jukebox," *Times Literary Supplement*, March 3, 2017, pp. 7–9.

93. Chaykovskiy, *Akademicheskoye polnoye sobraniye sochineniy. Seriya III. T. 3*, cxxxviii.

94. Ibid., cxxxviii–cxlii.

95. Ibid., cxxxviii.

96. "Letter 488,"Tchaikovsky Research Net, July 27, 1876, https://en.tchaikovsky-research.net/pages/Letter_488.

97. Leo Tolstoy, *Anna Karenina*, trans. Rosemary Edmonds (New York: Penguin, 1978), 809–11.

98. Duncan Richardson, "Mikhail Skobelev: The Creation and Persistence of a Legend" (Master's thesis, Ohio State University, 2019), 29.

99. P. I. Chaykovskiy and P. I. Yurgenson, *Perepiska. Tom 1: 1866–1885*, ed. P. I. Vaydman (Moscow: Yurgenson, 2011), 31 (letter to Jurgenson dated November 27, 1877).

100. Ibid., 50–51.

101. Zvantsov made his own Russian-language translation of Canto V. RGALI f. 763, op. 1, yed. khr. 4.

102. "Letter 447," trans. Brett Langston, Tchaikovsky Research Net, February 11, 1876, https://en.tchaikovsky-research.net/pages/Letter_488.

103. Kashkin, *Vospominaniya*, 106–07.

104. RGIA f. 678, op. 1, d. 58 (Otrïvki iz vospominanii A. E. Molchanova), l. 3.

105. Eduard Nápravník composed a *Francesca da Rimini* opera in 1902. Based on a play by Englishman Stephen Phillips, it was derisively nicknamed "Francesca da Petrograd" in the press owing to its complete indifference to Dante's Renaissance Italian context (K. N. Rïbakov, "Teatr i muzïka," *Novoye vremya*, September 14, 1916, p. 7). Sergey Rachmaninoff's *Francesca da Rimini* opera, premiered three years after Nápravník's, is based on Modest Tchaikovsky's adaptation of Dante. It too was panned by critics and fizzled at the box office.

106. "Letter 481," Tchaikovsky Research Net, July 3, 1876, https://en.tchaikovsky-research.net/pages/Letter_481. "My only consolation is to correspond with you. *Nessun dolor[e] maggior che ricordarsi del tempo felice nella miseria!* [There is no greater sorrow than the remembrance of happiness within misery!] The anguish that gnaws at me is yet more terrible because the three days spent with you in Lyon are so vivid in my memory." Dante Alig'eri, *Bozhestvennaya komediya. Ad'*, trans. V. A. Petrov (St. Petersburg: Tipografiya A. Morigerovskago, 1872); Kristina Landa, *"Bozhestvennaya Komediya" v zerkalakh russkikh perevodov: K istorii retseptsii dantovskogo tvorchestva v Rossii* (St. Petersburg: RKhGA, 2020), 159–65.

107. Dante's gendering of characters is more nuanced than this language suggests. Virgil is referred to as a mother in sections of the Inferno, and Beatrice is gendered male in Purgatorio, described there as a stern admiral and hailed with a masculine grammatical marker on the word *benedictus*. She is not comforting when judging the protagonist. My thanks to the Dante scholar Simone Marchesi for these details (email communication, February 18, 2020).

108. Joan Acocella, "What the Hell: Dante in Translation and in Dan Brown's New Novel," *The New Yorker*, May 20, 2013, https://www.newyorker.com/magazine/2013/05/27/what-the-hell (accessed March 1, 2020).

109. "The Love Story of Lancelot and Guinevere," *History and Women*, October 22, 2010, https://www.historyandwomen.com/2010/10/love-story-of-lancelot-and-guinevere.html.

110. Princeton Dante Project, accessed February 4, 2023, https://dante.princeton.edu/pdp.

111. "As to the whirlwind," he told his brother Modest, "I could have written something more like Doré's picture, but that wasn't really how I wanted it to turn out." "Letter 505," Tchaikovsky Research Net, October 14, 1876, https://en.tchaikovsky-research.net/pages/Letter_505.

112. Catherine Coppola, "The Elusive Fantasy: Genre, Form, and Program in Tchaikovsky's 'Francesca da Rimini,'" *19th-Century Music* 22, no. 2 (Autumn 1998): 183–85.

113. P. I. Chaykovskiy, "Bayreytskoye muzikal'noye torzhestvo. IV," in *Muzikal'nïye fel'yetoni i zametki (1868–1876 g.)*, ed. G. A. Larosh (Moscow: S. P. Yakovlev, 1898), 345, 347.

114. Ibid., 352.

115. Coppola, "Elusive Fantasy," 183.

116. Ibid., 188.

117. "Letter 412," trans. Anna-Maria Leonard, Tchaikovsky Research Net, September 10, 1875, https://en.tchaikovsky-research.net/pages/Letter_412.

118. Chaykovskiy, *Dnevniki*, 198; "Letter 681," trans. Luis Sundkvist, Tchaikovsky Research Net, December 7, 1877, https://en.tchaikovsky-research.net/pages/Letter_681. The *"moment of absolute happiness"* came during a concert performance of *Swan Lake* in Prague on February 9, 1888.

119. Alexander Poznansky, *Tchaikovsky: The Quest for the Inner Man* (New York: Schirmer, 1999), 175; see also Roland John Wiley, *Tchaikovsky's Ballets: Swan Lake, Sleeping Beauty, Nutcracker* (Oxford: Clarendon Press, 1985), 40–41.

120. Skromnïy nablyudatel', "Nablyudeniya i zametki," *Russkiye vedomosti*, February 26, 1877, p. 2; see also V. Krasovskaya, *Russkiy baletnïy teatr vtoroy polovinï XIX veka* (Leningrad and Moscow: Iskusstvo, 1963), 199.

121. Krasovskaya, *Russkiy baletnïy teatr vtoroy polovinï XIX veka*, 199; see also Wiley, *Tchaikovsky's Ballets*, 55.

122. RGIA f. 678, op. 1, d. 1058, ll. 49–50 (from De Lazari's memoir, a bouquet to Tchaikovsky and all the "hugs, kisses, chatter, and laughter" they shared).

123. Kashkin, *Vospominaniya*, 101. The composer received 400 rubles up front for the music, and then, upon submitting the first three acts to the Bolshoi on April 12, 1876, he requested the remaining 400 rubles due. The payment was "disbursed from the receipts for the first four performances of the ballet *Swan Lake* (accordingly, 100 rubles each evening)" (RGALI f. 659, op. 3, yed. khr. 3065, l. 36).

124. P. I. Chaykovskiy, *Lebedinoye ozero. Balet v 4-x deystviyakh. Postanovka v Moskovskom Bol'shom teatre 1875-1883. Skripichnïy repetitor i drugiye dokumentï*, ed. and comp. Sergey Konayev and Boris Mukosey (St. Petersburg: Kompozitor, 2015), 9.

125. Arlene Croce, "'Swan Lake' and Its Alternatives," in *Going to the Dance* (New York: Alfred A. Knopf, 1982), 184.

126. Chaykovskiy, *Lebedinoye ozero. Balet v 4-x deystviyakh. Postanovka v Moskovskom Bol'shom teatre 1875–1883*, 32.

127. Kashkin, *Vospominaniya*, 103.

128. Chaykovskiy, *Lebedinoye ozero. Balet v 4-x deystviyakh. Postanovka v Moskovskom Bol'shom teatre 1875–1883*, 87, 91.

129. Hansen liked the scenario of *Swan Lake* but not the music. He restaged it as *The Swans*, with music by Georges Jacobi, in 1884 in London and Paris.

130. Alastair Macaulay, "'Swan Lake' Discoveries Allow for a Deeper Dive into Its History," *New York Times*, October 13, 2015, sec. C, p. 1.

131. Chaykovskiy, *Lebedinoye ozero. Balet v 4-x deystviyakh. Postanovka v Moskovskom Bol'shom teatre 1875–1883*, 210.

132. D[mitriy] I[vanovich] Mukhin, "Kniga o balete," Muzey Bakhrushina f. 181, no. 1, l. 255.

133. U rampï, "Pochemu balet padayet? II.," *Russkiy listok*, November 22, 1900, p. 3.

134. Ibid.

135. Later this dance was inserted into another ballet, *The Little Humpbacked Horse*.

136. P. I. Chaykovskiy, *Perepiska s N. F. von-Mekk*, ed. V. A. Zhdanov and N. T. Zhegin, 3 vols. (Moscow and Leningrad: Academia, 1934–36), 2:298.

137. N. K[ashki]n, "Muzïkal'naya khronika," *Russkiye vedomosti*, March 3, 1877, p. 1.

138. Zub', "Bol'shoy teatr. Benefis g-zhi Karpakoy 1-oy—'Lebedinoye ozero', balet Reyzingera, muzïka Chaykovskago," *Sovremennïye izvestiya*, February 26, 1877, p. 1.

139. K. F. Val'ts, *65 let v teatre* (Leningrad: Academia, 1928), 108. In the draft of the Soviet-era memoirs from which these lines come, Valts adds that "none of this is in the current [circa 1926] production; everything is simplified" (Muzey Bakhrushina f. 43, op. 3, no. 3, l. 10 ob.). Since imperial-era ballet could not be seen as superior to Soviet-era ballet in any respect, Valts's complaint was excluded from the published text.

140. My thanks to Sergey Konaev for this observation.
141. N. K[ashki]n, "Muzïkal'naya khronika," *Russkiye vedomosti*, February 25, 1877, p. 1; see also Wiley, *Tchaikovsky's Ballets*, 57.
142. Simultaneously, the black swan became part of productions in Russia, England, and the United States.
143. Aleksey Barabanov, "Niti sud'bï," *Klinskaya nedelya*, June 10, 2019, https://nedelka-klin.ru/2019/06/10/niti-sudby/.
144. MarinaM, "Moskovskiy zhenskiy Elizaventiskiy institut," Genealogicheskiy forum VGD, October 18, 2013, https://forum.vgd.ru/1410/46846/10.htm?a=stdforum_view&o=.
145. V. O. Novichkov, "Znacheniye smïslova aktsenta. K voprosu interpretatsii romansa P. I. Chaykovskogo 'Net, tol'ko tot, kto znal' Vladimirom Atlantovïm i Pavlom Lisitsianom," in *Chaykovskiy v prostranstve i vremeni: Materialï Mezhdunarodnoy nauchno-prakticheskoy konferentsii, posvyashchennoy 175-letiyu so dnya rozhdeniya kompozitora* (Lugansk: Izd-vo LGAKI imeni M. L. Matusovskogo, 2015), 59. The text of the 1869 song is by Goethe as translated by Lev Mey.
146. Poznansky, *Tchaikovsky through Others' Eyes*, 116: "[*Eugene Onegin*] is good because it was written under the influence of love. It is based directly on us. He himself is Onegin and I am Tatyana."
147. Poznanskiy, *Pyotr Chaykovskiy. Biografiya*, 1:453.
148. Ibid., 1:427.
149. Kostalevsky, *Tchaikovsky Papers*, 255–56 n.65.
150. Poznansky, *Tchaikovsky through Others' Eyes*, 116.
151. Ibid., 112–13.
152. Kostalevsky, *Tchaikovsky Papers*, 264 n.164.
153. RGIA f. 678, op. 1, d. 58, ll. 2–3.
154. *Tchaikovsky through Others' Eyes*, 110.
155. Ibid., 109.
156. Ibid., 110.
157. Zinaída Pronchenko, "Tsvet nesvobodï: O chem fil'm 'Zhena Chaykovskogo' Kirilla Serebrennikova," *afishaDaily*, June 30, 2022, https://daily.afisha.ru/cinema/23445-cvet-nesvobody-o-chem-film-zhena-chaykovskogo-kirilla-serebrennikova/.
158. Chaykovskiy, *Perepiska s N. F. von-Mekk*, 1:3.
159. See Robert Pincus-Witten, *Occult Symbolism in France: Joséphin Péladan and the Salons de la Rose-Croix* (New York: Garland, 1976).
160. Poznanskiy, *Pyotr Chaykovskiy. Biografiya*, 1:405.
161. RGALI f. 279, op. 2, yed. khr. 283.
162. Galina von Meck, *As I Remember Them* (London: Dennis Dobson, 1973), 34–42.
163. P. E. Vaydman, ed., *P. I. Chaykovskiy—N. F. fon Mekk. Perepiska*, 4 vols. (Chelyabinsk: Music Production International, 2007–), 2:565–82.
164. "Brailov," Tchaikovsky Research Net, last modified December 31, 2022, https://en.tchaikovsky-research.net/pages/Brailov.
165. Vaydman, *P. I. Chaykovskiy—N. F. fon Mekk. Perepiska*, 2:200.
166. "Nadezhda von Meck," Tchaikovsky Research Net, last modified August 18, 2023, https://en.tchaikovsky-research.net/pages/Nadezhda_von_Meck.

167. Kostalevsky, *Tchaikovsky Papers*, 128 (January 9, 1878).
168. Poznanskiy, *Pyotr Chaykovskiy. Biografiya*, 2:15–17.
169. Zoran Minderovic, "Henryk Wieniawski Biography," AllMusic, accessed June 11, 2023, http://www.allmusic.com/artist/mn0001505198/biography.
170. Poznanskiy, *Pyotr Chaykovskiy. Biografiya*, 2:120; letter of August 7, 1880.
171. Francis Maes, *A History of Russian Music: From Kamarinskaya to Babi Yar*, trans. Arnold J. Pomerans and Erica Pomerans (Berkeley: University of California Press, 2002), 141.
172. Vaydman, *P. I. Chaykovskiy—N. F. fon Mekk. Perepiska*, 1:182, 184.
173. See Esti Sheinberg and Marina Ritzarev, "'The Infinite Grace of Jesus': Massenet's 'Marie-Magdeleine' and Tchaikovsky's Blessed Tears," *Music and Letters* 91, no. 2 (May 2010): 171–97.
174. RGIA f. 468, op. 16, d. 1124, l. 5 ob.
175. Poznanskiy, *Pyotr Chaykovskiy. Biografiya*, 2:418.
176. Kashkin, *Vospominaniya*, 107–09.
177. Aleksandr Mikhaílovich Belkin, "P. I. Chaykovskiy i sem'ya Shilovskikh," tambovlib.ru, accessed April 10, 2023, http://www.tambovlib.ru/?view=conferenc.2010.chaikovskij_tambkraj.belkin.
178. Wiley, *Tchaikovsky*, 171.
179. Muzïkal'nïy klassik, "Teatral'nïy kur'yer," *Peterburgskiy listok*, December 28, 1878, p. 3.
180. B. V. Asaf'yev, *"Yevgeniy Onegin," liricheskiye stsenï P. I. Chaykovskogo: Opït intonatsionnogo analiza stilya i muzïkal'noy dramaturgii* (Moscow and Leningrad: Muzgiz, 1944), 6–7. Some of the costumes were recycled from other productions; the new ones came out of the budget of the IRMS. In an unpublished letter, Kashkin describes Tchaikovsky traveling back from Europe on the day of the dress rehearsal, hotfooting it from Smolensk (Belarus) Station just in time. The March 17, 1879, premiere at the Malïy Theater was toasted at an after-midnight banquet for the composer, conductor, performers, and the dignitaries who came down from St. Petersburg for the opera. RGIA f. 678, op. 1, d. 360 (letter to Molchanov, October 4, 1893).
181. "Teatral'nïy kur'yer," *Peterburgskiy listok*, April 24, 1883, p. 2.
182. Information in this paragraph from Aleksandr Vasil'yev Kirovich, "Opera P. I. Chaykovskogo 'Yevgeniy Onegin' na russkoy stsene 1879–1991 gg. Postanovochnïye printsipï tantseval'nïkh i massovïkh stsen" (PhD diss., Rossiyskiy institut istorii iskusstv, 2019), 37, 46, 48, 59.
183. G. A. Laroche, "Tchaikovsky's *Eugene Onegin* in the Conservatoire's Production," March 22, 1879, in Campbell, *Russians on Russian Music, 1830–1880*, 246.
184. RGIA f. 947, op. 1, d. 62, ll. 8 ob.–9.
185. Quoted in Emily Frey, "Nowhere Man: *Evgeny Onegin* and the Politics of Reflection in Nineteenth-Century Russia," *19th-Century Music* 36, no. 3 (Spring 2013): 211, 217. Another indictment comes from Isaiah Berlin, "Tchaikovsky, Pushkin and Onegin," *Musical Times* 121, no. 1645 (1980): 163–68.
186. Asaf'yev, *"Yevgeniy Onegin,"* 8.
187. John Bayley, preface to Alexander Pushkin, *Eugene Onegin: A Novel in Verse*, trans. Charles Johnston; introd. Michael Basker (New York: Penguin 2003), xv, Kindle.

NOTES

188. M[ichael] B[asker], "A Note on the Text," in Pushkin, *Eugene Onegin* (2003), xx.
189. James Meek, "The Village Life," *London Review of Books* 41, no. 11 (June 6, 2019), https://www.lrb.co.uk/the-paper/v41/n11/james-meek/the-village-life.
190. The duet is a setting of another Pushkin text, the first and last stanzas of his elegy "The Singer" ("Pevets", 1816). Tchaikovsky's original plan for Act I, scene 1, was to have Olga and Tatyana sing an elegy by Zhukovsky, not Pushkin, as their mother and the nursemaid reflect on their salad days (while making jam).
191. Frey, "Nowhere Man," 224.
192. Caryl Emerson, "Tatyana," in *A Plot of Her Own: The Female Protagonist in Russian Literature*, ed. Sona Stephan Hoisington (Evanston: Northwestern University Press, 1995), 14–19, 133 n.19.
193. The ditches are rhymed with witches in Anthony Kline's translation of *Eugene Onegin*, Poetry in Translation, accessed May 28, 2023, https://www.poetryintranslation.com/PITBR/Russian/Onegin7.php. On the narrator's digressions see James Wood, "Bobbery," *London Review of Books*, 25, no. 4 (February 20, 2003), https://www.lrb.co.uk/the-paper/v25/n04/james-wood/bobbery.
194. Richard Taruskin, "*Yevgeny Onegin*," in Sadie, *New Grove Dictionary of Opera*, 4:1193.
195. Ts. A. Cui, "Notes on Music: *Eugene Onegin*," November 4, 1884, in Campbell, *Russians on Russian Music, 1830–1880*, 250, 252.
196. Wiley, *Tchaikovsky*, 178–79; Asaf'yev, "*Yevgeniy Onegin*," 59.
197. I am indebted to Ritvik Agnihotri and Gabrielle Hooper for the following comparison (from a March 9, 2023, presentation in Princeton University Music Department seminar MUS 514: Tchaikovsky).
198. Alexander Pushkin, *Eugene Onegin*, trans. James E. Falen (New York: Oxford University Press, 1998), 75.
199. Ibid., 202.
200. Ibid., 142. Tchaikovsky's librettistic adaptation of *Eugene Onegin*, and his annotations of the 1838 edition of the novel in his library, are described in detail by N. Rukavishnikov, "Pushkin v biblioteke P. Chaykovskogo," *Sovetskaya muzika*, no. 1 (1937): 60–70.
201. Taruskin, "*Yevgeny Onegin*," 4:1193.
202. Asaf'yev, "*Yevgeniy Onegin*," 27–33; Taruskin, "*Yevgeny Onegin*," 4:1194.
203. Asaf'yev, "*Yevgeniy Onegin*," 9.
204. The final line in the libretto, Onegin's expression of despair over his "wretched fate" was supplied to Tchaikovsky by an actor friend: Ivan Samarin. Wiley, *Tchaikovsky*, 172.
205. The fact that there is a conversation between the two of them, one that makes her doubt herself, is a major departure from Pushkin; and Laroche was the first to complain that Tchaikovsky "had made Tatyana show a weakness in her meeting with Onegin for which we would look in vain in the original poem" ("Tchaikovsky's *Eugene Onegin* in the Conservatoire's Production," 246). "As in the letter scene," Frey clarifies, "Tchaikovsky forces Tatiana to struggle: she agonizes over her choice, at one point nearly giving in before pushing Eugene away. Once again, Tchaikovsky's textual interpolations emphasize Tatiana's real-time mental processing—and her sympathy for her interlocutor.

Immediately before she reveals that she still loves Eugene, she begins to refer to him by his first name, her resolve clearly attenuating. Even as she finally sends Eugene on his way, Tchaikovsky's Tatiana admits inner turmoil ("Nowhere Man," 221).

206. Garry Wills, "The Lions of Venice," *The American Scholar* 68, no. 2 (Spring 1999): 49.
207. "Letter 799," trans. Luis Sundkvist, Tchaikovsky Research Net, March 27, 1878, https://en.tchaikovsky-research.net/pages/Letter_799. "In essence my symphony is an imitation of Beethoven's Fifth, that is, I was imitating not his musical thoughts, but the fundamental idea." Taneyev had a lot of complaints about the symphony, including one that Tchaikovsky rejected out of hand: the references to ballet music. "By ballet music do you mean every cheerful melody with a dance rhythm? But in that case you shouldn't be able to reconcile yourself to the majority of Beethoven's symphonies, in which one continually comes across such melodies. Are you trying to say that the trio in my Scherzo is written in the style of Minkus, Gerber, and Pugni? This, however, I think it does not deserve. Indeed, I simply cannot understand why there should be anything at all reprehensible in the expression ballet music!"
208. Aleksey Apukhtin, "Sud'ba (k 5-oy simfonii Betkhovena)," Askbuka literaturï, accessed April 19, 2023, https://www.askbooka.ru/stihi/aleksey-apuhtin/sudba.html.
209. Robert Gauldin, "Theory and Practice of Chromatic Wedge Progressions in Romantic Music," *Music Theory Spectrum* 26, no. 1 (Spring 2004): 1–22, esp. 13.
210. Piero Weiss and Richard Taruskin, *Music in the Western World: A History in Documents* (Belmont, CA: Thomson Higher Education, 2008), 338–42.
211. Taruskin, *Defining Russia Musically*, 297–302.
212. "Letter 763," trans. Brett Langston, Tchaikovsky Research Net, February 17, 1878, https://en.tchaikovsky-research.net/pages/Letter_763.
213. Ibid.
214. Kislova, "Russkiy detskiy muzïkal'nïy fol'klor," 147.
215. "Letter 763" (translation adjusted).
216. Kostalevsky, *Tchaikovsky Papers*, 125 (January 17, 1878).
217. Ibid., 116–17 (October 16, 1877).
218. Ibid., 117 (October 27, 1877).
219. Ibid., 120–21 (December 11, 1877), 126–27 (January 9, 1878).
220. Ibid., 122 (December 12, 1877).
221. Hans Keller, "Peter Ilyich Tchaikovsky," in *The Symphony*, vol. 1, *Haydn to Dvořák*, ed. Robert Simpson (Harmondsworth: Penguin, 1967), 345–46.
222. Taruskin, *Defining Russia Musically*, 253–60.
223. Alexander Pushkin, "Count Nulin," trans. Betsy Hulick, StoSvet, accessed June 12, 2023, http://www.stosvet.net/12/hulick/.
224. E. E. Filippova, "Proyavleniye russkogo natsional'nogo mirovospriyatiya v tsikle p'es P. I. Chaykovskogo 'Vremena goda,'" in *IV Vserossiyskiy festival' nauki. XVIII Mezhdunarodnaya konferentsiya studentov, aspirantov i molodïkh uchenïkh 'Nauka i obrazovaniye' (21–25 aprelya 2014 g.),"* ed. T. E. Zaytseva (Tomsk: TGPU, 2014), 35–38.
225. Taruskin, *Defining Russia Musically*, 269.

226. Aleksandr Komarov, "Syuita No. 1," kul'tura.rf, accessed April 18, 2023, https://www.culture.ru/catalog/tchaikovsky/ru/item/article/syuita-no-1.

227. Brooke Burkhart notes that Tchaikovsky relies on perfect cadences in the former and imperfect, half cadences in the latter. The harmonic language is more magically, spectrally elusive in the overture, involving applied dominants, eleventh and ninth chords, and third inversions. The march keeps things simpler ("An Exploration of Tchaikovsky's Affection for Dance Movements with a Specific Comparison of Orchestral Suite No. 1 and *The Nutcracker*," research paper for Princeton University Music Department seminar MUS 514: Tchaikovsky, submitted May 9, 2023).

228. O. L-n, "Muzïkal'naya khronika," *Russkiye vedomosti*, December 15, 1879, p. 1.

229. Philip Bullock, *Pyotr Tchaikovsky* (London: Reaktion Books, 2016), 127: "Its opening gestures suggest a stylized version of some rococo serenade, and thereafter its constructional principle is sectional and contrastive, rather in the manner of a baroque concerto grosso."

230. Liszt made several such arrangements in his later years; he and his publishers profited handsomely from them. According to the manuscript preserved in Moscow at the Glinka Museum, Liszt made the arrangement of the polonaise in 1879, just after Tchaikovsky completed the opera.

231. "Moskovskiy listok," *Petersburgskiy listok*, March 28, 1881, p. 1.

232. The preceding information from Dmitriy Vladimirovich Belyak, "Kontsertï P. I. Chaykovskogo v kontekste pozdneromanticheskogo fortepiannogo iskusstva" (PhD diss., Gnesin Russian Academy of Music, 2022), 23–29, 42–43, 165.

    The world premiere of the Second Piano Concerto was in New York City with Madeline Schiller as soloist. "It was a brilliant piece of pianism, the only regret being that her efforts had not been devoted to a more interesting work." ("The Philharmonic Society," *New York Times*, November 13, 1881, p. 8.) It fell to Taneyev to introduce the work to the Russian public with Anton Rubinstein conducting, and Taneyev convinced Tchaikovsky to make three small cuts for the performances that the composer conducted with a different soloist, Vasily Sapelnikov, whose interpretation he preferred to Taneyev's.

233. A. I. Klimovitskiy, "Motsart Chaykovskogo: Fragmentï syuzheta," in *Pyotr Il'yich Chaykovskiy. Kul'turnïye predchuvstviya. Kul'turnaya pamyat'. Kul'turnïye vzaimodeystviya* (St. Petersburg: Petropolis/Rossiyskiy institut istorii iskusstv, 2015), 159.

234. The Serenade inspired Tchaikovsky's student Taneyev to compose a C-major score of his own. Tchaikovsky dismissed it as "a captivating thing, but nothing more than a play of sounds," adding that the "aim of art is to please the heart and soul, not just the ears." Ibid., 170 (in reference to Taneyev's Overture in C major "On a Russian Theme" [1882]).

235. He sent a pile of letters to Sofronov expressing concern, as he did to von Mekk. These latter go into greater detail about the composer's efforts to ease Sofronov's situation; the former, because they had to pass through the military censors, do not. Sometimes the letters are hopeful, like this one from December 14, 1880, to von Mekk:

My Alyosha, thanks to the involvement of a certain General Klemm, commander of the Moscow troops, to whom I happened to render services in the past in the form of correcting Romances that he composed, was transferred to Moscow and should be here, if not today, then tomorrow. He'll be billeted with the Yekaterinoslav Grenadier Regiment and then seconded to the clerk class. This is a great relief for him, since his biggest fear was that he would be sent somewhere distant.

He continued the letter three days later, his mood soured:

My poor, poor Alyosha! Yesterday I visited him in the Pokrovsky garrison. The stuffy, dirty barracks, the defeated and pitiful sight of Alyosha, already dressed like a soldier, deprived of his liberty and made to march around from early morning until evening—all this made a heavy and depressing impression on me!

On December 28, he wrote the following from his sister's residence:

I've been receiving gloomy letters from Alyosha, and this circumstance greatly poisons the pleasure I've been experiencing in my warm little corner here. In addition to the hardships and deprivations associated with Alyosha's new posting, fate has assigned him a cruel and unfair supervising officer. The sergeant major of the regiment where he's stationed has shown himself to be a terrible tyrant. For some reason he took a dislike to my poor young man and insults him however he likes. But I hope that that this will soon come to an end. Fortunately, the regimental commander loves my music, and I've received word to the effect that that he's willing to protect Alyosha. I don't know what form the protection will take, but this news gives me great hope.

"Letter 1648," Tchaikovsky Research Net, December 14, 1880, https://en.tchaikovsky-research.net/pages/Letter_1648; "Letter 1658," Tchaikovsky Research Net, December 28, 1880, https://en.tchaikovsky-research.net/pages/Letter_1658.

236. "Letter 1718," Tchaikovsky Research Net, March 20, 1881, https://en.tchaikovsky-research.net/pages/Letter_1718.

237. "Letter 1410," Tchaikovsky Research Net, January 19, 1880, https://en.tchaikovsky-research.net/pages/Letter_1410.

238. The quote was added to the Wikipedia page about Ravel's *Tombeau de Couperin* in 2005 by a user named Antandrus, who falsely sources it to a 2001 reprint edition of the score published in 1919 by Durand.

239. "Teatral'nïy kur'yer," *Peterburgskiy listok*, July 18, 1891, p. 3.

240. Balanchine's *Serenade* became more abstract over time. In 1940, the centennial of Tchaikovsky's birth, Balanchine symbolically reversed the order of the last two movements, turning the work into a *tombeau* (monument) to the composer.

241. Wiley, *Tchaikovsky*, 237.

242. Taruskin, *Defining Russia Musically*, 268, 275.

243. "Letter 834," Tchaikovsky Research Net, May 21, 1878, https://en.tchaikovsky-research.net/pages/Letter_834. Volkmann's Cello Concerto was performed in St. Petersburg on February 11, 1867, on the same IRMS program as the andante and scherzo movements of Tchaikovsky's First Symphony.

244. Chaykovskiy, *Perepiska s N. F. von-Mekk*, 1:343.

245. His modest career is traced by Viktor von Herzfeld, "Robert Volkmann (1815–1883)," *The Musical Quarterly* 1, no. 3 (1915): 336–49. Volkmann had some success in the United States: the New York Philharmonic performed his music several times beginning in 1867, and the Boston Symphony Orchestra followed suit in 1882.

246. Karl Galle, "The Triumph of Melancholy: 500 Years of Dürer's Most Enigmatic Print," *The Guardian*, May 16, 2014, https://www.theguardian.com/science/the-h-word/2014/may/16/-triumph-melancholy-anniversary-durer-history-science.

247. Ibid.

248. David Thomas Salkowski, "Music for an Imagined Liturgy: Rethinking the Sound of Orthodoxy in Late Imperial Russia" (PhD diss., Princeton University, 2021), 79, 137–44.

249. Michael Graves, *Biblical Interpretation in the Early Church* (Minneapolis: Fortress Press, 2017), 197.

250. Tchaikovsky made three other arrangements of the Cherubic Hymn, the last of them after seeing the dying Kotek. The arrangements are included in his *Nine Sacred Pieces* of 1884–85.

251. John Ahern, "The Politics and Personality of Tchaikovsky's 'Cherubic Hymn' from *Liturgy of St. John Chrysostom*" (research paper for Princeton University Music Department seminar MUS 513: Tchaikovsky, submitted January 31, 2018).

252. "Composer's Preface" to "All-Night Vigil: An Essay in Harmonizing Liturgical Chants," op. 52 (1881), in *Monuments of Russian Sacred Music: Peter Tchaikovsky; The Complete Sacred Choral Works*, ed. Vladimir Morosan (Madison, CT: Musica Russica, 1996), 99.

253. Pyotr Il'yich Chaykovskiy, *Akademicheskoye polnoye sobraniye sochineniy. Seriya V. T. 1. Liturgiya Svyatogo Ioanna Zlatoustogo: dlya chetïrekhgolosnogo smeshannogo khora: soch. 41*, ed. Mitropolit Ilarion (Alfeyev) (Chelyabinsk: Music Production International, 2016), lxii, lxv.

254. Salkowski, "Music for an Imagined Liturgy," 45; N. A. Troitskiy, *Korifei rossiyskoy advokatï* (Moscow: Tsentrpoligraf, 2006), 50 (on Dmitri Stasov).

255. RGIA f. 776, op. 2, d. 19, l. 337.

256. RGIA f. 796, op. 160, d. 834, l. 4.

257. RGIA f. 499, op. 1, d. 2941 (correspondence between 1869 and 1870), ll. 165, 168.

258. *Kratkiy uchebnik garmoniy. Prisposoblennïy k chteniyu dukhovno-muzikal'nïkh sochineniy v Rossiy*, commissioned by the *Obshchestvo lyubiteley drevnerusskogo iskusstva* (Society for Lovers of Ancient Russian Art).

259. RGIA f. 797, op. 90, d. 46, l. 7.

260. The *Liturgy* was also heard at Komissarov College in Moscow. Chaykovskiy, *Akademicheskoye polnoye sobraniye sochineniy. Seriya V. T. 1.*, lxxi.

NOTES

261. Ibid., lxxiii; O. L-n, "Muzïkal'naya khronika," *Russkiye vedomosti*, January 8, 1881, p. 1.
262. RGIA f. 797, op. 52, d. 60.
263. Starïy moskovskiy svyashchennosluzhitel', "Dukhovnïy kontsert v zale Rossiyskago Blagorodnago Sobraniya 18-go dekabrya," *Rus'*, January 3, 1881, p. 14, quoted in M. Chaykovskiy, *Zhizn' Petra Il'yicha Chaykovskogo*, 2:441n.
264. P. I. Chaykovskiy, *Polnoye sobraniye sochineniy. Literaturnïye proizvedeniya i perepiska*, 17 vols. (Moscow: Muzïka, 1953–81), 10:265 (letter of November 9, 1881).
265. See Frolova-Walker, *Russian Music and Nationalism*, 291–92, 295.
266. RGIA f. 1119, op. 1, d. 3, l. 81 (Smolensky's diary entry for December 3, 1893, forty days after Tchaikovsky's death).
267. "Our Father" from Tchaikovsky's *Liturgy of St. John Chrysostom* was included on a packed program of older and newer sacred pieces by Bortnyansky, Stepan Degtyarev, Dmitri Solovyov, and others at St. Petersburg's Assembly of the Nobility on March 12, 1889. The sold-out concert ended with "loud and unanimous applause for the singers and their energetic, talented conductor, F[yodor] F[yodorovich] Bekker. The ovation was a richly deserved award for the aesthetic pleasure given to the listener by the beautiful, fully and wholly artistic singing of the Russian opera chorus and the excellence with which Bekker carried out his difficult task." "Teatral'nïy kur'yer," *Peterburgskiy listok*, March 14, 1889, p. 3.
268. "Letter 840," Tchaikovsky Research Net, May 23, 1878, https://en.tchaikovsky-research.net/pages/Letter_840.
269. After Tchaikovsky's death, Taneyev worked up the draft ideas into an operatic scene.
270. Raymond N. MacKenzie, "Trop Dandy," *London Review of Books*, 45, no. 5 (March 2, 2023), https://www.lrb.co.uk/the-paper/v45/n05/raymond-n.-mackenzie/trop-dandy.
271. John Pendergast, "Sisters in Sublime Sanctity: Schiller's *Jungfrau*, Euripides's Iphigenia Plays, and Joan of Arc on the Stage" (PhD diss., City University of New York, 2015), 287.
272. Elsa Bienenfeld, "Verdi and Schiller," *The Musical Quarterly* 17, no. 2 (April 1931): 204.
273. "Letter 1065," Tchaikovsky Research Net, January 10, 1879, https://en.tchaikovsky-research.net/pages/Letter_1065. Pendergast notes that Tchaikovsky also consulted historian Henri-Alexandre Wallon's *Jeanne d'Arc* (1860), a gift from von Mekk. Its account of Joan's death gutted him, as he related to Modest: "When I reach the trial, condemnation, and the execution itself (she screamed horribly the whole time, when they led her out, and begged them to cut off her head, and not burn her), I bawled terribly. I was suddenly so sick and sorry for humanity and overwhelmed by inexpressible sadness. Along with this, I suddenly imagined that all of you were sick or dead, and that I was such a *little wretch* (just as though I had been viciously banished here), etc." "Sisters in Sublime Sanctity," 289–90.
274. Pendergast, "Sisters in Sublime Sanctity," 276.
275. Ibid., 296.

276. As the line originally read in Zhukovsky's translation of Schiller. Ibid., 298.

277. The argument began right after the premiere, with Osip Levenson claiming that, by his count, only 60 of the 460 pages of the piano-vocal score had escaped foreign influence. The rest "flattered the coarse tastes of the masses, contrary to the calling of a true artist" ("Muzïkal'naya khronika," *Russkiye vedomosti*, February 21, 1881, p. 1).

278. Marina Frolova-Walker, "A Ukrainian Tune in Medieval France: Perceptions of Nationalism and Local Color in Russian Opera," *19th-Century Music* 35, no. 2 (2011): 117. Tchaikovsky took the tune from his 1878 *Children's Album*.

279. J. L. Nelson, "What a Woman!" *London Review of Books* 22, no. 20 (October 19, 2000), https://www.lrb.co.uk/the-paper/v22/n20/j.l.-nelson/what-a-woman.

280. Ibid.

281. Sophie Brady, "'My Name Is Joan': Musical Borrowings and National Identity in *The Maid of Orleans*" (research paper for Princeton University Music Department seminar MUS 513: Tchaikovsky, submitted January 31, 2018).

282. Nelson, "What a Woman!"

283. Ilya Vinitsky, "Go! Creating the Russian Jeanne D'Arc," paper presented at the Association for Slavic, East European, and Eurasian Studies conference, November 10, 2017, Chicago.

284. Ivan Turgenev, "Threshold" ("Porog," 1878), quoted in Vinitsky, "Go!"

285. Samuel Kucherov, "The Case of Vera Zasulich," *Russian Review* 11, no. 2 (April 1952): 86–96, esp. 86.

286. Vinitsky, "Go!"

287. RGIA f. 497, op. 2, d. 24637, l. 2 (March 26, 1880).

288. Rossiyskiy institut istorii iskusstv (henceforth RIII) f. 21, op. 1, d. 225, ll. 42 ob.–43.

289. Robert Ignatius Letellier, Meyerbeer's *Le Prophète: A Parable of Politics, Faith and Transcendence* (Newcastle: Cambridge Scholars Press, 2018), 30.

290. Rutger Helmers, *Not Russian Enough? Nationalism and Cosmopolitanism in Nineteenth-Century Russian Opera* (Rochester: University of Rochester Press, 2014), 91–95, esp. 94.

291. Ibid., 83: "[Tchaikovsky] gave up his individuality and began to copy the public's favorites, adapting himself to their tastes. This picture of the gifted composer humiliating himself for their favor is a depressing one."

292. Ibid., 95.

293. RIII f. 21, op. 1, d. 225, l. 44.

Part III Imperialism

1. Chaykovskiy and Yurgenson, *Perepiska*, 220 (letter of July 3, 1880).

2. "Letter 1350," trans. Brett Langston, Tchaikovsky Research Net, November 22, 1879, https://en.tchaikovsky-research.net/pages/Letter_1350.

3. "Letter 1603," Tchaikovsky Research Net, September 28, 1880, https://en.tchaikovsky-research.net/pages/Letter_1603.

4. Information in this paragraph from N. I. Teterina, "Problemï rekonstruktsii zhivïkh kartin k 25-letiyu tsarstvovaniya imperatora Aleksandra II," in *Chaykovskiy i XXI vek: Dialogi vo vremeni i prostranstve. Materialï*

mezhdunarodnoy nauchnoy konferentsii. Moskva—Klin 12–14 noyabrya 2014 goda, ed. A. V. Komarov (St. Petersburg: Kompozitor, 2017), 49–62, esp. 52–53.

5. Review in *Golos*, August 17, 1882, quoted in Wiley, *Tchaikovsky*, 240–41.

6. Tchaikovsky's manuscript is calibrated for indoor performances and calls for large bells of the same pitch and a suspended drum, ferociously whacked, as the replacement for cannons. There's also an option to include a brass band in the coda. "*1812 god. Torzhestvennaya uvertyura*," kul'tura.rf, accessed January 11, 2023, https://www.culture.ru/catalog/tchaikovsky/ru/item/archiv/1812-god-torzhestvennaya-uvertyura.

7. Mariya Fyodorovna, *Opisaniye svyashchennogo koronovaniya ikh imperatorskikh velichestv gosudarya imperatora Aleksandra Tret'yevo i gos. Imp. Marii Fyodorovnï vseya Rossii 1883 g.* (St. Petersburg: Kartogr. Zav. A. Il'yina, 1883), 60.

8. Dmitri Sidorov, "National Monumentalization and the Politics of Scale: The Resurrections of the Cathedral of Christ the Savior in Moscow," *Annals of the Association of American Geographers* 90, no. 3 (September 2000): 557.

9. In its new location the cathedral was surrounded by "low dilapidated buildings containing dubious-looking taverns and other types of drinking establishments—brothels for people of suspicious reputation." The neighborhood was called "The Valley of the Wolves" and the faithful "feared going there at night" (Belousov, *Ushedshaya Moskva*, 29–30).

10. Andrew Gentes, "The Life, Death and Resurrection of the Cathedral of Christ the Savior, Moscow," *History Workshop Journal* 46, no. 1 (1998): 72.

11. This information comes from the memoirs of Konstantin Pobedonostsev's wife Yekaterina Alekseyevna Pobedonostseva, RGIA f. 1754, op. 1, d. 29, l. 79: "We provided aid to P. I. Tchaikovsky. He was poor and on request of K. P. the sovereign gave him 3,000."

12. Poznanskiy, *Pyotr Chaykovskiy. Biografiya*, 2:208.

13. Sergey S., "Moskovskiy triumf P. I. Chaykovskogo v mae 1883 goda," *Usad'ba Dem'yanovo g. Klin*, April 30, 2015, https://klin-demianovo.ru/http:/klin-demianovo.ru/analitika/100211/.

14. E. V. Perevalov, "Torzhestvennïy koronatsionnïy marsh P. I. Chaykovskogo: Otkrïtiye E. Svetlanova-Dirizhyora," elibrary.ru, October 16, 2018, https://www.elibrary.ru/item.asp?id=36974894&selid=36974910.

15. He renamed it "Marche Solennelle" but no one was fooled.

16. S., "Moskovskiy triumf."

17. M. Ivanov, "Muzïkal'noye obozreniye," *Nuvellist*, no. 2 (February 1884): 5.

18. "Czar's Adviser, Mestchersky, Dies," *New York Times*, July 24, 1914, p. 9.

19. Evgenii Bershtein, "The Russian Myth of Oscar Wilde," in *Self and Story in Russian History*, ed. Laura Engelstein and Stephanie Sandler (Ithaca: Cornell University Press, 2000), 173.

20. See G. A. Moiseyev, "Chaykovskiy i Konstantinovichi. Neizvestnïye faktï istorii vzaimootnosheniy s avgusteyshimi pokrovitelyami IRMO," in Komarov, *Chaykovskiy i XXI vek*, 32–48.

21. Givens, "Shakespeare and Russian Literature," 5.

22. Information in this paragraph is from Vera Tsarevna Brauner, *Autographs Don't Burn: Letters to the Bunins* (Boston: Academic Studies Press, 2020), 25–30.

23. K. R. (Velikiy Knyaz' Konstantin Romanov), *Dnevniki. Vospominaniya. Stikhi. Pis'ma*, ed. Ella Matonina (Moscow: Iskusstvo, 1998), 78–79.

24. "By *Andantino in modo di canzona* did you mean a short and clear piece without any excess?" K. R. asked. "I think I heard two themes in it, one alternating with the other. First the violins, then the bassoon, and finally the cello, and in between the whole orchestra enters. In the first movement, the initial, fatal trumpet sounds strongly affected me, so successfully repeated in the finale, like an indelible memory of the past. I also really liked the disturbing theme [the waltz!]; there is so much excitement, struggle and despair. The oboe and flute didn't sound very good." (V. E. Andreyev, "Muzïka v Mramornom dvortse (shtrikhi k portretam velikikh knyazey Konstantina Nikolayevicha i Konstantina Konstantinovicha)," in *'Muzïka vse vremya protsvetala ...' Muzïkal'naya zhizn' imperatorskikh dvortsov. Materialï nauchno-prakticheskoy konferentsii*, ed. S. A. Astakhovskaya and E. V. Minkina (St. Petersburg: Lesnik-Print, 2015), 44–45.

25. "Song of the Gypsy," to words by Polonsky, describes a girl–boy romance that for the girl, allegorized as a gypsy, has ended in sadness and anger. The opening stanza likens the end of the relationship to a campfire whose sparks expire in the cold of the night. It also mentions a bridge, which places it in an urban environment. There are no fortune cards, necklace beads, or sharp knives; the one gypsy prop is a shawl, which the boy has wrapped tight around the girl before rejecting her, consigning her to nomadic sisterhood. She asks him to remember her when the next girl sits on his lap and sings to him. In this, the penultimate stanza, she breaks out of her banal-cheerful recitational mode to become an actual singer. It's a defiant moment of heartache that points out what he'll be missing. And if she's to be treated like a gypsy, she'll be tough and proud and beg for nothing. Her aim is to leave a mark, an imprint in his memory, like the piano part's insistent downbeats. The song is cast in E minor (representing inner truth) with an E-major frame (outer appearance).

26. Grigoriy Moiseyev, "Romansï P. I. Chaykovskogo dlya imperatritsï Marii Fyodorovnï: Neizvestnaya avtorizovannaya rukopis'," *Nauchnïy vestnik Moskovskoy konservatorii*, no. 3 (2015): 106–45, esp. 117.

27. Andreyev, "Muzïka v Mramornom dvortse," 45–48.

28. Sergey Tyulenev, "Speaking Silence and Silencing Speech: The Translations of Grand Duke Konstantin Romanov as Queer Writing," in *Queering Translation, Translating the Queer*, ed. Brian James Baer and Klaus Kaindl (New York: Routledge, 2018), 102–18.

29. G. A. Moiseyev, "P. I. Chaykovskiy i velikiy knyaz' Konstantin Konstantinovich: posmertnïy dialog," *Observatoriya kul'turï* 17, no. 5 (2020): 496–509.

30. Ibid., 503–04.

31. RGIA f. 497, op. 2, d. 25300, ll. 15–20.

32. Chaykovskiy, *Polnoye sobraniye sochineniy. Literaturnïye proizvedeniya i perepiska*, 7: 334.

33. Marius Petipa's first wife Mariya Surovshchikova, for example, received a pension of 1,140 rubles annually following her retirement in 1869 (RGIA f. 468, op. 16, d. 1124, l. 1). Tchaikovsky began to receive the pension in 1888, in recognition of his "outstanding service to Russian music" and the "first place" he occupied "among other representatives of this profession." The paperwork granting the pension also recorded Tchaikovsky's 1859–67 service as a "titular counselor" in St. Petersburg's halls of justice, for which he received a pittance

(RGIA f. 497, op. 5, d. 3391, ll. 2, 3, 6). In 1890, the year von Mekk ended her support, Tchaikovsky earned about 8,000 rubles in royalties for his operas, hefty works that he composed at a fast clip. The 1888 commission for the ballet *The Sleeping Beauty*, sales of printed scores, and payments for conducting engagements pushed his income much higher.

34. Muzikal'niy klassik, "Teatral'niy kur'yer," *Peterburgskiy listok*, June 22, 1882, p. 3.

35. Ya. Yu. Gurova, *Ivan Aleksandrovich Vsevolozhskiy i yego znacheniye v istorii russkogo muzikal'nogo teatra* (St. Petersburg: Skifiya, 2015), 27.

36. "Если же флейтист хорош, я очень рад его принять—тем более, что Министру угодно, чтобы немцев и жидов было по возможности менее": RIII f. 44, op. 1, d. 58, l. 37 (July 25, 1887).

37. "Если она выйдет замуж, то, вероятно, за негра": RGIA f. 678, op. 1, d. 58, l. 11.

38. Gurova, *Vsevolozhskiy*, 123-25.

39. "Neizvestnïye pis'ma P. I. Chaykovskogo," *Sovetskaya muzïka*, no. 8 (1939): 55.

40. Tchaikovsky also worked with private opera companies, like the one bankrolled by St. Petersburg entrepreneur Alexei Kartavov, who organized the Latvian premiere of *Eugene Onegin* on October 17, 1888.

41. N. N. Kalinichenko, "Astrakhanskiye episodï v biografii Chaykovskogo," in Komarov, *Chaykovskiy i XXI vek*, 63–65.

42. "Tiflisskaya zhizn'," *Kavkaz*, April 20, 1886, p. 3.

43. Из медных утюгов огонь я достаю,
Чтоб тут же закурить потухшую мою
Сигару—здесь курить начальство позволяет;
Пожаров никогда в Тифлисе не бывает,
В Тифлисе просто нечему гореть.

    Ya. P. Polonskiy, "Progulka po Tiflisu" (1846), in *Stikhotvoreniya i poemï*, ed. B. M. Eykhenbaum (Moscow: Sovetskiy pisatel', 1935), 40–41.

44. G. Kor-nov, "Izyashchnïya iskusstva," *Kavkaz*, December 12, 1886, p. 3.

45. RGIA f. 1412, op. 55, d. 9, ll. 1–2 (July 3, 1887, sent from Borzhom, Georgia).

46. Ibid., ll. 6–24, esp. 8 (October 5, 1887).

47. Campbell Shiflett, "Tchaikovsky: Second Suite for Orchestra, Op. 53" (analysis for Princeton University Music Department seminar MUS 513: Tchaikovsky, submitted September 30, 2017).

48. Iya Nemirovskaya, "Ad libitum (Ves'ma zhelatel'nïy, no ne neobkhodimï)," paper presented at the conference "Sozdaniya kul'turnoy sredï: Iz veka XIX v vek XXI," October–December, 2013, Samara, Russia, http://www.sgubern.ru/img/illustration4/Ad_libitum.pdf.

49. M. Lepekhin, "Burenin Viktor Petrovich," Knizhnaya Lavka Pisateley, accessed May 19, 2023, https://lavkapisateley.spb.ru/enciklopediya/b/burenin-.

50. Aynbinder, *Pyotr Chaykovskiy*, 261–62; Chernaya, "Kamenka," 26.

51. Viktor Voynov, "Chaykovskiy, Mikhail Illiaronovich (Sadïk-pasha)," *Bol'shaya biograficheskaya entsiklopediya*, 2009, https://dic.academic.ru/dic.nsf/enc_biography/15592/Чайковский.

52. Dimitri Horbay, trans., "The Duma of Hetman Mazepa," *Svoboda*, March 22, 1958, p. 3.

53. Voltaire, *History of Charles XII, King of Sweden*, trans. Winifred Todhunter (London: J. M. Dent and Sons, 1908), 190–91. My thanks to Chester Dunning for this reference.

54. RGIA f. 497, op. 2, d. 25300, ll. 9–11 (correspondence with the Imperial Theaters office between November 5 and December 22, 1883); RIII f. 44, op. 1, d. 56, l. 83 ob.

55. David Brown, "Tchaikovsky's Mazeppa," *The Musical Times* 125, no. 1702 (December 1984): 697: "And just as, in *Onegin*, the nominal hero was the agent of Fate in Tatyana's life, so in *Mazeppa* the Cossack leader was Fate's surrogate in Maria's existence. The point is abruptly made in the very first sounds in the orchestra, for the terse and forceful invention of the first two bars (Mazeppa's own very special musical embodiment) immediately gives way to that ubiquitous Tchaikovskyan symbol of Fate—the descending scale." The descending scales might be ubiquitous, but their association with Fate is Brown's and Brown's alone.

56. RGIA f. 497, op. 2, d. 25300, l. 6 (September 10, 1883).

57. Ol'ga Nikolayevna Gavrilina, "Teatr muzïkal'noy dramï v Peterburge: Istoriya i istochniki," in *Muzïkal'noye naslediye Peterburga: Proyektï po sokhraneniyu i populyarizatsii: materialï XIV nauchno-prakticheskoy konferentsii po informatsionnim resursam peterburgovedeniya 11–12 marta 2021 g.*, ed. A. V. Savel'yeva (St. Petersburg: Tsentr. gor. publ. b-ka im. V. V. Mayakovskogo, 2021), 33.

58. RGIA f. 777, op. 3, d. 30 (O nepechatannom v Moskve libretto operï "Mazepa").

59. V, "Bol'shoy teatr. 'Mazeppa.' Opera v 3-kh deystviyakh i 6 kartinakh. Muzïka P. I. Chaykovskago (Okonchaniye)," *Peterburgskiy listok*, February 9, 1884, p. 3.

60. Tchaikovsky received the compliment in the afterglow of the ceremony awarding him the Order of Saint Prince Vladimir. *Eugene Onegin* was happening at the Bolshoi, and the tsar, who had seen the opera before, attended. "After the wedding dinner," Tchaikovsky wrote to von Mekk on January 18, 1885, in reference to singer Alexandra Panayeva's marriage to one of his cousins, "I went straight to the Bolshoi Theater, where the fifteenth performance of *Onegin* was taking place in the presence of the Sovereign, the Empress and other members of the royal family. The Emperor wished to see me, spoke with me for quite a while, was extremely affectionate and favorable to me, and with greatest sympathy asked in all sorts of detail about my life and my musical activities, after which he brought me to the Empress, who, in turn, showed me greatly moving attention." "Letter 2646," Tchaikovsky Research Net, January 18, 1885, https://en.tchaikovsky-research.net/pages/Letter_2646.

61. RIII f. 44, op. 1, d. 56, l. 81.

62. Roland John Wiley, "The Dances in 'Eugene Onegin,'" *Dance Research* 6, no. 2 (Autumn 1988): 52.

63. Ye. A. Skripkina, "Khorovïye stsenï iz I kartinï operï P. I. Chaykovskogo 'Yevgeniy Onegin,'" in *Tvorchestvo P. I. Chaykovskogo v ispolnitel'skoy podgotovke pedagoga muzïkanta*, ed. G. P. Stulova and A. P. Yudin (Moscow: Izdatel'stvo Ritm, 2021), 105–06.

64. Wiley, "Dances," 54.

65. Ibid., 56.

66. Ibid.

67. Chaykovskiy and Yurgenson, *Perepiska*, 522–23 (letter of August 21, 1885).
68. Harold Bloom, "Pilgrim to Eros," *The New York Review of Books*, September 24, 2009, https://www.nybooks.com/articles/2009/09/24/pilgrim-to-eros/.
69. M. O. Tsetlin, *Pyatero i drugiye* (Moscow: Direkt-Media, 2000), 208.
70. Miliy Alekseyevich Balakirev, *Vospominaniya i pis'ma*, ed. Emiliya Lazarevna Frid (Leningrad: Gosudarstvennoye muzïkal'noye izdatel'stvo, 1962), 167.
71. "Letter 2158," trans. Luis Sundkvist, Tchaikovsky Research Net, November 12, 1882, https://en.tchaikovsky-research.net/pages/Letter_2158.
72. N. Gerbel', ed., *Sochineniya lorda Bayrona v perevodakh russkikh poetov* (St. Petersburg: Gerbel', 1883).
73. "Letter 2580," trans. Luis Sundkvist, Tchaikovsky Research Net, October 31, 1884, https://en.tchaikovsky-research.net/pages/Letter_2580.
74. [Untitled], *Moskovskiye vedomosti*, March 13, 1886, p. 3.
75. "Letter 2912," trans. Luis Sundkvist, Tchaikovsky Research Net, March 13, 1886, https://en.tchaikovsky-research.net/pages/Letter_2912.
76. Wye Jamison Allanbrook, *Rhythmic Gesture in Mozart: Le Nozze Di Figaro and Don Giovanni* (Chicago: University of Chicago Press, 1983), 197–98, referenced in Cora Palfy, "Anti-hero Worship: The Emergence of the 'Byronic Hero' Archetype in the Nineteenth Century," *Indiana Theory Review* 32, nos. 1–2 (Spring/Fall 2016): 174–75.
77. Palfy, "Anti-hero Worship," 182–86.
78. Ts. A. Cui, "P. Tchaikovsky's *Manfred* Symphony," in *Russians on Russian Music, 1880–1917: An Anthology*, ed. and trans. Stuart Campbell (Cambridge: Cambridge University Press, 2003), 11. The review is dated December 31, 1886, weeks after the premiere. Cui delayed writing it pending scrutiny of the score, hence his harmonic factoids and details of orchestration.
79. Ibid., 12.
80. RIII f. 21, op. 1, d. 226, ll. 38–43, 58–60.
81. N. Kashkin, "Bol'shoy teatr. 'Charodeyka,' opera v 4-kh deystviyakh P. I. Chaykovskago, libretto I. V. Shpazhinskogo," *Artist* 6 (February 1890): 106. Vsevolozhsky made no secret of his dislike of *The Enchantress*, invidiously likening it to Camille Saint-Saëns's "horrible" opera *Ascania* (RIII f. 44, op. 1, d. 60, l. 45ob).
82. The origins of the word are unclear. Kuma might derive from *kuna*, the name of an ancient coin which is in turn named after an animal, a *kunitsa* (marten), whose pelts served as currency in Old Rus.
83. Even a preview of the opera noted this problem. See "Teatral'nïy kur'yer," *Peterburgskiy listok*, October 20, 1887, pp. 2–3.
84. RGIA f. 497, op. 8, d. 423 (Montirovka operï "Charodeyka").
85. The following information and quotations are from B. Asaf'yev, "'Charodeyka.' Opera P. I. Chaykovskogo. Opït raskrïtiya intonatsionnaya soderzhaniya," in *O muzïke Chaykovskogo* (Leningrad: Muzïka, 1972), 162–97, esp. 168.
86. The reviewer both praised the production (except for the libretto's "quasi-folkloric language") and defended Tchaikovsky from the claim, "made by some Russian, or more precisely, St. Petersburg critics," that the composer's lyricism didn't make for great drama. G. Kor-nov, "Izyashchnïya iskusstva," *Kavkaz*, December 14, 1887, p. 3.
87. Asaf'yev, "'Charodeyka.' Opera P. I. Chaykovskogo," 191.

88. "Letter 3392," Tchaikovsky Research Net, October 28, 1887, https://en.tchaikovsky-research.net/pages/Letter_3392.

89. "Letter 4177," Tchaikovsky Research Net, July 17, 1890, https://en.tchaikovsky-research.net/pages/Letter_4177.

90. P. I. Chaykovskiy, "Avtobiograficheskoye opisaniye puteshestviya za granitsu v 1888 godu," in Larosh, *Muzïkal'nïye fel'yetonï i zametki*, 370–72, 386–87.

91. "Symphony No. 5," Tchaikovsky Research Net, last modified May 29, 2023, https://en.tchaikovsky-research.net/pages/Symphony_No._5.

92. John Warrack, *Tchaikovsky Symphonies and Concertos* (London: British Broadcasting Corporation, 1974), 29.

93. Donald Seibert, "The Tchaikovsky Fifth: A Symphony without a Programme," *The Music Review* 51, no. 1 (February 1990): 45.

94. Timothy Jackson, "Aspects of Sexuality and Structure in the Later Symphonies of Tchaikovsky," *Music Analysis* 14, no. 1 (1995): 3, 5.

95. Dylan J. Principi, "The Program Problem: Interpreting the Cyclic Motto in Tchaikovsky's Fifth Symphony" (research paper for Princeton University Music Department seminar MUS 513: Tchaikovsky, submitted January 31, 2018).

96. Ibid.

97. Wiley, *Tchaikovsky*, 334.

98. According to Aleksandr Komarov, the composer and his brother Modest had tried to hire a carriage from a stationmaster in the hamlet of Sumy but were told that all the horses were out. It was early in the morning, and Pyotr was feeling the effects of the vodka he had imbibed with breakfast. "Do you have any idea who you're talking to?" he fumed. The station master didn't react, and Pyotr asked to file a complaint, which he signed not with his own name but that of a high-ranking diplomat: Prince Alexander Volkonsky. Suddenly, the horses appeared. He and Modest made it to Vorozhba to catch the train to Kyiv. Pyotr, however, realized that he'd left his wallet and passport back in Sumy. He told Modest to go on without him and slept with the rats. He returned to Sumy at sunrise, confident that the station master had looked through his papers and discovered that he was not, in fact, Prince Volkonsky. But the stationmaster hadn't peeked. Or so he said. Pyotr thanked him and asked for his name. "Tchaikovsky," the stationmaster replied. "Pis'mo k M. I. Chaykovskomu. Vorozhba, 17–18 iyulya 1872 goda," kul'tura.rf, accessed June 17, 2023, https://www.culture.ru/catalog/tchaikovsky/ru/item/article/pismo-k-m-i-chaykovskomu-vorozhba-17-18-iyulya-1872-goda).

99. N. N. Kondrat'yeva, "Vospominaniya o P. I. Chaykovskim," in Protopopov, *Vospominaniya o P. I. Chaykovskim*, 102–18, esp. 109.

100. Poznanskiy, *Pyotr Chaykovskiy. Biografiya*, 2:299–303.

101. "Muzïkal'noye obozreniye," *Nuvellist*, no. 8 (December 1888): 3.

102. "Teatral'nïy kur'yer," *Peterburgskiy listok*, November 7, 1888, p. 3.

103. "Letter 3589," Tchaikovsky Research Net, June 11, 1888, https://en.tchaikovsky-research.net/pages/Letter_3589.

104. RIII f. 44, op. 1, d. 59, l. 53; see also Nadine Meisner, *Marius Petipa: The Emperor's Ballet Master* (New York: Oxford University Press, 2019), 225.

105. Gurova, *Vsevolozhskiy*, 242–43.

106. Roland John Wiley, *The Petersburg Noverre: Marius Petipa in Russia* (forthcoming; reproduced with permission from Anthem Press, London).
107. Arlene Croce, "On Beauty 'Bare,'" *The New York Review of Books*, August 12, 1999, https://www.nybooks.com/articles/1999/08/12/on-beauty-bare/.
108. Meisner, *Marius Petipa*, 227.
109. "The responses to maestro Tchaikovsky's music for *The Sleeping Beauty* are ecstatic. Besides its melodiousness and the mass of delightful individual morceaux, the composer has written tens [dozens] of purely 'balletic' numbers whose sounds will ease the dancers' burden." "Teatral'nïy kur'yer," *Peterburgskiy listok*, October 9, 1889, p. 3.
110. Wiley, *Tchaikovsky's Ballets*, 175; see also Sally Banes, *Dancing Women: Female Bodies Onstage* (New York: Routledge, 1998), 55.
111. Most of the notation is in Nicholas Sergeyev's hand, though some parts are documented by his two assistants. Almost the entire ballet is present in the notation, albeit in different degrees of completeness. Red Riding Hood and the Wolf and the Sarabande are missing, so too the Fairies' and Carabosse's attendants. Doug Fullington describes this and other sources in "La notation Stepanov et *La belle au bois dormant*: Des productions historiquement documentées et de quelques particularités" (Stepanov notation and *The Sleeping Beauty*: Historically informed productions and some peculiarities), in *À la recherche de Marius Petipa II: Entre romantisme, orientalisme et avant-garde*, ed. Tiziana Leucci and Pascale Melani (Pessac: Maison des Sciences de l'Homme d'Aquitaine [MSHA], forthcoming).
112. Croce, "On Beauty."
113. Alastair Macaulay, "*The Sleeping Beauty*: A Hundred and Twelve Questions, a Hundred and Twelve Answers," September 10, 2021, https://www.alastairmacaulay.com/all-essays/.
114. Liane Fisher, "Mythology in Sleeping Beauty," Fisher Ballet Productions, 2016, https://fisherballet.com/mythology-in-sleeping-beauty/.
115. Ned Sublette, *Cuba and Its Music: From the First Drums to the Mambo* (Chicago: Chicago Review Press, 2004), 53, 78–81.
116. Ewa Kociszewska, "War and Seduction in Cybele's Garden: Contextualizing the *Ballet des Polonais*," *Renaissance Quarterly* 65, no. 3 (Fall 2012): 811, 815–16, 821–26.
117. Taruskin, *Defining Russia Musically*, 282–84.
118. Wiley, *Tchaikovsky's Ballets*, 132 and 134.
119. Ibid., 144, 149–50.
120. Lucia Denk, "Rhetorical Agency of the Piano in Act III of *The Sleeping Beauty*" (research paper for Princeton University Music Department seminar MUS 514: Tchaikovsky, submitted May 9, 2023).
121. Reginald Gerig, *Famous Pianists and Their Technique* (Bloomington: Indiana University Press, 1974), 287. I am grateful to Lucia Denk for this reference.
122. Denk, "Rhetorical Agency."
123. Tim Scholl, "Genre Trouble," in *Sleeping Beauty: A Legend in Progress* (New Haven and London: Yale University Press, 2004), 1–29.
124. Ibid., 175.
125. Ibid., 176.

126. Ibid., 179.
127. Ibid., 177.
128. Ibid., 49–60.
129. Fullington, "Notation Stepanov."
130. Scholl, *Sleeping Beauty*, 33.
131. Ibid., 32.
132. Ibid., 219 n.5.
133. Alexandre Benois, *Reminiscences of the Russian Ballet*, trans. Mary Britnieva (London: Putnam, 1945), 123–24, 131–32.
134. Poznanskiy, *Pyotr Chaykovskiy. Biografiya*, 2:379; Aynbinder, *Pyotr Chaykovskiy*, 334–36.
135. Von Mekk kept out of sight at her Villa Oppenheim, which is now a luxury hotel. Hershey Felder, "Our Great Tchaikovsky," *The Florentine*, December 5, 2020, https://www.theflorentine.net/2020/12/05/our-great-tchaikovsky-florence/.
136. For Italian content there is Tchaikovsky's 1878 song "Pimpinella" and his *Italian Capriccio* of 1880. The latter composition was inspired by Glinka's 1851 *Souvenir d'une nuit d'été à Madrid*, which is based on Spanish dances in triple meter and attests, in general, to Glinka's two-year immersion in Spanish culture. Tchaikovsky's Italian "potpourri" was derided at the time of its premiere as an exercise in emptiness, "lacking internal content," as opposed to Glinka's more integrated Iberian conception. "Teatr i muzïka," *Novoye vremya*, January 7, 1881, p. 3.
137. "Letter 351," Tchaikovsky Research Net, April 27, 1874, https://en.tchaikovsky-research.net/pages/Letter_351.
138. "Teatral'nïy kur'yer," *Peterburgskiy listok*, September 18, 1890, p. 3.
139. "*Souvenir de Florence*," Tchaikovsky Research Net, last modified February 12, 2023, https://en.tchaikovsky-research.net/pages/Souvenir_de_Florence; Wiley, *Tchaikovsky*, 405–6.
140. Benedict Taylor, "Temporality in Nineteenth-Century Russian Music and the Notion of Development," *Music and Letters* 94, no. 1 (February 2013): 112.
141. According to Neil Cornwell, Saint-Germain was an actual person, "a highly educated, sophisticated and engaging conversationalist who spread, or was reputed to have spread, bizarre rumors of both his antiquity and his powers. He was an accomplished musician (having been compared to Paganini as a violinist!), and even a composer. There is a tradition that one of his compositions ended up in the hands of Tchaikovsky, leading to speculation that it may even have featured among the quotations from eighteenth-century music included in his opera *The Queen of Spades*. He was apparently of unlimited but mysterious wealth, he may have been an occult scholar, a fanatical chemist, and an alchemical adept, and he was certainly a brilliant dyer and mixer of colors (to a secret formula which he refused to divulge), as well as a keen herbalist" ("'You've heard of the Count Saint-Germain ...'—in Pushkin's 'The Queen of Spades' and Far Beyond," *New Zealand Slavonic Journal* [2002]: 52).
142. In faro, or *banque*, the banker holds a limited pack of cards and the player another. The player selects a card and lays it face down; the banker lays cards face down on each side of it. The three cards are turned over. If the card on

the right has the same value as the player's card, the banker wins; if the card on the left has the same value the player wins.

143. N. F. Solov'yov, "Otrïvki iz vospominaniy," *Yezhegodnik imperatorskikh teatrov,* nos. 6–7 (1909): 16.

144. G. Dombayev, *Tvorchestvo Pyotra Il'yicha Chaykovskogo v materialakh i doku-mentakh,* ed. Gr. Bernandt (Moscow: Gosudarstennoye muzïkal'noye izdatel'stvo, 1958), 169.

145. Poznanskiy, *Pyotr Chaykovskiy. Biografiya,* 2:349–50.

146. Chaykovskiy, *Dnevniki,* 252–56.

147. Kostalevsky, *Tchaikovsky Papers,* 278, 182 (Modest to Pyotr, February 23, 1890; Pyotr to Modest, March 14, 1890).

148. Chaykovskiy, *Polnoye sobraniye sochineniy. Literaturnïye proizvedeniya i perepiska,* 15B:236 (letter of August 5, 1890).

149. Chaykovskiy, *Dnevniki,* 258.

150. Chaykovskiy, *Polnoye sobraniye sochineniy. Literaturnïye proizvedeniya i perepiska,* 15B:87 (letter of March 3, 1890).

151. Poznansky, *Tchaikovsky through Others' Eyes,* 191.

152. Malcolm Forbes, "The Moving Tide of Abundance: *Petersburg* by Andrei Bely," *The Quarterly Conversation,* December 5, 2011; http://quarterly conversation.com/the-moving-tide-of-abundance-petersburg-by-andrei-bely.

153. Aynbinder, *Pyotr Chaykovskiy,* 326.

154. The great soprano Medeya Figner (1859–1952), Nikolay's wife, would take the part of Liza for the premiere.

155. The accident happened on November 29, 1890, at a performance of *Eugene Onegin.* He sang the part of Lensky and tripped onto his back during the duel. RGIA f. 472, op. 44, d. 24, l. 148. Vladimir Pogozhev's description of the ill-fortuned *Queen of Spades* rehearsal is included in Poznansky, *Tchaikovsky through Others' Eyes,* 153–54: "In the scene at the guardhouse, despite the choir's wonderful recital of the funeral motif 'I pour out my prayers to the Lord,' at the moment when the countess' ghost appears, Figner, illustrating Herman's horror, accidentally knocked a candlestick with a burning candle from the table behind which he was moving. It rolled across the floor and, as if on purpose, stopped with its flame under the edge of the curtain of the backdrop of the set. The candle continued to burn and, of course, the public's attention, attracted by the sound of the falling candlestick, was riveted to the candle's flame and to the curtain, which had already begun to smoke." Still, Figner triumphed, as the high-ranking government official Anatoly Koni reported: "He understood and presented Herman as a complete clinical picture of mental disorder . . . I must say that I have practical familiarity with every possible kind of mad display on account of my profession as a member of the judiciary. But when I saw Figner I was amazed. I was amazed at the extent to which he correctly and deeply depicted the madness . . . and how it developed." Quoted in Juliet Forshaw, "Russian Opera Rebels: Fyodor Komissarzhevsky, Nikolai Figner and the Rise of the Tenor Antihero," in *Masculinity in Opera,* ed. Philip Purvis (New York: Routledge, 2013), 77–78.

156. Nápravník complained about this problem to Vsevolozhsky on April 27, 1890: "My report on P. I. Tchaikovsky's *Queen of Spades* will be short and to

the point. When he arrived in St. Petersburg, P. I. only had with him only the printed proofs of the first two scenes, and it wasn't easy persuading him to play them for us on the third day [of rehearsal]. Such hasty familiarization gives me pause" (RGIA f. 652, op. 1, d. 472, l. 27).

157. RGIA f. 678, op. 1, d. 58, l. 4.
158. Vsevolozhsky's conception of the staging, as recalled by Pogozhev: RIII f. 44, op. 1, d. 7, l. 17.
159. The dancers are listed in RGIA f. 497, op. 8, d. 432, l. 1 (Montirovka operï "Pikovaya dama").
160. Wiley, *The Petersburg Noverre*, (forthcoming).
161. N. Sin'kovskaya, "Brat'ya Chaykovskiye v rabote nad libretto 'Pikovoy damï,'" in *Chaykovskiy. Voprosï i teorii. Vtoroy sbornik statey*, ed. Yu. A. Rozanova (Moscow: Moskovskaya gosudarstvennaya dvazhdï ordena Lenina konservatoriya im. P. I. Chaykovskogo, 1991), 25.
162. Caryl Emerson, "Tchaikovsky's Tatiana," in Kearney, *Tchaikovsky and His World*, 216–19.
163. Caryl Emerson, "The Three Worlds of Tchaikovsky's 'Pikovaya Dama,'" paper presented at the American Association for the Advancement of Slavic Studies, Seattle, November 21, 1997.
164. "Teatral'nïy kur'yer," *Peterburgskiy listok*, December 12, 1890, p. 3.
165. "Peterburgskiy kaleydoskop," *Peterburgskiy listok*, January 18, 1891, p. 3.
166. Solovyov also held a grudge against Tchaikovsky for dissing his opera *Cordelia* (1885), based on a drama by Victorien Sardou called *La Haine* (Hatred, 1874). See Irakliy Andronikov, "Pis'mo Chaykovskogo," *Sovetskaya muzïka*, no. 4 (1956): 117–21.
167. N. Solov'yov, "Teatr i muzïka. 'Pikovaya dama,' opera P. Chaykovskago," *Novosti i birzhevaya gazeta*, December 9, 1890, p. 3.
168. F. B. Miller, trans., "Doch' korolya Rene. Liricheskaya drama Genrika Gertsa," *Russkiy vestnik* 163 (February 1883): 653.
169. Ibid.
170. "Letter 4415," Tchaikovsky Research Net, June 18 or 19, 1891, https://en.tchaikovsky-research.net/pages/Letter_4415.
171. V. V. Yakovlev, "Chaykovskiy v poiskakh opernogo libretto," in *Muzïkal'noye nasledstvo. Sbornik materialov po istorii muzïkal'noy kul'turï v Rossii. Vïp. 1*, ed. M. V. Ivanov-Boretskiy (Moscow: Muzgiz, 1935), 73.
172. G. B., "Beseda s P. I. Chaykovskim," *Peterburgskaya zhizn'* 2 (November 12, 1892): 16–19; see also "Zabïtoye interv'yu s P. I. Chaykovskim," *Sovetskaya muzïka*, no. 7 (1949): 59–61.
173. "Letter 4364," Tchaikovsky Research Net, April 3, 1891, https://en.tchaikovsky-research.net/pages/Letter_4364.
174. RGIA f. 652, op. 1, d. 607, l. 28 (April 3, 1891).
175. RGIA f. 652, op. 1, d. 472, ll. 12 ob.–13.
176. RGIA f. 497, op. 4, d. 3307, l. 1 ob. (Pospektal'naya plata avtoram i perevodchikam). He received 4 percent of the box-office receipts for *Iolanta*, and an advance payment of 1,000 rubles for the opera and the ballet on November 3, 1892.
177. "The World of Ibn Al-Haytham," 1001 Inventions, accessed January 7, 2023, https://www.ibnalhaytham.com/discover/who-was-ibn-al-haytham/.

NOTES

178. Antonina Leonidovna Makarova, "Misterial'nïye proobrazï v opernom tvorchestve P. I. Chaykovskogo" (PhD diss., Magnitogorsk State Conservatory, 2017), 28 (of the abstract).
179. "Letter 4804," Tchaikovsky Research Net, November 11, 1892, https://en.tchaikovsky-research.net/pages/Letter_4804.
180. Victor Borovsky, "Modest Tchaikovsky—Dramatist, Librettist, Critic, Translator," *New Zealand Slavonic Journal* (1997): 150–51.
181. RIII f. 21, op. 1, d. 227, l. 33 ob.
182. Modeste Tchaikovsky, *The Life and Letters of Peter Ilich* Tchaikovsky, ed. and trans. Rosa Newmarch (London: John Lane the Bodley Head, 1906), 696.
183. M. Ivanov, "Muzïkal'nïye nabroski," *Novoye vremya*, December 14, 1892, p. 2.
184. N. A. Rimskiy-Korsakov, *Letopis' moyey muzïkal'noy zhizni*, ed. A. N. Rimskiy-Korsakov (Moscow: Gosudarstvennoye izdatel'stvo Muzïkal'nïy sektor, 1928), 304.
185. Ibid., 318.
186. Richard Taruskin, "Tchaikovsky, Pyotr Il'yich," in Sadie, *The New Grove Dictionary of Opera*, 4:669.
187. The notice appears on page 4 of the April 3, 1891, issue of *Novoye vremya*.
188. His twenty-five days in the United States (April 14/26 to May 9/21, 1891) were confined to the Northeast. He conducted in New York, Baltimore, and Philadelphia, and took a sightseeing trip to Niagara Falls. For the details of his reception in, and impressions of, Gilded Age America, see Elkhonon Yoffe, *Tchaikovsky in America: The Composer's Visit in 1891*, trans. Lidya Yoffe (Oxford: Oxford University Press, 1986); and Carol J. Binkowski, *Opening Carnegie Hall: The Creation and First Performances of America's Premier Concert Stage* (Jefferson, NC: McFarland & Company, 2016).
189. Roland John Wiley, "On Meaning in 'Nutcracker,'" *Dance Research* 3, no. 1 (Autumn 1984), 12–15.
190. Wiley, *The Petersburg Noverre*, (forthcoming) (ballerina Olga Preobrazhensky's recollection).
191. V. S. Maksimenko, *P. I. Chaykovskiy i Odessa: Istoriko-dokumental'nïy ocherk* (Odessa: Astroprint, 2001), 27.
192. "U P. I. Chaykovskago," *Odesskiy listok*, January 13, 1893, quoted in "With P. I. Tchaikovsky," Tchaikovsky Research Net, last modified March 10, 2023, https://en.tchaikovsky-research.net/pages/With_P._I._Tchaikovsky.
193. Kevin Tuite, "The Violet and the Rose: A Georgian Lullaby as Song of Healing and Socio-Political Commentary," 2009, http://www.mapageweb.umontreal.ca/tuitekj/publications/IavnanaTUITE.pdf.
194. Alexander Poznansky and Brett Langston, *The Tchaikovsky Handbook: A Guide to the Man and his Music*, 2 vols. (Bloomington: Indiana University Press, 2002), 1:117–18.
195. Wiley, "On Meaning," 20–21; and Wiley, *Tchaikovsky*, 415.
196. My thanks to Alastair Macaulay for this observation.
197. Arkadii Klimovitsky, "Tchaikovsky and the Russian 'Silver Age,'" in *Tchaikovsky and His World*, ed. Leslie Kearney (Princeton: Princeton University Press, 1998), 327. The author expands his account of Tchaikovsky's Silver Age connections in the 2008 Russian version of this article, included in Klimovitskiy, *Pyotr Il'yich Chaykovskiy*, 379–411.

198. Damien Mahiet, "The Aesthetics and Politics of Wonder in the First *Nutcracker*," *19th-Century Music* 40, no. 2 (Fall 2016): 132–33; on the broader political context, see Damien Mahiet, "The First *Nutcracker*, the Enchantment of International Relations, and the Franco-Russian Alliance," *Dance Research* 34, no. 2 (2016): 119–49.

199. Sara Cutler, "Performance Practice of Three Tchaikovsky Ballet Cadenzas: A Discussion of the Current Editing Practice of the Waltz of the Flowers, White Swan, and Rose Adagio Harp Cadenzas," *American Harp Journal* 27, no. 1 (Summer 2019): 16. I am grateful to harpist Joshua Velasquez for this reference, and for the technical information in this paragraph.

200. Cutler, "Performance Practice," 17.

201. *Shchelkunchik. Balet-feyeriya v 2-kh deystviyakh, 3-kh kartinakh,* kul'tura.rf, accessed January 7, 2023, https://www.culture.ru/catalog/tchaikovsky/ru/item/archiv/shchelkunchik-balet-feeriya-v-2-h-deystviyah-3-h-kartinah-2017-08-17.

202. Wiley, *The Petersburg Noverre,* (forthcoming).

203. The typophone is organologically related to the dulcitone, a Scottish rather than a French invention.

204. P. I. Chaykovskiy and P. I. Yurgenson, *Perepiska. Tom 2: 1886–1893,* ed. P. I. Vaydman (Moscow: Yurgenson, 2013), 377–78.

205. Siloti emboldened himself to remove a section of the first movement and shrink the second movement by half. Tchaikovsky resisted the changes but had no say after he died. In 1898, Jurgenson published Siloti's edition, which reduced the concerto from forty-five minutes in length to thirty-five; it was mistakenly considered the authorized version through the first half of the twentieth century. Balanchine choreographed this version in 1941 under the title *Ballet Imperial.* In 1951, the longer, harder original version fell into the hands of Tatyana Nikolayeva, who recorded it with the USSR State Symphony as a demonstration of Soviet pianistic fortitude. Four years later, the original was included in the Soviet edition of Tchaikovsky's complete works and subsequently found its way into the international piano competition repertoire.

206. "*The Voyevoda* (Symphonic Ballad)," Tchaikovsky Research Net, last modified August 27, 2023, https://en.tchaikovsky-research.net/pages/The_Voyevoda_(symphonic_ballad).

207. Aynbinder, *Pyotr Chaykovskiy,* 349.

208. "Teatral'nïy kur'yer," *Peterburgskiy listok,* July 10, 1892, p. 3, and July 19, 1892, p. 4.

209. Polina Dimova, "Polar Fantasies: Valery Bryusov and the Russian Symbolist Electric Aesthetic," in *Russian Energy Culture: Work, Power, and Waste in Russia and the Soviet Union,* ed. Jillian Porter and Maya Vinokur (London: Palgrave Macmillan, 2023), 91.

210. *Ukazatel' pervoy elektricheskoy vïstavke* (Moscow: Tovarishchestvo Skoropechatni A. A. Levenson, 1892), esp. 3, 5, 24.

211. "Teatral'nïye i muzïkal'nïye izvestiya," *Moskovskiye vedomosti,* July 6, 1892, pp. 4–5.

212. "Many Popular Concerts: Chicago Orchestra Concerts Will Present Brighter Music—Some of the Selections," *Chicago Daily Tribune,* October 2, 1892, p. 36; "Local Musical Matters," *Detroit Free Press,* November 13, 1892, p. 8.

213. B., "Teatral'noye ekho," *Peterburgskaya gazeta*, December 7, 1892, p. 3. The review in *Peterburgskiy listok* was a rave by comparison. The sole critique, a peculiar one, was that the luxuriousness of the production detracted from the listening experience. R-t., "Teatral'nïy kur'yer," *Peterburgskiy listok*, December 7, 1892, p. 3.
214. S., "Teatr i muzïka," *Novoye vremya*, December 7, 1892, p. 3.
215. B. Asaf'yev, "Shchelkunchik," in *O balete. Stat'i. Retsensiy. Vospominaniya* (Leningrad: Muzïka, 1974), 194–97.
216. RGIA f. 1119, op. 1, d. 3, l. 56: "On that same day [April 26, 1892], P. I. Tchaikovsky came to hear the children's orchestra. He was extremely kind to the young musicians and took an interest in our children's instruments. He examined and tried them all. The children who played for him almost jumped out of their skin trying to sound artistic."

Part IV Matters of Life and Death

1. R. V. Iyezuitova, "A. N. Apukhtin i Pushkin," in *Pushkin: Issledovaniya i materialï*, ed. N. N. Skatov et al. (St. Petersburg: Nauka, 2004), 337.
2. Ibid., 338.
3. Aleksandr Amfiteatrov, "Chaykovskiy i Apukhtin—druz'ya (K sorokaletiyu ikh konchinï)," *Sevodnya*, September 8, 1933, p. 2.
4. Bullock, "Ambiguous Speech," 112–19.
5. Amfiteatrov, "Chaykovskiy i Apukhtin."
6. "Pokhoronï A. N. Apukhtina," *Peterburgskiy listok*, August 21, 1893, p. 3.
7. Aleksey Apukhtin, "Rekviyem," kul'tura.rf, accessed April 21, 2023, https://www.culture.ru/poems/7146/rekviem.
8. Petr Il'ič Čajkovskij, *Symphony No. 6 in B Minor, op. 74 (ČW 27): Pathétique: Critical Report*, ed. Thomas Kohlhase, with Polina Vajdman (Mainz: Schott, 2003), 3, 5.
9. "Letter 4767," trans. Brett Langston, Tchaikovsky Research Net, September 7 and 10, 1892, https://en.tchaikovsky-research.net/pages/Letter_4767.
10. Čajkovskij, *Symphony No. 6 in B Minor, op. 74 (ČW 27): Pathétique: Critical Report*, 7–8.
11. Jackson, "Aspects of Sexuality," 19.
12. Lucia Denk, "'Mid Bleak Days,' 'Средь мрачных дней,' from Tchaikovsky's *Six Romances*, Opus 73: Memorializing the Ephemeral" (analysis for Princeton University Music Department seminar MUS 514: Tchaikovsky, submitted April 5, 2023).
13. "Letter 4996," trans. Brett Langston, Tchaikovsky Research Net, August 1, 1893, https://en.tchaikovsky-research.net/pages/Letter_4996.
14. Marina Ritzarev, *Tchaikovsky's Pathétique and Russian Culture* (Burlington: Ashgate, 2014), esp. 21, 30–31, 69.
15. Wiley, *Tchaikovsky*, 425. As noted, Wiley also hears the hymn—its rhythm—in *Eugene Onegin*.
16. Ian Almond, "Derrida and the Secret of the Non-secret: On Respiritualising the Profane," *Literature and Theology* 17, no. 4 (December 2003): 465.
17. Petr Il'ič Čajkovskij, *Symphony No. 6 in B Minor, op. 74 (ČW 27): Pathétique: Autograph Draft (Facsimile) and Critical Notes*, ed. Thomas Kohlhase, with Polina Vajdman (Mainz: Schott, 1993), 52–63.

18. "Moskovskiy fel'yeton," *Novoye vremya*, January 3, 1870, p. 3.
19. "Teatr i muzïka," *Novoye vremya*, October 18, 1893, p. 3.
20. V. B., "Teatral'noye ekho," *Peterburgskaya gazeta*, October 18, 1893, p. 3.
21. E. K. Rozenov, "Concert in Aid of the Fund for Artists' Widows and Orphans," February 14, 1896, in Campbell, *Russians on Russian Music, 1880–1917*, 40.
22. "Miss Aus der Ohe Praised. Her Touching Story of the Death of Tschaikowsky," *Chicago Sunday Tribune*, February 25, 1894, p. 25.
23. Tchaikovsky awarded control of his estate to a grandnephew, Georgy (Georges-Léon) Tchaikovsky (1883–1940), who was the illegitimate child of a niece, his sister's daughter Tatyana. Tchaikovsky looked after Tatyana in Paris during her pregnancy, and arranged for her and the baby's care. Later, with Tchaikovsky's help, Georgy was adopted into the family of his older brother Nikolay. The will instructs Georgy to provide a seventh of the value of the estate to Tchaikovsky's servant, "reserve corporal Alexei Sofronov." Bob Davïdov received his foreign and domestic performance royalties, with a fifth of the royalties for *The Queen of Spades* and *Iolanta* going to Modest, as the author of their librettos. Tchaikovsky adds a line about Modest receiving the same amount for other librettos from future collaborations. He specifies that Modest was to receive no less than 1,800 rubles a year, obliging Bob to top up the amount from other royalties from other works if need be. Since Milyukova remained his wife, he instructed Bob to pay her 1,200 rubles a year from the royalties, so too Georgy, with Alexei collecting 600 rubles. His personal possessions—"furniture, clothes, shoes, linen, tools, books, notes, metal-leaf wreaths and gifts"—all went to his servant. He made his publisher the executor of the will. RGIA f. 468, op. 16, d. 1124, ll. 5–6.
24. This fake "last photograph" of the composer is on Facebook and other social media sites and in Claudio Casini and Maria Delogu's *Čajkovskij* (Milan: Rusconi, 1993).
25. Alexander Poznansky, *Tchaikovsky's Last Days: A Documentary Study* (Oxford and New York: Oxford University Press, 1996), 71.
26. Frank Clemow, *The Cholera Epidemic of 1892 in the Russian Empire* (London and New York: Longmans, Green, and Co., 1893), 55; https://archive.org/details/39002086311652.med.yale.edu.
27. RIII f. 44, op. 1, d. 61, ll. 19–20 (July 9, 1892), 35 (August 24), 38 (August 27).
28. "Bolezn' P. I. Chaykovskago," *Peterburgskiy listok*, October 24, 1893, p. 3.
29. V. Baskin, "P. I. Chaykovskiy," *Niva* 24, no. 45 (November 6, 1893): 1031.

SUGGESTIONS FOR FURTHER READING

Alexander Poznansky, *Pyotr Chaykovskiy. Biografiya v 2-kh tomakh* (St. Petersburg: Vita Nova, 2009).

Poznansky's capacious biography of the composer focuses on his social and private life. The major instrumental works receive brief discussions, with emphasis placed on their reception (Nikolay Rubinstein's panning of the First Piano Concerto, for example). The coverage of the operas and ballets is richer. The biography is most valuable for its letters-based descriptions of the institutions that educated and employed the composer—the St. Petersburg and Moscow Conservatories—and the plethora of information concerning Tchaikovsky's relationship with his peers and his sexuality.

Alexander Poznansky and Brett Langston, *The Tchaikovsky Handbook: A Guide to the Man and His Music*, vol. 1, *Thematic Catalogue of Works, Catalogue of Photographs, Autobiography*, vol. 2, *Catalogue of Letters, Genealogy, Bibliography* (Bloomington: Indiana University Press, 2002).

In addition to considering recently discovered pieces (including a previously unknown aria from the opera *The Oprichnik* and a chorus titled "Spring") and providing thematic incipits for his entire output, the first volume of the catalogue includes Tchaikovsky's brief autobiography of 1889, written in response to a request from a German advocate and devotee of his music. For Poznansky and Langston, the autobiography is noteworthy for what it does not discuss: the composer's abruptly curtailed marriage to Antonina Milyukova and the chief source of his income after his resignation from the Moscow Conservatory, Nadezhda von Mekk. The annotated catalogue of photographs in volume 1 is marvelous, the meticulous bibliography in volume 2 indispensable.

Richard Taruskin, "Tchaikovsky, Pyotr Il'yich," in *The New Grove Dictionary of Opera*, ed. Stanley Sadie, 4 vols. (London: Macmillan, 1994), 4:662–69.

This article highlights the diversity of Tchaikovsky's ten operas, the fourth of which (*Vakula the Smith/Cherevichki*) exists in two versions. The generic and stylistic admixture, exceeding that of the superprolific Nikolay Rimsky-Korsakov and Anton Rubinstein, includes folk tale and fairytale settings, Russian and non-Russian historical dramas, and erotic and psychological explorations. Taruskin notes Tchaikovsky's creative misfires but approaches the repertoire as an advocate.

Polina Vaydman, ed., *P. I. Chaykovskiy, P. I. Yurgenson: Perepiska v dvukh tomakh; 1866–1893*, 2 vols. (Moscow: P. Yurgenson, 2011).

Vaydman chronicles the publication and premieres of the bulk of Tchaikovsky's oeuvre as represented in the 1,200 letters he exchanged with his main publisher over twenty-seven years. The letters are hardly businesslike: Pyotr Yurgenson (Jurgenson) is a master ironist, and Tchaikovsky opines, with profane candor, about people, places, and events they have in common.

Roland John Wiley, *Tchaikovsky's Ballets:* Swan Lake, Sleeping Beauty, Nutcracker. Oxford Monographs on Music (Oxford: Clarendon Press, 1985).

Wiley is the chief guide to the sources, genesis, reception, and legacies of Tchaikovsky's three canonic ballets. His book relies on extensive archival research while also addressing matters of musical and choreographic symbolism and historical reconstruction (the appendixes contain scenario drafts and facsimiles of choreographic notation in the hand of the St. Petersburg Imperial Theaters regisseur Nicholas Sergeyev).

Tchaikovsky Research Net, www.tchaikovsky-research.net

Established in 2006 by a musicological collective headed by Brett Langston, Tchaikovsky Research Net includes many of the 5,359 known letters written by the composer to his 394 known correspondents, with places and dates of each letter as well as links to related publications. English translations of the letters are being posted. Other essential features of the site include a chronicle of the composer's life and a separate, entertainingly revealing list of the places he traveled to. Derived from the *Thematic Catalogue*, the work list includes a superabundance of information about dates of composition, premiere performances, location of manuscripts (including musical sketches, scenarios, and libretti), durations, recordings, publications, and details about the compositional genesis of his works. Likewise illuminating are the miniature biographies of people in Tchaikovsky's life, a section of the database still in progress. The database also hosts a forum on subjects as arcane as Tchaikovsky's best French horn solos and his love of macaroni, along with the *Tchaikovsky Research Bulletin*, a listing of articles commissioned for the database in February and April 2001, and January 2012.

INDEX

"PT" refers to Pyotr Tchaikovsky.

Fifth Symphony, 144, 149, 313 n.207
Ninth Symphony, 25–6
Begichev, Vladimir, 108–9
Bekker, Fyodor, 317 n.267
Belgium, 18, 24, 41, 111
Belïy, Andrey, 268
  Petersburg (novel), 253
Bellermann, Heinrich
  Kontrapunkt, Der, 28
Bellini, Vincenzo, 167
bellringing, 184, 298 n.28
Benois, Alexandre, 244–5
berceuse, 95, 204–5, 268
Berlin, 18, 20
Berlioz, Hector, 5, 211–12, 214, 216
  Fantastic Symphony, 215
  Harold in Italy, 215
  Romeo and Juliet, 215
  Treatise on Instrumentation and Orchestration, 24
Bernard, Nikolay, 150–1
Bertenson, Lev, 292
Bessel, Vasily, 78, 81, 82, 305 n.56
Bevignani, Enrico, 131
Bezborodko, Alexander, 88
bïlina, 187
Bizet, Georges
  Carmen, 81, 215, 219, 250
  Ivan IV, 305 n.61
Blok, Alexander, 268
Bloom, Harold, 211
Boccherini, Luigi
  Night Music of the Streets of Madrid, 306 n.80
Bolsheviks, 15, 17, 293
  See also Soviet Union
Bolshoi Theater, 46, 190, 250
  Begichev, repertoire inspector for, 109, 129
  Catherine the Great and, 256
  PT and, 194, 259
    1812 Overture, 183
    Enchantress, 216–17
    Eugene Onegin, 130–1, 132, 322 n.60
    "Montenegro", 182
    op. 19 Theme and Variations, 91
    Polytechnic Exhibition Cantata, 5

Snow Maiden, 71–2, 109
Swan Lake, 105, 106, 108–14, 129, 293, 309 n.123
Undina, 69
Vakula the Smith, 83
Voyevoda/Cherevichki, 61–2, 64, 192
Borjomi, 197
Borodin, Alexander, 186, 298 n.28
  In the Steppes of Central Asia, 182
  Prince Igor, 205
Bortnyansky, Dmitri, 80, 164, 165, 317 n.267
  "How Glorious", 184
Boucher, François, 255
boyars, 26, 76, 77, 79, 129
Brady, Sophie, 174
Brahms, Johannes, 10, 154, 228, 247
Braïliv, 124–5, 127, 130, 248
Brianza, Carlotta, 242
Bronzino, 248
Brown, Dan
  Inferno, 101
Brown, David, 38, 43, 204, 300 n.67, 302 n.9, 322 n.55
Bulgaria, 71–2, 98
Bullock, Philip Ross, 9, 280, 295 n.6, 301 n.79, 314 n.229
Bülow, Cosima von, 90
Bülow, Hans von, 90–2
Burenin, Viktor, 200–1, 203
Butakova, Vera, 191
Byron, Lord, 4
  "Childe Harold", 211
  "Manfred", 211–16, 256
  "Mazeppa", 201
  "The Prisoner of Chillon", 259
Byzantine Empire, 161, 166, 187–8

cadenza, 96, 153, 154, 269–70, 283
café chantant, 48
cannons, 181, 183–4, 186, 319 n.6
cantata *see K radosti*; Moscow Cantata; Polytechnic Exhibition Cantata
canzone, 146, 320 n.24
capriccio, 79, 274, 326 n.126
Catherine the Great (Catherine II, empress of Russia), 31, 152
  amateur playwright, 39

Pchelnikov, Pavel, 208
Péladan, Joséphin
  Salons de la Rose-Croix, 122
peniye, 187
People's Will, 175, 178
Pereletsky, Pavel, 196
Perrault, Charles
  belle au bois dormant, La, 235–6, 239,
    243
Peter the Great (tsar of Russia), 32, 57,
    294, 296 n.8
  bicentennial, 4
  Mazeppa and, 202, 206
  pretend court of the young, 198
  St. Petersburg, founding of, 218
  war with Sweden, 202–3
Petipa, Marie, 244
Petipa, Marius
  Don Quixote, 234
  first wife of, 320 n.33
  King's Command, The, 234
  PT and, 69
    Nutcracker, 110, 266, 268, 270,
      275–6
    Queen of Spades, 254
    Sleeping Beauty, 110, 234–6, 238,
      239, 244
    Swan Lake, 113, 234, 292
  Undina, 69
Petrov, V. A., 100
Phillips, Stephen, 307 n.105
piano, 3, 93–6, 124, 330 n.205
  arrangements, 121, 165
  competitions, 4, 94, 330 n.205
  pieces for children, 105, 125, 147
  Anton Rubinstein and, 19, 20, 22,
    30
  Nikolay Rubinstein and, 20, 30, 47,
    89
  Russian pianism, 241–2
  Sleeping Beauty, 241–2
  vocal score for *Eugene Onegin*, 130
  vocal score for *Maid of Orleans*,
    318 n.277
  vocal score for *Queen of Spades*, 252,
    255
  See also Eighteen Pieces for Solo
    Piano; First Piano Concerto;

Seasons, The; Second Piano
  Concerto; *Souvenir d'un lieu
  cher*
Piccioli, Luigi, 18
"Pimpinella" (PT), 326 n.136
plagal cadence, 162, 214, 223, 230
Pleshcheyev, Alexei, 300 n.64
Pobedonostsev, Konstantin, 185, 319
  n.11
Pogozhev, Vladimir, 195, 234, 250, 291,
  327 n.155, 328 n.158
pogroms, 8, 185
Poland, 2, 9, 165, 203, 240–1, 272
  polonaise, 240, 306 n.80
  uprising, 201
Polenov, Nikolay, 39
Polignac, Prince and Princesse de, 122
Polish-Lithuanian Commonwealth, 36
polka, 90, 110–11
polonaise, 25, 241
  Eugene Onegin, 153, 210, 314 n.230
  Fourth Symphony, 145–6, 147, 192,
    240
  Mazeppa, 206
  Queen of Spades, 256
  Sleeping Beauty, 240–1
  Third Symphony, 306 n.80
  Vakula the Smith, 86, 274
Polonsky, Yakov, 197
  "Night", 262
  libretto for Polytechnic Exhibition
    Cantata, 84, 295–6 n.8
  libretto for *Vakula the Smith*, 84–6,
    87
  "Song of the Gypsy", 320 n.25
Polytechnic Exhibition Cantata (PT),
  4–5, 84, 295–6 n.8
Popov, Sergey, 64–6
Poznansky, Alexander, 120, 128, 231,
  246
Principi, Dylan, 229–31
program music, 4, 39, 45, 233, 272
Prokofiev, Sergey
  Classical Symphony of 1917, 152–3
Prokunin, Vasily, 48
  *Russian Folksongs for Solo Voice with
    Piano Accompaniment*, 48
Prussia, 32